COVID-19: Causes, Transmission, Diagnosis, and Treatment

Edited by

Mohammad Sufian Badar
Department of Bioengineering, University of California
Riverside, CA, USA

COVID-19: Causes, Transmission, Diagnosis, and Treatment

Editor: Mohammad Sufian Badar

ISBN (Online): 978-981-5256-53-6

ISBN (Print): 978-981-5256-54-3

ISBN (Paperback): 978-981-5256-55-0

First published in 2024.

need for a court order if at any point you breach any terms of this License Agreement. In no event will any delay or failure by Bentham Science Publishers in enforcing your compliance with this License Agreement constitute a waiver of any of its rights.

3. You acknowledge that you have read this License Agreement, and agree to be bound by its terms and conditions. To the extent that any other terms and conditions presented on any website of Bentham Science Publishers conflict with, or are inconsistent with, the terms and conditions set out in this License Agreement, you acknowledge that the terms and conditions set out in this License Agreement shall prevail.

Bentham Science Publishers Pte. Ltd.
80 Robinson Road #02-00
Singapore 068898
Singapore
Email: subscriptions@benthamscience.net

BENTHAM SCIENCE

CONTENTS

PREFACE i

LIST OF CONTRIBUTORS ii

CHAPTER 1 HISTORY OF CORONAVIRUSES 1
Mohammad Sufian Badar, Umme Hania Irfan, Zaid Hussain Siddique, Ahmad Masroor Karimi, Mairaj Ahmed Ansari, Fahim Ahmad and Faiyaz Ahmad
    INTRODUCTION 2
    ORIGIN 4
        Animal Origin 4
            SARS-CoV 7
            MERS-CoV 7
            SARS-CoV-2 8
            Community-acquired HCoVs 8
        Interspecies Transmission 9
        Endemic Origin 10
            SARS-CoV 11
            MERS-CoV 11
            SARS-CoV-2 12
    NOMENCLATURE 13
    CLASSIFICATION OF VARIANTS 13
        Alpha Variant 13
        Beta Variant 14
        Gamma Variant 14
        Delta Variant 15
        Omicron Variant 15
            Variants of Concern (VOC) 16
            Variants of Interest (VOI) 16
            Variants Being Monitored (VBM) 16
            Variants of High Consequence (VOHC) 17
    TYPES OF CORONAVIRUSES 17
        HCoV-229E 20
        HCoV-NL63 20
        HCoV-OC43 20
        HKU1 (beta-coronavirus) 21
        MERS-CoV 21
        SARS-CoV 22
        SARS-CoV-2 22
    GENOMIC EVOLUTION 23
    BIOLOGICAL EVOLUTION OF CORONAVIRUS SPIKE PROTEIN 25
    CONCLUSION 28
    TAKE-HOME MESSAGES 29
    WHAT YOU WILL LEARN 30
    LIST OF ABBREVIATIONS 31
    REFERENCES 32

CHAPTER 2 EPIDEMIOLOGY OF CORONAVIRUS 37
Mohammad Sufian Badar, Ibtesaam Hafeez, Imtshan Nawaz, Mohammad Rehan Badar and Sadia Saba
    INTRODUCTION OF EPIDEMIOLOGY OF CORONAVIRUS 38
    ETIOLOGY OF CORONAVIRUS 38

ORIGIN/DISEASE BACKGROUND 39
GEOGRAPHICAL DISTRIBUTION 39
EPIDEMIOLOGICAL DETERMINANTS OF CORONAVIRUS 39
    Variants of Coronavirus 39
    Risk Factors 40
TRANSMISSION 41
    Transmissibility of SARS-CoV2 41
    Transmission Routes 42
        Respiratory Transmission 42
        Faecal-oral Route of Transmission 42
        Vertical Route of Transmission 43
        Sexual Route of Transmission 44
        Ocular Route of Transmission 44
        Incubation Period and Serial Interval 45
    Period of Infectivity / Infectious Period 45
CLINICAL MANIFESTATIONS AND SEVERITY OF THE DISEASE 46
    Asymptomatic Cases 46
    Mild Cases 46
    Moderate Cases 47
    Severe Cases 47
CASE FATALITY RATE 47
    Based on Gender 48
    Based on the Age Factor 49
CONCLUSION 49
TAKE-HOME MESSAGE 50
WHAT YOU WILL LEARN 51
LIST OF ABBREVIATIONS 51
REFERENCES 52
CHAPTER 3 REPLICATION AND PATHOGENESIS OF CORONAVIRUSES 58
Mohammad Sufian Badar, Onaiza Ansari, Anam Mursaleen, Asrar Ahmad Malik,
Javaid Ahmad Sheikh and *Aamir Nehal*
INTRODUCTION 58
    Genomic Organisation of SARS-CoV-2 60
    Structural Proteins of the SARS-CoV-2 60
        Spike Protein 60
        Envelope Protein 62
        Membrane Protein 63
        N Protein 63
    Replication of SARS-CoV-2 Genome 64
        Entry of Coronavirus inside the Host Cell 64
    SARS-CoV-2 Infection via CD16 Receptor 65
    SARS-CoV-2 Replicates inside the Macrophages in the Human Lungs 65
        Genome Multiplication 66
        Viral Assembly and Release 68
    The SARS-CoV-2 Pathogenesis 69
        Direct Cytopathic Effect of SARS-CoV-2 70
        Initiation of Innate Immune Response 70
        Adaptive Immune Response 71
        SARS-CoV-2 Activates Inflammasomes 73
        Hypercytokinemia and Organ Damage 75

Renin-angiotensin System in COVID-19 76

CONCLUSION 77

SUMMARY 78

REFERENCES 79

CHAPTER 4 TRANSMISSION CYCLE OF SARS-COV-2 86

Mohammad Sufian Badar, Tahira Khan ,Harsha Negi, Abul Kalam Najmi and Junaid Alam

INTRODUCTION 86

Transmission Cycle 87

MECHANISM OF SARS-COV-2 ENTRY INTO THE HUMAN CELL 89

Modes of Transmission 89

Animal-to-Human Transmission 89

Human-to-Human Transmission 91

Horizontal Transmission 92

Fomite Transmission 94

Oral-Fecal Route of Transmission 94

Nosocomial Transmission 94

Environmental Transmission 95

Air Pollution 96

Water Pollution 97

Weather-related Parameters 97

PREVENTIVE MEASURES TO COMBAT TRANSMISSION 98

CONCLUSION 98

TAKE HOME MESSAGE 99

REFERENCES 99

CHAPTER 5 SYMPTOMS AND DIAGNOSTIC TECHNIQUES OF COVID-19 102

Mohammad Sufian Badar, Aamir Nehal, Barka Basharat and Nushrat Jahan

INTRODUCTION 103

Asymptomatic Illness 104

Moderate Illness 105

Severe Illness 105

Critical Illness 105

Other Symptoms 105

Neurological Symptoms 106

Olfactory and Gustatory Dysfunction 107

Altered Mental Status/confusion/delirium 107

Myalgia 108

Cerebrovascular Diseases 108

Stroke 108

Cerebral Venous (sinus) Thrombosis 108

Encephalitis, Meninges-encephalitis, and Meningitis 109

Acute Myelitis 109

Gastrointestinal Manifestations 109

Myocardial Symptoms 110

Renal Manifestations 110

Hepatobiliary Manifestations 111

Diagnostic Techniques for COVID-19 111

Nucleic Acid Amplification Test 112

REVERSE TRANSCRIPTASE REAL-TIME POLYMERASE CHAIN REACTION (RT-QPCR) 112

REVERSE TRANSCRIPTION LOOP-MEDIATED ISOTHERMAL AMPLIFICATION (RT-LAMP) 113
CRISPR-BASED DIAGNOSIS 114
CARTRIDGE-BASED NUCLEIC ACID AMPLIFICATION TEST (CBNAAT) 116
TRUNAT 116
SEROLOGICAL ASSAYS 117
LATERAL FLOW IMMUNOASSAY 118
ENZYME-LINKED IMMUNOSORBENT ASSAY 119
CHEMILUMINESCENCE IMMUNOASSAY (CLIA) 119
    Chemiluminescence Immunoassay for Testing SARS-CoV-2 Specific Antibody 119
    Chemiluminescence Immunoassay for Testing Serum SARS-CoV-2 N Antigen 120
DISCUSSION 120
CONCLUSION 121
WHAT YOU WILL LEARN 122
REFERENCES 122

CHAPTER 6 TREATMENT OPTIONS FOR COVID-19 INFECTED PATIENTS 125
M. Anju, Vivas Salim, Azfar Kamal, Ekbal Ahmed and Ravindra Kumar
INTRODUCTION 125
IMPORTANT TARGETS FOR PHARMACEUTICAL TREATMENT 127
TREATMENT STRATEGIES 130
    Pharmacological Interventions 130
        Antiviral Drugs 130
        Convalescent Plasma Therapy 132
        Monoclonal Antibody Therapy 133
        Immunomodulator Therapy 134
        CRISPR-Cas13 Therapy 135
        Vaccines 137
    Non-Pharmacological Interventions 139
CHALLENGES ASSOCIATED WITH VARIOUS TREATMENTS 140
TAKE HOME MESSAGE 141
CONCLUSION 142
WHAT YOU WILL LEARN 142
REFERENCES 143

CHAPTER 7 CHALLENGES POSED BY COVID-19 148
Mohammad Sufian Badar, Waseem Ali, Onaiza Ansari, Asrar Ahmad Malik,
Javaid Ahmad Sheikh and Anam Mursaleen
INTRODUCTION 149
    Challenge: Mental Health of Healthcare Workers 150
        Risk Factors Associated with Challenges Related to Mental Health Due to COVID-19
        Outbreak 151
    Infomania 151
    Restriction Measures 152
    Changes in Daily Habits 152
    Current or Past Medical History- 152
    Challenge: Vaccine 153
        Major Hurdles in Vaccine Development against Global COVID-19 Pandemic 154
    Challenge: COVID-19 Diagnosis 156
        Factors Interfering Diagnosis of COVID-19 157
    Unavailability of Effective Diagnostic Tool 158
    Specialized Laboratory Settings 158

False Results 158
Sampling Error 159
Shortage of kits/limited Supply of the Reagents 159
Challenge: Identification of Potential of Drug Candidates Against COVID-19 159
    Why Drug Discovery is a Challenge? 160
    COVID-19 Complexities 162
    Cost and Risk 162
Challenge: Antimicrobial Resistance 162
FACTORS RESPONSIBLE FOR THE RISE IN AMR DUE TO COVID-19 PANDEMIC 163
High Rate of Antimicrobial Utilization 163
Disruption of Healthcare 163
Antibiotic Availability 163
    Challenge: Economical Burden 164
Challenge: High morbidity and Mortality 165
    Risk Factors Resulting in Higher Morbidity and Mortality Rates 165
Age 165
Gender 166
Co-morbidities: (Bacterial co-infection, viral co-infection, and non-communicable diseases) 166
The Co-morbidities Associated with Severity and Greater Mortality during COVID-19
Pandemic 167
    Obesity 167
    Hypertension 167
    Diabetes 168
    Bacterial/Viral co-infection 168
    COVID-19 Vaccination 168
CONCLUSION 169
FUTURE PERSPECTIVES 169
Resilience, Rest and Recover 169
Vaccination Drives 170
Multivalent Vaccine 170
Private-public Collaborations 170
Monitoring Approaches 171
Drug Repurposing 171
Point-of-care Diagnostic Devices/standardization of New Protocols for Better Diagnostic
Approaches 171
REFERENCES 172

**CHAPTER 8 THE IMPACT OF COVID-19 ON THE ECONOMY AND ROADBLOCKS TO
RECOVERY** 177
Mohammad Sufian Badar, Ankita Pati, Labeebah Rizwan Badar and K. Shruti Lekha
COVID-19 INFECTION 178
STATISTICS OF COVID-19- MORBIDITY, MORTALITY 178
THE OVERALL IMPACT OF COVID-19 179
IMPACT OF COVID-19 ON MACROECONOMICS AND MACROECONOMICS 181
Manufacturing 181
Employment 182
Travel 182
Economic activities 182
**RESPONSE TO THE IMPACT OF COVID-19 ON MACROECONOMICS AND
MICROECONOMIES BY AUTHORITIES** 183

IMPACT OF COVID-19 AT AN INDIVIDUAL LEVEL 188
WHAT YOU WILL LEARN 189
REFERENCES 189

CHAPTER 9 AI-BASED DIAGNOSIS OF NOVEL CORONAVIRUS USING RADIOGRAPH IMAGES 190
Mohammad Sufian Badar, Aisha Idris, Areeba Khan, Md Mustafa and Farheen Asaf
INTRODUCTION 191
COVID 19- ETIOLOGY, CLINICAL IMAGING, AND PROGNOSIS 192
 Chest Imaging 193
  Ground-glass opacity (GGO) 194
  Peripheral or posterior distribution 194
  Crazy-paving appearance 194
  Air bronchograms 194
  Fibrous lesions 194
  Halo sign 194
COMPUTATIONAL DIAGNOSIS FOR COVID-19 196
 Techniques Used in Diagnosis of Covid 19 196
  Nucleic Acid Amplification Test 198
  Serological tests 198
  Biosensors 198
  Radiology Imaging 199
  Microfluidic approach 199
ML BASED APPROACHES [35] 200
 Role of ML in COVID-19 Diagnosis 200
 Circumstantial Use of ML 201
  Patient Diagnosis through Radiology Images 201
  Tracking of COVID-19 201
  Tracking Patient Health Condition 202
  Use of ML in Vaccine and Drug Development 202
 ML Algorithms Used to Combat COVID-19 203
  Decision tree 204
  Random Forest 204
  Naive Bayes 205
  Support vector machine 205
  k-Nearest-Neighbor (KNN) 205
  Gradient-boosted Decision Tree (GBDT) 205
  Logistic regression 206
  Artificial Neural Network 206
 Different Models and Networks of ML Used in COVID-19 Diagnosis 206
  LR Model 206
  XGBoost Model 206
  Boosted RF Model 207
  Deep Forest Model 207
  Truncated Inception Net 207
CASE STUDIES 208
 CASE I 208
 CASE II 208
 CASE III 208
 CASE IV 209

CHALLENGES AND FUTURE DIRECTIONS 209
TAKE AWAY HOME MESSAGE 210
CONCLUSION 211
WHAT YOU WILL LEARN 212
REFERENCES 212

CHAPTER 10 USE OF MACHINE LEARNING IN DIAGNOSING COVID-19 INFECTION 218
Mohammad Sufian Badar, Bipasa Kar, Budheswar Dehury, Sarbani Mishra and
Shamim Ahmed Shamim
INTRODUCTION 219
ROLE OF MODERN TECHNIQUES IN THE DIAGNOSIS OF COVID-19 220
.... 221
    Nucleic acid Amplification Tests 221
    Serological Tests 222
    Biosensors 222
    Radiology Imaging 223
    Microfluidic Approach 223
    ML based Approaches 224
ML AND ITS ROLE IN COVID-19 DIAGNOSIS 224
    Circumstantial use of ML 225
        Patient Diagnosis Through Radiology Images 225
        Tracking of COVID-19 225
        Tracking Patient Health Condition 226
        Use of ML in Vaccine and Drug Development 226
    ML Algorithms used to Combat COVID-19 227
        Decision tree 228
        Random forest 229
        Naive Bayes 229
        Support Vector Machine 229
        k-Nearest-Neighbor (KNN) 229
        Gradient-boosted Decision Tree (GBDT) 229
        Logistic Regression 230
        Artificial Neural Network 230
    Different Models and Networks of ML used in COVID-19 Diagnosis 230
        LR Model 230
        XGBoost Model 231
        Boosted RF Model 231
        Deep Forest Model 231
        Truncated Inception Net 232
CASE STUDIES 232
    CASE I 232
    CASE II 233
    CASE III 233
    CASE IV 233
CHALLENGES AND FUTURE DIRECTIONS 233
CONCLUSION 234
REFERENCES 235

CHAPTER 11 FUTURE TECHNOLOGIES FOR CORONAVIRUSES (COVID-19) 243
Mohammad Sufian Badar, Alia, Kamakshi Srivastava, Zara Khan, Himanshu Dagar,
Faiz Akram Siddiqui, Punit Kaur and Nadeem Zafar Jilani
EXPLORATION OF ROBOTICS IN PANDEMIC MITIGATION STRATEGIES 243

Integration of Robotics in Combating Coronaviruses 243
Robotics Techniques and Tools 244
COUGH RECOGNITION NETWORK (CRN) 244
AUTOMATED AMBU VENTILATOR 245
AUTONOMOUS ROBOTIC POINT-OF-CARE ULTRASOUND IMAGING FOR
MONITORING OF COVID–19–INDUCED PULMONARY DISEASES 245
ROBOT-ASSISTED ULTRAVIOLET (UV) DISINFECTION IN RADIOLOGY 247
ROBOTIC-ASSISTED SURGERY FOR AUTOPSY 247
ULTRASOUND SCANNING ROBOT 247
MEDICAL TELEROBOTIC SYSTEMS 247
DRONES REDEFINING PANDEMIC SURVEILLANCE AND RESPONSE 248
Unmanned Aerial Vehicles (UAVs) 248
Technological Advancements in Drones to Combat COVID-19 250
BLOCKCHAIN 250
WEARABLE SENSING 250
ARTIFICIAL INTELLIGENCE AND MACHINE LEARNING 250
EDGE-COMPUTING-BASED DRONE TECHNOLOGY 251
GENETIC ENGINEERING AT THE FOREFRONT: CRISPR-CAS, GENE THERAPY,
RNAI 251
CRISPR/Cas9 252
Diagnosis and Therapy 252
RNAi 253
Gene Therapy 253
Repurposed Drugs 254
PRECISION PANDEMIC INTERVENTION THROUGH ADVANCED
NANOTECHNOLOGY APPLICATIONS 255
Nanoparticles to Combat COV19/SARSCOV2 255
Vaccine Delivery Methods via Nanocarriers 256
Future Prospect 257
CONCLUSION 258
TAKE HOME MESSAGE 258
WHAT YOU WILL LEARN 258
REFERENCES 259

SUBJECT INDEX 263

PREFACE

Since the ongoing pandemic has affected every individual, we need a book that is simple, precise, and easy to comprehend. I feel that very few books are available in the market aimed at the common person. Most books are written for college-going students, academicians, or researchers. This book covers all the aspects required to understand the present situation.

Generally, books are written for students, academicians, or researchers. However, this book is intended for the ordinary person to raise awareness. Therefore, it is written in a way that is coherent and understandable to the average person. Furthermore, the chapters' names and the contents' language are straightforward.

As we have already mentioned, the primary audience is the general masses. This book is written to include the role of all emerging technologies like Artificial Intelligence and Machine Learning, for predicting and diagnosing COVID-19 infection. Therefore, this book takes care of the primary and secondary audiences, without compromising the need and availability of the required material.

Since the primary audience is the general masses, we need to design the content so they can understand it easily and not lose interest. Readers will also learn all they need to know about emerging technologies (Machine Learning, Artificial Intelligence, Blockchain), so they can understand how these technologies can be used to diagnose and fight COVID-19. Due to this coherency, the reader goes to a higher level of understanding without realizing it.

Three key features:

1. Generally, books are written for students, academicians, and researchers. This is the only book written based on the needs of the general masses of the population. Since this pandemic has affected every strata of society, many people want to learn more about the causative Coronaviruses, the viral agent that causes this disease. For that, they will need to learn about the basics of cause, epidemiology, pathogenicity, transmission, diagnosis, treatment, and challenges. The above-mentioned characteristics are explained in detail in the first few chapters.

2. The book is organized in a way that the reader acquires knowledge from basic to advanced levels. After learning about the biology of the coronaviruses, readers will learn how Machine Learning, a common buzzword that everyone uses, is used to diagnose and fight COVID-19 infection. This book will also discuss the challenges we face in using these technologies to carry out such a task.

3. Along with Machine Learning, Artificial Intelligence (AI) and the Internet of Things (IoT) can also be used in the fight against COVID-19. This book will also use Blockchain technology to find and control the socioeconomic and educational post-pandemic impacts of COVID-19.

Mohammad Sufian Badar
Department of Bioengineering, University of California
Riverside, CA, USA

List of Contributors

Aisha Idris	Department of Biotechnology, Jamia Hamdard, New Delhi, India
Areeba Khan	Department of Biotechnology, Jamia Hamdard, New Delhi, India
Alia	Department of Computer Science, Jamia Millia Islamia, New Delhi, India
Ankita Pati	Centre for Biotechnology, Siksha'O'Anusandhan University, Bhubaneswar, Odisha, India
Ahmad Masroor Karimi	Clinical Oncology, South West Wales Cancer Centre, Swansea Bay University Health Board, Swansea, UK
Anam Mursaleen	Department of Biotechnology, Jamia Hamdard, New Delhi, India
Asrar Ahmad Malik	Department of Biotechnology, Jamia Hamdard, New Delhi, India
Aamir Nehal	Consultant Physiotherapist, Bank Road, Motihari, Bihar, India
Abul Kalam Najmi	Department of Pharmacology, SPER, Jamia Hamdard, New Delhi, India
Azfar Kamal	Postgraduate Diploma in Orthopedics, Senior Consultant, District Hospital, Sambhal, India
Bipasa Kar	Bioinformatics Division, ICMR-Regional Medical Research Centre, Odisha, India
Budheswar Dehury	Bioinformatics Division, ICMR-Regional Medical Research Centre, Odisha, India
Barka Basharat	Department of Biotechnology, Jamia Hamdard University, New Delhi, India
Faiz Akram Siddiqui	AIIMS, New Delhi, India
Fahim Ahmad	Department of Pathology, University of Maryland School of Medicine, Baltimore, MD, USA
Faiyaz Ahmad	Madhubani Medical College & Hospital (MMCH), Madhubani, Bihar, India
Farheen Asaf	Max Super Speciality Hospital, New Delhi, India
Harsha Negi	Department of Pharmacology, SPER, Jamia Hamdard, New Delhi, India
Himanshu Dagar	Department of Computer Science, Jamia Millia Islamia, New Delhi, India
Ibtesaam Hafeez	Department of Biotechnology, Jamia Hamdard, New Delhi, India
Imtshan Nawaz	Department of Biotechnology, Jamia Hamdard, New Delhi, India
Junaid Alam	Division of Trauma Surgery & Critical Care, AIIMS Jai Prakash Narayan Apex Trauma Center, New Delhi, India
Javaid Ahmad Sheikh	Department of Biotechnology, Jamia Hamdard, New Delhi, India
Kamakshi Srivastava	Department of Computer Science, Jamia Millia Islamia, New Delhi, India
K. Shrutilekha	Centre for One Health Education, Research, and Development (COHERD), Indian Institute of Public Health Gandhinagar (IIPHG), Gandhinagar, Gujarat, India IMS&SH, SOA University, Bhubaneswar, Odisha, India

Labeebah Rizwan Badar   Badar Medical Centre, New Delhi, India

Md Mustafa   Department of Biotechnology, Jamia Hamdard, New Delhi, India

Mohammad Sufian Badar   Department of Bioengineering, University of California, Riverside, CA, USA
Universal Scientific Education and Research Network (USERN), Tehran, Iran
Director (Academic), SPI Darbhanga, India
Department of Computer Science and Engineering (Bioinformatics), School of Engineering Sciences and Technology (SEST), Jamia Hamdard, New Delhi, India

Mairaj Ahmed Ansari   Department of Biotechnology, Jamia Hamdard, New Delhi, India

M. Anju   Department of Bioscience and Engineering, National Institute of Technology, Kerala, India

Nadeem Zafar Jilani   Department of Pediatric Emergency, Sidra Medicine, Ar-Rayyan, Qatar

Nushrat Jahan   Department of Biotechnology, Jamia Hamdard, New Delhi, India

Onaiza Ansari   Department of Biotechnology, Jamia Hamdard, New Delhi, India

Punit Kaur   AIIMS, New Delhi, India

Ravindra Kumar   Department of Bioscience and Engineering, National Institute of Technology Calicut, Kerala, India

Sadia Saba   Department of Neurology, Indiana University School of Medicine, Indianapolis, USA

Sarbani Mishra   Bioinformatics Division, ICMR-Regional Medical Research Centre, Odisha, India

Shamim Ahmed Shamim   Department of Nuclear Medicine, AIIMS, New Delhi, India

Sushim Harish Mathur   Medical Officer, New Delhi Municipal Council, New Delhi, India

Tahira Khan   Department of Pharmacology, SPER, Jamia Hamdard, New Delhi, India

Umme Hania Irfan   Department of Biotechnology, Jamia Hamdard, New Delhi, India

Vivas Salim   Department of Bioscience and Engineering, National Institute of Technology, Kerala, India

Waseem Ali   Department of Molecular Medicine, Jamia Hamdard, New Delhi, India

Zaid Hussain Siddique   Department of Biotechnology, Jamia Hamdard, New Delhi, India

Zara Khan   Department of Computer Science, Jamia Millia Islamia, New Delhi, India

CHAPTER 1

History of Coronaviruses

Mohammad Sufian Badar[1,2,3,4,*], Umme Hania Irfan[5], Zaid Hussain Siddique[5], Ahmad Masroor Karimi[6], Mairaj Ahmed Ansari[5], Fahim Ahmad[7] and Faiyaz Ahmad[8]

[1] Department of Bioengineering, University of California, Riverside, CA, USA

[2] Universal Scientific Education and Research Network (USERN), Tehran, Iran

[3] Director (Academic), SPI Darbhanga, India

[4] Department of Computer Science and Engineering (Bioinformatics), School of Engineering Sciences and Technology (SEST), Jamia Hamdard, New Delhi, India

[5] Department of Biotechnology, Jamia Hamdard, New Delhi, India

[6] Clinical Oncology, South West Wales Cancer Centre, Swansea Bay University Health Board, Swansea, UK

[7] Department of Pathology, University of Maryland School of Medicine, Baltimore, MD, USA

[8] Madhubani Medical College & Hospital (MMCH), Madhubani, Bihar, India

Abstract: Over the past two decades, coronavirus-associated diseases such as SARS and MERS have challenged the public health systems globally. Around 2002-2003, a near-pandemic of a previously unknown β-coronavirus, named SARS-CoV, arose in China and 29 other countries. Not much attention was paid to it post-disappearance of this outbreak. An understanding of the coronavirus began only after alarming predictions of the virus's re-emergence began in 2007. Identification from previous studies revealed that bats have proven to be a major reservoir of animal coronavirus. SARS-related bat coronaviruses have all the essential components of SARS-virus, have along with similar genome sequences to that of SARS-CoV and SARS-CoV-2, and thus, are able to cause infection and transmit between humans directly. Later in 2012, another unknown β-coronavirus named Middle East respiratory syndrome (MERS-CoV), with close relation to the SARS-CoV, caused an epidemic limited to the Middle-East. The emergence of yet another bat-origin coronavirus, α-coronavirus, in China caused epizootic disease in pigs, thus named swine acute diarrhea syndrome coronavirus (SADS-CoV). Subsequently, unattended warnings of 12 years led to the most fatal bat-derived sarbecovirus, recognized as SARS CoV-2, springing up in November 2019, sweeping the globe. The predictions of SARS-CoV-2 to be a natural event with association to transmission directly from bats to humans or through an intermediate host have been essentially proven to be true. SARS-Cov-2 shares genetic properties with many other sarbecoviruses; this slies fully within their genetic cluster and is, thus, a naturally emerged virus.

---

* Corresponding author Mohammad Sufian Badar: Department of Bioengineering, University of California, Riverside, CA, USA; E-mail: sufianbadar@gmail.com

Based on the genomic structure coronavirus is mainly divided into four subgroups alpha, beta, gamma, and delta.

CoVs are fall under the family Coronaviridae, and subfamily Orthocoronavirinae. The virus is protected by receptor binding domain (RBD) that binds to ACE2 receptor found in kidneys, lungs, heart and gastrointestinal tract, which that promote viral entry into target cells.

Domestic animals can act as intermediary hosts in the transmission of viruses from natural hosts to people. Porcine Epidemic Diarrhea CoV(PEDC), which originated in pigs, was found to be similar to SADS-CoV. It has been transferred from bats to pigs. SADS-CoV was first found in rhinolophids or horseshoe bat, before the SARS epidemic Recombination of bat SARSr-CoVs, or recombined virus, infected and adapted to civets and humans. MERS-CoV is a zoonotic virus. It was transferred from dromedary camels to humans. The first confirmed cases of SARS-CoV-like viruses were found in raccoon dogs in live animal markets and palm civets. Another bat coronavirus, CoV RaTG13, was isolated from the *Rhinolophus affinis* bats.

Corona variants are classified into variants of concern (VOCS), variants of interest (VOI), variants of high consequence (VOHC), and variants being monitored (VBM).

Some common coronaviruses of human are 229E, NL63, OC43, and HKU1, which infect the upper-respiratory tract.

Keywords: ACE2 receptor, A570Y, ARCoV-2, APN, AIBV, BALF, CTD, CEACAM1, CoV-HKU5 strains, D614G, DPP4, Fatal pneumonia, GISAID, HCoV, HKU1, HCoV-OC43, MERS-CoV, NL63, N5014, Nsp, NTD, Orthocoronavirinae, Orf1a, PL-pro, PEPV, RaTG13, Rf4092, RBd, SARS-CoV-2, Spike (S1), SARS-CoV, SADS-CoV, SARS-CoV-2, SARsr-CoVs, TMPRSS2, TCOV(TECoV), TGEV, VOI, VBM, VOCs, VOHC, WIV16.

INTRODUCTION

Coronaviruses are enclosed, unsegmented, and single-stranded positive RNA genomes. They are identifiable by crown-like protrusions on their surface (the term "corona" comes from the Latin word "crown"). They belong to the Nidovirales subfamily within the Coronaviridae family. Coronaviruses are categorized into four groups: alpha, beta, gamma, and delta. Typically, alpha and beta coronaviruses impact mammals, causing respiratory issues in humans and gastroenteritis in various animal species [1].

B.1.1.7 (Alpha): The first problematic variant was labeled in the UK at the end of December 2020.

B.1.351 (Beta): First stated in South Africa in December 2020.

P.1 (Gamma): First identified in Brazil in January 2021.

B.1.617.2 (Delta): First identified from India in December 2020.

B.1.1.529 (Omicron): First identified in South Africa in November 2021 [2].

Among the four beta-coronaviruses known to infect people, the most serious pathogens are the SARS-CoV and MERS-CoV [3].

Till December 2019, only six different coronaviruses had been identified with capability of infecting humans. Among these, four coronaviruses (HCoV-NL63, HCoV-229E, HCoV-OC43, and HKU1) usually induced mild flu-like signs in individuals with a healthy immune system. The remaining two coronaviruses had caused global pandemics in the preceding two decades [4]. The first case of covid was reported as a common cold in 1960. According to a Canadian study in 2001, about 500 patients had a flu-like symptoms. Around 17-18 cases were confirmed by PCR to be infected with the coronavirus strain [5].

The SARS outbreak, which occurred between 2002 and 2003, was characterized by the development of the severe acute respiratory syndrome coronavirus (SARS-CoV) and had a 10% death rate. Likewise, in 2012, the Middle East Respiratory Syndrome Coronavirus (MERS-CoV) gave rise to a substantial pandemic with a notably high fatality rate of 37 percent [6].

Hundreds of different classes of bats found around the world have become a huge reservoir of coronaviruses. SARS-CoV, MERS-CoV, and SARSCoV-2, all cluster as closely associated coronaviruses in the SARS-like virus's arbovirus and merbecovirus (MERS-like viruses) phylogenetic groups. These two SARS viruses, like SADS-CoV, are derived from viruses that infect rhinolophids (Rhinolophus genus) or horseshoe bats. During the previous 15 years, scientists have also discovered worldwide reservoirs of coronaviruses over the past 15 years (in Africa, the Americas, the Middle East, Asia, and Southeast Asia, with a particular focus on China, which has been the epicenter of three out of the four recent crises).

Bats, belonging to many widespread genera and species, have now been identified as an important source of animal coronaviruses. According to a study in 20 countries with more than 19k species, mainly primates, and bats. These regions represented over 98% of the reported cases of coronavirus infections, with nearly 9% of over 12,000 randomly sampled bats found to be carrying one or more coronaviruses [7].

The virus known as the 2019 novel coronavirus (2019-nCoV), commonly referred to as the Wuhan coronavirus, was initially pinpointed as the primary factor behind a cluster of pneumonia cases that emerged in late 2019 in Wuhan, located in Hubei province, China. The China 2019-nCoV shared approximately 79.5% of its genetic sequence with SARS-CoV, which triggered the epidemic in 2002-2003 when its genomes were sequenced. The International Committee on Taxonomy of Viruses reclassified 2019-nCoV and renamed it as SARS-CoV-2 [8]. Various receptor- domain (RBD) spike proteins in SARS-related coronaviruses act as protective measures. This RBD binds particularly to the ACE-2 receptor, which is found in a variety of tissues or body parts including the kidneys, lungs, heart, and gastrointestinal system. This binding relationship aids the virus' entrance into target cells. According to genome sequencing, the RaTG13 virus isolated from bats (*Rhinolophus affinus*) appears to be the nearby relative of SARS-RBD CoV-2s [9].

ORIGIN

Coronaviruses (CoVs) are encapsulated viruses with a positive sense RNA, that is the single-stranded genome. They get their name from the crown-like appearance of the viral envelope under an electron microscope, which is caused by spike glycoproteins, as shown in Fig. (**1**) [10]. Coronaviruses (CoVs) are categorized within the order Nidovirales, the family Coronaviridae, and the subfamily Orthocoronavirinae [11]. Coronaviruses, which had previously spread in humans but primarily caused minor infections in immunocompetent people, were responsible for the SARS outbreak in Guangdong Province, China, in 2002 and 2003. MERS-CoV, which is also a highly pathogenic coronavirus, made its first appearance in Middle Eastern countries a decade following the emergence of SARS [12].

Animal Origin

Existing sequence databases show that entire human coronaviruses are descended from animals. As mentioned in Fig. (**2**), SARS-CoV, MERS-CoV, HCoV-NL63, and HCoV-229E are believed to have their origins in bats, while HCoV-OC43 and HKU1 are thought to have emerged from rodent species [13]. Domestic animals can act as intermediary reservoirs or carriers in the spread of viruses from natural reservoirs to people. Furthermore, domestic animals may contract diseases from coronaviruses that are spread by bats or other related species. The PEDV (Porcine Epidemic Diarrhea CoV) genomes are strikingly similar to those of bats, and more recently, SADS-CoV has been transferred from bats to pigs [13]. Only four of the nine beta-coronaviruses species and seven of the eleven alpha-coronavirus species have been recognised as hosts by the The International Committee on Taxonomy of Viruses (ICTV). It follows that bats are most possibly the main source of alpha- and beta-coronaviruses [12].

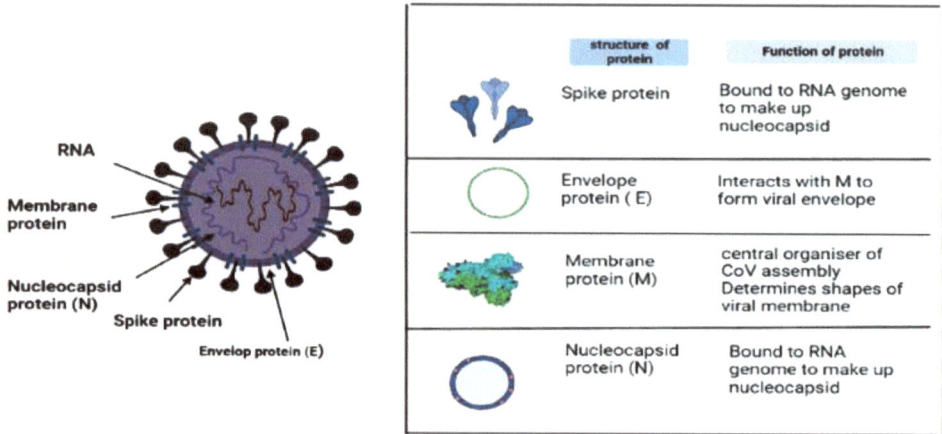

	structure of protein	Function of protein
	Spike protein	Bound to RNA genome to make up nucleocapsid
	Envelope protein (E)	Interacts with M to form viral envelope
	Membrane protein (M)	central organiser of CoV assembly Determines shapes of viral membrane
	Nucleocapsid protein (N)	Bound to RNA genome to make up nucleocapsid

Fig. (1). Coronavirus protein spike protein, envelope protein (E), membrane protein (M), and nucleocapsid structure and function

Genetically diverse coronavirus	Intermediate host	Natural host	Human host
	camel	bat	HCoV-229E
	rat	cow	HCoV-OC43
	?	mouse	HCoV-HKU1
	pig	bat	SADS-CoV
	bat	camel	MERS-CoV
	bat	fox	SARS-CoV
	?	bat	HCoV-NL63

Fig. (2). A visual representation illustrating the various animal categories serving as natural hosts and potential intermediary hosts for the six coronaviruses discovered in humans.
(Source: Victor M. Corman, Doreen Muth, Daniela Niemeyer *et al.*)

The establishment of the coronavirus associated with severe acute respiratory syndrome (SARS-CoV) was aided by recombination events involving bat SARS-related coronaviruses (SARSr-CoVs) [14]. The recombined virus had previously infected and adapted to both civets and humans before the SARS epidemic [15]. Since at least 30 years ago, dromedary camels have frequently been visible to the Middle East respiratory syndrome coronavirus (MERS-CoV) [16], with bats being the most likely source of transmission. HCoV-229E and HCoV-NL63 typically cause minor contaminations in humans with a healthy immune system. Given that HCoV-229E's ancestors have newly been discovered in African bats, camelids are most likely the virus' intermediate hosts. Both HKU1 and HCoV-OC43, which are generally safe for humans, likely originated in rodents [17]. The swine acute diarrhea syndrome (SADS) has recently appeared in piglets. This disease is brought on by the SADS coronavirus (SADS-CoV), a brand-new variation of the HKU2 Rhinolophus bat coronavirus [18].

According to the reports of two different teams, new coronaviruses related to the human SARS-CoV were identified in horseshoe bats (genus Rhinolophus) in 2005 as SARS-related viruses or SARS-like coronaviruses. These results suggest that bats might be the virus' natural carrier and that civets were merely transmission hosts for the SARS-CoV.

Direct transmission to humans with bat coronaviruses is infrequent because of the limited direct contact between bats and humans. It has been hypothesized that the transmission of SARS-CoV-2 from bats to humans requires an unidentified intermediary host that may aid in its transmission to humans [19].

The viral strains identified in this one place also contain all of the heritable components required to produce SARS-CoV. Given the lack of an immediate ancestor of SARS-CoV discovered in bat groups or communities despite searches lasting 15 years and given the frequency of RNA recombination amongst coronaviruses, it is most plausible that SARS-CoV arose relatively recently by the recombination of multiple bat SARS-CoVs, presumably within the aforementioned bat caves or other yet-to-be-identified places [19].

The idea that the civet SARS-CoV variant SZ3 was produced by the recombination of the bat SARS-CoV strains WIV16 and Rf4092 received additional strong support from recombination analysis. The closest SARS-CoV relative discovered in bats, WIV16, was probably produced by the recombination of two additional common SARS-CoV strains found in bats [20]. The genetic area before orf8, which contains an additional amino acid, and the S gene, which expresses the spike (S) protein with the receptor-binding domain (RBD), are both of great relevance, are and the regions with the most recombination breakpoints. Due to the prevalence of bat SARSr-CoVs, their substantial genetic diversity, the close closeness of these genetic components, as well as the frequent occurrence of recombination events in coronaviruses, are important considerations, and it is anticipated that new variants will emerge in the future. The original source of SARS-CoV is believed to have emerged through genetic recombination within bats, subsequently transmitting to farmed civets or another animal. The virus was then passed to civets through fecal-oral transmission. This theory is bolstered by the absence of SARS cases in the Yunnan province during the SARS outbreak, the Guangdong virus spread among market civets before it infected people and underwent further mutations [20].

SARS-CoV

The first confirmed cases of biruses similar to SARS-CoV were discovered in masked palm civets (Paguma larvata) and a raccoon dogs in live animal markets. Reports indicate that masked palm civets, whether from the wild or farms without any contact with live animal markets, predominantly tested negative for SARS-CoV. This suggests that these animals may primarily serve as intermediate amplifying hosts rather than being the natural reservoirs of SARS-CoV [20].

A closely similar bat coronavirus termed SARS-related Rhinolophus bat coronavirus HKU3. (SARSr-Rh-BatCoV HKU3) was detected in Chinese horseshoe bats after extensive research on the natural animal reservoir of SARS-CoV [21]. Both the SARSr-Rh-BatCoV HKU3 genome sequence and anti-SAR--CoV antibodies are positive in these bats. These bat CoVs and SARS-CoV have nucleotide sequence homologies of 88–92%. The human Angiotensin-converting enzyme 2 (ACE2) is recognized as the SARS-CoV receptor. It has been shown that WIV1 derived from bat feces uses the human ACE2 receptor, the civet receptor, and the bat receptor for cell entry. With 95% nucleotide sequence homology, WIV1 represents the SARS-CoV in bats' closest relative [22].

MERS-CoV

Evolutionary or genetic relationship analysis investigation places MERS-CoV in the same group as the bat-derived CoV-HKU4 and CoV-HKU5 variants [22]. MERS-CoV and bat CoV-HKU4 both enter the host through the dipeptidyl peptidase 4 (DPP4) receptor [23]. Only 87% of MERS-CoV and its counterpart bat coronavirus, CoV-HKU25 counterparts' genomic sequences are comparable. According to the research performed in the Middle East, dromedary camels had positive serological results for MERS-CoV-specific neutralizing antibodies, echoing the situation with camels from the Middle East living in different African nations [24]. Camels are a confirmed reservoir host of MERS-CoV, as evidenced by the isolation of live MERS-CoV from dromedary camels' nasal swabs, it is identical to the virus originating in humans [23].

SARS-CoV-2

SARS-CoV-2 and a bat CoV RaTG13, obtained from *Rhinolophus affinis* bats, have 96.2% nucleotide homology [25]. Given that the Huanan Seafood Wholesale Market was related to a substantial number of the early COVID-19 cases, it means that the intermediary animal host of SARS-CoV-2 may also exist there, indicating the possibility of transmission from animals to people [26]. The nucleotide sequences of these novel pangolin CoV genomes and SARS-CoV-2 are 85–92% similar [27]. However, they share roughly 90% of RaTG13's nucleotide sequence identity, making them equally related to that gene [28]. In the phylogenetic tree, they are divided between two sub-lineages of SARS-CoV-2-like infectious agents, one of which has 97.4% sequence amino acid similarity with SARS-CoV-2 and a more comparable receptor binding domain (RBD) [27]. Even less distance exists between SARS-CoV-2 and RaTG13 than between SARS-CoV-2 and beta-CoVs related to pangolin SARS-CoV-2. SARS-CoV-2's evolutionary history in bats, pangolins, and other mammals is still unknown. The RBDs between SARS-Co--2 and pangolin have the maximum sequence homology. However, the most significant similarity in terms of genome-wide sequence homology is observed among beta coronaviruses associated with SARS-CoV-2, including SARS-CoV-2 itself and RaTG13 [29]. The remarkable similarity observed in the receptor-binding domains (RBDs) of pangolin SARS-CoV-2-related beta-coronaviruses and SARS-CoV-2 is likely the result of hypothesized convergent evolution driven by selective pressures [24]. An opposing viewpoint suggests that recombination could have occurred between a beta-CoV closely related to SARS-CoV-2 in pangolins and RaTG13 within a different animal species, potentially the third intermediate host. Recombination is common amid beta-CoVs and is a major force in evolution. SARS-CoV-2's immediate zoonotic origin is still up for debate [30].

Community-acquired HCoVs

Rodents have been shown to have the ancestors of human coronaviruses HCoV-OC43 and HCoV-HKU1. However, evolutionary data implies that both HCoV-NL63 and HCoV-229E emerged in bat coronaviruses, namely ARCoV2 (Appalachian Ridge CoV), identified in North American tri-colored bats, and HCoV-NL63, which had a reportedly close relationship. However, HCoV-229E shared genetic similarities that exist with another bat coronavirus known as GhanaKwam /Hipposideros /19/2008, which was discovered in Ghana. Additionally, it has been suggested that camelids could serve as potential intermediate hosts for the virus [31].

Interspecies Transmission

The coronavirus family can be divided into at least three different groups of coronaviruses. These groups cause different kinds of illnesses in animals like pets, wild animals, birds, and even in human. Some of these illnesses are mild, while others can be severe. In humans, some coronaviruses can even cause common colds. SARS-CoV is quite different genetically from other known coronaviruses. When scientists study its genetic relationships using a rooted tree method, they classify it as either a new group called "IV" or sometimes as a subgroup of group II. Recent genetic studies have identified two wild animal coronaviruses (civet cats and raccoon dogs) as belonging to the SARS-CoV group. Each group of coronaviruses has varying degrees of genetic and antigenic similarity, and several of them exhibit interspecies transmission.

Given previous research on the transmission between different species of animal coronaviruses and the identification of wildlife reservoirs for coronaviruses, it is not unexpected that SARS-CoV is a zoonotic disease, with the potential for transmission from wild animals to humans. For instance, Table **1** clearly depicts that there are cases like porcine CoVs (TGEV) and canine and feline CoVs, which demonstrate how these viruses can infect pigs, dogs, and cats, leading to different levels of disease manifestation and offering some level of cross-protection in hosts that are different from their primary reservoir. These three related CoVs reportedly evolved from an ancestral CoV through host range mutations. Wildlife reservoirs were recognized prior to SARS for CoVs. Wild ruminants kept in captivity are known to harbor domestic calf-infected wild ruminant isolates as well as bovine CoVs that are antigenically similar to them. The infection of both humans and dogs by CoV strains that share genetic identities exceeding 97% highlights the adaptability and versatility of bovine CoV. The discovery that bovine CoV may infect and cause sickness (especially diarrhea) in a wide range of phylogenetically distinct species, including avian hosts, baby turkeys, but not newborn chicks, is significant, the situation is even more striking compared to the contagion of mammalian hosts by bovine CoVs. It is noteworthy that the baby turkeys infected with bovine CoV in the latter study also spread the viruses to the control birds, who had no interaction with the infected turkeys. Although the causes of the bovine CoVs' wide host range are unknown, it is possible that hemagglutinin and its potential function in binding to various cell types are related.

Current data shows that the SARS-CoV may have a variation of hosts in addition to humans. Civet cats and raccoon dogs both harbors genetically related CoVs. SARS-CoV sub-clinically infected cats as well as macaques, ferrets, and other animals in experimental studies. The SARS-CoV spread to exposed contacts in the latter two species, proving that it can spread to a new host species. Therefore, while earlier research has shown the introduction of novel animal coronavirus (CoV) strains and the wide range of hosts that certain CoVs may infect, the parameters governing host range specificity among CoVs remain unknown [32].

Table 1. This table divides Coronaviruses into genetic groups (I, II, III, IV, and IIA) and gives the viral names as well as the hosts they infect. The organization of genetic groupings and their related viruses provides insights into the variety of coronaviruses and their host range. The chart also offers further information on the sources of certain CoVs and the tissues they affect.

Genetic group	Virus	Host
I	HCoV-229E	Human
-	TGEV	Pig
-	PRCV	Pig
-	PEDV	Pig
-	F1pV	Cat
-	FCoV	Cat
-	CCoV	Dog
-	RaCoV	Rabbit
II	HCoV-OC43	Human
-	NUN	Mouse
-	RCoV(sialodocry-adenitis)	Rat
-		Pig
-	BEV	Cattle
-	BCOV	
III	IBV	Chicken
-	TCOV(TECoV)	Turkey
IV ?	SARS	Human
IIA	Civet cat CoV	Himalayan civet(palm)
-	Raccoon dog	Raccoon dog

A= SIintestine(small);?? = BCoV-like Corona virus from a child; =unknown
:-CNS(central nervous system)
(Source: Weiss & Navas-Martin, 2005)

Endemic Origin

Humans have been found to harbor six different CoVs. The first descriptions of regional human CoV (HCoV) were published in the 1960s, around the time HCoV-OC43 and -229E were first identified [33]. Only recently, in the years 2004 and 2005, were HCoV-NL63 and HCoV-HKU1 identified. Severe acute respiratory syndrome (SARS)-CoV and the Middle East Respiratory Syndrome (MERS)-CoV, identified in 2003 and 2012, respectively [34], represent two widespread CoVs that have emerged in humans in the past twenty years apart from these four endemic HCoVs. Both of these viruses were accountable for outbreaks characterized by significant case fatality rates and belong to the beta-coronaviruses genus. In 2002–2003, a viral pneumonia outbreak was triggered by SARS-CoV. At least 8000 people were impacted by this outbreak, which had a 10% case fatality rate overall. According to the main idea, the SARS-CoV epidemic lineage was spread by predatory wild animals such as civet cats, which are likely to have first acquired the virus *via* rhinolophid bats [35].

HCoV-NL63 and HCoV-229E, two human alpha coronaviruses, share only 65% identical nucleotides. In 1967, HCoV-229E was first discovered. After being isolated from a baby who had bronchiolitis and conjunctivitis, the latter was first discovered in 2003. Contrary to HCoV-OC43, which has been around since the 1960s, HCoV-HKU1 was first identified in a 71-year-old man undergoing treatment for pneumonia in Hong Kong in 2005 [35].

SARS-CoV

On January 2, 2003, two cases of atypical pneumonia were linked to the infection of several hospital staff members in the city of Heyuan, located in Guangdong Province. Clusters of cases were discovered as a result of an investigation by the Guangdong Provincial Center for Disease Control and Prevention between November 2002 and mid-January 2003 in six additional municipalities: Foshan, Jiangmen, Zhongshan, Guangzhou, Shenzhen, and Zhaoqing. A mandatory atypical pneumonia case reporting requirement using a standardized case definition and reporting form was implemented across the entire province on February 3, 2003. On March 12, 2003, the WHO issued a worldwide alert concerning unusual pneumonia cases reported in China's Guangdong Province, the Hong Kong Special Administrative Region, and Vietnam. Coronavirus infection is the cause of the sickness, which is now referred to as Severe Acute Respiratory Syndrome (SARS) and it subsequently spread quickly throughout the world [36].

MERS-CoV

The Middle East Syndrome associated-CoV (MERS-CoV) was originally discovered in a Saudi Arabian patient in September 2012 who had severe, fatal pneumonia. It was later discovered in Jordan in April 2012. According to the WHO, the vast majority of the 2,040 confirmed cases and 712 fatalities to date have happened in the Kingdom of Saudi Arabia, and one significant travel-related outbreak took place in South Korea. Since 2012, 26 nations have been impacted, whichinclude regions spanning the Middle East, Africa, Europe, Asia, and North America [37]. About 75% of cases are said to have originated in the Middle East.

SARS-CoV-2

According to epidemiological statistics, the Huanan Seafood Wholesale Market located in Wuhan emerged as a prominent and early focal area of SARS-CoV-2 infection. Approximately 28% of all cases recorded in December 2019, as well as two of the first three known cases of coronavirus illness (COVID-19), had direct ties to this market that dealt in the sale of wild animals [38]. The Huanan or other markets in Wuhan were involved in overall cases in December 2019, with these cases being more common in the first half of the month [39]. SARS-CoV-2 was named due to its association with severe acute respiratory syndrome, stemming from its structural similarity to related coronaviruses [40]. There have been 2,791 fatalities and 78,959 authenticated instances of SARS-CoV-2 infection in China as of February 28, 2020. A significant obstacle to successful containment is the fact that outside of China, over 3,664 confirmed cases have been reported in 46 countries and regions. Additionally, the genomic sequences of SARS-CoV-2 viruses isolated from different patients display sequence similarities of over 99.9%, indicating a very recent transmission to the human host [41].

It is generally acknowledged that a great number of diseases have long occurred in their natural habitats. Modern farming practices and urbanization, for example, have a significant influence on the continuous transfer of viruses from their hosts in nature to people and other animals. In accordance with the "one health" idea, keeping the borders between reservoirs of nature and human settlements is the most effective strategy to prevent zoonotic illnesses [20]. When viruses enter the body, they cling to cells, penetrate them, and copy their RNA, allowing them to spread. Errors in the replication process, on the other hand, cause changes to the RNA [42].

Despite the proofreading capabilities, viruses may undergo rapid mutations on replication. Mutations either lead to virus deletion or have no effect at all. The silent mutation, one with no effect, may either alter only the nucleotide sequences while exempting amino acid sequences or they are conservative with similar properties of amino acid side chains. However, the virus proliferates rapidly and becomes the dominant variant, thus giving the selective advantage.

The SARS-CoV-2 genome has 1,516 nucleotide-level changes, according to genome-wide annotation programs.

The WIVO4/2019 sequence of strain is considered to be the original sequence or considered to be the original 'sequence zero' by GISAID, which stands for the Global Initiative on Sharing Avian Influenza Data.

A symptomatic patient's broncho-alveolar lavage fluid (BALF) was used to isolate this strain. It has also demonstrated the sequence of the earliest genome from a patient in China. Before this, the occurrence of SARS-CoV was identified in a live sample from two deceased Malayan pangolins that exhibited frothy liquid in their lungs, indicating the occurrence of pulmonary fibrosis [43]. WHO brought together health professionals, virologists, epidemiologists, and bioinformatics experts to establish a worldwide network for monitoring and studying the mutations and variants of SARS-CoV-2 from the beginning.

NOMENCLATURE

GISAID, Nextstrain & PANGO are used extensively for naming and tracking the SARS-CoV-2, the virus responsible for COVID-19 variant in the Greek alphabet. WHO has recommended Greek alphabets for easy and unambiguous discussion [44].

CLASSIFICATION OF VARIANTS

The World Health Organization (WHO) has designated certain variants of the virus as "Variants of Concern" (VOCs). This declaration is based on exhibiting altered transmissibility or immune escape and eventually warrants closure monitoring. The transmissions exhibited by VOCs were advantageous and dominating over the preceding variants either in the case of regional variants, which included:

- Alpha (PANGO lineages B.1.1.7) in Europe
- Beta (B.1.351) in South Africa
- Gamma (P.I) in South America

or global transmission cases, including

- Delta variant (B.1.617.2/AY sublineages)
- Omicron variant (B.1.1.529/BA sublineages, including BA.1, BA.2, and BA.5) [45].

Alpha Variant

Alpha variant (B.1.1.7), alternatively referred to as BOI/501.VI is the first variant to be highly publicized. It first appeared in November 2020 and surged its infections in December. It was classified by C.D.C. as a variant of concern when dominated in the US. 23 mutations of this variant were reported, among which 17 were severe mutations with 13 non-synonymous and 4 deletions, making them capable of manifesting the disease severely [45].

The mutations of spike protein include deletion at 69-70, deletion at 144 & several substitutions such as N501Y, A570D, D614G, P681H [46].

i. D614G Mutation

The original Wuhan virus possessed an aspartic acid at 614-position of amino acid in the receptor-binding region of the S1 subunit of the spike protein (614D). The mutation with glycine at that position made it more infectious and led to its rapid spread [42].

i. N501Y Mutation

This is a mutation in the receptor-binding domain (RBD) of the S protein, causing a change from asparagine to tryptophan [42].

i. A570Y Mutation

This is also a receptor-binding domain mutation that changes Ala to Asp. This change is non-conservative as an acidic polar amino acid replaces a neutral polar amino acid.

Beta Variant

Beta/B.1,35/5014.V2 variant emerged as a dominant and more transmissible variant in South Africa, following South England at the end of 2020. The spike protein possesses eight lineages mutations, among which are as follows:

  i. K417N (changes of Lys to Asn)
 ii. EH84K (change of Glu to Lys)
iii. N501Y (change of Asn to Tyr)

Gamma Variant

P.1/gamma/501Y.V3 variant rose in Manaus with more transmissibility than the original virus. It was known to bear 17 specific amino acid changes with insertion, deletion as well as few synonymous mutations. The concern emerged by mutations in the receptor binding site of the S protein as in the other variant. By

January 2021, Japan, Germany, and the US were infected with the P.1 variant.

i. Mutations in P.1

i. N501

The spike protein readily binds to the ACE-2 receptor on the cell surface, thereby increasing the virus's ability to infect cells.

i. E484

It is the mutation of amino acid 484 from Glu to Lys. Referred to as escape mutation, it allows the virus to escape the previous P.1 infection-generated antibodies partially [47].

Delta Variant

The Delta variant was first identified in India in April 2021 and subsequently linked to a significant outbreak in the United Kingdom. This new wave of infections led to the emergence of various viral lineages, with some, like AY49, exhibiting higher transmissibility.

This variant exhibits mutations in the spike protein, which includes various mutations like T19R, Δ157158, L452R, T478K, D614G, P681R, and D950N. These mutations affect the antigenic regions of the receptor-binding protein and N-terminal domain deletion. Strains with deletions at specific sites may lead to increased replication, higher viral loads and ultimately increased transmission.

Omicron Variant

For more than a year, Omicron/B.1.1.529 and its sub-variants have dominated. Omicron distinguishes itself *via* its changed entrance behavior, considerable immune evasion skills, and capacity to contaminate individuals who have received vaccinations or were previously infected.

Omicron has already established significant genetic diversity before to its discovery. It is currently categorized into five main lineages, specifically BA.1, BA.2, BA.3, BA.4, and BA.5, with multiple sub-lineages forming, all of which are accruing additional alterations in their antigenic characteristics. BA.1 initially produced a global rise in infections at the end of 2021. However, by early 2022, it had been overtaken by BA.2. Additional BA sublineages, BA.4 and BA.5, were discovered in April 2022, and as of September 2022, BA.5 was responsible for a new worldwide Omicron revival. The Omicron lineages have extensive interactions with one another, suggesting that several recombination events occurred within the Omicron Variant of Concern (VOC) prior to its identification. For instance, BA.4 and BA.5 have essentially comparable sequences at the 5'-end of their genetic material until the M gene, but then they differ significantly, indicating a recent recombination event. BA.3 might also be the consequence of recombination between the original BA.1 and BA.2 viruses.

Variants of Concern (VOC)

A variant:

- with a rise in transmissibility
- increase in a fatality
- decrease in the effectiveness of vaccine therapy [45]

Examples include the B.1.6.1.7 variant with mutations E484D & L452R.

At present, there are no designated variants of SARS-CoV-2 classified as Variants of Interest (VOI) [48].

Variants of Interest (VOI)

A variant with the genetic capabilities of

- disease severity
- immune escape
- transmissibility
- diagnostic escape
- community transmission of consequential volume [45]

Examples of these include the Omicron (B.1.1.529, BA.1, BA.1.1, BA.2, BA.3, BA.4, and BA.5) lineages [48].

Variants Being Monitored (VBM)

A variant with

- approved medical countermeasures
- no longer detected or level of transmission [45]

Examples include:

- Alpha variant (B.1.1.7 and Q lineages)
- Beta variant (B.1.351 and its descendant lineages)
- Gamma variant (P.1 and its descendant lineages)
- Delta variant (B.1.617.2 and AY lineages)
- Epsilon variant (B.1.427 and B.1.429)
- Eta variant (B.1.525)
- Iota variant (B.1.526)
- Kappa variant (B.1.617.1)
- 1.617.3
- Mu variant (B.1.621, B.1.621.1)
- Zeta variants (P.2) [48]

Variants of High Consequence (VOHC)

A variant with

- a decrease in the effectiveness of vaccines
- an increase in clinical disease severity

No SARS-CoV-2 variant has been classified as VOHCs yet [45].

TYPES OF CORONAVIRUSES

The distinctive corona-like spikes on the surface of coronaviruses play a pivotal role in naming these viruses. They are categorized into four primary coronavirus subgroups: alpha, beta, gamma, and delta, which are displayed in Fig. (**3**).

- Two types of human viruses, Human Coronaviruses HCoV-229E and HCoV-NL63, associate to the alpha-coronavirus genus. Similar to other animal alpha coronaviruses, HCoV-229E primarily utilizes aminopeptidase-N (APN) as a receptor, as shown in Fig. (**4**). Contrarily, HCoV-NL63 utilizes angiotensin-converting enzyme-2 (ACE-2) like SARS-CoV and SARS-CoV-2, both belonging to the beta-coronaviruses [49]. Pig-transmissible gastroenteritis viruses and feline infectious peritonitis viruses are two significant animal alpha coronaviruses. The alpha coronaviruses also include a number of closely related bat coronaviruses.
- Two human beta-coronaviruses species that do not cause SARS, HCoV-OC43 and HCoV-HKU1, exhibit hemagglutinin-esterase activity and most likely utilize sialic acid residues as receptors [50]. Furthermore, within this particular

genus, various bat viruses exist, such as MERS-CoV, SARS-CoV, and SARS-CoV-2. It is crucial to emphasize that the latter three viruses are genetically separate and distinct from HCoV-OC43 and HCoV-HKU1 [51].

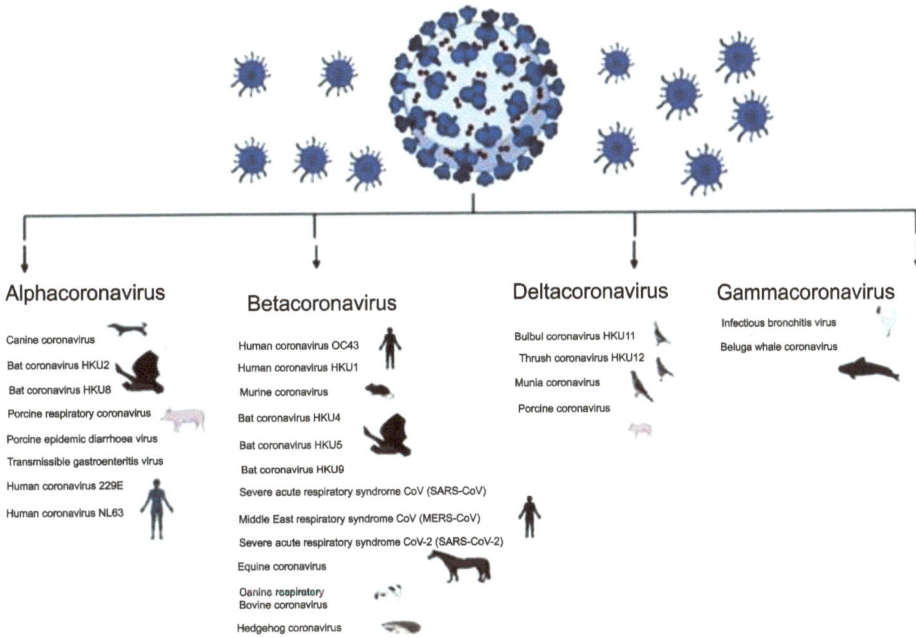

Fig. (3). Diagram illustrating the classification hierarchy of the Coronaviridae family, as per the guidelines of the International Committee on Taxonomy of Viruses (ICTV). The six coronaviruses identified in humans are categorized under the alpha- and beta-coronaviruses genera respectively.

Significant animal beta-coronaviruses comprise the mouse hepatitis virus and the bovine coronavirus, both of which are associated with viral hepatitis and demyelinating central nervous system diseases in laboratory settings. Due to their high degree of similarity, bovine coronavirus and HCoV-OC43 have been categorized as a single species, referred to as beta-coronaviruses 1. Interestingly, it was once believed, as recently as 1890, that HCoV-OC43 had the capacity to switch between different animal hosts.

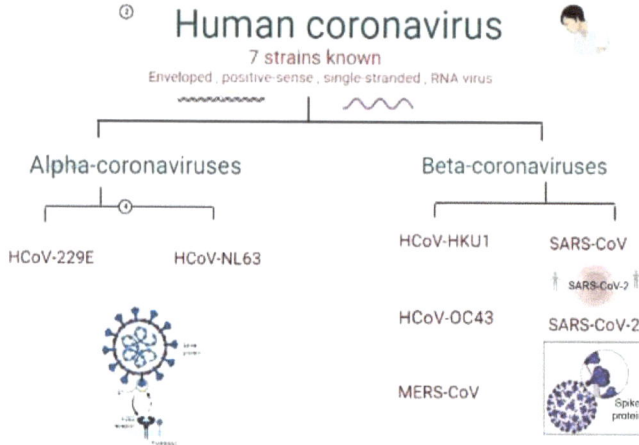

Fig. (4). A well-known group of enveloped, positive-sense, single-stranded RNA virus strains within human coronaviruses.

- Avian infectious bronchitis virus (AIBV), a significant veterinary pathogen that causes respiratory and reproductive tract diseases in chickens, is the most notable member of the genus of avian coronaviruses found in the gamma-coronavirus.
- There are several species of songbirds that carry the recently identified avian coronaviruses that make up the delta-coronavirus genus. Table **2** provides the list of coronaviruses along with the infection caused by them.

Table 2. The list below includes the numerous human coronaviruses and the diseases they cause. It provides information on the severity of each virus's diseases, ranging from mild respiratory ailments to more serious disorders like Middle East Respiratory Syndrome (MERS) and Severe Acute Respiratory Syndrome (SARS). It also shows the most current coronavirus, SARS-CoV-2, which was responsible for the COVID-19 epidemic.

HUMAN CORONAVIRUSES	SICKNESSES
HCoV-229E	Usually, mild respiratory illness
HCoV-NL63	-
HCoV-OC43	-
HKU1	-
MERS-CoV	Middle East Respiratory Syndrome (MERS)
SARS-CoV	Severe Acute Respiratory Syndrome (SARS)
SARS-CoV-2	COVID-19

HCoV-229E

When Dorothy Hamre, a researcher at the University of Chicago, examined tissue cultures from students who had colds, she found a novel virus that she named 229E.

In the meantime, a group of scientists working under the direction of Dr. David Tyrrell in England found a virus that resembled one that had been found in chickens with bronchitis in the 1930s. It was the first coronavirus to be linked to human infection [52].

The populations at highest risk of contracting HCoV-229E are the elderly, young children under the age of 2, and people who are immunosuppressed for any reason. Inoculation of the mucosal surfaces of the respiratory tract leads to the onset of HCoV-229E infections. The degree of the symptoms is correlated with the quantity of nasal mucosal plasma exudate and elevated interferon (IFN) levels in nasal lavage specimens [53].

HCoV-NL63

The initial isolation of HCoV-NL63 took place in Amsterdam in 2004, where it was obtained from the nasopharyngeal aspirate of a seven-month-old infant. Phylogenetic analysis classifies HCoV-NL63 as a Group I coronavirus [54].

It is a positive-sense, single-stranded, enveloped RNA virus that enters its host cell by attaching to ACE2. The likelihood of the emergence of a recombinant virus variant is high due to the virus's high prevalence and the potential for recombination through co-infection. In a heavily populated area, direct transmission is the main way that HCoV-NL63 spreads [55].

HCoV-OC43

It was first found in the nasopharynx of a patient with cold symptoms in 1967 by NIH researchers. In the 18th or 19th century, it most likely spread from cattle to people. One of the major important organizational proteins of HCoV-OC43, the spike (S) protein, is essential for the attachment and entry of the virus as well as for pathogenicity and host tropism.

In children, the elderly, or immune-compromised adults, HCoV-OC43 infection can result in fatal encephalitis or severe lower respiratory conditions like bronchiolitis, asthma, and pneumonia in addition to mild upper respiratory symptoms [56].

HKU1 (beta-coronavirus)

In 2004, a 71-year-old man traveling from Shenzhen City, Guangdong Province, to Hong Kong SAR, China, was found to have the coronavirus HCoV-HKU1, which causes human respiratory tract infections. The virus was discovered at the University of Hong Kong, hence named after it [57].

Similar to other HCoVs, HCoV-HKU1's spike (S) protein is crucial to the recognition of the virus and the invasion of host cells. Before binding to cellular receptors, the S protein goes through structural changes that produce a fusion precursor that enables the virus to bind to receptors and fuse with cell membranes [58].

The coronavirus can infect both humans and animals due to its high frequency of recombination and distinct replication mechanism.

It affects the upper respiratory tract and results in pneumonia, lung bronchiolitis, fever, and colds [59].

MERS-CoV

Middle East Respiratory Syndrome (MERS) is a viral respiratory illness brought about by the Middle East respiratory syndrome coronavirus (MERS-CoV), initially discovered in Saudi Arabia in 2012. In 2015, the Republic of Korea experienced the most significant outbreak of Middle East Respiratory Syndrome (MERS) outside of the Arabian Peninsula [60].

Considering the investigation of various virus genomes, the virus is thought to be a zoonotic pathogen that first appeared in bats and later spread to camels. The virus's genesis is not fully understood, though. The examination revealed that virus samples obtained from the Egyptian tomb bat, *Taphozous perforatus*, exhibited a 100% similarity with MERS-CoV in Saudi Arabia. This discovery was made in a situation where bat feces were confirmed to contain MERS-CoV nucleic acids [61].

In order to attach to host cells and fuse with them, the MERS-CoV spike protein interacts with CD26, which is also known as DPP4 (Dipeptidyl peptidase-4). MERS-CoV infection leads to extensive apoptosis of infected respiratory cells within 24 hours. Through the use of real-time RT-PCR, the virus in respiratory secretions can be detected and employed for the initial diagnosis of MERS-CoV infection [62].

SARS-CoV

The Severe Acute Respiratory Syndrome (SARS) epidemic was caused by beta-coronaviruses. This virus is commonly referred to as SARS-CoV, which evolved in South China in November 2002 and eventually spread to 29 different nations. The SARS epidemic, prior to its eventual containment in July 2003, led to 8,000 reported infections and 774 fatalities [63]. SARS-CoV, based on its genome sequence, appeared to have a very close genetic relationship to another virus found in Himalayan palm civets, suggesting that it may have originated from this source. Subsequently, civets were believed to be an intermediate host for SARS-CoV, while bats were identified as the natural host of the virus [64]. Following its introduction to the Guangdong market, the virus spread within civets and underwent additional mutations before eventually being transmitted to humans [65].

SARS-CoV-2

SARS-CoV-2, the virus responsible for the COVID-19 pandemic, was initially identified in humans in December 2019. in Wuhan, China. However, due to the virus's high capacity for transmission, the infection was practically widespread within a few months.

The majority of the first 27 recorded hospitalized patients had epidemiological ties to Huanan Seafood Market, a wet market in the heart of Wuhan that sells live animals in addition to seafood, including poultry and wildlife [66].

On January 10, the Virological website published the novel coronavirus's first genome sequence. On January 12, the GISAID database made available additional nearly complete genome sequences determined by various research institutions. The World Health Organization assigned the name "SARS-CoV-2" to the new coronavirus, while the International Committee on Taxonomy of Viruses named the associated disease "COVID-19" on February 11th. SARS-CoV-2, a novel beta coronavirus, shares about 79% of its genome sequence with SARS-CoV and 50% with MERS-CoV24. Its genomic structure is similar to that of other beta-coronaviruses. The virus's genetic information is organized into six functional open reading frames (ORFs) arrayed in sequence from 5' to 3': replicase (ORF1a/ORF1b), spike (S), envelope (E), membrane (M), and nucleocapsid (N). While bats are most likely the virus's primary reservoir host, other mammalian species may have functioned as intermediary hosts, aiding in the accumulation of mutations essential for optimal human transmission. In Malayan pangolins, viruses with receptor-binding domains similar to SARS-CoV-2 have been found, one of the presumed intermediate hosts, and share a 97% amino acid sequence with SARS-CoV-2. These coronaviruses have mutations that are thought to facilitate binding to the Angiotensin-converting enzyme 2 (ACE2) receptor. However, the genomic similarity to SARS-CoV-2 was lower at the whole genome level (91%) [66].

The majority of the SARS-CoV-2-encoded proteins have lengths that are comparable to those of the SARS-CoV with the exception of the S gene, which diverges. The four structural genes in SARS-CoV-2 exhibit over 90% similarity in terms of amino acid composition when compared to SARS-CoV.

GENOMIC EVOLUTION

According to reports, the genetic composition of SARS-CoV-2 shares genetic similarity of more than 80% with the original human coronavirus (the SARS-like bat CoV). This genetic likeness encompasses the four structural genes responsible for encoding the structural proteins. The components of the coronavirus structure include the spike (S), envelope (E), membrane (M), and nucleocapsid (N). The major genetic factor in SARS-CoV-2, orf1ab, codes for the pp1ab protein as well as 15 nsps. The orf1a gene encodes for the pp1a protein, which contains 10 non-structural proteins (NSPs). The phylogenetic tree demonstrates a close relationship between SARS-CoV-2 and the SARS-coronavirus family. Recent investigations have exposed notable distinctions between SARS-CoV and SARS-CoV-2. These distinctions include the absence of the 8a gene in the former and alterations in the amino acid composition of the 8b and 3c proteins in the latter. Additionally, according to reports, the SARS-CoV-2 spike glycoprotein comprises genetic components from the bat SARS-CoV as well as an unnamed beta-CoV. Fluorescent investigation has revealed that SARS-CoV-2 enters host cells *via* the same ACE2 (angiotensin-converting enzyme 2) cell receptor and mechanism as SARS-CoV. Surprisingly, a single N501T change in the SARS-CoV-2 spike protein appears to have significantly increased the virus's capacity to attach to ACE2 [67].

The evolutionary domains constitute a part of the RNA helicase found in the Orthocoronavirinae family. Furthermore, the Macro domain, along with the genus-specific domains CoV_peptidase and NSP3_C are components of the Papain-like peptidase protein (PL-pro) found in Orthocoronavirinae. In addition to some Herpesvirales (dsDNA viruses), The Hema_esterase domain may also be found in Nidovirales members such as Embecovirus and Torovirus, as well as Influenza C and D viruses. The Haemagglutinin-esterase fusion glycoprotein in Embecoviruses consists of the Hema_esterase domain and the Hema_HEF domain. Haemagglutinin-esterases are thought to have evolved from lectins of viral hosts, although it is unknown whether this occurred through a common ancestor virus followed by speciation and gene loss or through many separate acquisitions. Although it has been found in various Orthocoronavirinae genomes, including the genomes analyzed in this work, the Corona_NS2A domain can be found in several members of the Riboviria supergroup. The Corona_NS2A domain is also present in Rotaviruses, which are double-stranded RNA viruses belonging to the Reoviridae family. In Rotaviruses, this domain, in conjunction with the Rotavirus_VP3 domain, constitutes a multifunctional enzyme called the VP3 protein, which plays a role in mRNA capping. The VP3 protein is a multifunctional enzyme that is found in Rotaviruses, double-stranded RNA viruses in the family *Reoviridae* and is made up of the Rotavirus_VP3 domain and Corona_NS2A domain. Interestingly, it is encoded as a single ORF in *Embecovirus* and *Luchacovirus*. The remaining five domains are exclusive to the Nidovirales group and can be found in specific members of the Tobaniviridae and Orthocoronavirinae families. These domains encompass the uridylate-specific endoribonuclease (CoV_NSP15_C), the 2′-O-methyltransferase (CoV_Methyltr_2), the RNA synthesis protein NSP10 (CoV_NSP10), and the S2 subunit of the spike protein (CoV_S2) [67].

The findings of this study suggest that the branch originating from Nidovirales to Orthocoronavirinae underwent the most notable increase in the number of acquired domains during the evolution of the Coronaviridae family, which is classified in Fig. (5). These gained domains encompass the small enveloped protein E (including the CoV_E domain), the Matrix/glycoprotein M (with the CoV_M domain), the nucleocapsid protein N (incorporating the CoV_nucleocap domain), and three spike glycoprotein domains (bCoV_S1_N, CoV_S1_C, and CoV_S2_C) [67].

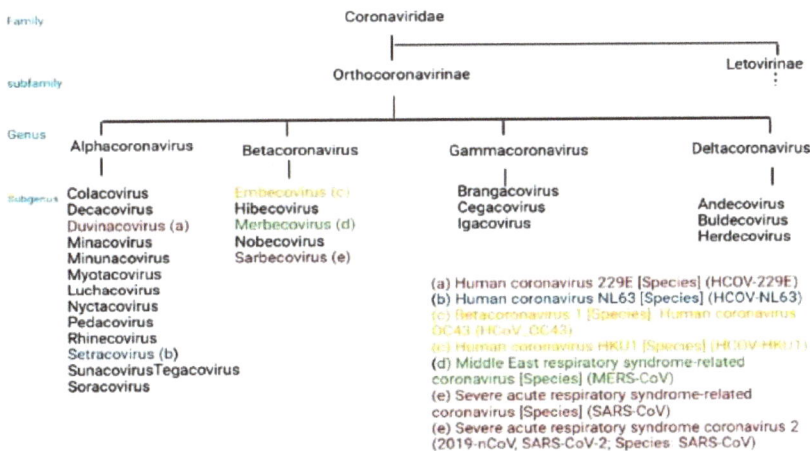

Fig. (5). Classification of the family Coronaviridae

BIOLOGICAL EVOLUTION OF CORONAVIRUS SPIKE PROTEIN

Insight to the structure, function, and history of corona spikes will help us better understand the source of viruses and the evolutionary connection between viruses and their host.

Fig. (**6**)shows that coronaviruses demonstrate a complex pattern when it comes to recognizing receptors. For instance, the zinc peptidase angiotensin-c enzyme 2 (ACE2) is recognized by both the beta-coronaviruses SARS-CoV and the alpha-coronavirus HCoV-NL63. Additionally, HCoV-NL63 and other alpha-coronaviruses exhibit receptor recognition diversity. For example, alpha-coronaviruses such as TGEV, PEDV, and PRCV are known to interact with aminopeptidase N (APN), a different zinc peptidase. Also, SARS-CoV and other beta-coronaviruses distinguish between various receptors: Dipeptidyl peptidase 4 (DPP4), a serine peptidase, is recognized by MERS-CoV and HKU4; MHV (Mouse Hepatitis Virus) recognizes the cell adhesion molecule Carcinoembryonic Antigen-Related Cell Adhesion Molecule 1 (CEACAM1), whereas BCoV and OC43 recognise sugar molecules. Additionally, the gamma-coronavirus IBV and the alpha-coronaviruses TGEV and PEDV use sugar as coreceptors or receptors. These coronavirus receptors serve a variety of physiological purposes in addition to their function in viral attachment. The variety of receptors used by coronaviruses is a remarkable characteristic [68].

A better understanding of coronavirus evolution is provided by their S1 domain. By recombining with alpha and gamma coronaviruses, beta-coronaviruses contribute to the evolution of coronaviruses. Beta-coronaviruses mutations make them more virulent and contribute to the deadly illnesses caused by SARS-CoV-1 and MERS-CoV.

The S1 protein consists of two sections: the N-terminal domain (NTD) and the C-terminal domain (CTD), both capable of interacting with receptors. For instance, SARS-CoV and MERS-CoV employ the S1-CTD to identify and attach to their specific target receptors. Beta-coronaviruses S1-NTDs exhibit a galectin fold, suggesting their likely origin from the host. However, the origin of COVID S1-CTDs is less straightforward and remains unclear [68].

With the limited details available in their structural configuration, it's possible that the rapid development of S1-CTDs has effectively erased their evolutionary traces. The dual-component structure of S1 offers coronaviruses two potential domains for binding to receptors, irrespective of their origin from host galectins: The S1-CTD, which evolves at a brisk pace, exploits new protein receptors, while the S1-NTD, which remains more structurally and functionally preserved, relies on sugars as an alternative receptor.

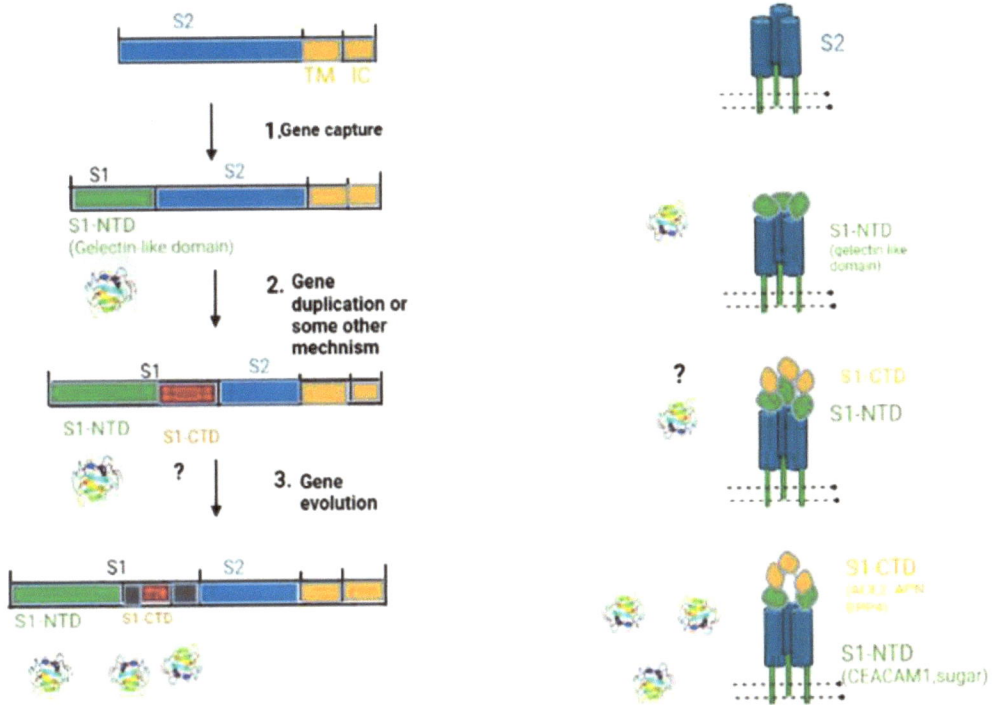

Fig. (6). Coronaviruses attach to the receptor surface of host cells *via* viral membrane proteins from the class I fusion protein group assisting the host cell in entering, thus, merging the host membrane and viral membrane. They can be found in various conformations. The six-bundle post-fusion tetrameric S2 has exposed fusion peptides and is helix-shaped. Another is S1-headed and has three pre-fusion trimeric spike receptor bindings. The host range and tissue tropism of coronaviruses are significant determinants of receptor identification and membrane fusion. It aids in understanding the intricate composition and operation of the spike coronavirus protein.
(Source: Structure, Function, and Evolution of Coronavirus Spike Proteins,Fang Li, Vol. 3 (2016), pp. 237–261).

Both the prefusion and postfusion conformations of S2 of the coronaviruses and other viral membrane fusion proteins classified as class I viruses display significant structural and functional similarity. They undergo similar conformational changes and are triggered by comparable mechanisms. The process of transitioning to postfusion six-helix bundle structures, where fusion peptides become exposed, appears remarkably consistent across both coronavirus S2 and other class I viral membrane fusion proteins. The complication and intricate characteristics of the membrane fusion process imply that class I viral sheath fusion proteins probably share a mutual evolutionary origin. However, it cannot be definitively ruled out that these viruses independently developed the same membrane fusion mechanism.

This research provides valuable insights into the evolutionary history of S1-CTDs in coronaviruses. Despite the distinct core structures found in alpha- and beta-coronaviruses S1-CTDs, characterized by a β-sandwich and a single-layer β-sheet, respectively, they exhibit a shared structural framework, suggesting a common evolutionary origin. S1-CTDs from different genera are believed to have undergone significant divergent evolution to develop their unique core structures. Within alpha-coronavirus S1-CTDs, the three RBM loops appear to have diverged, resulting in ACE2-binding RBMs in HCoV-NL63 and APN-binding RBMs in PRCV. Similarly, the RBM subdomain of S1-CTDs in beta-coronaviruses seems to have diversified, leading to the emergence of an ACE2-binding RBM in SARS-CoV and a DPP4-binding RBM in MERS-CoV. Despite structural disparities, both alpha-coronavirus HCoV-NL63 and beta-coronaviruses SARS-CoV S1-CTDs connect to the same region on ACE2, depicted in Fig. (7), which may be influenced by a shared virus-binding hotspot on ACE2. The tertiary structures of S1-CTDs in gamma- and delta-coronaviruses remain undisclosed, but it is probable that they share similarities with the folds found in alpha- and beta-coronaviruses S1-CTDs. The intricate evolutionary connections among S1-CTDs from various genera highlight the substantial evolutionary pressures that have shaped this domain [68].

The resemblances in both structure and function amid coronavirus S2 and other class I viral membrane fusion proteins are striking. These proteins all have two distinct conformations, one before and one after fusion. They exhibit comparable triggers for transitioning from their pre-fusion to post-fusion states, undergo analogous structural rearrangements, and ultimately form nearly identical post-fusion six-helix bundle structures, exposing fusion peptides. While it's not entirely impossible that these viruses independently evolved the same membrane fusion mechanism, the intricate nature of this mechanism strongly suggests that class I viral membrane fusion proteins likely divide a common evolutionary ancestor.

The research sheds light on the development of S1-CTDs in coronaviruses. While alpha- and beta-coronaviruses S1-CTDs have distinct core structures - a single-layer β-sheet and β-sandwich, respectively - they exhibit a similar structural arrangement, implying a shared evolutionary heritage. S1-CTDs across various species probably experienced significant divergent evolution to acquire their distinct core structures. The three RBM loops found in alpha-coronavirus S1-CTDs appear to have undergone further differentiation, leading to ACE2-binding RBMs in HCoV-NL63 and APN-binding RBMs in PRCV. Similarly, in beta-coronaviruses, the RBM subdomain of S1-CTDs has likely diversified into ACE2-binding RBM in SARS-CoV and DPP4-binding RBM in MERS-CoV. Contempt to these varying structural features, the S1-CTDs of alpha-coronavirus HCoV-NL63 and beta-coronaviruses SARS-CoV still interact with a shared region on ACE2, possibly due to a common virus-binding site on ACE2. The tertiary configurations of S1-CTDs in gamma- and delta-coronaviruses are currently unknown, but it is probable that they share similarities with the structures found in alpha- and beta-coronaviruses S1-CTDs. The intricate evolutionary connections among S1-CTDs from various genera underscore the significant evolutionary forces influencing this domain [68].

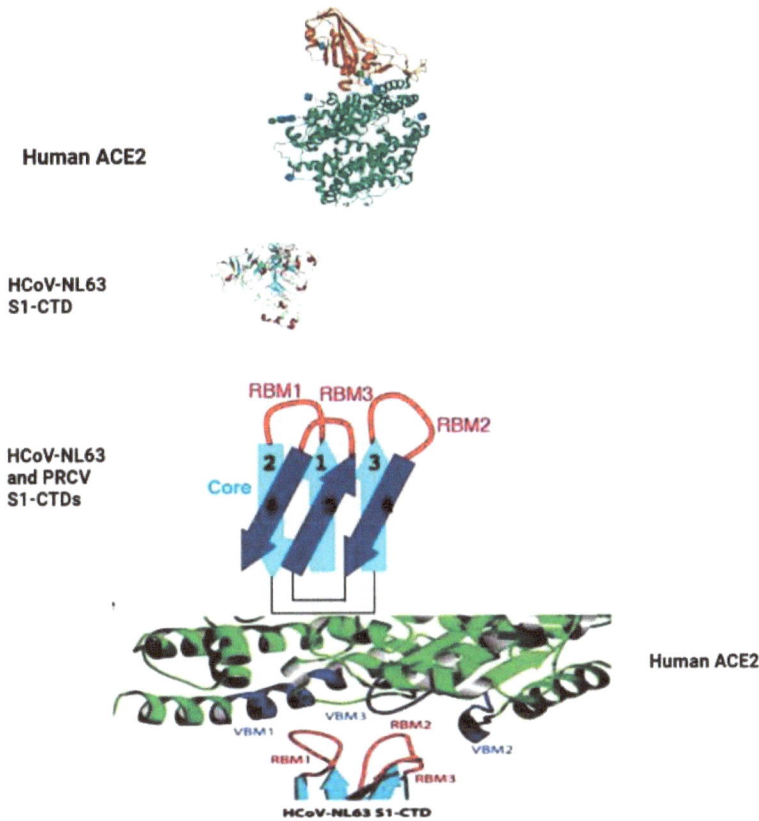

Fig. (7). NL63 S1-CTD (Human coronavirus) complexed with human ACE2, interface between HCoV-NL63 S1-CTD and ACE2 human. The binding motifs of virus (VBMs) on ACE2 are highlighted in purple. RBMs on S1-CTD are depicted in red, as is the structural topology of alpha-coronavirus S1-CTDs. Strands are represented by arrows. (Li 2016)

CONCLUSION

Coronaviruses are crown-like spike glycoproteins protein with positive sense single stranded RNA virus that infects millions of people belonging to the family. Coronaviridae and subfamily Nidovirales. The four coronavirus subgroups of alpha, beta, gamma, and delta are categorized based on the genomic structure of the virus. Receptor-binding domain (RBD) spike proteins provide protection for coronaviruses associated with SARS. The ACE-2 receptor present in the kidneys, lungs, heart, and gastrointestinal system binds with RBD and promotes easy entrance into target cells.

This research focuses on coronavirus introduction, various subgroups based on genomic structure, reports cases with an overall deaths and fatality rate. It also provides an insight to how coronavirus facilitates infection when bind to RBD, regional or geographical origin (endemic origin) of different human coronaviruses like HCoV-OC43, HCoV-229E, HCoV-NL63, HKU1, SARS-CoV, MERS-CoV, infection mechanism, host interaction with epidemiology of different human coronaviruses, adaptive nature of coronaviruses and their ability to undergo genetic changes that give rise to new strains. This also includes their origins, mutations, and potential implications for transmission and vaccine efficacy by emphasizing the need for ongoing surveillance and research to effectively respond to their evolution.

This study also highlights the nomenclature of SARS-CoV-2 according to GISAID, Nextstrain & PANGO in the Greek alphabet to identify different variants. The chapter continues to focus on the detailed discussion of genomic evolution of coronaviruses, a brief mechanism on how the coronavirus spike protein evolves and similarities between coronaviruses S1 and S2 membrane fusion protein.

In conclusion, this review article provides a thorough overview of the history, epidemiology, variations, kinds, and evolution of coronaviruses. It is clear that combating the existing and upcoming problems caused by these viruses' calls for an expanded strategy. We are better able to create successful solutions that protect the health and well-being of all people by combining historical context, present epidemiological knowledge, genetic variants, and evolutionary trajectories.

TAKE-HOME MESSAGES

Coronavirus is an enveloped, non-segmented, single-stranded positive RNA viruses belonging to the Coronaviridae subfamily Nidovirales of the Coronaviridae family.

Crown-like spikes on the surface of coronaviruses play a major role in inserting the virus genome into the host.

Innate and adaptive immune systems are intricate in SARS-CoV-2 infection. They have four main subgroups based on their genomic structure: alpha, beta, gamma and delta. Alpha- and beta-coronaviruses infect only mammals and usually cause respiratory symptoms in humans and gastroenteritis in other animals.

The four structural genes are spike (S), envelope (E), membrane (M), and nucleocapsid (N) are responsible for encoding the structural proteins.

The largest gene in SARS-CoV-2, orf1ab, encodes the pp1ab protein as well as 15 nsps. The *orf1a* gene encodes for pp1a protein containing 10 nsps.

There are four major coronaviruses that have been identified, namely SARS-CoV, MERS-CoV, HCoV-NL63 and HCoV-229E, which are thought to have originated in bats, while HCoV-OC43 and HKU1 most likely originated in rodents.

There are several types of COVID-19 vaccines. Genetic vaccine for COVID-19 contains virus genetic material that codes for specific protein, inactivated vaccines contain killed SARS-CoV virus, attenuated vaccines contain weakened SARS-CoV virus, and protein vaccines contain protein fragments that provoke immunity, while viral vector vaccines for COVID-19 contain vectors for delivering the altered genetic material.

WHAT YOU WILL LEARN

• A brief introduction of coronaviruses, different subgroups based on genomic structure year of first reported case, including no of cases with mortality and fatality rate.

• Origin and classification of coronaviruses including animal origin of coronavirus strains from different animals, intermediate host, human host.

• Region in which protein binds and encodes the spike protein and genetic diversity.

• Genetic groups of coronaviruses and their host.

• Regional or geographical origin (endemic origin) of different human coronaviruses like HCoV-OC43, HCoV-229E, HCoV-NL63, HKU1, SARS-CoV, MERS-CoV with discovery dates.

• Nomenclature of SARS-CoV-2.

• Classification of five different variants like Variants of Concern (VOC), Variants of Interest (VOI), Variants Being Monitored (VBM), Variants of High Consequence (VOHC), Variants of interest (VOI).

• Different types of coronaviruses, including alpha, beta, gamma, delta and coronaviruses with different strains, such as HCoV-229E, HCoV-NL63, HCoV-HKU1, HCoV-OC43, SARS-CoV, SARS-CoV-2, MERS-CoV.

• Genomic evolution of coronaviruses, a brief mechanism on how the coronavirus spike protein evolves and similarities between coronaviruses S1 and S2 membrane fusion protein.

LIST OF ABBREVIATIONS

SARS-CoV	Severe Acute Respiratory Syndrome Coronavirus
MERS-CoV	Middle East Respiratory Syndrome Coronavirus
HCoV	Human Coronavirus
HKU1	Hong Kong University 1.
PEPV	Porcine Epidemic Diarrhea Coronavirus
ACE2	Angiotensin-converting Enzyme 2
AIBV	Avian Infectious Bronchitis Virus
BALF	Broncho-alveolar Lavage Fluid
WIV16	Wuhan Institute of Virology 16
APN	Aminopeptidase N
ATP	Adenosine Triphosphate
BCoV	Beta-coronaviruses
CEACAM1	Carcinoembryonic Antigen-Related Cell Adhesion Molecule 1
CCL	Chemokine ligand
CoVs	Coronaviruses
DNA	Deoxyribonucleic Acid
DPP4	Dipeptidyl peptidase 4
E	Envelope
GISAID	Global Initiative on Sharing Avian Influenza Data
ORFs	Open Reading Rrames
PLpro	Papain-like protease
TGEV	Transmissible Gastroenteritis Virus
VOC	Variants of Concern
VOI	Variants of Interest
VOHC	Variants of High Consequences
VBM	Variants Being Monitored
CTD	C-Terminal Domain
NTD	N-Terminal Domain
RBD	Receptor-binding Domain
mRNA	Messenger RNA
TGEV	Transmissible Gastroenteritis Virus

| WHO | World Health Organization |
| HEF | Haemagglutinin-esterase Fusion Glycoprotein |

REFERENCES

[1]   Rabi FA, Al Zoubi MS, Kasasbeh GA, Salameh DM, Al-Nasser AD. SARS-CoV-2 and Coronavirus Disease 2019: What We Know So Far. Pathogens 2020; 9(3): 231.
[http://dx.doi.org/10.3390/pathogens9030231] [PMID: 32245083]

[2]   Cascella M, Rajnik M, Aleem A, Dulebohn S C, Di Napoli R. Di Napoli, Features, Evaluation, and Treatment of Coronavirus (COVID-19). 2023.

[3]   Koh D. Occupational risks for COVID-19 infection. Occup Med (Lond) 2020; 70(1): 3-5.
[http://dx.doi.org/10.1093/occmed/kqaa036] [PMID: 32107548]

[4]   Rabi FA, Al Zoubi MS, Kasasbeh GA, Salameh DM, Al-Nasser AD. SARS-CoV-2 and Coronavirus Disease 2019: What We Know So Far. Pathogens 2020; 9(3): 231.
[http://dx.doi.org/10.3390/pathogens9030231] [PMID: 32245083]

[5]   Kumar D. Corona Virus: A Review of COVID-19. Eurasian J Med Oncol 2020; 4(1): 8-25.
[http://dx.doi.org/10.14744/ejmo.2020.51418]

[6]   Abdelghany TM, Ganash M, Bakri MM, Qanash H, Al-Rajhi AMH, Elhussieny NI. SARS-CoV-2, the other face to SARS-CoV and MERS-CoV: Future predictions. Biomed J 2021; 44(1): 86-93.
[http://dx.doi.org/10.1016/j.bj.2020.10.008] [PMID: 33602634]

[7]   Morens DM, Breman JG, Calisher CH, *et al.* The Origin of COVID-19 and Why It Matters. Am J Trop Med Hyg 2020; 103(3): 955-9.
[http://dx.doi.org/10.4269/ajtmh.20-0849] [PMID: 32700664]

[8]   Ludwig S, Zarbock A. Coronaviruses and SARS-CoV-2: A Brief Overview. Anesth Analg 2020; 131(1): 93-6.
[http://dx.doi.org/10.1213/ANE.0000000000004845] [PMID: 32243297]

[9]   Rabi FA, Al Zoubi MS, Kasasbeh GA, Salameh DM, Al-Nasser AD. SARS-CoV-2 and Coronavirus Disease 2019: What We Know So Far. Pathogens 2020; 9(3): 231.
[http://dx.doi.org/10.3390/pathogens9030231] [PMID: 32245083]

[10]   Dutta A, Roy A, Roy L, Chattopadhyay S, Chatterjee S. Immune response and possible therapeutics in COVID-19. RSC Advances 2021; 11(2): 960-77.
[http://dx.doi.org/10.1039/D0RA08901J] [PMID: 35423713]

[11]   Rabi FA, Al Zoubi MS, Kasasbeh GA, Salameh DM, Al-Nasser AD. SARS-CoV-2 and Coronavirus Disease 2019: What We Know So Far. Pathogens 2020; 9(3): 231.
[http://dx.doi.org/10.3390/pathogens9030231] [PMID: 32245083]

[12]   Cui J, Li F, Shi ZL. Origin and evolution of pathogenic coronaviruses. Nat Rev Microbiol 2019; 17(3): 181-92.
[http://dx.doi.org/10.1038/s41579-018-0118-9] [PMID: 30531947]

[13]   Cui J, Li F, Shi ZL. Origin and evolution of pathogenic coronaviruses. Nat Rev Microbiol 2019; 17(3): 181-92.
[http://dx.doi.org/10.1038/s41579-018-0118-9] [PMID: 30531947]

[14]   Lau SKP, Luk HKH, Wong ACP, *et al.* Possible Bat Origin of Severe Acute Respiratory Syndrome Coronavirus 2. Emerg Infect Dis 2020; 26(7): 1542-7.
[http://dx.doi.org/10.3201/eid2607.200092] [PMID: 32315281]

[15]   Wang LF, Eaton BT. Bats, civets and the emergence of SARS. Curr Top Microbiol Immunol 2007; 315: 325-44.
[http://dx.doi.org/10.1007/978-3-540-70962-6_13] [PMID: 17848070]

[16] Ludwig S, Zarbock A. Coronaviruses and SARS-CoV-2: A Brief Overview. Anesth Analg 2020; 131(1): 93-6.
[http://dx.doi.org/10.1213/ANE.0000000000004845] [PMID: 32243297]

[17] Cui J, Li F, Shi ZL. Origin and evolution of pathogenic coronaviruses. Nat Rev Microbiol 2019; 17(3): 181-92.
[http://dx.doi.org/10.1038/s41579-018-0118-9] [PMID: 30531947]

[18] Edwards CE, Yount BL, Graham RL, *et al.* Swine acute diarrhea syndrome coronavirus replication in primary human cells reveals potential susceptibility to infection. Proc Natl Acad Sci USA 2020; 117(43): 26915-25.
[http://dx.doi.org/10.1073/pnas.2001046117] [PMID: 33046644]

[19] Cui J, Li F, Shi ZL. Origin and evolution of pathogenic coronaviruses. Nat Rev Microbiol 2019; 17(3): 181-92.
[http://dx.doi.org/10.1038/s41579-018-0118-9] [PMID: 30531947]

[20] Cui J, Li F, Shi ZL. Origin and evolution of pathogenic coronaviruses. Nat Rev Microbiol 2019; 17(3): 181-92.
[http://dx.doi.org/10.1038/s41579-018-0118-9] [PMID: 30531947]

[21] York A. Searching for relatives of SARS-CoV-2 in bats. Nat Rev Microbiol 2021; 19(8): 482-2.
[http://dx.doi.org/10.1038/s41579-021-00595-8] [PMID: 34145421]

[22] Ye ZW, Yuan S, Yuen KS, Fung SY, Chan CP, Jin DY. Zoonotic origins of human coronaviruses. Int J Biol Sci 2020; 16(10): 1686-97.
[http://dx.doi.org/10.7150/ijbs.45472] [PMID: 32226286]

[23] Han HJ, Yu H, Yu XJ. Evidence for zoonotic origins of Middle East respiratory syndrome coronavirus. J Gen Virol 2016; 97(2): 274-80.
[http://dx.doi.org/10.1099/jgv.0.000342] [PMID: 26572912]

[24] Ye ZW, Yuan S, Yuen KS, Fung SY, Chan CP, Jin DY. Zoonotic origins of human coronaviruses. Int J Biol Sci 2020; 16(10): 1686-97.
[http://dx.doi.org/10.7150/ijbs.45472] [PMID: 32226286]

[25] Zhou P, Yang XL, Wang XG, *et al.* A pneumonia outbreak associated with a new coronavirus of probable bat origin. Nature 2020; 579(7798): 270-3.
[http://dx.doi.org/10.1038/s41586-020-2012-7] [PMID: 32015507]

[26] Huang C, Wang Y, Li X, *et al.* Clinical features of patients infected with 2019 novel coronavirus in Wuhan, China. Lancet 2020; 395(10223): 497-506.
[http://dx.doi.org/10.1016/S0140-6736(20)30183-5] [PMID: 31986264]

[27] Lam TTY, Jia N, Zhang YW, *et al.* Identifying SARS-CoV-2-related coronaviruses in Malayan pangolins. Nature 2020; 583(7815): 282-5.
[http://dx.doi.org/10.1038/s41586-020-2169-0] [PMID: 32218527]

[28] Zhang T, Wu Q, Zhang Z. Probable Pangolin Origin of SARS-CoV-2 Associated with the COVID-19 Outbreak. Curr Biol 2020; 30(7): 1346-1351.e2.
[http://dx.doi.org/10.1016/j.cub.2020.03.022] [PMID: 32197085]

[29] Zhu Z, Lian X, Su X, Wu W, Marraro GA, Zeng Y. From SARS and MERS to COVID-19: a brief summary and comparison of severe acute respiratory infections caused by three highly pathogenic human coronaviruses. Respir Res 2020; 21(1): 224.
[http://dx.doi.org/10.1186/s12931-020-01479-w] [PMID: 32854739]

[30] Lytras S, Hughes J, Martin D, *et al.* Exploring the Natural Origins of SARS-CoV-2 in the Light of Recombination. Genome Biol Evol 2022; 14(2): evac018.
[http://dx.doi.org/10.1093/gbe/evac018] [PMID: 35137080]

[31] Ye ZW, Yuan S, Yuen KS, Fung SY, Chan CP, Jin DY. Zoonotic origins of human coronaviruses. Int

J Biol Sci 2020; 16(10): 1686-97.
[http://dx.doi.org/10.7150/ijbs.45472] [PMID: 32226286]

[32]   Saif LJ. Animal coronavirus vaccines: lessons for SARS. Dev Biol (Basel) 2004; 119: 129-40.
[PMID: 15742624]

[33]   Bahadur S, Long W, Shuaib M. Human coronaviruses with emphasis on the COVID-19 outbreak.
Virusdisease 2020; 31(2): 80-4.
[http://dx.doi.org/10.1007/s13337-020-00594-y] [PMID: 32399479]

[34]   Abdel-Moneim AS. Middle East respiratory syndrome coronavirus (MERS-CoV): evidence and
speculations. Arch Virol 2014; 159(7): 1575-84.
[http://dx.doi.org/10.1007/s00705-014-1995-5] [PMID: 24515532]

[35]   Corman VM, Muth D, Niemeyer D, Drosten C. Hosts and Sources of Endemic Human Coronaviruses.
Adv Virus Res 2018; 100: 163-88.
[http://dx.doi.org/10.1016/bs.aivir.2018.01.001] [PMID: 29551135]

[36]   Xu RH, He JF, Evans MR, *et al.* Epidemiologic clues to SARS origin in China. Emerg Infect Dis
2004; 10(6): 1030-7.
[http://dx.doi.org/10.3201/eid1006.030852] [PMID: 15207054]

[37]   WHO Health Emergencies Programme (WHE), World Health Organization, 2022.

[38]   Worobey M, *et al.* The Huanan Seafood Wholesale Market in Wuhan was the early epicenter of the
COVID-19 pandemic. Science (1979) 2022; 377(6609): 951-9.
[http://dx.doi.org/10.1126/science.abp8715]

[39]   Michaeleen Doucleff, Goats and Soda Stories of life in a changing world, Feb. 28, 2023.

[40]   Pal M, Berhanu G, Desalegn C, Kandi V. Severe Acute Respiratory Syndrome Coronavirus-2 (SARS-
CoV-2): An Update. Cureus 2020; 12(3): e7423.
[http://dx.doi.org/10.7759/cureus.7423] [PMID: 32337143]

[41]   Tang X, Wu C, Li X, *et al.* On the origin and continuing evolution of SARS-CoV-2. Natl Sci Rev
2020; 7(6): 1012-23.
[http://dx.doi.org/10.1093/nsr/nwaa036] [PMID: 34676127]

[42]   CORONA VIRUSES: COLDS, SARS, MERS AND COVID-19. 2021.

[43]   Zhang T, Wu Q, Zhang Z. Probable Pangolin Origin of SARS-CoV-2 Associated with the COVID-19
Outbreak. Curr Biol 2020; 30(7): 1346-1351.e2.
[http://dx.doi.org/10.1016/j.cub.2020.03.022] [PMID: 32197085]

[44]   O'Toole Á, Pybus OG, Abram ME, Kelly EJ, Rambaut A. Pango lineage designation and assignment
using SARS-CoV-2 spike gene nucleotide sequences. BMC Genomics 2022; 23(1): 121.
[http://dx.doi.org/10.1186/s12864-022-08358-2] [PMID: 35148677]

[45]   https://www.cdc.gov/coronavirus/2019-ncov/variants/varian-
-classifications.html#anchor_16790594849542023.
https://www.cdc.gov/dotw/sars/index.html#:~:text=Key%20Facts%201%20SARS%20was%20caused
%20by%20a,successfully%20contain%20the%20outbreak%20in%202003.%20More%20items

[46]   Akkiz H. Implications of the Novel Mutations in the SARS-CoV-2 Genome for Transmission, Disease
Severity, and the Vaccine Development. Front Med (Lausanne) 2021; 8: 636532.
[http://dx.doi.org/10.3389/fmed.2021.636532] [PMID: 34026780]

[47]   Virology - chapter twenty five corona viruses: Colds, Sars, Mers and COVID-19
2021.https://www.microbiologybook.org/book/welcome.htm

[48]   Shukri AMA, Wang SM, Chia SL, Nawi SFAM. The SARS-CoV-2 Variants and their Impacts. J Pure
Appl Microbiol 2022; 16(3): 1409-24.
[http://dx.doi.org/10.22207/JPAM.16.3.45]

[49] Liu YC, Kuo RL, Shih SR. COVID-19: The first documented coronavirus pandemic in history. Biomed J 2020; 43(4): 328-33.
[http://dx.doi.org/10.1016/j.bj.2020.04.007] [PMID: 32387617]

[50] Vlasak R, Luytjes W, Spaan W, Palese P. Human and bovine coronaviruses recognize sialic acid-containing receptors similar to those of influenza C viruses. Proc Natl Acad Sci USA 1988; 85(12): 4526-9.
[http://dx.doi.org/10.1073/pnas.85.12.4526] [PMID: 3380803]

[51] Severe respiratory illness associated with a novel coronavirus--Saudi Arabia and Qatar, 2012. MMWR Morb Mortal Wkly Rep 2012; 61(40): 820.
[PMID: 23051613]

[52] The secret history of the first coronavirus 2020. https://www.forbes.com/sites/alexknapp/2020/04/11/the-secret-history-of-the-first-coronavirus-229e/?sh=62a1e91471d6

[53] Poutanen SM. Human Coronaviruses. Principles and Practice of Pediatric Infectious Diseases. Elsevier 2018; pp. 1148-1152.e3.
[http://dx.doi.org/10.1016/B978-0-323-40181-4.00222-X]

[54] Liu DX, Liang JQ, Fung TS. Human Coronavirus-229E, -OC43, -NL63, and -HKU1 (Coronaviridae). Encyclopedia of Virology. Elsevier 2021; pp. 428-40.
[http://dx.doi.org/10.1016/B978-0-12-809633-8.21501-X]

[55] Abdul-Rasool S, Fielding BC. Understanding Human Coronavirus HCoV-NL63~!2009-11-13~!2-10-04-09~!2010-05-25~! Open Virol J 2010; 4(1): 76-84.
[http://dx.doi.org/10.2174/1874357901004010076] [PMID: 20700397]

[56] Keshavarz Valian N, Pourakbari B, Asna Ashari K, Hosseinpour Sadeghi R, Mahmoudi S. Evaluation of human coronavirus OC43 and SARS-COV-2 in children with respiratory tract infection during the COVID-19 pandemic. J Med Virol 2022; 94(4): 1450-6.
[http://dx.doi.org/10.1002/jmv.27460] [PMID: 34786736]

[57] Liu W, Liu P, Liu WJ, Wang Q, Tong Y, Gao GF. Origins of HIV, HCoV-HKU1, SFTSV, and MERS-CoV and Beyond. China CDC Wkly 2022; 4(37): 823-7.
[http://dx.doi.org/10.46234/ccdcw2022.171] [PMID: 36284537]

[58] Chen X, Zhu Y, Li Q, *et al.* Genetic characteristics of human coronavirus HKU1 in mainland China during 2018. Arch Virol 2022; 167(11): 2173-80.
[http://dx.doi.org/10.1007/s00705-022-05541-4] [PMID: 35840864]

[59] HCoV-HKU1 https://www.cusabio.com/m-171.html

[60] 2021.https://www.who.int/emergencies/disease-outbreak-news/item/2021-DON333

[61] Mohd HA, Al-Tawfiq JA, Memish ZA. Middle East Respiratory Syndrome Coronavirus (MERS-CoV) origin and animal reservoir. Virol J 2016; 13(1): 87.
[http://dx.doi.org/10.1186/s12985-016-0544-0] [PMID: 27255185]

[62] Alnuqaydan AM, Almutary AG, Sukamaran A, *et al.* Middle East Respiratory Syndrome (MERS) Virus—Pathophysiological Axis and the Current Treatment Strategies. AAPS PharmSciTech 2021; 22(5): 173.
[http://dx.doi.org/10.1208/s12249-021-02062-2] [PMID: 34105037]

[63] SARS (10 Years After) https://www.cdc.gov/dotw/sars/index.html#print

[64] Helmy YA, Fawzy M, Elaswad A, Sobieh A, Kenney SP, Shehata AA. The COVID-19 Pandemic: A Comprehensive Review of Taxonomy, Genetics, Epidemiology, Diagnosis, Treatment, and Control. J Clin Med 2020; 9(4): 1225.
[http://dx.doi.org/10.3390/jcm9041225] [PMID: 32344679]

[65] Cui J, Li F, Shi ZL. Origin and evolution of pathogenic coronaviruses. Nat Rev Microbiol 2019; 17(3): 181-92.

[http://dx.doi.org/10.1038/s41579-018-0118-9] [PMID: 30531947]

[66]   Hu B, Guo H, Zhou P, Shi ZL. Characteristics of SARS-CoV-2 and COVID-19. Nat Rev Microbiol 2021; 19(3): 141-54.
[http://dx.doi.org/10.1038/s41579-020-00459-7] [PMID: 33024307]

[67]   Zmasek CM, Lefkowitz EJ, Niewiadomska A, Scheuermann RH. Genomic evolution of the Coronaviridae family. Virology 2022; 570: 123-33.
[http://dx.doi.org/10.1016/j.virol.2022.03.005] [PMID: 35398776]

[68]   Li F. Structure, Function, and Evolution of Coronavirus Spike Proteins. Annu Rev Virol 2016; 3(1): 237-61.
[http://dx.doi.org/10.1146/annurev-virology-110615-042301] [PMID: 27578435]

CHAPTER 2

Epidemiology of Coronavirus

Mohammad Sufian Badar[1,2,3,4,*], **Ibtesaam Hafeez**[5], **Imtshan Nawaz**[5], **Mohammad Rehan Badar**[6] and **Sadia Saba**[7]

[1] *Department of Bioengineering, University of California, Riverside, CA, USA*

[2] *Universal Scientific Education and Research Network (USERN), Tehran, Iran*

[3] *Director (Academic), SPI Darbhanga, India*

[4] *Department of Computer Science and Engineering (Bioinformatics), School of Engineering Sciences and Technology (SEST), Jamia Hamdard, New Delhi, India*

[5] *Department of Biotechnology, Jamia Hamdard, New Delhi, India*

[6] *Consultant, Apollo Hospital, Delhi, India*

[7] *Department of Neurology, Indiana University School of Medicine, Indianapolis, USA*

Abstract: More than 600 million people have contracted the COVID-19, and a substantial level of fatalities have occurred on a global scale. The pandemic has grown to pose a serious risk to humankind. Gaining knowledge about the dynamics of virus transmission and clinical manifestation, as well as possible causes of severe illness and mortality, requires an understanding of coronavirus epidemiology. To create global health policies that work, it is imperative to understand these elements. It is believed that bats are the original host of the coronavirus that causes severe acute respiratory syndrome. The most prevalent means of transmission is through airborne droplets. Other potential routes of infection include the fecal-oral pathway, sexual transmission, the vertical chain, and so forth. The incubation period of COVID-19 is two to fourteen days, during which asymptomatic carriers may spread the virus to other people. From mild symptoms like fever, coughing, and fatigue to life-threatening illness necessitating hospitalization, COVID-19 respiratory illness can range widely in severity. The impacts of the disease are more likely to affect the elderly and people with underlying medical disorders including Type 2 diabetes, obesity, or chronic heart disease. New strains of SARS-CoV-2 have evolved as the pandemic has expanded, wreaking havoc on countries with weak healthcare systems and low incomes. Social isolation, the use of masks, and vaccination campaigns have all helped reduce the spread of the virus.

Keywords: Aerosols, Coronavirus, COVID-19, Epidemiology, Fecal-oral route, Respiratory Syndrome, Respiratory infection, Symptoms, SARS-CoV-2, Transmission.

* **Corresponding author Sufian Badar:** Department of Bioengineering, University of California, Riverside, CA, USA; E-mail: sufianbadar@gmail.com

INTRODUCTION OF EPIDEMIOLOGY OF CORONAVIRUS

Coronavirus is among the most common pathogens that are related to mild and moderate respiratory disorders [1, 2]. Despite the fact that coronaviruses have been isolated from a wide variety of animals, bats are generally considered to be their primary natural reservoir. The virus emerged at the tail end of 2019 [3, 4]. On March 11, 2020, a declaration was made by WHO labeling Coronavirus as a global pandemic in response to swift dissemination of the SARS-CoV-2. This beta coronavirus had never been observed before, but it is related to other coronaviruses, such as severe acute respiratory syndrome (SARS). It has also been associated with Middle East Respiratory Syndrome (MERS) [5, 6]. There are multiple ways that SARS-CoV-2 can spread from one person to another in a community; respiratory droplets are the most common [7]. COVID-19 manifests with a variety of severity levels and symptoms. Some patients develop an adverse type of disease that is characterized by acute respiratory distress syndrome and adverse effects on other organs. However, the vast majority of the disease is less severe or without symptoms [8, 9]. As a result of the COVID-19 pandemic, millions of people were infected, and thousands of lives were lost all over the world. This chapter discusses the epidemiology, geographical distribution, and clinical manifestations of COVID-19.

ETIOLOGY OF CORONAVIRUS

The name "Coronavirus" comes from the Latin term "corona," which literally translates to "crown". It is named so because of the appearance of cloverleaf structures, such as glycoproteins and proteins, on the surface of the virus when viewed through an electron microscope that looks like spherical particles with a ring of projections around them, like the corona of the sun [10, 11]. These single-stranded viruses with 80-120 nm diameters belong to the family Orthocoronaviridae. They are enveloped, non-segmented, positive-sense viruses and were first isolated from humans in 1965. They commonly cause mild respiratory diseases in humans [12]. The virus was officially named SARS-CoV-2 on February 11, 2020. This decision was based on evolutionary history and taxonomic classification. The viral spike (S) glycoproteins are accountable for mediating the cellular entry of the virus. These glycoproteins consist of two subunits, S1 and S2. S1 is in charge of binding to the receptor on host cells. S2 is responsible for the fusing of the viral and cellular membranes. An infection caused by the virus is dependent on the ability of the host cell receptor, angiotensin-converting enzyme 2, to bind to the virus. High levels of ACE2 are found in alveolar epithelia, making them a crucial target for SARS-CoV-2. The disease that occurs due to this virus has been named Coronavirus disease by the World Health Organization (WHO) [13].

ORIGIN/DISEASE BACKGROUND

Initial reports from the Chinese Centre for Disease Control (CDC) in early 2019 described a cluster of patients in Wuhan, China, with pneumonia of unknown origin. In these patients' lower respiratory tract epithelial cells, an unidentified beta-coronavirus, known as the 2019 novel Coronavirus (2019–nCoV), was found using genetic sequencing. It was also theorized that the virus was initially found in bats and "naturally" spread to humans, most likely through contact with infected aquatic and living animals at the Huanan seafood wholesale market. Within a matter of months following the original outbreak, the pandemic had spread to dozens of additional countries and territories around the world [14]. The principal mode of viral transmission from an individual who is infected to another individual is by direct or through respiratory droplets. As compared to coronaviruses that infect humans, the novel Coronavirus showed a higher degree of phylogenetic relatedness to two bat-derived coronavirus strains, such as a 79% similarity with SARS and a 50% similarity with MERS that have led to large outbreaks of varying clinical severity, ranging from mild illness that goes away on its own to illness that can kill. COVID-19 has caused a previously unseen human and health disaster and brought about a global financial crisis that will take a long time to recover from [15, 16].

GEOGRAPHICAL DISTRIBUTION

The disease outbreak caused by the Coronavirus rapidly spread throughout China and 229 other countries and territories. Some of these countries were geographically close to China, such as Thailand, Taiwan, Japan, Singapore, and South Korea. Due to its very high transmissibility rates, the virus's spread was not limited to countries near China or even the Asian continent. France was the first European country involved, and all patients there apparently had contact with their Chinese counterparts [17]. On January 30, 2020, the first coronavirus case in India was reported in the Thrissur district of Kerala. The patient was a student who had recently returned from studying at Wuhan University in China [18]. As of March 5, 2023, the Coronavirus COVID-19 has caused 680,656,727 confirmed cases and 6,805,186 deaths around the world [19]. The United States has the highest number of COVID cases, followed by India [20]. About a third of all cases were presumed to have happened in South Asia (including India).

EPIDEMIOLOGICAL DETERMINANTS OF CORONAVIRUS

Variants of Coronavirus

Viruses tend to mutate genetically to adapt to even minor changes in the environment and transfer from one host to another. Mutations help the virus to gain characteristics that aid in its replication or reproduction by evading the immune system of a host, various treatments, and prevention measures such as vaccines. Owing to their rapid emergence in populations and evidence of enhanced transmissibility or virulence, decreased neutralization by natural infection or vaccination-derived antibodies, evasion of detection, or decrease in therapeutic or vaccination efficacy, certain variants have received much attention. The World Health Organization (WHO) has assigned the Greek alphabets such as Alpha, Beta, Delta, and Gamma to each variant [21, 22].

Alpha (B.1.1.7)- It was one of the first widely publicized variants. It was not until December 2020 that infections began to skyrocket in the UK, making the Alpha strain a growing cause for concern. When compared to other strains, Alpha has a transmission rate that is 50-75% higher.

Beta (B.1.351 lineage)- South Africa was the first region to discover and prioritize this second COVID-19 variant. It is also known as GH/501Y.V2. A higher transmission risk has been associated with this variation.

Gamma (P.1 lineage)- This variant was first identified in Brazil in early 2021. Concerns about an increase in the variant's transmissibility, as well as its impact on the immune system, have been raised as a result of several mutations in the variant.

Delta variant (B.1.617.2)- Tt first appeared in India in 2020 and soon became the most widespread variant all over the world and remained so until the appearance of the Omicron variant. It is highly transmissible and may also cause more severe illness than other variants.

Other variants identified include Zeta, Theta, Eta, Epsilon, Kappa, Iota, and Lambda. These variants differ in terms of mutations and characteristics, which may influence their response to treatments and vaccines, severity, and transmissibility [21, 23].

Risk Factors

There are several risk factors for COVID-19, including:

1. Age: The Coronavirus poses a greater danger to elderly people, particularly those who are over the age of 65.

2. Underlying medical conditions: People with prior health issues such as diabetes, complications of the lungs and the heart, obesity, and compromised immune systems are more likely to develop severe disease symptoms.

3. Smoking: Smoking can cause damage to the lungs and make it more difficult for the body to fight off infections, including COVID-19.

4. Occupation: People who work in healthcare environmental setups, transportation, retail, and other important industries may be at higher risk for infection due to close association with others.

5. Crowded living conditions: People living in densely populated living conditions such as nursing homes and prisons or individuals who participate in activities that entail proximity to others may face an increased susceptibility to contracting COVID-19.

6. Travel: People who have recently travelled to areas with high levels of COVID-19 transmission have more chances of contracting and spreading the virus [24, 25].

TRANSMISSION

The virus can replicate and disseminate depending on certain aspects of its structure as well as its robustness as a whole. Researchers found that coronavirus has one of the thickest and most protective outer membranes of any coronavirus. It is believed that this leads to viral particles that are most stable, which in turn results in greater resistance in bodily fluids [26]. SARS-CoV-2 can spread directly (via aerosols and person-to-person transmission) as well as indirectly through contaminated objects and airborne contagion. The infection could spread through personal protective equipment (PPE) as well [27, 28]. In the past, researchers believed that COVID-19 was transmitted through aerosols; however, more recent studies have brought to light the possibility of other transmission pathways. Multiple samples or fluids testing positive for viral RNA raise the possibility of additional routes of transmission, including blood borne, urinary, and feculent [29].

Transmissibility of SARS-CoV2

The basic reproduction number (R_0), is the predicted number of secondary cases that could result from one case in a susceptible population, and it provides an indication of the danger of an epidemic spreading. The R_0 for SARS-CoV2 has been estimated in most studies to be between 2.0 and 3.0 [11]. The secondary attack rate among the close contacts of the primary patient is the other factor that determines the infectious potential of SARS-CoV-2. The secondary attack rate and, in turn, the transmissibility of the SARS-CoV-2 is influenced by risk factors such as the age of household contacts and their spousal relationship to the index case [30].

Transmission Routes

Respiratory Transmission

The early manifestation of Coronavirus is an infection of the respiratory system. Lower respiratory tract infection is an early symptom of this virus, and it typically manifests with classic fever, shortness of breath, and cough [29]. This virus has an aerodynamic diameter of about 120 nm (0.12 μm). The virus needs a protein coating in order to replicate, so it can only survive in human respiratory droplets or other protein-rich environments [31, 32]. Droplets of respiratory fluids of varying sizes are expelled during a variety of bodily functions, such as exhaling, talking, coughing, and sneezing. This fluid is secreted from the body, and viral infection is spread via these droplets [33].

Transmission through the droplets occurs when an infected person's respiratory droplets (typically > 5-10 m in diameter) are inhaled by another person within 1 m of the infected person's nose or mouth. **29]** [34]. The term "airborne transmission" is used to describe the spread of an infectious agent from one person to another via the inhalation of minute aerosols droplets breathed by an infected individual nearby [32]. When particles are aerosolized, they become a threat in the air, especially during critical procedures like endotracheal intubation, bronchoscopy, and cardiopulmonary resuscitation [29, 34]. The largest droplets fall out of the air relatively quickly, taking anywhere from a few seconds to a few minutes. When these droplets rapidly dry out, very fine droplets and particles form. These particles are so small that they are able to float in the air for minutes or even hours [33]. Infection can occur not only through the inhalation of microbe particles but also through direct contact with objects that are infected or through fomites. A study that was documented in the New England Journal of Medicine (NEJM) suggested that viruses can spread through fomites as well as aerosols. This is due to the fact that the virus can remain viable for hours as aerosols, whereas it remains active on the surface for days (depending on the amount of inoculum shed) [35].

Faecal-oral Route of Transmission

Typically, respiratory symptoms characterize the infection, indicating droplet transmission. However, studies show that there are chances of fecal-oral route as well. Many researchers have documented the presence of viral RNA or live infectious viruses in the feces of patients. These claims have been supported by relevant GI symptoms and evidence [36]. Coronavirus RNA has been discovered in clinical analyses of non-traditional specimens such as anal or rectal swabs, blood, and stool, as well as conventional specimens such as nasopharyngeal or oropharyngeal swabs [37]. In 2020, researchers synthesized data from a Hong

Kong cohort and discovered that 17.6% of patients experience gastrointestinal symptoms and that 48.1% of fecal samples from patients with the virus tested positive for viral RNA [38, 39]. The viruses infect cells by binding to the ACE2 receptor, which allows it to enter the cell membrane. Absorbing enterocytes from the ileum and colon, as well as upper and stratified epithelial cells of the oesophagus, contain ACE2 [40]. Diarrhea, nausea, vomiting, and abdominal discomfort have been reported as the main gastrointestinal symptoms. The probability of gastrointestinal distress varies widely, from 2% to 57% [41, 42]. Other gastrointestinal manifestations include heartburn, GI bleeds, bloody diarrhea, constipation, and melena [39].

Various studies have linked respiratory viral infections to altered gut microbiota composition. Several case studies have been conducted to investigate changes in the fecal microbiota of patients infected with the virus during hospitalization. Comparing 15 patients with COVID-19 to healthy controls, researchers found an increase in opportunistic pathogens like *Clostridium hathewayi* and *Actinomyces viscosus* and a decrease in beneficial commensals like the *Ruminococcaceae* and *Lachnospiraceae* [39, 43].

It is unknown whether the viral particles shed in the stool for an extended period of time are infectious and can be spread faecal-orally. Yong Zhang and colleagues conducted a study that demonstrated the presence of live viruses in stool. The researchers managed to isolate the virus from a stool specimen of patients with severe COVID-19 pneumonia [44]. These results suggested that feces-borne virus transmission might be a factor. New evidence suggests extreme caution is required when dealing with Coronavirus patients' feces [29].

Vertical Route of Transmission

The potential for vertical transmission of Coronavirus exists and appears to occur in a limited number of instances involving maternal COVID-19 infection during the third trimester. The rates of infection demonstrate similarities to those observed in other pathogens that are responsible for congenital infections [45]. Several studies have provided evidence supporting the possibility of vertical transmission. It is indicated by the presence of elevated IgM antibodies in babies born to mothers who were tested positive for Coronavirus. In addition to detecting viral RNA and protein in the placenta, the research team led by Alexandre J. Vivanti also found viral RNA in amniotic fluid and neonatal blood samples taken shortly after birth, providing the strongest evidence to date for transplacental transmission of SARS-CoV-2 [46]. Huaping Zhu and his team observed that potential Coronavirus infection could lead to detrimental outcomes in neonates. The study involved a group of 10 infants born from nine mothers with the disease.

The neonates exhibited various adverse effects, including fetal distress, premature birth, breathing difficulties, thrombocytopenia, dysfunctional liver, and, in certain cases, mortality [47]. Although these findings support the theory of vertical transmission occurring in utero, the fetal infection could only be proven conclusively by demonstrating the presence of the virus in fetal tissues [45]. Large-scale studies are needed to address numerous questions pertaining to the vertical transmission of this novel Coronavirus.

Sexual Route of Transmission

The presence of Coronavirus was tested in the vaginal fluid and semen of COVID-19 positive patients to investigate the potential for sexual transmission. Based on the findings of a recent study conducted by Diangenge Li and his team, it was observed that Coronavirus was detected in the seminal fluid of six out of thirty-eight male individuals diagnosed with COVID-19 [48]. Among these cases, four were identified during the acute phase of infection, while the remaining two were observed during the recovery phase. Kelvin Kai-Wang To and his team of researchers showed that the novel Coronavirus was present in the saliva samples of 11 of 12 patients, with three patients' saliva samples testing positive for the presence of live viruses via viral culture [49]. Oral sex and the use of saliva as a lubricant can aid in the transmission of COVID-19. The presence of ACE2 receptors on the epithelium lining the oral cavity and the rectum, as well as viral particle shedding through saliva and feces, supports this [50].

Ocular Route of Transmission

The ocular surface can act as a reservoir and source of coronavirus infection. This disease can spread to other systems through the nasolacrimal route and hematogenous metastasis after entering the ocular surface through hand-eye contact and aerosols [51]. In a recent study, out of 216 children whose COVID-19 status was confirmed, researchers found that 49 (22.7%) of them had ocular manifestations. Conjunctival discharge, itchiness, and conjunctival congestion are the most common of these symptoms. Children who had systemic symptoms or a cough were more susceptible to developing ocular symptoms, which were mild and could be treated with a few drops of eye drops or by self-healing [52]. In a different case study of 38 COVID-19 patients, 12 of them had ocular symptoms like epiphora, conjunctival congestion, or chemosis, which were more prevalent in those who had more severe systemic symptoms. Patients with ocular abnormalities had more significant changes in blood test values [53]. Consequently, it is impossible to rule out the possibility of Coronavirus ocular transmission.

Incubation Period and Serial Interval

The primary epidemiological parameters that determine the transmission dynamics of Coronavirus infection are the serial interval and incubation period [54]. The incubation period is the time it takes for a disease to develop after an individual has been infected by the infectious agent. Knowing the incubation period is crucial for defining the cases, managing new threats, estimating follow-up time for contact tracing and secondary case detection, and developing public health programs to curb local transmission [55].

Researchers conducted a systemic review of studies reporting the Coronavirus incubation period published between January 1, 2020, and January 10, 2021 [56]. According to the findings, the average incubation period of SARS-CoV-2 is 6.38 days, ranging from 2.33 to 17.60 days. The incubation period is affected by both the immune response and the infectious dose [57]. According to a study conducted by researchers, the reduced incubation period of COVID-19 observed in individuals who travelled to Hubei, as opposed to those who did not travel, was attributed to their increased exposure to a higher viral load in Hubei, which is considered the epicenter of the outbreak [58]. The longer incubation period observed by Kong (2020) [57] in older adults can be attributed to age-related immunosenescence.

A serial interval can be defined as the time interval between the appearance of infection in the first patients and the onset of symptom in a second patient [54]. The average serial interval is estimated to be 4–5 days [11]. A serial interval of shorter duration than the incubation period may indicate pre-symptomatic transmission and should be considered when developing intervention strategies. SARS-CoV-2 serial interval estimates are also shorter than SARS-CoV and MERS-CoV, implying that containing the spread is more difficult than with other coronaviruses [59].

Period of Infectivity / Infectious Period

A patient's period of infectivity also called the infectious period, is the time during which they can spread COVID-19 to others. In most cases, the natural history of an infection's progression over time can only be inferred indirectly through methods like contact tracing, repeated diagnostic virological studies, and modeling because of how challenging it is to measure the infectious period [60]. Patients may continue to shed the virus long after their symptoms have subsided [11]. Although studies of viral loads suggest that peak viral loads occur within a week or so of the first appearance of symptoms (possibly within 1–7 days), it is unclear whether this typically occurs before, during, or after symptom onset [60]. According to previous research, the mean serial intervals are approximated to range between 4 and 5 days. The presence of pre-symptomatic spread should be considered when formulating prevention plans, as evidenced by a serial interval that is shorter than the incubation period [61]. Pre-symptomatic transmission was observed in Singapore, and when taken together with evidence from other studies, it strengthens the likelihood that viral shedding can occur asymptomatically and ahead of the onset of symptoms. The duration of the infectious period has been reported to range from 3 to 20 days by various research papers [60].

CLINICAL MANIFESTATIONS AND SEVERITY OF THE DISEASE

Coronavirus has a broad range of clinical manifestations and appears less than 14 days after virus exposure. Most patients have mild or no symptoms that include persistent dry cough, fever, difficulty breathing, muscle or body aches accompanied by headaches, loss of taste or smell that can last for several days or weeks, sore throat, runny nose or congestion, and gastrointestinal symptoms [62, 63]. Others develop a severe or critical illness such as acute respiratory distress syndrome (ARDS), pneumonia, organ failure, or sepsis. The severity of the disease is influenced by several risk factors, including age and underlying medical conditions [64, 65]. It is crucial to continue practicing social isolation and wearing protective clothing as well as getting vaccination shots to slow the spread of the virus and protect susceptible people.

Asymptomatic Cases

Asymptomatic individuals infected with the virus either do not develop any or have inconsistent symptoms. This means they can unknowingly spread the virus to others, which is why testing and contact tracking are crucial on a global scale [66].

Mild Cases

Mild instances of COVID-19 pertain to individuals who manifest symptoms, including fever, cough, fatigue, headache, loss of taste or smell, and sore throat. There is no dyspnoea or abnormal chest imaging and, therefore, do not require hospitalization. It is often possible to treat mild cases at home by getting plenty of rest, drinking adequate amounts of water, and taking over-the-counter medications to treat any symptoms that may arise.

However, even these cases of COVID-19 can have long-term health effects, such as fatigue, shortness of breath, and cognitive issues. Therefore, it is essential to take precautions to prevent the spread of the virus [29].

Moderate Cases

In moderate cases, the symptoms are common respiratory symptoms and fever, which usually resolve within a week or two.

These individuals typically have oxygen saturation (SpO2) $\geq$ 94% on room air at sea level and inflammation in the bottom portion of their lungs. The symptoms of an intermediate COVID-19 case include fever, exhaustion, headache, and prolonged and intense coughing. Adverse effects including nausea, vomiting, and diarrhea are possible for certain persons. Smell and taste loss can very seldom occur along with general sickness. The majority of patients can get better without being hospitalized. However, they should stay away from other people to stop the transmission of the infection [66 - 68].

Severe Cases

Symptoms like hypoxemia, tachypnea, dyspnea, persistent fever over 38 degrees Celsius, and pale lips or cheeks are indicative of a severe case. When inhaling regular air at sea level, people often have oxygen saturation levels (SPO2) below 94% and lung infiltrates more than 50%. Acute respiratory distress syndrome may emerge from these circumstances. Breathing becomes challenging due to the condition's inflammation and pulmonary fluid accumulation. It could be required to use breathing devices to keep the patient alive due to the severity of this damage. Apart from these potentially lethal consequences, acquiring COVID-19 can also lead to sepsis, heart failure, liver failure and kidney failure.

The elderly and people with underlying medical issues such as diabetes, obesity, heart disease, lung diseases or weakened immune systems are more respectable to sever cases of COVID-19.

The life-sustaining treatment for COVID-19 includes hospitalization, oxygen therapy, and supportive care such as fluid management, pain relief, and treatment of secondary infections. When breathing assistance is required, two methods can be used: extracorporeal membrane oxygenation (ECMO) and mechanical ventilation [66, 69].

CASE FATALITY RATE

The severity and subsequent influence on public health are key features of an infectious disease caused by a newly discovered pathogen, such as SARS-CoV-2. This is defined by the Case Fatality Rate, which is a measure of the proportion of deaths among documented cases of COVID-19 [70]. With its help, we can comprehend disease fatality, identify populations at risk, and evaluate the quality of healthcare to be provided [71].

$$\textbf{Case Fatality Rate (in \%) - } \frac{No.\ of\ deaths\ from\ disease\ x\ 100}{No.\ of\ confirmed\ cases\ of\ disease}$$

The drawback of this formula is that it is used only after all the cases have been resolved and, therefore, cannot be used for ongoing outbreaks. However, for an ongoing pandemic, a modified formula can be used that takes into account only the resolved cases.

$$\textbf{Case Fatality Rate (in \%) - } \frac{No.Of\ deaths\ from\ disease\ x\ 100}{No.\ of\ deaths\ caused\ by\ disease + No.Of\ recovered\ from\ the\ disease}$$

As of April 13, 2020, the WHO's situation report stated that the overall rate of case fatalities was 6.3. The CFR decreased as more cases were identified, and testing became more widely

available. A lower CFR is also important since healthcare providers have gained more expertise in treating COVID-19 patients and have access to more effective therapies and treatments. Because COVID-19 mortality is a multifactorial process, factors like age, policy decisions regarding the allocation of quality healthcare systems in various nations and regions, gender, and pre-existing health conditions may all have an impact on CFR rates [72].

It is essential to keep in mind that the CFR does not accurately reflect the impact that COVID-19 has on public health. It only takes into account cases that have been confirmed, but many cases go unnoticed or are not reported, which can lead to an underestimation of the disease's true impact.

Based on Gender

According to global data, men are highly susceptible to COVID-19 case fatalities than women. In a few countries, women are more likely than men to die from a Coronavirus case, including India, which was one of the most severely affected nations. However, the majority of nations that have data point to a male-to-female case fatality ratio that is greater than 1.0. According to a data from around the world, men are considered to be more likely to develop serious health complications and die from COVID-19 than women are. This is due to both biological risk factors, such as stronger immune responses, and behavioural risk factors, such a smoking cigarette and leading a very unhealthy lifestyle. The differing results regarding the association between gender and the disease mortality can be associated to several factors, including insufficient COVID-19 data throughout various geographic areas, possible prejudice towards case recognition based on gender, and the presence of demographic factors that may increase the vulnerability of women in certain countries [73].

Based on the Age Factor

The disease occurs at a significantly higher rate in nations with more older citizens. Patients in Italy averaged 62 years old, while COVID-19-related deaths averaged 78 years old. It is also common knowledge that the effectiveness of COVID-19 prevention efforts among these age groups has a direct impact on countries' mortality rates. Early Chinese reports suggested that older patients, especially those over 80, could die three times more often. In an Italian study, ICU mortality was 26%, and after age 65, it was 36%. Another key finding was the fact that the median time between the first appearance of symptoms and mortality was shorter for patients who were older [74 - 76].

In conclusion, CFR determines the number of deaths and it varies across the world. It is influenced by age, gender, and underlying health conditions. Although the CFR is a useful gauge of the disease's severity, it does not accurately reflect the disease's impact on public health [77].

CONCLUSION

In December of 2019, COVID-19 was first detected in Wuhan, China. The very high infectivity rate of the virus resulted in a global public health crisis of unprecedented scale and effects. Epidemiological studies have enabled us to understand the transmission dynamics of COVID-19, risk factors, clinical manifestations, and severity of the disease. The WHO has assigned Greek alphabets such as Alpha, Beta, Delta, and Gamma to each variant of the virus according to their virulence, transmissibility, detection, and treatment. Risk factors for COVID-19 include age, smoking, occupation, living conditions, *etc*. Historically, it was believed that respiratory droplets were the means of COVID-19 transmission. Nonetheless, recent research has verified that COVID-19 can spread via numerous pathways. The presence of SARS-CoV-2 in various bodily fluids, including saliva, feces, and urine, suggests that there may be several channels of transmission, including fecal-oral and sexual routes. COVID-19 may or may not cause symptoms, depending on the individual. It can also cause significant impairment. The World Health Organisation (WHO) defined the case fatality rate (CFR) as a way to measure the severity of a disease based on age, gender, and the effect it has on public health in different parts of the world. The worldwide community has taken significant attempts to curb the spread of COVID-19, but there is still significant concern about the virus's impact on public health. The COVID-19 epidemiology emphasizes the need for quick response times, public health preparedness, and the creation of potent treatments.

TAKE-HOME MESSAGE

- The coronavirus is one of the most common viruses that cause mild respiratory illness.
- The SARS-CoV-2 virus is characterized by single-stranded RNA, a positive-sense RNA genome. The diameter ranges between 80 and 120 nm. It was initially found in humans in 1965 and belongs to the family Orthocoronaviridae.
- Angiotensin-converting enzyme 2 functions as a host cell receptor for SARS-CoV-2 infection and is abundantly expressed in alveolar epithelia.
- The World Health Organization (WHO) has named several strains of the virus, including alpha, beta, delta, and gamma. Alpha was a highly publicized variant when it first appeared in the UK in November 2020.
- South Africans with COVID-19 beta form were shown to have a greater risk of transmission. Early in 2021, researchers in Brazil discovered the new gamma strain of the virus, and they believe it may be potentially more contagious than the original. The Delta variant emerged in India in late 2020, is highly transmissible, and may also cause more severe illness than other variants.
- COVID-19 is associated with a number of risk factors, including age, underlying medical conditions, smoking, occupational occupation, crowded living conditions, and travel.
- Elderly people, particularly those over the age of 65, are more susceptible to severe illness and death, and those with pre-existing medical conditions are more susceptible to developing severe symptoms.
- With its strong outer protective shell, SARS-CoV-2 is the most infectious coronavirus and therefore the most stable.
- Airborne contagion, aerosols, direct human-to-human contact, indirect contact with contaminated objects, and third-party contamination are examples of potential mechanisms of transmission.
- When an infected individual coughs, sneezes, or speaks with someone who is vulnerable to the virus, droplet transmission takes place.
- Several studies have provided evidence supporting the possibility of vertical transmission, as indicated by the presence of elevated IgM antibodies in infants born to women who were tested positive for COVID-19.
- Sexual contact can transfer the COVID-19 virus. This is further supported by the fact that viral particles are present in feces and saliva, and that the epithelium of the rectum and oral cavity has ACE2 receptors.
- SARS-CoV-2 can spread through the nasal-lacrimal and hematogenous pathways, resulting in ocular infection.
- COVID-19 transmission kinetics are influenced by both the incubation period

and the serial interval. The average incubation period of SARS-CoV-2 is 6.38 days, with a range spanning from 2.33 to 17.60 days.

- Pre-symptomatic transmission should be considered in intervention attempts if the serial interval is shorter than the incubation period.
- Depending on the person, COVID-19 might cause mild to severe symptoms.
- People who do not exhibit any symptoms of the virus themselves may unintentionally spread it to others.
- In mild cases, the symptoms are common respiratory symptoms and fever, inflammation in the lower lungs, gastrointestinal symptoms, and loss of taste or smell. Even the patients with mild symptoms are advised to be isolated.
- Weariness, shortness of breath, and a dry cough are signs of a mild case that can be managed at home with over-the-counter drugs.
- The case fatality rate is a useful tool for assessing the severity of COVID-19 infection.
- In accordance with global data, men are more at risk of catching an infectious disease than women. However, in a few countries, such as India, women are at a higher risk.
- Nations that have a significant percentage of older citizens have shown that older people have a higher fatality rate.

WHAT YOU WILL LEARN

• A detailed understanding of the structure of Coronavirus, its origin from the Wuhan seafood market in China, emergence, and geographical distribution around the world impacting millions of individuals.

• A brief account of the epidemiological determinants of Coronavirus, such as the transmissibility and severity of various variants of Coronavirus, as well as highlighting the risk factors involved in Coronavirus.

• A detailed analysis of how Coronavirus infection spreads, focusing on the various routes of manifestation of the virus and how long it can remain infectious.

• Additionally, the chapter also discusses the clinical manifestations of the disease and classifies various symptoms according to their severity, together with the fatality rates of the disease.

LIST OF ABBREVIATIONS

SARS-CoV-2 Severe Acute Respiratory Syndrome Coronavirus 2

MERS Middle East Respiratory Syndrome

SARS Severe Acute Respiratory Syndrome

COVID-19 Coronavirus Disease 2019

WHO	World Health Organization
CDC	Center for Disease Control
2019–nCoV	2019-novel Coronavirus
R_0	Basic reproduction number
PPE	Personal protective equipment
NEJM	New England journal of medicine
RNA	Ribonucleic Acid
ACE2	Angiotensin-Converting Enzyme 2
AT2	Alveolar Type 2
GI	Gastrointestinal
IgM	Immunoglobulin M
MERS CoV	Middle East Respiratory Syndrome
SARS CoV	Severe Acute Respiratory Syndrome
ARDS	Acute Respiratory Distress Syndrome
SpO$_2$	Saturation of Peripheral Oxygen
ECMO	Extracorporeal Membrane Oxygenation
CFR	Case Fatality Rate

REFERENCES

[1] Bulut C, Kato Y. Epidemiology of COVID-19. Turk J Med Sci 2020; 50(SI-1): 563-70.
[http://dx.doi.org/10.3906/sag-2004-172] [PMID: 32299206]

[2] Rothan HA, Byrareddy SN. The epidemiology and pathogenesis of coronavirus disease (COVID-19) outbreak. J Autoimmun 2020; 109: 102433.
[http://dx.doi.org/10.1016/j.jaut.2020.102433] [PMID: 32113704]

[3] Cui J, Li F, Shi ZL. Origin and evolution of pathogenic coronaviruses. Nat Rev Microbiol 2019; 17(3): 181-92.
[http://dx.doi.org/10.1038/s41579-018-0118-9] [PMID: 30531947]

[4] Yu P, Hu B, Shi ZL, Cui J. Geographical structure of bat SARS-related coronaviruses. Infect Genet Evol 2019; 69: 224-9.
[http://dx.doi.org/10.1016/j.meegid.2019.02.001] [PMID: 30735813]

[5] Hu B, Guo H, Zhou P, Shi ZL. Characteristics of SARS-CoV-2 and COVID-19. Nat Rev Microbiol 2021; 19(3): 141-54.
[http://dx.doi.org/10.1038/s41579-020-00459-7] [PMID: 33024307]

[6] Niemi MEK, Daly MJ, Ganna A. The human genetic epidemiology of COVID-19. Nat Rev Genet 2022; 23(9): 533-46.
[http://dx.doi.org/10.1038/s41576-022-00478-5] [PMID: 35501396]

[7] Rahman S, Montero MTV, Rowe K, Kirton R, Kunik F Jr. Epidemiology, pathogenesis, clinical presentations, diagnosis and treatment of COVID-19: a review of current evidence. Expert Rev Clin Pharmacol 2021; 14(5): 601-21.
[http://dx.doi.org/10.1080/17512433.2021.1902303] [PMID: 33705239]

[8] Huang C, Wang Y, Li X, *et al.* Clinical features of patients infected with 2019 novel coronavirus in

Wuhan, China. Lancet 2020; 395(10223): 497-506.
[http://dx.doi.org/10.1016/S0140-6736(20)30183-5] [PMID: 31986264]

[9]   Zhou F, Yu T, Du R, *et al.* Clinical course and risk factors for mortality of adult inpatients with COVID-19 in Wuhan, China: a retrospective cohort study. Lancet 2020; 395(10229): 1054-62.
[http://dx.doi.org/10.1016/S0140-6736(20)30566-3] [PMID: 32171076]

[10]   Salahshoori I, Mobaraki-Asl N, Seyfaee A, *et al.* Overview of COVID-19 Disease: Virology, Epidemiology, Prevention Diagnosis, Treatment, and Vaccines. Biologics 2021; 1(1): 2-40.
[http://dx.doi.org/10.3390/biologics1010002]

[11]   Dhar Chowdhury S, Oommen A M. Epidemiology of COVID-19. Journal of Digestive Endoscopy 11(1): 3-7.2020;
[http://dx.doi.org/10.1055/s-0040-1712187]

[12]   Rauf A, Abu-Izneid T, Olatunde A, *et al.* COVID-19 Pandemic: Epidemiology, Etiology, Conventional and Non-Conventional Therapies. Int J Environ Res Public Health 2020; 17(21): 8155.
[http://dx.doi.org/10.3390/ijerph17218155] [PMID: 33158234]

[13]   Jiang MD, Zu ZY, Schoepf UJ, *et al.* Current Status of Etiology, Epidemiology, Clinical Manifestations and Imagings for COVID-19. Korean J Radiol 2020; 21(10): 1138-49.
[http://dx.doi.org/10.3348/kjr.2020.0526] [PMID: 32767867]

[14]   Mohan BS, Vinod N. COVID-19: An Insight into SARS-CoV2 Pandemic Originated at Wuhan City in Hubei Province of China. Journal of Infectious Diseases and Epidemiology 2020; 6: 4.
[http://dx.doi.org/10.23937/2474-3658/1510146]

[15]   Lu R, Zhao X, Li J, *et al.* Genomic characterisation and epidemiology of 2019 novel coronavirus: implications for virus origins and receptor binding. Lancet 2020; 395(10224): 565-74.
[http://dx.doi.org/10.1016/S0140-6736(20)30251-8] [PMID: 32007145]

[16]   Bolsen T, Palm R, Kingsland JT. Framing the Origins of COVID-19. Sci Commun 2020; 42(5): 562-85.
[http://dx.doi.org/10.1177/1075547020953603] [PMID: 38603006]

[17]   Delgosha MS, Ahmadi K, Dashti MF. Geographical distribution of COVID-19 in the World and Iran; Investigation of possible transmission roots. J Family Med Prim Care 2020; 9(8): 4473-5.
[http://dx.doi.org/10.4103/jfmpc.jfmpc_733_20] [PMID: 33110890]

[18]   Rawat M. Coronavirus in India: tracking country's first 50 COVID-19 cases; what numbers tell. https://www.indiatoday.in/india/story/coronavirus-in-india-tracking-country-s-first-50-COVID-19-cases-what-numbers-tell-1654468-2020-03-12

[19]   Countries where Coronavirus has spread - Worldometer (nd) https://www.worldometers.info/ coronavirus/countries-where-coronavirus-has-spread/

[20]   Chakraborty I, Maity P. COVID-19 outbreak: Migration, effects on society, global environment and prevention. Sci Total Environ 2020; 728: 138882.
[http://dx.doi.org/10.1016/j.scitotenv.2020.138882] [PMID: 32335410]

[21]   Aleem A, Samad AA, Slenker AK. Emerging Variants of SARS-CoV-2 And Novel Therapeutics Against Coronavirus (COVID-19) StatPearls Publishing, 01, 01 https://www.ncbi.nlm.nih.gov/ books/NBK570580/ 2021.

[22]   UpToDate (nd) UpToDate https://wwwuptodatecom/contents/COVID-19-epidemiology-virology-and-prevention#H3544233796

[23]   Katella K. Omicron, Delta, Alpha, and More: What To Know About the Coronavirus Variants Yale Medicine https://wwwyalemedicineorg/news/COVID-19-variants-of-concern-omicron 2023.

[24]   COVID-19 and Your Health (2020, February 11) Centers for Disease Control and Prevention https://wwwcdcgov/coronavirus/2019-ncov/your-health/risks-getting-very-sickhtml 2020.

[25]   Who Is at High Risk for Severe Coronavirus Disease? https://www.hopkinsmedicine.org/health/

conditions-and-diseases/coronavirus/coronavirus-and-covid19-who-is-at-higher-risk 2022.

[26]   Goh GKM, Dunker AK, Foster JA, Uversky VN. Shell disorder analysis predicts greater resilience of the SARS-CoV-2 (COVID-19) outside the body and in body fluids. Microb Pathog 2020; 144: 104177.
[http://dx.doi.org/10.1016/j.micpath.2020.104177] [PMID: 32244041]

[27]   Liu Y, Ning Z, Chen Y, *et al.* 2020.Aerodynamic Characteristics and RNA Concentration of SARS-CoV-2 Aerosol in Wuhan Hospitals during COVID-19 Outbreak. BioRxiv
[http://dx.doi.org/10.1101/2020.03.08.982637]

[28]   Lotfi M, Hamblin MR, Rezaei N. COVID-19: Transmission, prevention, and potential therapeutic opportunities. Clin Chim Acta 2020; 508: 254-66.
[http://dx.doi.org/10.1016/j.cca.2020.05.044] [PMID: 32474009]

[29]   Patel KP, Vunnam SR, Patel PA, *et al.* Transmission of SARS-CoV-2: an update of current literature. Eur J Clin Microbiol Infect Dis 2020; 39(11): 2005-11.
[http://dx.doi.org/10.1007/s10096-020-03961-1] [PMID: 32638221]

[30]   Li W, Zhang B, Lu J, *et al.* Characteristics of Household Transmission of COVID-19. Clin Infect Dis 2020; 71(8): 1943-6.
[http://dx.doi.org/10.1093/cid/ciaa450] [PMID: 32301964]

[31]   Lim Y, Ng Y, Tam J, Liu D. Human Coronaviruses: A Review of Virus–Host Interactions. Diseases 2016; 4(3): 26.
[http://dx.doi.org/10.3390/diseases4030026] [PMID: 28933406]

[32]   Zhao X, Liu S, Yin Y, Zhang TT, Chen Q. Airborne transmission of COVID-19 virus in enclosed spaces: An overview of research methods. Indoor Air 2022; 32(6): e13056.
[http://dx.doi.org/10.1111/ina.13056] [PMID: 35762235]

[33]   Coronavirus Disease 2019 (COVID-19) (2020, February 11) Centers for Disease Control and Prevention   https://wwwcdcgov/coronavirus/2019-ncov/science/science-briefs/sars-c-v-2-transmissionhtml 2020.

[34]   World Health Organization (2020) Modes of transmission of virus causing COVID-19: implications for   IPC   precaution   recommendations: scientific   brief,   27   March   2020 https://appswhoint/iris/handle/10665/331601 2020.

[35]   van Doremalen N, Bushmaker T, Morris DH, *et al.* Aerosol and Surface Stability of SARS-CoV-2 as Compared with SARS-CoV-1. N Engl J Med 2020; 382(16): 1564-7.
[http://dx.doi.org/10.1056/NEJMc2004973] [PMID: 32182409]

[36]   Hindson J. COVID-19: faecal–oral transmission? Nat Rev Gastroenterol Hepatol 2020; 17(5): 259.
[http://dx.doi.org/10.1038/s41575-020-0295-7] [PMID: 32214231]

[37]   Mohammad Khalid P. Gut Feeling: The Plausible Faecal-Oral Transmission Route of COVID-19. Journal of Infectious Diseases and Epidemiology 2020; 6: 4.
[http://dx.doi.org/10.23937/2474-3658/1510141]

[38]   Cheung KS, Hung IFN, Chan PPY, *et al.* Gastrointestinal Manifestations of SARS-CoV-2 Infection and Virus Load in Fecal Samples From a Hong Kong Cohort: Systematic Review and Meta-analysis. Gastroenterology 2020; 159(1): 81-95.
[http://dx.doi.org/10.1053/j.gastro.2020.03.065] [PMID: 32251668]

[39]   Guo M, Tao W, Flavell RA, Zhu S. Potential intestinal infection and faecal–oral transmission of SARS-CoV-2. Nat Rev Gastroenterol Hepatol 2021; 18(4): 269-83.
[http://dx.doi.org/10.1038/s41575-021-00416-6] [PMID: 33589829]

[40]   Zhang H, Kang Z, Gong H, *et al.* The digestive system is a potential route of 2019-nCov infection: a bioinformatics analysis based on single-cell transcriptomes. BioRxiv 2020.
[http://dx.doi.org/10.1101/2020.01.30.927806]

[41]　Ferm S, Fisher C, Pakala T, *et al.* Analysis of Gastrointestinal and Hepatic Manifestations of SARS-CoV-2 Infection in 892 Patients in Queens, NY. Clin Gastroenterol Hepatol 2020; 18(10): 2378-2379.e1.
[http://dx.doi.org/10.1016/j.cgh.2020.05.049] [PMID: 32497637]

[42]　Mao R, Qiu Y, He JS, *et al.* Manifestations and prognosis of gastrointestinal and liver involvement in patients with COVID-19: a systematic review and meta-analysis. Lancet Gastroenterol Hepatol 2020; 5(7): 667-78.
[http://dx.doi.org/10.1016/S2468-1253(20)30126-6] [PMID: 32405603]

[43]　Zuo T, Zhang F, Lui GCY, *et al.* Alterations in Gut Microbiota of Patients With COVID-19 During Time of Hospitalization. Gastroenterology 2020; 159(3): 944-955.e8.
[http://dx.doi.org/10.1053/j.gastro.2020.05.048] [PMID: 32442562]

[44]　Zhang Y, Chen C, Zhu S, *et al.* Isolation of 2019-nCoV from a Stool Specimen of a Laboratory-Confirmed Case of the Coronavirus Disease 2019 (COVID-19). China CDC Weekly 2020; 2(8): 123-4.
[http://dx.doi.org/10.46234/ccdcw2020.033] [PMID: 34594837]

[45]　Kotlyar AM, Grechukhina O, Chen A, *et al.* Vertical transmission of coronavirus disease 2019: a systematic review and meta-analysis. Am J Obstet Gynecol 2021; 224(1): 35-53.e3. b
[http://dx.doi.org/10.1016/j.ajog.2020.07.049] [PMID: 32739398]

[46]　Vivanti AJ, Vauloup-Fellous C, Prevot S, *et al.* Transplacental transmission of SARS-CoV-2 infection. Nat Commun 2020; 11(1): 3572. b
[http://dx.doi.org/10.1038/s41467-020-17436-6] [PMID: 32665677]

[47]　Zhu H, Wang L, Fang C, *et al.* Clinical analysis of 10 neonates born to mothers with 2019-nCoV pneumonia. Transl Pediatr 2020; 9(1): 51-60.
[http://dx.doi.org/10.21037/tp.2020.02.06] [PMID: 32154135]

[48]　Li D, Jin M, Bao P, Zhao W, Zhang S. Clinical Characteristics and Results of Semen Tests Among Men With Coronavirus Disease 2019. JAMA Netw Open 2020; 3(5): e208292.
[http://dx.doi.org/10.1001/jamanetworkopen.2020.8292] [PMID: 32379329]

[49]　To KKW, Tsang OTY, Yip CCY, *et al.* Consistent Detection of 2019 Novel Coronavirus in Saliva. Clin Infect Dis 2020; 71(15): 841-3.
[http://dx.doi.org/10.1093/cid/ciaa149] [PMID: 32047895]

[50]　Cipriano M, Giacalone A, Ruberti E. Sexual Behaviors During COVID-19: The Potential Risk of Transmission. Arch Sex Behav 2020; 49(5): 1431-2.
[http://dx.doi.org/10.1007/s10508-020-01757-0] [PMID: 32504235]

[51]　Qu JY, Xie HT, Zhang MC. Evidence of SARS-CoV-2 Transmission Through the Ocular Route. Clin Ophthalmol 2021; 15: 687-96.
[http://dx.doi.org/10.2147/OPTH.S295283] [PMID: 33658750]

[52]　Ma N, Li P, Wang X, *et al.* Ocular Manifestations and Clinical Characteristics of Children With Laboratory-Confirmed COVID-19 in Wuhan, China. JAMA Ophthalmol 2020; 138(10): 1079-86.
[http://dx.doi.org/10.1001/jamaophthalmol.2020.3690] [PMID: 32845280]

[53]　Wu P, Duan F, Luo C, *et al.* Characteristics of Ocular Findings of Patients With Coronavirus Disease 2019 (COVID-19) in Hubei Province, China. JAMA Ophthalmol 2020; 138(5): 575-8.
[http://dx.doi.org/10.1001/jamaophthalmol.2020.1291] [PMID: 32232433]

[54]　Alene M, Yismaw L, Assemie MA, Ketema DB, Gietaneh W, Birhan TY. Serial interval and incubation period of COVID-19: a systematic review and meta-analysis. BMC Infect Dis 2021; 21(1): 257.
[http://dx.doi.org/10.1186/s12879-021-05950-x] [PMID: 33706702]

[55]　Nishiura H, Mizumoto K, Ejima M, Zhong Y, Cowling BJ, Omori R. Incubation period as part of the case definition of severe respiratory illness caused by a novel coronavirus. Euro Surveill 2012; 17(42):

20296.
[http://dx.doi.org/10.2807/ese.17.42.20296-en] [PMID: 23098822]

[56] Elias C, Sekri A, Leblanc P, Cucherat M, Vanhems P. The incubation period of COVID-19: A meta-analysis. Int J Infect Dis 2021; 104: 708-10.
[http://dx.doi.org/10.1016/j.ijid.2021.01.069] [PMID: 33548553]

[57] Kong T. Longer incubation period of coronavirus disease 2019 (COVID-19) in older adults. Aging Med (Milton) 2020; 3(2): 102-9.
[http://dx.doi.org/10.1002/agm2.12114] [PMID: 32661509]

[58] Leung C. The difference in the incubation period of 2019 novel coronavirus (SARS-CoV-2) infection between travelers to Hubei and nontravelers: The need for a longer quarantine period. Infect Control Hosp Epidemiol 2020; 41(5): 594-6.
[http://dx.doi.org/10.1017/ice.2020.81] [PMID: 32183920]

[59] Park M, Cook AR, Lim JT, Sun Y, Dickens BL. A Systematic Review of COVID-19 Epidemiology Based on Current Evidence. J Clin Med 2020; 9(4): 967.
[http://dx.doi.org/10.3390/jcm9040967] [PMID: 32244365]

[60] Byrne AW, McEvoy D, Collins AB, et al. Inferred duration of infectious period of SARS-CoV-2: rapid scoping review and analysis of available evidence for asymptomatic and symptomatic COVID-19 cases. BMJ Open 2020; 10(8): e039856.
[http://dx.doi.org/10.1136/bmjopen-2020-039856] [PMID: 32759252]

[61] Liu Y, Yan LM, Wan L, et al. Viral dynamics in mild and severe cases of COVID-19. Lancet Infect Dis 2020; 20(6): 656-7.
[http://dx.doi.org/10.1016/S1473-3099(20)30232-2] [PMID: 32199493]

[62] Tsai PH, Lai WY, Lin YY, et al. Clinical manifestation and disease progression in COVID-19 infection. J Chin Med Assoc 2021; 84(1): 3-8.
[http://dx.doi.org/10.1097/JCMA.0000000000000463] [PMID: 33230062]

[63] Kutsuna S. Clinical Manifestations of Coronavirus Disease 2019. Japan Med Assoc J 2021; 4(2): 76-80.
[http://dx.doi.org/10.31662/jmaj.2021-0013] [PMID: 33997439]

[64] Baj J, Karakuła-Juchnowicz H, Teresiński G, et al. COVID-19: Specific and Non-Specific Clinical Manifestations and Symptoms: The Current State of Knowledge. J Clin Med 2020; 9(6): 1753.
[http://dx.doi.org/10.3390/jcm9061753] [PMID: 32516940]

[65] Kordzadeh-Kermani E, Khalili H, Karimzadeh I. Pathogenesis, clinical manifestations and complications of coronavirus disease 2019 (COVID-19). Future Microbiol 2020; 15(13): 1287-305.
[http://dx.doi.org/10.2217/fmb-2020-0110] [PMID: 32851877]

[66] Clinical Spectrum | COVID-19 Treatment Guidelines (nd) COVID-19 Treatment Guidelines https://wwwcovid19treatmentguidelinesnihgov/overview/clinical-spectrum/

[67] Mbe SJ. Coronavirus: what are asymptomatic and mild COVID-19? Patient https://patientinfo/news-and-features/coronavirus-what-are-asymptomatic-and-mild-COVID-19 2021.

[68] Lowth M. Coronavirus: what are moderate, severe and critical COVID-19? Patient https://patientinfo/news-and-features/coronavirus-what-are-moderate-severe-and-critical-COVID-19 2020.

[69] How to tell if your coronavirus symptoms are mild, moderate, or severe The Checkup https://wwwsinglecarecom/blog/news/coronavirus-symptoms-and-incubation-period/ 2022.

[70] Alimohamadi Y, Tola HH, Abbasi-Ghahramanloo A, Janani M, Sepandi M. Case fatality rate of COVID-19: a systematic review and meta-analysis. J Prev Med Hyg 2021; 62(2): E311-20. b
[http://dx.doi.org/10.15167/2421-4248/jpmh2021.62.2.1627] [PMID: 34604571]

[71] World Health Organization: WHO (2020, August 4) Estimating mortality from COVID-19

https://wwwwhoint/news-room/commentaries/detail/estimating-mortality-from-COVID-19 2020.

[72]   Ji Y, Ma Z, Peppelenbosch MP, Pan Q. Potential association between COVID-19 mortality and health-care resource availability. Lancet Glob Health 2020; 8(4): e480.
[http://dx.doi.org/10.1016/S2214-109X(20)30068-1] [PMID: 32109372]

[73]   Dehingia N, Raj A. Sex differences in COVID-19 case fatality: do we know enough? Lancet Glob Health 2021; 9(1): e14-5.
[http://dx.doi.org/10.1016/S2214-109X(20)30464-2] [PMID: 33160453]

[74]   Wu Z, McGoogan JM. Characteristics of and Important Lessons From the Coronavirus Disease 2019 (COVID-19) Outbreak in China. JAMA 2020; 323(13): 1239-42.
[http://dx.doi.org/10.1001/jama.2020.2648] [PMID: 32091533]

[75]   Grasselli G, Zangrillo A, Zanella A, *et al.* Baseline Characteristics and Outcomes of 1591 Patients Infected With SARS-CoV-2 Admitted to ICUs of the Lombardy Region, Italy. JAMA 2020; 323(16): 1574-81.
[http://dx.doi.org/10.1001/jama.2020.5394] [PMID: 32250385]

[76]   Wang W, Tang J, Wei F. Updated understanding of the outbreak of 2019 novel coronavirus (2019-nCoV) in Wuhan, China. J Med Virol 2020; 92(4): 441-7.
[http://dx.doi.org/10.1002/jmv.25689] [PMID: 31994742]

[77]   Dudel C, Riffe T, Acosta E, van Raalte A, Strozza C, Myrskylä M. Monitoring trends and differences in COVID-19 case-fatality rates using decomposition methods: Contributions of age structure and age-specific fatality. PLoS One 2020; 15(9): e0238904.
[http://dx.doi.org/10.1371/journal.pone.0238904] [PMID: 32913365]

CHAPTER 3

Replication and Pathogenesis of Coronaviruses

Mohammad Sufian Badar[1,2,3,4], **Onaiza Ansari**[5,*], **Anam Mursaleen**[5], **Asrar Ahmad Malik**[5], **Javaid Ahmad Sheikh**[5] and **Aamir Nehal**[6]

[1] *Department of Bioengineering, University of California, Riverside, CA, USA*

[2] *Universal Scientific Education and Research Network (USERN), Tehran, Iran*

[3] *Director (Academic), SPI Darbhanga, India*

[4] *Department of Computer Science and Engineering (Bioinformatics), School of Engineering Sciences and Technology (SEST), Jamia Hamdard, New Delhi, India*

[5] *Department of Biotechnology, Jamia Hamdard, New Delhi, India*

[6] *Consultant Physiotherapist, Bank Road, Motihari, Bihar, India*

Abstract: The COVID-19 pandemic has led to widespread illness, death, and economic disruption worldwide, leading to a critical need for effective treatments, vaccines, and diagnostic tools. SARS-CoV-2, belonging to the class of β-CoVs, is the virus accountable for COVID-19, and mediates entry into the host cell via its surface spike protein. Understanding its replication and pathogenesis is crucial for developing effective treatments and curbing the microbe's spread. Here, we dive deep into the genomic organisation of the SARS-Cov2 virion and its various structural components, highlighting the molecular mechanism involved in replication, ultimately leading to pathogenesis.

Keywords: COVID-19, Diagnostic, Genomics, Pandemic, Pathogenesis, SARS-CoV-2, Vaccines.

INTRODUCTION

Infecting both mammals and birds, coronavirus (CoV) is a zoonotic virus. This virus family induces respiratory tract infections (RTI) that range from mild to severe. It was first reported in 1937 and termed "coronavirus" for its crown-like appearance observed under the microscope in 1965. These viruses are non-segmented and enveloped, with a massive positive-sense genome. It is a member of the family Coronaviridae, the Orthocoronaviridae subfamily of the Nidovirales order. In addition, the subfamily is categorised into four genera: alpha coronavirus (α-CoV), beta coronavirus (β-CoV), gamma coronavirus (γ-CoV), and delta coro-

---

* **Corresponding author Onaiza Ansari:** Department of Biotechnology, Jamia Hamdard, New Delhi, India; E-mail: ozansari8@gmail.com

navirus (δ-CoV). Their hosts can be bovis, pigs, humans, avians, *etc.* and they suffer from various sorts of infections such as pneumonia, diarrhea, enteric indication, renal failures, and so on. Both, α-CoV and β-CoV infections are prevalent in mammals. However, γ-CoV and δ-CoV infections are predominant in birds [1].

The coronavirus is not new to human beings and has existed for decades. Since the dawn of the 21st century, it has become a great threat to human life, necessitating immediate, researchful, and effective remedies. Pathogenic human coronavirus was first recognised in 2002 with the discovery of severe acute respiratory syndrome-CoronaVirus (SARS-CoV). To date, 7 human coronaviruses have been identified with disease severities ranging from mild to lethal. Human coronavirus associated with mild diseases is 229E and OC-43 (belonging to genera α-CoV) and NL-63 and HKU-1 (belonging to β-CoV). The two extremely detrimental human CoV (hCoV) are SARS-CoV, accountable for causing severe acute respiratory syndrome (SARS), and MERS-CoV, liable for triggering Middle East Respiratory Syndrome (MERS), both belonging to genera β-CoV [2].The outbreaks of SARS-CoV and MERS-CoV had a significant impact on human life in 2002 and 2012, respectively. The SARS-CoV outbreak first appeared in China in 2002, infecting 8422 people and resulting in 916 deaths. In 2012, the MERS-CoV outbreak originated in Arabian countries, with approximately 1800 individuals being infected [3].

Recently, in late December 2019, a novel virus surfaced in China, causing severe pneumonia-like symptoms in patients, predominantly those who had visited the seafood market in the city of Wuhan. The pathogen was certified to be a virus using Polymerase Chain Reaction (PCR) and Next Generation Sequencing (NGS) techniques, which revealed that the virus was new and distinct from any previously known viruses, as it did not demonstrate complete similarity to any known virus. Also, the clinical symptoms were much more severe and distinguishable from any of the other known viruses [3]. It has caused a great infestation influencing almost all countries across the globe and killing millions of people [4]. SARS-CoV-2 (β-coronavirus) is a virus that is closely related to SARS-CoV. The SARS-CoV-2 NGS result shows 79% homology with SARS-CoV and 50% with MERS CoV. However, SARS-CoV-2 has a higher transmission and infectivity rate than SARS-CoV and MERS-CoV [5].

Both the corona viruses, MERS-CoV and SARS CoV were discovered in bats and inflicted human beings through different intermediate hosts; civet cats in case of SARS-CoV and the intermediate in MERS CoV were dromedary camels [6, 7]. Furthermore, SARS-CoV-2 shares 88% of homology with two bat-derived coronaviruses, bat-SL-CoVZC45 and bat-SL-CoVZXC21.

Genomic Organisation of SARS-CoV-2

CoVs have the largest genomic size of any RNA virus, ranging in length from 26 to 32 Kbp. SARS-CoV-2 being the largest CoVs have positive, single-stranded RNA genome of 29,891 nucleotides and 9,860 amino acids present within the nucleocapsid, which is further encapsulated by an envelope [8, 9]. Club-shaped spikes protrude from the surface, like a solar corona. The GC content is only 38%, which is very low compared to other CoVs.

The ORF number differs across CoVs. However, the SARS CoV-2 genome consists of 10 ORFs; out of which ORF-1 is the longest and accounts for 2/3rd of viral RNA. It encodes for polyprotein-1a, polyprotein-1b and 1-16 non -structural genes. ORF1b overlaps with 1a followed by shorter sub-gRNA (sgRNA). The remaining 9 ORF are involved in encoding structural gene-protein Spike (S), Envelope (E), Nucleocapsid (N), Membrane(M) and other accessory proteins [10].

Structural proteins are located at the 3' end of the remaining one-third of the genome. Generally, 4 structural genes are required by most CoV to produce a functional and complete viral particle. Some CoVs may encode additional structural proteins like Hemagglutinin Esterase (HE) protein, which, however, is lost in SARS-CoV-2 [11]. Not just limited to structure formation, these genes are also involved in other aspects such as entry inside the host, replication, *etc*.

The coronavirus genome is structured as 5' UTR-Replicase-S-E-M-N-3' UTR followed by a poly A tail. The structural genes are present with genes that code for auxiliary proteins. For SARS-CoV-2, five ORFs that encode accessory genes have been identified as ORF6, ORF7a, ORF3a, ORF7b, and ORF8. Also, ORF3b and ORF9b are formed due to the leaky translation of sgRNA of the nucleocapsid protein [12 - 14].

Structural Proteins of the SARS-CoV-2

Spike Protein

The SARS-CoV-2 virion membrane features glycoprotein projections known as the spike protein, which belongs to the class I type of transmembrane protein. This protein plays a critical role in identifying the host cell receptor, mediating binding to it, and subsequently merging with the membrane to enter the host cell. The spike protein comprises homotrimers of the S protein, with each corona virion typically containing around 50 to 100 of these trimers. The S protein has a molecular weight of 150KDa and is divided into three regions being the outer ectodomain region, intracellular region which has a short tail (C fragment) and a transmembrane region. Within the ectodomain region, there are two subunits: the S1 and S2 subdomain (Fig. **1**).

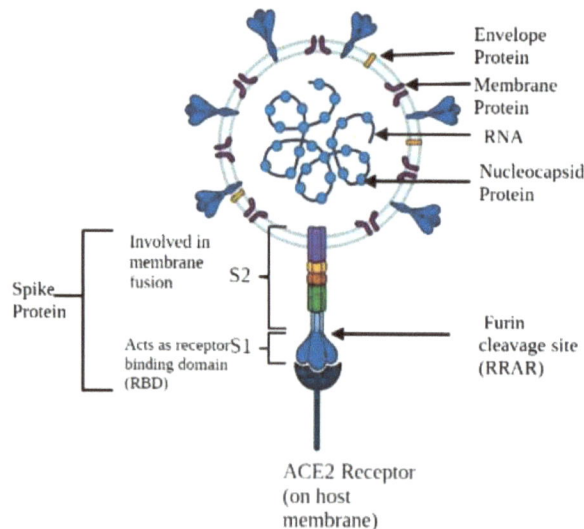

Fig. (1). Diagrammatic representation of SARS-CoV-2 structural protein.

• S1 subunit is a crucial antigen consisting of two: C-terminal domain (CTD) and the N-terminal domain (NTD), with the S1-CTD functioning as the receptor binding domain (RBD) [14]. The RBD is responsible for binding to 18 residues of human Angiotensin Converting Enzymes-II(ACEII). Because the RBDs are concealed by glycosylation, the S protein must undergo a conformational change to bind with the host receptor. The RBDs exhibit two conformations, "up" and "down," with up-conformation RBDs binding with greater affinity. Three RBDs trimerize and rotate upwards to achieve a receptor-accessible conformation.

• The S2 domain of the spike protein is responsible for facilitating the membrane fusion. It comprises several components, including the fusion peptide (FP), central helix (CH), heptad repeat1 (HR1), heptad repeat2 (HR2), connector domain (CD), and transmembrane domain (TD) (Fig. **2**). The HRs trimerize to create a coiled-coil structure that pulls the viral envelope towards the host cell membrane, ultimately enabling fusion of the two.

The two subunits of the spike protein, S1 and S2 resemble a clove-like structure, with three S1 subunits forming the head and three S2 subunits forming the stem [17]. The boundary between the S1 and S2 subunits is marked by the furin cleavage site (RRAR), which distinguishes SARS-CoV-2 from other CoVs (Fig. **2**). Another less-studied motif, the GTNGTKR motif, also appears to be in the S1 subunit, which binds to other receptors like sugar or protein [18]. The similarity between the RBD regions of SARS-CoV and SARS-CoV-2 has decreased to 74%, which explains their binding with different receptors on the host cell. Additionally, the glycosylation patterns of the two virions differ.

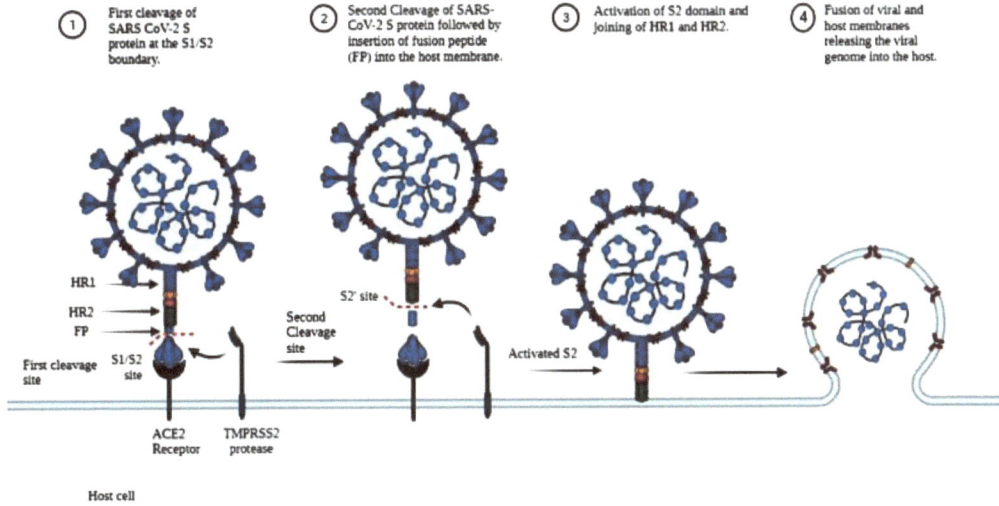

Fig. (2). Activation of Spike protein.

Also, an important aspect of the S protein is mediating cell-to-cell fusion between infected cells and adjacent non-infected cells, thereby forming multinucleated giant cells, a phenomenon well observed in viral cells to spread infections [15]. Because these protruding proteins form the initial contact with the host cell, many therapeutic strategies can be designed and employed to limit binding to the receptor and entry of the pathogen inside the host cell.

Envelope Protein

E protein or the Envelope protein is a small integral membrane protein which is constituted of three components: NTD called the ectodomain, a hydrophobic domain present in the cytoplasm and a chain at CTD referred to as the endodomain, which comprises 76-109 amino acid residue [16]. The molecular mass lies between 8-12KDa [17]. Its NTD ranges from the 1st-9th amino acid, from the 10th-37th position is the hydrophobic portion and the C terminal lies in the 38th-76th position in the amino acid sequence [18]. Structural E gene expression forms viroporin, a small hydrophobic viral protein. These proteins are essential for viral assembly and release and help mediate cell cytotoxicity [19]. The C-terminal tail lies in the cytosolic end and interacts with the cis-Golgi trans face with the aid of proline residue. An ion gradient is generated in the ERGIC compartment and Golgi apparatus with the assistance of the E protein that further mediates the viral exit [20]. Experimentation on the SARS CoV2 genome revealed that mutation of the structural E gene hampers viral development, inhibiting viral maturation and production; thereby demonstrating the significance of the E protein [21, 22].

Membrane Protein

Amongst all the structural proteins of the SARS-CoV-2 genome, M protein is the most abundant [27]. The length is approximately 220-260 amino acids and has a short N-terminal tail associated with a triple transmembrane domain. The triple transmembrane domain is further linked to the CTD, which is an N-linked glycosylated protein having a 12-amino acid conserved domain [28]. Structural studies have revealed the existence of two different configurations of the M protein: long and compact forms. These two conformations of long and compact forms are homodimers of either the C-terminal endodomain or N-terminal ectodomain with different conformations. The endodomain can undergo elongation and compression, resulting in the formation of long and compact forms, respectively. Both the forms contain the M protein suggesting their role in spike installation. The tyrosine amino acid at position 211 provides stability to the M protein, aiding in membrane bending and giving it a spherical structure to enclose the ribonucleoprotein [29]. The translation of M protein occurs in polysomes bound to the membrane, fused with the endoplasmic reticulum (ER), and transported to the Golgi apparatus, where it encounters the E protein, generating pathogenic virus particles.

N Protein

Nucleocapsid (N) proteins are another abundant viral protein after the M protein and are expressed during the initial phase of infection. Viral RNA forms a core with the ribonuclear protein that mediates entry into the host cell [23]. The N protein is the only type of protein that interacts with RNA. Its structure consists of two defined domains: C-terminal domain (CTD) and the the N-terminal domain (NTD). Both components are of paramount importance for the protein to be able to bind to RNA molecules [31]. SARS CoV and SARS CoV2 N protein shows 90% sequence similarity [24]. Replication of viral RNA is enhanced upon binding of the N protein with heterologous nuclear riboprotein (hnRNPA1) [25]. N protein of SARS-CoV-2 activates cyclooxygenase-2 (COX2), which mediates inflammation in the lung tissue [26]. Phosphorylation of the B23 phosphoprotein is a key step for the progression of the cell cycle during centrosome duplication. N protein is involved in inhibiting the phosphorylation of B23 and obstructing cell cycle progression [27]. It can also bind with the p42 proteasome, a complex that degrades the viral protein [28]. It also inhibits the secretion of type I interferons

(INF1), which reduces the immune response generated by the host [29]. Cell line experiments have demonstrated that the N protein can inhibit cyclin-dependent cell cycle (cCDK) progression to the S phase [38]. The N-terminal domain of the nucleocapsid protein interacts with the RNA sequence at the N45-181 region [30], with the existence of arginine (R) at position 94 and tyrosine (Y) at position 122 in the NTD playing a crucial role in the interaction with the negatively charged RNA genome [40]. The existence of the basic amino acid, arginine (R) at position 94 and Tyrosine (Y) at position 122 in the NTD plays a significant role in interaction with the negatively charged RNA genome [31]. After the spike protein, the N protein exhibits several phenomena that are essential for the proper functioning and proliferation of the virus.

Replication of SARS-CoV-2 Genome

Entry of Coronavirus inside the Host Cell

The virus enters host cells through the interaction between its spike protein and specific receptors in the host's body. ACE II receptors have been identified as the primary facilitators of entrance since the emergence of SARS-CoV in 2002. The spike protein's S1 subunit serves as the receptor-binding domain (Fig. **1**), that binds with ACE II receptors expressed in several organs, including lungs, kidneys, arteries, heart, and intestine. The expression profile of ACE II receptors in different organs can indicate their susceptibility to infection. Studies have shown that ACE II receptor expression levels increase with number of years and are frequently greater in males than females. Viral infection can also enhance ACE II receptor expression via interferon signalling, which is one of the mechanisms of host's primary defenses against the virus. Single-cell RNA sequencing (scRNA-seq) studies have identified Type II pneumocytes, myocardial cells, upper oesophagus and stratified epithelial cells, and the digestive system as having high ACE II receptor expression [41, 42]. Furthermore, the analysis of mucosa transcriptomes in the oral cavity has revealed high ACE II receptor expression, suggesting this as a possible route of entry for the virus [32].

In addition to receptor binding, entry of the virus into host cells requires the activation of the S protein, which is facilitated by its proteolytic cleavage by the host Type II Transmembrane Serine protease (TMPRSS2) (Fig. **2**). This receptor is found in the respiratory tract of humans and is accountable for the development and pathogenesis of SARS-CoV-2. The S protein undergoes two sequential cleavages, with the first cleavage occurring at the boundary of S1-S2 (R685) and the subsequent cleavage site being S2' (R815) (Fig. **2**). The first cleavage site comprises multiple basic amino acids (arginine residues) that are responsible for high cleavability [44]. Subsequently, after the second cleavage at the S2 site, the fusion peptide is inserted into the membrane, and then the two heptad repeats are joined, ultimately generating a six-helix bundle that are in antiparallel orientation. The construction of this six-helix bundle results in fusion and, finally, the release of the viral genome into the cytoplasm.

The presence of both ACE II and TMPRSS2 receptors is crucial for the pathogenesis of SARS-CoV. Through co-expression analyses of ACE II and TMPRSS2 proteins in various human cells, three cell types have been recognised as potential hosts for SARS-CoV: type II pneumocytes, nasal goblet epithelial cells and enterocytes [45]. The S protein priming is enhanced by the presence of a furin cleavage site. Furthermore, the co-expression of ACE II, TMPRSS2 and FURIN is observed in lung tissue, which responds to the high multiplicity of the virion in the lungs [33].

SARS-CoV-2 Infection *via* CD16 Receptor

A little proportion of monocytes circulating in the blood that express CD16 (FcRIII) are activated and far more enhanced in patients with COVID-19. These receptors could very well detect viral particles that are opsonized by an antibody and expedite their entry through antibody-dependent phagocytosis (ADP) [34]. The Fc moiety of the antibody binds with a wide variety of surface Fcγ receptors (FcγRs) expressed by immune cells. These interaction results in several pathological functions. The severity of COVID-19 depends upon the interaction between the IgG antibody with the IgG-Fc receptor. The interaction is mediated by CD16 expressed on the surface of macrophages [35].

SARS-CoV-2 Replicates inside the Macrophages in the Human Lungs

To identify the cellular site of viral RNA replication and accumulation, the researchers analysed the level of gRNA and sgRNA in three different samples: lung tissue, lung epithelial cell and human immune cell from infected MISTRG6-hACEII mice and concluded that the level of gRNA was abundant and similar in epithelial cells and immune cells; however, the sgRNA level cannot be determined. SARS-CoV-2 RNA-dependant RNA polymerase (RdRp) was localised in macrophages in association with the spike protein. The autopsy report of human lung macrophages infected with the SARS-CoV-2 virus confirmed the presence of RdRp and spike protein in human macrophages, validating the phenomenon observed in the mouse model. The expression of ACEII receptors in infected human macrophages and epithelial cells increases when the virus enters the host. Thus, the study demonstrated the virus replication inside the human macrophage [35].

Macrophages play a critical role in the innate immune response and are the primary target of SARS-CoV replication. Both MERS-CoV and SARS-CoV are capable of directly infecting human innate immune cells particularly macrophages and dendritic cells, generating the proinflammatory cytokines and chemokines [36], implicating that PAMP-PRR signalling results in the secretion of pro-inflammatory mediators in COVID-19.

Genome Multiplication

The initiation of the replication cycle is marked by the release of the viral genome into the host cytoplasm. Positive-stranded viral RNA is then translated into a polypeptide utilizing the host cell machinery. Translation of ORF1a and ORF1b from the genomic RNA at the 5' end produces two polypeptides, pp1a and pp1b. Co-translation and post-translation events of pp1a/b, followed by cleavage by two cysteine derived proteases, releasing sixteen non-structural proteins (nsp). Within nsp3, lies the papain like protease while the chymotrypsin-like protease, known as the main (M) protein, is located within nsp5. The nsps assemble to form a replication-transcriptase complex (RTC), which provides an environment suitable for viral replication.

• The first non-structural protein to be cleaved and released is Nsp1, which is involved in hijacking the translation machinery of the host cell [50].

• Nsp2-16 forms the viral replication-transcriptase complex (RTC), where nsp2-11 is involved in accommodating the RTC and nsp12-16 performs a main enzymatic function in RNA synthesis like proofreading, modification, *etc.* Nsp7,8,12 is involved in RNA synthesis using (nsp12) RNA- dependant RNA Polymerase (RdRp) [37]. Nsp14 provides unique proofreading activity through its 3'-5' exonuclease activity [38].

The replication cycle of the virus begins with the production of a negative-sense RNA from the positive-sense genomic RNA. The newly synthesized negative-sense RNA then acts as a template for the synthesis of new positive strands of genomic RNA (gRNA) and sub-genomic RNA (sgRNA) (Fig. **3**). These newly synthesized gRNAs are then translated to generate multiple copies of RTC and nsp, which are subsequently processed into a packaged viral particle. Additionally, coronavirus undergoes discontinuous transcription to produce nested 3' and 5' co-terminal sgRNA, which encode structural and accessory proteins. During the synthesis of a negative strand of sgRNA, transcription mechanism is interrupted by the RTC, which binds to the Transcription regulatory sequence (TRS) located upstream near the 3' end of the viral genome. Transcription resumes at the adjacent TRS of the leader sequence (TRS-L) that lies at 70 nucleotides from the 5' end of the genome [53 - 55]. The next step involves complementary base-pairing between the TRS of the nascent negative strand RNA and the +ve strand of the genomic RNA (TRS-L). When, at TRS-L region, the RNA synthesis resumes, a negative-strand copy of the leader sequence is fused to the nascent RNA of the sgRNA. This discontinuous RNA synthesis step generates several copies of nascent sgRNA, which serve as templates for synthesizing positive sg mRNA coding for structural and accessory proteins [53].

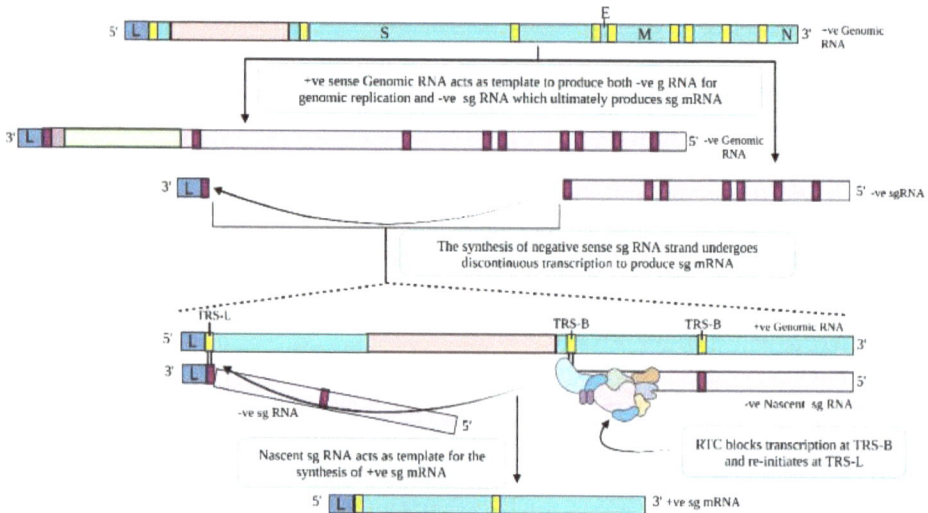

Fig. (3). Continuous and discontinuous transcription of coronavirus genome.

The nsp12 protein contains the RdRp, which is essential for the replication and transcription of sgRNA in the RTC of SARS-CoV-2. The structure of SARS-CoV-2 RdRp, along with its co-factors nsp7 and nsp8, is similar to that of SARS-CoV, with over 95% identical amino acid sequences except for changes in the nucleotidyl transferase domain. The RdRp active site shares structural similarity with various positive-stranded viruses, which suggests the probability of using drugs that prove to be efficacious against RNA viruses. One such drug is remdesivir (RDV), which competes with ATP and serves as a substrate for the viral RNA dependant polymerases [39]. SARS-CoV-2 RdRp selectively incorporates RDV instead of ATP, which delays replication termination [40]. Even after adding RDV, the RdRp continues to incorporate three nucleotides before termination. The nsp14 protein contains an exonuclease domain that limits the effectiveness of RDV by proofreading [41].

Viral evolution is significantly impacted by the strand-switching ability of RdRp, as it allows for both homologous and non-homologous recombination in the coronavirus [42, 43].

Viral Assembly and Release

Following replication and transcription of viral sgRNA and gRNA, the structural and accessory proteins are synthesized and assembled. SARS-CoV-2 uses host cell machinery to translate viral mRNA (Fig. **4**), and it becomes oblivious that they adapt to host cell codon usage. It has been discovered that SARS-CoV-2 has modified its codon usage and the level of GC percent in accordance with genes that are expressed in the lungs of humans [44]. The presence of many viral transcripts suppresses the translation of human RNA. Proteins S, M, E, and N that make up the structure of the Coronavirus are synthesized and integrated into the membrane of the endoplasmic reticulum (ER) (Fig. **4**). Then, these proteins undergo through the secretory pathway and are carried from the ER to the ERGIC (endoplasmic reticulum-Golgi intermediate compartment) [45, 46]. M protein facilitates viral protein-protein interaction, which is crucial for the assembly of the viral-like particle (VLP). The formation of viral-like particles (VLPs) requires the co-expression of the M protein along with the E protein, which work together to facilitate the formation of the viral envelope [47]. E protein induces membrane curvature [48] and prevents the aggregation of M protein [49]. These secretory proteins must be retained near the ERGIC for proper assembly [50]. They consist of ER retention signal present at the C terminal of the S protein [42]. In between these events, gRNA transcribed before, will interact with the N protein, and form a ribonuclear (RNP) complex. N protein complexes with the RNA that resembles a "beads on string" conformation. In the host cell, the N protein and the RNA bimolecular condensates undergo phase separation.

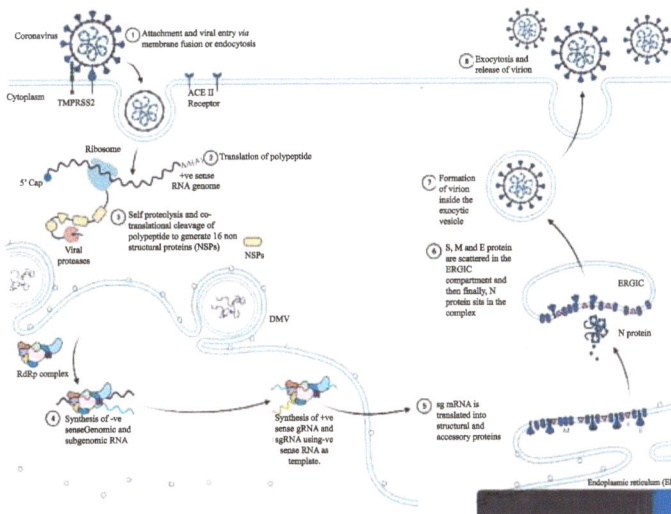

Fig. (4). The coronavirus replication and transportation inside the host cell.

The N and C terminals of the protein are highly disorganized and contain a high concentration of basic amino acids such as arginine and lysine, which promote binding to the negatively charged RNA backbone. The presence of a serine-arginine residue is known to promote phase separation. Ultimately, this complex associates with the M protein [51]. The fully organized viral particle assembled within the vesicle is released by exocytosis to the cell membrane.

The SARS-CoV-2 Pathogenesis

The transmission of the SARS-CoV-2 virus occurs through respiratory droplets and aerosols, which are produced by an infected person and can be inhaled by a healthy person. Upon inhalation, the virus interacts the nasal epithelial cells in the upper part of the respiratory tract and binds to the receptor. In particular, the ACE2 receptors are abundant in adult nasal epithelial cells and are frequently utilized by the virus for entry [52, 53]. The virus increases its copy number by undergoing local replication, thereby infecting nearby ciliated epithelial cells and further propagating the infection to the conducting airways. The viral load at the early stage is low which lasts for a few days, and the immune mechanism provoked at this point is also restricted, but the individual is highly capable of transmitting the infection. This phase is called the **asymptomatic phase** but can be detected by examination of the nasal swab.

Following entry into the nasal epithelial cells, the virus then spreads to the respiratory tract through the conducting airways. This involvement of the upper region of the respiratory tract results in the manifestation of mild symptoms such as fever and dry cough. The body responds to the viral infection by generating an increased immune response, which includes the release of different mediators from infected cells like C-X-C motif chemokine ligand 10 (CXCL10) and interferons (INF-β and INF-λ) [54].

The immune response that is produced is adequate in limiting the spread of infection, and most patients can successfully control the disease at this stage. However, approximately 20% of patients who may have compromised immune systems or underlying medical conditions will progress to the lower respiratory tract and experience symptoms of acute respiratory distress syndrome (ARDS). The virus infiltrates type 2 alveolar epithelial cells and replicates, producing additional copies of the nucleocapsid. A strong innate immune reaction is generated by recognising and encountering with the pathogen by pattern recognition receptors (PRRs) (Fig. **5**). The infected cells release various cytokines and inflammatory markers such as interleukins, interferons, CXCL10, *etc.*

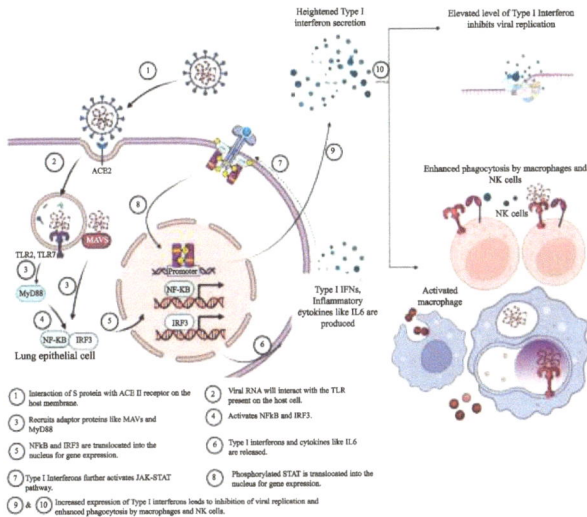

Fig. (5). Innate immune response to SARS-CoV-2 infection.

Direct Cytopathic Effect of SARS-CoV-2

Once replication is complete, the viral particle assembles near the ER and is exocytosed out of the cell. Infected cells will interact with the adjacent normal cells to form giant syncytial cells thereby, aiding the spread of the infection. Following an initial encounter with the virus, the immune system generates an antiviral response inside the host by releasing interferons and other mediators to combat the infection. Also, externally providing antiviral therapy at this point will help in limiting the progression of the disease and reduce the mortality rate [55].

Immune cells, such as macrophages and lymphocytes also express ACEII receptors [56], but it is not yet known if SARS-CoV-2 can directly infect these cells. Since immune cells move throughout the body, they may facilitate the spread of the infection. Research conducted using the COVID-19 model has shown that the immune system and spleen can also be impacted by the damage caused by the SARS-CoV-2 virus. Cytokine activation can lead to lymphoid atrophy, suggesting that the immune system may be damaged directly by the SARS-CoV-2 infection [57 - 60].

Initiation of Innate Immune Response

The innate immune response, being the first line of defense against any pathogen, including viruses, recognises the foreign pathogen by means of Pattern recognition receptors (PRRs) and bind to its receptor. The level of the immune retaliation by the host and the amount of inflammatory mediators produced depend on various factors such as the virus type, strength of immune system of the host's body, viral load, and the age of the host [61]. Specific PRRs such as toll-like receptor (TLR), nod-like receptor (NLR), C-reactive protein (CRP) and Mannose-binding lectin (MBL), detect the viral RNA on the membrane or in secretory form. These PRRs recognize the pathogen-associated molecular pattern (PAMP) expressed on the surface of the virus, which results in the secretion of type I interferons (IFN1), pro-inflammatory cytokines, and chemokines. This leads to the initiation of several signaling pathways and the recruitment of adaptor proteins such as mitochondrial antiviral signaling protein (MAVS), interferon β (INFβ), and STING protein, as well as the activation of downstream signaling cascades like MyD88 adaptor molecule [62] (Fig. **5**). Transcription factors like NF-κB, IRF3 are also activated, which helps in nuclear localization. Once into the nucleus, type1 interferons and various inflammatory cytokines especially IL6 are produced [63]. Type1 interferons initiate the JAK-STAT signalling mechanism and the transcription of the interferon-stimulated gene (ISGs). An elevated level of Type1 interferon prevents viral replication and promotes phagocytosis by macrophages and NK cells. However, if the JAK-STAT signalling is somehow blocked or the level of type 1 interferons is decreased, it will have a direct impact on viral survival [63]. Also, if the SARS-CoV-2 viral replication is robust and the INF response is delayed, it will progress to the development of severe acute respiratory syndrome (SARS).

In addition to virus-induced damage, necrosis and cell damage can also generate damage-associated molecular patterns (DAMPs) in the form of proteins, DNA, RNA, and heat-shock proteins. These DAMPs are recognized by specific PRRs, thereby, releasing different cytokines and chemokines that can exacerbate the inflammatory reaction and cause further cell damage [64]. Severe cases of the disease can result in organ failure and cell damage.

In addition to virus-induced damage, necrosis and cell damage can also generate damage-associated molecular patterns (DAMPs) in the form of proteins, DNA, RNA, and heat-shock proteins. These DAMPs are recognized by specific PRRs, thereby, releasing different cytokines and chemokines that can exacerbate the inflammatory reaction and cause further cell damage [64]. Severe cases of the disease can result in organ failure and cell damage.

Adaptive Immune Response

Adaptive immunity provides a highly specific immune response and is activated after recognizing the pathogen. Two different cells namely, B cells and T cells are involved and are activated in secondary lymphoid organs following encounters with the antigen. Antigen-presenting cells (APCs) present the antigenic peptide to B lymphocytes (B cells) and T lymphocytes (T cells) for specific recognition and thereby induce cellular and humoral immunity. Studies have shown that SARS-CoV-2-specific B and T cells are generated in patients who recovered from COVID-19 [65]. When the naïve T cell first encounters an antigen complexed with an MHC molecule, then it produces a plethora of T cells depending on the type of MHC presented. MHCI interacts with the CD8 receptor present on the T cell and differentiates into Cytotoxic T cell (CTL) each having the same antigenic specificity as the parent cell type and memory T cell; MHCII interacts with the CD4 receptor present on the Tcell and differentiates into helper T cell (Th cell). CTLs recognize the endogenous peptide and upon activation induce the apoptosis of target cells. The Th1-mediated immune mechanism plays an important role in viral-infected cells. They can secrete a cluster of enzymes like granzyme and perforin, which mediates the killing of the virus. The CD4+ helper T cells assist the CTLs and provide an adaptive immune response. B cells mediate humoral immunity and produce neutralizing antibodies, thereby protecting the host body and impeding reinfection.

Studies have revealed that the severity of the disease is marked by increased levels of cytokines and chemokines such as interleukins (IL1, IL2, IL4, IL7, IL10, IL12, IL13, and IL17), Macrophage-colony-stimulating factor (MCSF), Granulocyte-CSF (GCSF), CXCL10, Monocyte chemoattractant protein (MCP1), hepatocyte growth factor (HGF), INFγ, TNFα, and others (Fig. **6**) [63]. The presence of a *"Cytokine storm"* and *"lymphopenia"* in SARS-CoV and MERS CoV suggests their role in SARS-CoV-2. This immune response is also involved in cancer cells and viral-infected cells and can promote apoptosis and necrosis of the infected cells. The "cytokine storm" triggers fibrin formation causing viral sepsis, leading to lung damage through inflammation and associated disorders such as ARDS, pneumonitis, respiratory defeat, septic shock, multi organ failure, and ultimately, death. A downfall in the level of circulating CD4+ cells, CD8+ cells, B cells, NK cells, and certain white blood cells like monocytes, eosinophils, and basophils is also linked to the severity of COVID-19 [66].

The humoral immune response also plays an effective role in eradicating the virus. Inside the host cell, specific antibodies are raised against the SARS-CoV-2 S protein, which are IgA, IgG, and IgM. On the 5th day of infection, IgA and IgM antibodies were detected and IgG was detected on the 14th day post the emergence of the symptoms [67]. Studies have revealed the importance of antibodies in the neutralization of the virus. A recent report suggests that an antibody from 3 recovered SARS patients, limits SARS-CoV-2 entry and progression of the disease, implying that antibodies specific to SARS-CoV spike protein can protect and provide immunity against SARS-CoV-2 infection [53]. It might also be used as a therapeutic or vaccine candidate like convalescent plasma from patients recovered from COVID-19 is used as potential therapy [68].

Antibody-dependant cell cytotoxicity (ADCC) is involved in cellular injury and tissue damage [69].

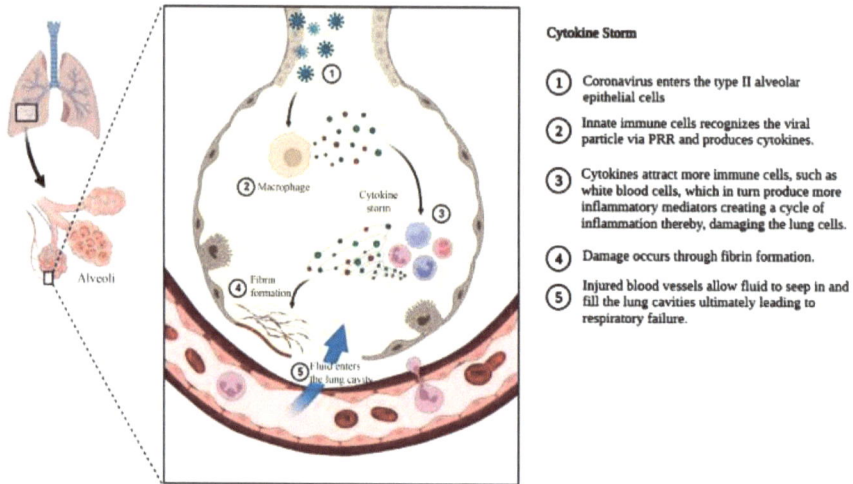

Fig. (6). Cytokine storm in infected alveoli leading to lung damage.

SARS-CoV-2 Activates Inflammasomes

The intrinsic growth rate and doubling time of the SARS-CoV-2 virus are very short and they can overtake the host tissue if they are not contained quickly enough. The body needs to have a molecular mechanism that can sense the threat and translate effector proteins that are specific to the pathogen and effective enough to fight the threat. To confront the microbe, the body needs to implement strategies that permit it to take decisive actions and warns other cells of the threat. One such mechanism is the formation of inflammasomes. Inflammasomes are dynamic, large multiprotein complex that recognises the threat and assembles to activate caspases (Fig. 7). An inflammasome consists of three major components: A sensor, a CARD domain, and inflammatory caspases. The sensor is involved in sensing the pathogenic or damage-associated signal, which however does not necessarily need to bind with the ligand, distinguishing it from PAMP and DAMP. The CARD domain can either bind directly to the sensor protein or can be found with the adaptor protein (ASC). This domain mediates the interaction of caspases with the inflammasome complex. Caspases are zymogen that activates upon cleavage. Caspase1,4 and 5 in humans are involved in the signalling cascade, where caspase1 undergoes autocatalytic cleavage to activate itself. Activated caspase1 can then cleave pro-IL-1β and pro-IL18 to activate them. When activated, IL-1β and IL-18 can trigger inflammation in other cells. IL-1β interacts with its IL-1 receptor, which has a TIR domain and interacts similarly to

TLR. This interaction downstream activates NFκB signaling through the MyD88 pathway thereby, secreting the proinflammatory cytokines like IL-6 and TNF-α. However, IL-18 is involved in inducing the vascular components of inflammation by inducing the secretion of IFN-γ and increasing the expression of cell adhesion molecules. Caspase1 also cleaves another host protein, Gasdermin D (GSDMD), which plays a role in mediating programmed cell death. The cleaved GSDMD interacts with the host membrane and forms pores, which release IL-18 and IL-1β, leading to cell lysis in an inflammatory form of programmed cell death known as pyroptosis, characterized by membrane blebbing.

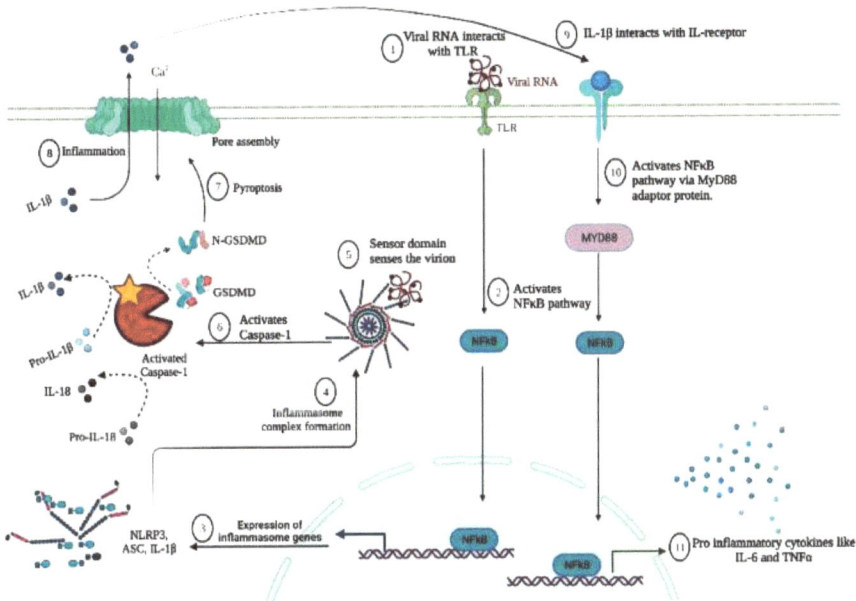

Fig. (7). Inflammasome activation and immune response.

Most of the inflammasome belongs to the Nod-like receptor (NLR) family of PRRs. NLRP3 also called cryopyrin, is involved in viral infection and is expressed in myeloid cell lineage like macrophages and dendritic cells. For the activation of NLRP3, it must be primed with the viral particle. So, when the virion binds with the TLR3/TLR7, it induces an increased expression of NLRP3 protein which will further aid in the activation of inflammasome complex. The co-expression profile of NLRP3 and ASC is enhanced characterizing severe SARS-CoV-2 infection. The level of lactate dehydrogenase (LDH) and GSDMD, which are biomarkers of pyroptosis is also enhanced multifold suggesting inflammatory cell lysis. Blocking the viral entry by blocking ACEII and CD16 receptors or by blocking viral replication by remdesivir or inhibiting caspase1and NLRP3, will inhibit the inflammasome activation pathway and downstream inflammasome cascade, thereby reducing the level of IL-1β, IL-18 and CXCL10. Also, blocking these pathways in vivo during the chronic phase of the disease has a direct effect in dampening the overactive inflammasome response [35].

Hypercytokinemia and Organ Damage

Hypercytokinemia is a phenomenon whereby, the body releases too many cytokines in a very short span of time on account of an immune evasion mechanism following an encounter with the pathogen. The SARS-CoV-2 infection leads to systemic inflammation and pulmonary damage leading to multiple organ dysfunction syndromes (**MODS**), especially in people with comorbidities [70]. ACEII receptors are not just confined to nasal epithelial cells but are also expressed in different organs.

The expression profile of ACEII receptors determines the involvement of organs and disease severity. Severe SARS-CoV-2 infection is diagnosed based on organ dysfunction. The most frequently observed dysfunctions in severe COVID-19 patients include ARDS, acute cardiac injury, liver injury, and chronic kidney dysfunction [65]. According to another clinical report, critically ill COVID-19 patients often experience multiple organ dysfunction, including ARDS accounting to 67%, acute kidney injury and liver dysfunction both approximating to 29% each and 23% of cardiac injury. Additionally, approximately 70% of these critical patients require medical ventilation support [71].

A study demonstrated that individuals who already have cardiovascular disease (CVD), diabetes, or hypertension are more susceptible to experiencing severe COVID-19. The study included 46,248 patients with existing comorbidities like hypertension (17%), CVD (5%) and diabetes (8%). Existing CVD increases the mortality rate, and it has been broadly accepted that COVID-19 has a disastrous effect on myocardial health and damages the heart. The high expression of ACEII in heart muscles leads to ACEII-dependent infection. Cardiac biomarkers are also enhanced suggesting the involvement of the cardiovascular system. Cytokine storm, resulting from inflammation and a hypoxic environment due to ARDS leads to excessive calcium deposition on the extracellular surface, which expedites the apoptosis of myocytes [72]. The elevated level of cytokines in the circulating blood and the increased demand for cardiovascular involvement in disease progression can cause atherosclerotic plaque instability and injury to the heart muscle ultimately leading to myocardial infarction. Hypertension and palpitation are observed in response to the infection [73, 74].

In patients with ARDS, there is often a progression to acute kidney injury (AKI), which is characterized by a sudden loss of kidney function due to an infection. This phenomenon has been observed in SARS-CoV and MERS-CoV infections and has also been observed in patients with COVID-19 [75]. The mechanism by which COVID-19 causes renal involvement is currently unknown. However, AKI can lead to sepsis and shock, finally progressing to multiorgan failure [76].

Liver injury is another complication prevalent in patients with severe SARS-Co--2 infection. Mild to moderate and sometimes severe liver damage is observed in individuals with COVID-19 infection. In an experiment conducted by Wong et al., 14.8-53.1% of infected individuals have an unusual level of liver enzymes like aspartate aminotransferase, alanine aminotransferase and bilirubin. It also demonstrated that the severity of the disease is proportional to COVID-19 [77].

Another common hurdle is disseminated intravenous coagulation (DIC) or defibrination syndrome, whereby clots are formed within the circulating blood that results in insufficient blood flow thereby leading to tissue death and eventually damaging the vital organs. Reportedly, individuals who did not survive COVID-19 had disseminated intravascular coagulation (DIC) at an estimated rate of 71.4%, whereas only 0.6% of survivors had this condition [78]. It is also reported that using low-weight anticoagulants like heparin enhanced survival in severe SARS-CoV-2 infection [79].

Renin-angiotensin System in COVID-19

The renin-angiotensin-aldosterone system (RAAS) is primarily involved in blood pressure regulation by balancing the blood volume through water and salt secretion and reabsorption. ACEII is a significant bit of the RAAS system that is involved in forming angiotensin 1-7 from angiotensin II and angiotensin I converts to angiotensin1-9 [80]. The role of ACEII inhibitor and blocker of ACE II receptor on the SARS-CoV-2 disease susceptibility and prognosis is disputable. Some reports suggest that increased expression of ACEII receptor promotes COVID-19 while other studies suggested its antithetical effect on decreasing lung injury [81].

The binding of Ang1 and Ang2 to their receptor has both opposing and contradictory roles. AngII binds to the AT1 receptor and leads to pro-inflammatory signals, causing vasoconstriction, pro-oxidative, and fibrotic effects. In contrast, Ang1-7 interacts with the MasR receptor and promotes anti-inflammatory signalling, producing antioxidant, and vasodilatory consequences [82]. According to a recent study, the binding of SARS-CoV-2 to its ACEII receptor reduces ACEII activity through internalization, which subsequently increases the expression of AngII. This increase leads to pulmonary infection and fibrosis, followed by organ damage, ultimately resulting in ARDS [83].

CONCLUSION

The COVID-19 pandemic has affected the world in unprecedented ways, causing widespread illness, death, economic disruptions, implication in healthcare system and severe disruptions in disease control programmes [84, 85]. As the virus continues to spread globally, scientists and medical professionals are racing to better understand the virus and develop effective treatments and vaccines. In this context, understanding the pathogenesis and replication of the SARS-CoV-2 virus is crucial.

SARS-CoV-2, the virus that causes COVID-19, enters the host cell through its surface spike protein, which encounters the ACE2 receptor on the surface of the host cell. Once inside the host's body, the virus begins to replicate, using host cellular machinery to transcribe and translate viral proteins. The viral RNA is inserted into the endoplasmic reticulum (ER) and then through the ERGIC pathway, it is expelled out of the cell.

The pathogenesis of SARS-CoV-2 begins with the infection of lung macrophages, where the viral RNA replication produces sgRNA, gRNA, RdRp, RTC, and other viral components. As viral replication and translation progress, the inflammatory response is activated, leading to the production of cytokines, chemokines, and interleukins. This inflammatory cascade ultimately leads to programmed cell death via pyroptosis, characterized by membrane blebbing. Severe infection is characterized by the increased expression of these inflammatory mediators, high expression of ACE2 receptors, and damage to other organs like the heart, kidneys, liver, and the brain.

Despite extensive research, many aspects of the mechanism and pathogenesis of the SARS-CoV-2 genome remain unclear. However, recent studies have provided new insights into the molecular mechanisms of the virus, including its interaction with the host and the activation of the host defense mechanism [86].

One promising area of research focuses on the development of effective treatments and vaccines for COVID-19. Vaccines are currently being developed and distributed globally, with the aim of providing widespread immunity against the virus. Meanwhile, scientists are also working to develop new antiviral drugs that can effectively target the virus and limit its spread.

In addition, effective diagnosis and proper medication are key to limiting the progression of the disease. Accurate and efficient diagnostic tests are essential for early detection and tracking of the virus. In the absence of specific antiviral drugs, supportive care remains the mainstay of treatment for COVID-19 patients. This includes monitoring of symptoms, providing supplemental oxygen, and ensuring adequate hydration and nutrition.

In conclusion, the pathogenesis and replication of the SARS-CoV-2 virus are complex and multi-faceted, involving a range of molecular and cellular mechanisms. Despite ongoing research efforts, many questions remain unanswered, highlighting the urgent need for further research into this highly infectious and deadly virus. Nevertheless, effective diagnosis, proper medication, and effective vaccination remain crucial in limiting the progression of COVID-19 and ultimately saving lives.

SUMMARY

The SARS-CoV-2 virus belongs to the member of β-CoV family, and has a single positive-stranded segmented genome. The virus causes COVID-19, which emerged in late 2019 in China and has spread globally, causing widespread havoc. The virus is highly infectious and transmissible, leading to the death of millions of people worldwide.

The genome of the SARS-CoV-2 virus consists of several regions, including a 5' UTR, replicase gene, accessory gene /structural gene, and 3' UTR, followed by a poly A tail. The replicase gene encodes enzymes responsible for viral replication and translation, while the structural gene produces various proteins, including S, M, E, and N proteins that mediate viral structure formation, assembly, and release. The viral S protein recognizes host ACEII receptors or CD16 receptors present on lung macrophages and initiates viral entry into the host cell. After entry into the host cytoplasm, viral genome triggers the replication process, whereby the positive sense RNA forms its complementary negative strand. After synthesizing viral sgRNA and gRNA, the structural and accessory proteins are assembled. The replicase gene encodes the pp1a/b protein, which undergoes proteolytic cleavage to produce sixteen nsp. These nsps assemble to form RTC, where RdRp is at the center, which is crucial for viral replication. The viral mRNA is translated in the ER and ultimately secreted out of the cell via exocytosis.

Upon entering the host's body, the immune system recognizes the virus and activates to eliminate it. The first line of defense is the innate immune system, which activates several PRRs like TLR, NLR, *etc*. The specific binding of these PRRs (NLRP3) to the viral RNA activates type 1 interferons and secretes inflammatory mediators like cytokines, IL-1β, IL-18, CXCL10, *etc*. It also recruits other immune cells like neutrophils and phagocytic cells like macrophages. The adaptive immune response is then activated, whereby viral RNA complexed with MHC1 interacts with the CD8 receptor expressed on CTL, which undergoes apoptosis of the virally infected cells. B cell will bind with the virus and produce neutralizing antibodies. The levels of IgA, IgG, and IgM antibodies raised depict the severity of COVID-19. Inflammasomes are activated, which cleave caspase1 to generate IL-18 and IL-1β. It also cleaves gasdermin and downstream activates NFκB signaling. The levels of pro-inflammatory cytokines, INF, and interleukins are enhanced several folds, owing to the severity of the disease. The disease at this stage is not just limited to the lungs and spreads to other organs like the kidneys, liver, heart, *etc.*, leading to MODS. People with co-morbidities are at a greater threat of developing severe COVID-19.

Effective vaccination, timely diagnosis, proper treatment, and medication are crucial for slowing down the growth rate and transmissibility of the infection.

REFERENCES

[1]   Tang Q, Song Y, Shi M, Cheng Y, Zhang W, Xia XQ. Inferring the hosts of coronavirus using dual statistical models based on nucleotide composition. Sci Rep 2015; 5(1): 17155.
[http://dx.doi.org/10.1038/srep17155] [PMID: 26607834]

[2]   Malik YA. Properties of Coronavirus and SARS-CoV-2. Malays J Pathol 2020; 42(1): 3-11.
[PMID: 32342926]

[3]   Zhu N, Zhang D, Wang W, *et al.* A Novel Coronavirus from Patients with Pneumonia in China, 2019. N Engl J Med 2020; 382(8): 727-33.
[http://dx.doi.org/10.1056/NEJMoa2001017] [PMID: 31978945]

[4]   Sheikh JA, Singh J, Singh H, *et al.* Emerging genetic diversity among clinical isolates of SARS-Co--2: Lessons for today. Infect Genet Evol 2020; 84: 104330.
[http://dx.doi.org/10.1016/j.meegid.2020.104330] [PMID: 32335334]

[5]   Rahman SA, Singh H, Singh J, *et al.* Mapping the genomic landscape & diversity of COVID-19 based on >3950 clinical isolates of SARS-CoV-2: Likely origin & transmission dynamics of isolates sequenced in India. Indian J Med Res 2020; 151(5): 474-8.
[http://dx.doi.org/10.4103/ijmr.IJMR_1253_20] [PMID: 32474554]

[6]   Thakur N, Das S, Kumar S, *et al.* Tracing the origin of Severe acute respiratory syndrome coronavirus-2 (SARS-CoV-2): A systematic review and narrative synthesis. J Med Virol 2022; 94(12): 5766-79.
[http://dx.doi.org/10.1002/jmv.28060] [PMID: 35945190]

[7]   Yuan S, Jiang SC, Li ZL. Analysis of Possible Intermediate Hosts of the New Coronavirus SARS-CoV-2. Front Vet Sci 2020; 7: 379.
[http://dx.doi.org/10.3389/fvets.2020.00379] [PMID: 32582786]

[8]   Chan JFW, Kok KH, Zhu Z, *et al.* Genomic characterization of the 2019 novel human-pathogenic coronavirus isolated from a patient with atypical pneumonia after visiting Wuhan. Emerg Microbes Infect 2020; 9(1): 221-36.
[http://dx.doi.org/10.1080/22221751.2020.1719902] [PMID: 31987001]

[9]   Li F. Structure, Function, and Evolution of Coronavirus Spike Proteins. Annu Rev Virol 2016; 3(1): 237-61.
[http://dx.doi.org/10.1146/annurev-virology-110615-042301] [PMID: 27578435]

[10]   Han Y, Du J, Su H, *et al.* Identification of Diverse Bat Alphacoronaviruses and Betacoronaviruses in China Provides New Insights Into the Evolution and Origin of Coronavirus-Related Diseases. Front Microbiol 2019; 10: 1900.
[http://dx.doi.org/10.3389/fmicb.2019.01900] [PMID: 31474969]

[11] Bakkers MJG, Lang Y, Feitsma LJ, *et al.* Betacoronavirus Adaptation to Humans Involved Progressive Loss of Hemagglutinin-Esterase Lectin Activity. Cell Host Microbe 2017; 21(3): 356-66.
[http://dx.doi.org/10.1016/j.chom.2017.02.008] [PMID: 28279346]

[12] Kim D, Lee JY, Yang JS, Kim JW, Kim VN, Chang H. The Architecture of SARS-CoV-2 Transcriptome. Cell 2020; 181(4): 914-921.e10.
[http://dx.doi.org/10.1016/j.cell.2020.04.011] [PMID: 32330414]

[13] Konno Y, Kimura I, Uriu K, *et al.* SARS-CoV-2 ORF3b Is a Potent Interferon Antagonist Whose Activity Is Increased by a Naturally Occurring Elongation Variant. Cell Rep 2020; 32(12): 108185.
[http://dx.doi.org/10.1016/j.celrep.2020.108185] [PMID: 32941788]

[14] Xu K, Zheng BJ, Zeng R, *et al.* Severe acute respiratory syndrome coronavirus accessory protein 9b is a virion-associated protein. Virology 2009; 388(2): 279-85.
[http://dx.doi.org/10.1016/j.virol.2009.03.032] [PMID: 19394665]

[15] Schoeman D, Fielding BC. Coronavirus envelope protein: current knowledge. Virol J 2019; 16(1): 69.
[http://dx.doi.org/10.1186/s12985-019-1182-0] [PMID: 31133031]

[16] Ruch TR, Machamer CE. The hydrophobic domain of infectious bronchitis virus E protein alters the host secretory pathway and is important for release of infectious virus. J Virol 2011; 85(2): 675-85.
[http://dx.doi.org/10.1128/JVI.01570-10] [PMID: 21047962]

[17] Fung TS, Liu DX. Post-translational modifications of coronavirus proteins: roles and function. Future Virol 2018; 13(6): 405-30.
[http://dx.doi.org/10.2217/fvl-2018-0008] [PMID: 32201497]

[18] Verdiá-Báguena C, Nieto-Torres JL, Alcaraz A, DeDiego ML, Enjuanes L, Aguilella VM. Analysis of SARS-CoV E protein ion channel activity by tuning the protein and lipid charge. Biochim Biophys Acta Biomembr 2013; 1828(9): 2026-31.
[http://dx.doi.org/10.1016/j.bbamem.2013.05.008] [PMID: 23688394]

[19] Ye Y, Hogue BG. Role of the coronavirus E viroporin protein transmembrane domain in virus assembly. J Virol 2007; 81(7): 3597-607.
[http://dx.doi.org/10.1128/JVI.01472-06] [PMID: 17229680]

[20] Liu DX, Yuan Q, Liao Y. Coronavirus envelope protein: A small membrane protein with multiple functions. Cell Mol Life Sci 2007; 64(16): 2043-8.
[http://dx.doi.org/10.1007/s00018-007-7103-1] [PMID: 17530462]

[21] DeDiego ML, Álvarez E, Almazán F, *et al.* A severe acute respiratory syndrome coronavirus that lacks the E gene is attenuated in vitro and in vivo. J Virol 2007; 81(4): 1701-13.
[http://dx.doi.org/10.1128/JVI.01467-06] [PMID: 17108030]

[22] Ortego J, Escors D, Laude H, Enjuanes L. Generation of a replication-competent, propagation-deficient virus vector based on the transmissible gastroenteritis coronavirus genome. J Virol 2002; 76(22): 11518-29.
[http://dx.doi.org/10.1128/JVI.76.22.11518-11529.2002] [PMID: 12388713]

[23] Huang Q, Yu L, Petros AM, *et al.* Structure of the N-terminal RNA-binding domain of the SARS CoV nucleocapsid protein. Biochemistry 2004; 43(20): 6059-63.
[http://dx.doi.org/10.1021/bi036155b] [PMID: 15147189]

[24] Gralinski LE, Menachery VD. Return of the Coronavirus: 2019-nCoV. Viruses 2020; 12(2): 135.
[http://dx.doi.org/10.3390/v12020135] [PMID: 31991541]

[25] Luo H, Chen Q, Chen J, Chen K, Shen X, Jiang H. The nucleocapsid protein of SARS coronavirus has a high binding affinity to the human cellular heterogeneous nuclear ribonucleoprotein A1. FEBS Lett 2005; 579(12): 2623-8.
[http://dx.doi.org/10.1016/j.febslet.2005.03.080] [PMID: 15862300]

[26] Yan X, Hao Q, Mu Y, *et al.* Nucleocapsid protein of SARS-CoV activates the expression of

cyclooxygenase-2 by binding directly to regulatory elements for nuclear factor-kappa B and CCAAT/enhancer binding protein. Int J Biochem Cell Biol 2006; 38(8): 1417-28.
[http://dx.doi.org/10.1016/j.biocel.2006.02.003] [PMID: 16546436]

[27]   Zeng Y, Ye L, Zhu S, *et al.* The nucleocapsid protein of SARS-associated coronavirus inhibits B23 phosphorylation. Biochem Biophys Res Commun 2008; 369(2): 287-91.
[http://dx.doi.org/10.1016/j.bbrc.2008.01.096] [PMID: 18243139]

[28]   Wang Q, Li C, Zhang Q, *et al.* Interactions of SARS Coronavirus Nucleocapsid Protein with the host cell proteasome subunit p42. Virol J 2010; 7(1): 99.
[http://dx.doi.org/10.1186/1743-422X-7-99] [PMID: 20478047]

[29]   Lu X, Pan J, Tao J, Guo D. SARS-CoV nucleocapsid protein antagonizes IFN-β response by targeting initial step of IFN-β induction pathway, and its C-terminal region is critical for the antagonism. Virus Genes 2011; 42(1): 37-45.
[http://dx.doi.org/10.1007/s11262-010-0544-x] [PMID: 20976535]

[30]   Chang C, Hou MH, Chang CF, Hsiao CD, Huang T. The SARS coronavirus nucleocapsid protein – Forms and functions. Antiviral Res 2014; 103: 39-50.
[http://dx.doi.org/10.1016/j.antiviral.2013.12.009] [PMID: 24418573]

[31]   McBride R, Van Zyl M, Fielding B. The coronavirus nucleocapsid is a multifunctional protein. Viruses 2014; 6(8): 2991-3018.
[http://dx.doi.org/10.3390/v6082991] [PMID: 25105276]

[32]   Xu H, Zhong L, Deng J, *et al.* High expression of ACE2 receptor of 2019-nCoV on the epithelial cells of oral mucosa. Int J Oral Sci 2020; 12(1): 8.
[http://dx.doi.org/10.1038/s41368-020-0074-x] [PMID: 32094336]

[33]   Lukassen S, Chua RL, Trefzer T, *et al.* SARS -CoV-2 receptor ACE 2 and TMPRSS 2 are primarily expressed in bronchial transient secretory cells. EMBO J 2020; 39(10): e105114.
[http://dx.doi.org/10.15252/embj.20105114] [PMID: 32246845]

[34]   Bournazos S, Gupta A, Ravetch JV. The role of IgG Fc receptors in antibody-dependent enhancement. Nat Rev Immunol 2020; 20(10): 633-43.
[http://dx.doi.org/10.1038/s41577-020-00410-0] [PMID: 32782358]

[35]   Sefik E, Qu R, Junqueira C, *et al.* Inflammasome activation in infected macrophages drives COVID-19 pathology. Nature 2022; 606(7914): 585-93.
[http://dx.doi.org/10.1038/s41586-022-04802-1] [PMID: 35483404]

[36]   Zhou J, Chu H, Chan JFW, Yuen KY. Middle East respiratory syndrome coronavirus infection: virus-host cell interactions and implications on pathogenesis. Virol J 2015; 12(1): 218.
[http://dx.doi.org/10.1186/s12985-015-0446-6] [PMID: 26690369]

[37]   Perlman S, Netland J. Coronaviruses post-SARS: update on replication and pathogenesis. Nat Rev Microbiol 2009; 7(6): 439-50.
[http://dx.doi.org/10.1038/nrmicro2147] [PMID: 19430490]

[38]   Eckerle LD, Lu X, Sperry SM, Choi L, Denison MR. High fidelity of murine hepatitis virus replication is decreased in nsp14 exoribonuclease mutants. J Virol 2007; 81(22): 12135-44.
[http://dx.doi.org/10.1128/JVI.01296-07] [PMID: 17804504]

[39]   Gao Y, Yan L, Huang Y, *et al.* Structure of the RNA-dependent RNA polymerase from COVID-19 virus. Science 2020; 368(6492): 779-82.
[http://dx.doi.org/10.1126/science.abb7498] [PMID: 32277040]

[40]   Gordon CJ, Tchesnokov EP, Woolner E, *et al.* Remdesivir is a direct-acting antiviral that inhibits RNA-dependent RNA polymerase from severe acute respiratory syndrome coronavirus 2 with high potency. J Biol Chem 2020; 295(20): 6785-97.
[http://dx.doi.org/10.1074/jbc.RA120.013679] [PMID: 32284326]

[41]   Ferron F, Subissi L, Silveira De Morais AT, *et al.* Structural and molecular basis of mismatch

correction and ribavirin excision from coronavirus RNA. Proc Natl Acad Sci USA 2018; 115(2): E162-71.
[http://dx.doi.org/10.1073/pnas.1718806115] [PMID: 29279395]

[42]   Keck JG, Makino S, Soe LH, Fleming JO, Stohlman SA, Lai MMC. RNA recombination of coronavirus. Adv Exp Med Biol 1987; 218: 99-107.
[http://dx.doi.org/10.1007/978-1-4684-1280-2_11] [PMID: 2829575]

[43]   Lai MM, Baric RS, Makino S, *et al.* Recombination between nonsegmented RNA genomes of murine coronaviruses. J Virol 1985; 56(2): 449-56.
[http://dx.doi.org/10.1128/jvi.56.2.449-456.1985] [PMID: 2997467]

[44]   Li Y, Yang X, Wang N, *et al.* GC usage of SARS-CoV-2 genes might adapt to the environment of human lung expressed genes. Mol Genet Genomics 2020; 295(6): 1537-46.
[http://dx.doi.org/10.1007/s00438-020-01719-0] [PMID: 32888056]

[45]   Krijnse-Locker J, Ericsson M, Rottier PJ, Griffiths G. Characterization of the budding compartment of mouse hepatitis virus: evidence that transport from the RER to the Golgi complex requires only one vesicular transport step. J Cell Biol 1994; 124(1): 55-70.
[http://dx.doi.org/10.1083/jcb.124.1.55] [PMID: 8294506]

[46]   Tooze J, Tooze S, Warren G. Replication of coronavirus MHV-A59 in sac- cells: determination of the first site of budding of progeny virions. Eur J Cell Biol 1984; 33(2): 281-93.
[PMID: 6325194]

[47]   Lam TTY, Jia N, Zhang YW, *et al.* Identifying SARS-CoV-2-related coronaviruses in Malayan pangolins. Nature 2020; 583(7815): 282-5.
[http://dx.doi.org/10.1038/s41586-020-2169-0] [PMID: 32218527]

[48]   Raamsman MJB, Locker JK, de Hooge A, *et al.* Characterization of the coronavirus mouse hepatitis virus strain A59 small membrane protein E. J Virol 2000; 74(5): 2333-42.
[http://dx.doi.org/10.1128/JVI.74.5.2333-2342.2000] [PMID: 10666264]

[49]   Boscarino JA, Logan HL, Lacny JJ, Gallagher TM. Envelope protein palmitoylations are crucial for murine coronavirus assembly. J Virol 2008; 82(6): 2989-99.
[http://dx.doi.org/10.1128/JVI.01906-07] [PMID: 18184706]

[50]   de Haan CAM, Vennema H, Rottier PJM. Assembly of the coronavirus envelope: homotypic interactions between the M proteins. J Virol 2000; 74(11): 4967-78.
[http://dx.doi.org/10.1128/JVI.74.11.4967-4978.2000] [PMID: 10799570]

[51]   Jack A, Ferro LS, Trnka MJ, *et al.* SARS-CoV-2 nucleocapsid protein forms condensates with viral genomic RNA. PLoS Biol 2021; 19(10): e3001425.
[http://dx.doi.org/10.1371/journal.pbio.3001425] [PMID: 34634033]

[52]   Wan Y, Shang J, Graham R, Baric RS, Li F. Receptor Recognition by the Novel Coronavirus from Wuhan: an Analysis Based on Decade-Long Structural Studies of SARS Coronavirus. J Virol 2020; 94(7): e00127-20.
[http://dx.doi.org/10.1128/JVI.00127-20] [PMID: 31996437]

[53]   Hoffmann M, Kleine-Weber H, Schroeder S, *et al.* SARS-CoV-2 Cell Entry Depends on ACE2 and TMPRSS2 and Is Blocked by a Clinically Proven Protease Inhibitor. Cell 2020; 181(2): 271-280.e8.
[http://dx.doi.org/10.1016/j.cell.2020.02.052] [PMID: 32142651]

[54]   Tang NLS, Chan PKS, Wong CK, *et al.* Early enhanced expression of interferon-inducible protein-10 (CXCL-10) and other chemokines predicts adverse outcome in severe acute respiratory syndrome. Clin Chem 2005; 51(12): 2333-40.
[http://dx.doi.org/10.1373/clinchem.2005.054460] [PMID: 16195357]

[55]   Yu X, Sun S, Shi Y, Wang H, Zhao R, Sheng J. SARS-CoV-2 viral load in sputum correlates with risk of COVID-19 progression. Crit Care 2020; 24(1): 170.
[http://dx.doi.org/10.1186/s13054-020-02893-8] [PMID: 32326952]

[56] He L, Ding Y, Zhang Q, *et al.* Expression of elevated levels of pro-inflammatory cytokines in SARS-CoV-infected ACE2 $^+$ cells in SARS patients: relation to the acute lung injury and pathogenesis of SARS. J Pathol 2006; 210(3): 288-97.
[http://dx.doi.org/10.1002/path.2067] [PMID: 17031779]

[57] Chen G, Wu D, Guo W, *et al.* Clinical and immunological features of severe and moderate coronavirus disease 2019. J Clin Invest 2020; 130(5): 2620-9.
[http://dx.doi.org/10.1172/JCI137244] [PMID: 32217835]

[58] Huang C, Wang Y, Li X, *et al.* Clinical features of patients infected with 2019 novel coronavirus in Wuhan, China. Lancet 2020; 395(10223): 497-506.
[http://dx.doi.org/10.1016/S0140-6736(20)30183-5] [PMID: 31986264]

[59] Bermejo-Martin JF, Almansa R, Menéndez R, Mendez R, Kelvin DJ, Torres A. Lymphopenic community acquired pneumonia as signature of severe COVID-19 infection. J Infect 2020; 80(5): e23-4.
[http://dx.doi.org/10.1016/j.jinf.2020.02.029] [PMID: 32145214]

[60] Chan JFW, Zhang AJ, Yuan S, *et al.* Simulation of the Clinical and Pathological Manifestations of Coronavirus Disease 2019 (COVID-19) in a Golden Syrian Hamster Model: Implications for Disease Pathogenesis and Transmissibility. Clin Infect Dis 2020; 71(9): ciaa325.
[http://dx.doi.org/10.1093/cid/ciaa325] [PMID: 32215622]

[61] van der Poll T, Opal SM. Host–pathogen interactions in sepsis. Lancet Infect Dis 2008; 8(1): 32-43.
[http://dx.doi.org/10.1016/S1473-3099(07)70265-7] [PMID: 18063412]

[62] Totura AL, Baric RS. SARS coronavirus pathogenesis: host innate immune responses and viral antagonism of interferon. Curr Opin Virol 2012; 2(3): 264-75.
[http://dx.doi.org/10.1016/j.coviro.2012.04.004] [PMID: 22572391]

[63] Chatterjee SK, Saha S, Munoz MNM. Molecular Pathogenesis, Immunopathogenesis and Novel Therapeutic Strategy Against COVID-19. Front Mol Biosci 2020; 7: 196.
[http://dx.doi.org/10.3389/fmolb.2020.00196] [PMID: 32850977]

[64] Eppensteiner J, Kwun J, Scheuermann U, *et al.* Damage- and pathogen-associated molecular patterns play differential roles in late mortality after critical illness. JCI Insight 2019; 4(16): e127925.
[http://dx.doi.org/10.1172/jci.insight.127925] [PMID: 31434802]

[65] Ni L, Ye F, Cheng ML, *et al.* Detection of SARS-CoV-2-Specific Humoral and Cellular Immunity in COVID-19 Convalescent Individuals. Immunity 2020; 52(6): 971-977.e3.
[http://dx.doi.org/10.1016/j.immuni.2020.04.023] [PMID: 32413330]

[66] Zhou Z, Ren L, Zhang L, *et al.* Heightened Innate Immune Responses in the Respiratory Tract of COVID-19 Patients. Cell Host Microbe 2020; 27(6): 883-890.e2.
[http://dx.doi.org/10.1016/j.chom.2020.04.017] [PMID: 32407669]

[67] Guo L, Ren L, Yang S, *et al.* Profiling Early Humoral Response to Diagnose Novel Coronavirus Disease (COVID-19). Clin Infect Dis 2020; 71(15): 778-85.
[http://dx.doi.org/10.1093/cid/ciaa310] [PMID: 32198501]

[68] Chen L, Xiong J, Bao L, Shi Y. Convalescent plasma as a potential therapy for COVID-19. Lancet Infect Dis 2020; 20(4): 398-400.
[http://dx.doi.org/10.1016/S1473-3099(20)30141-9] [PMID: 32113510]

[69] Fu Y, Cheng Y, Wu Y. Understanding SARS-CoV-2-Mediated Inflammatory Responses: From Mechanisms to Potential Therapeutic Tools. Virol Sin 2020; 35(3): 266-71.
[http://dx.doi.org/10.1007/s12250-020-00207-4] [PMID: 32125642]

[70] Chen T, Wu D, Chen H, *et al.* Clinical characteristics of 113 deceased patients with coronavirus disease 2019: retrospective study. BMJ 2020; 368: m1091.
[http://dx.doi.org/10.1136/bmj.m1091] [PMID: 32217556]

[71]   Yang X, Yu Y, Xu J, *et al.* Clinical course and outcomes of critically ill patients with SARS-CoV-2 pneumonia in Wuhan, China: a single-centered, retrospective, observational study. Lancet Respir Med 2020; 8(5): 475-81.
[http://dx.doi.org/10.1016/S2213-2600(20)30079-5] [PMID: 32105632]

[72]   Aggarwal G, Cheruiyot I, Aggarwal S, *et al.* Association of Cardiovascular Disease With Coronavirus Disease 2019 (COVID-19) Severity: A Meta-Analysis. Curr Probl Cardiol 2020; 45(8): 100617.
[http://dx.doi.org/10.1016/j.cpcardiol.2020.100617] [PMID: 32402515]

[73]   Khashkhusha TR, Chan JSK, Harky A. ACE inhibitors and COVID-19: We don't know yet. J Card Surg 2020; 35(6): 1172-3.
[http://dx.doi.org/10.1111/jocs.14582] [PMID: 32340070]

[74]   Liu K, Fang YY, Deng Y, *et al.* Clinical characteristics of novel coronavirus cases in tertiary hospitals in Hubei Province. Chin Med J (Engl) 2020; 133(9): 1025-31.
[http://dx.doi.org/10.1097/CM9.0000000000000744] [PMID: 32044814]

[75]   Naicker S, Yang CW, Hwang SJ, Liu BC, Chen JH, Jha V. The Novel Coronavirus 2019 epidemic and kidneys. Kidney Int 2020; 97(5): 824-8.
[http://dx.doi.org/10.1016/j.kint.2020.03.001] [PMID: 32204907]

[76]   Zaim S, Chong JH, Sankaranarayanan V, Harky A. COVID-19 and Multiorgan Response. Curr Probl Cardiol 2020; 45(8): 100618.
[http://dx.doi.org/10.1016/j.cpcardiol.2020.100618] [PMID: 32439197]

[77]   Wong SH, Lui RNS, Sung JJY. COVID-19 and the digestive system. J Gastroenterol Hepatol 2020; 35(5): 744-8.
[http://dx.doi.org/10.1111/jgh.15047] [PMID: 32215956]

[78]   Tang N, Li D, Wang X, Sun Z. Abnormal coagulation parameters are associated with poor prognosis in patients with novel coronavirus pneumonia. J Thromb Haemost 2020; 18(4): 844-7.
[http://dx.doi.org/10.1111/jth.14768] [PMID: 32073213]

[79]   Tang N, Bai H, Chen X, Gong J, Li D, Sun Z. Anticoagulant treatment is associated with decreased mortality in severe coronavirus disease 2019 patients with coagulopathy. J Thromb Haemost 2020; 18(5): 1094-9.
[http://dx.doi.org/10.1111/jth.14817] [PMID: 32220112]

[80]   Shenoy V, Ferreira AJ, Qi Y, *et al.* The angiotensin-converting enzyme 2/angiogenesis-(1-7)/Mas axis confers cardiopulmonary protection against lung fibrosis and pulmonary hypertension. Am J Respir Crit Care Med 2010; 182(8): 1065-72.
[http://dx.doi.org/10.1164/rccm.200912-1840OC] [PMID: 20581171]

[81]   Meng J, Xiao G, Zhang J, *et al.* Renin-angiotensin system inhibitors improve the clinical outcomes of COVID-19 patients with hypertension. Emerg Microbes Infect 2020; 9(1): 757-60.
[http://dx.doi.org/10.1080/22221751.2020.1746200] [PMID: 32228222]

[82]   Arabi YM, Arifi AA, Balkhy HH, *et al.* Clinical course and outcomes of critically ill patients with Middle East respiratory syndrome coronavirus infection. Ann Intern Med 2014; 160(6): 389-397.
[http://dx.doi.org/10.7326/M13-2486] [PMID: 24474051]

[83]   Henry BM, Vikse J, Benoit S, Favaloro EJ, Lippi G. Hyperinflammation and derangement of renin-angiotensin-aldosterone system in COVID-19: A novel hypothesis for clinically suspected hypercoagulopathy and microvascular immunothrombosis. Clin Chim Acta 2020; 507: 167-73.
[http://dx.doi.org/10.1016/j.cca.2020.04.027] [PMID: 32348783]

[84]   Shariq M, Sheikh JA, Quadir N, Sharma N, Hasnain SE, Ehtesham NZ. COVID-19 and tuberculosis: the double whammy of respiratory pathogens. Eur Respir Rev 2022; 31(164): 210264.
[http://dx.doi.org/10.1183/16000617.0264-2021] [PMID: 35418488]

[85]   Sheikh JA, Malik AA, Quadir N, Ehtesham NZ, Hasnain SE. Learning from COVID-19 to tackle TB pandemic: From despair to hope. Lancet Regional Health - Southeast Asia 2022; 2: 100015.

[http://dx.doi.org/10.1016/j.lansea.2022.05.004] [PMID: 35769164]

[86]   Shariq M, Malik AA, Sheikh JA, Hasnain SE, Ehtesham NZ. Regulation of autophagy by SARS-Co-
        -2: The multifunctional contributions of ORF3a. J Med Virol 2023; 95(7): e28959.
        [http://dx.doi.org/10.1002/jmv.28959] [PMID: 37485696]

CHAPTER 4

Transmission Cycle of SARS-CoV-2

Mohammad Sufian Badar[1,2,3,4], **Tahira Khan**[5,*], **Harsha Negi**[5], **Abul Kalam Najmi**[5] and **Junaid Alam**[6]

[1] *Department of Bioengineering, University of California, Riverside, CA, USA*

[2] *Universal Scientific Education and Research Network (USERN), Tehran, Iran*

[3] *Director (Academic), SPI Darbhanga, India*

[4] *Department of Computer Science and Engineering (Bioinformatics), School of Engineering Sciences and Technology (SEST), Jamia Hamdard, New Delhi, India*

[5] *Department of Pharmacology, SPER, Jamia Hamdard, New Delhi, India*

[6] *Division of Trauma Surgery & Critical Care, AIIMS Jai Prakash Narayan Apex Trauma Center, New Delhi, India*

Abstract: The COVID-19 infection caused by severe acute respiratory syndrome coronavirus 2 (SARS-CoV-2), progressed to a global pandemic and led to millions of deaths worldwide over the years since its COVID-19 origin. Coronavirus transmission is a zoonotic spillover, which means that virus transmission can occur from a vertebrate animal to a human host. The CoV genome underwent continuous recombination and evolution, which resulted in interspecies transmission and the virus' recurrent emergence as a pandemic. The SARS-CoV-2 infection primarily results in respiratory symptoms, like pneumonia, that range from mild to severe in severity, along with alveolar injury ultimately leading to acute respiratory distress syndrome (ARDS) and death. This chapter outlines the SARS-CoV-2 transmission pathways, how the disease spreads by infected people, and the consequences for the prevention and control of infection, both inside and outside healthcare facilities. This section also covers modes of transmission like horizontal, fomite, fecal-oral, nosocomial, and animal-to-human transmission of SARS-CoV-2.

Keywords: COVID -19, Modes of transmission, SARS-CoV-2, Transmission cycle.

INTRODUCTION

In December 2019, researchers discovered an unexplained source of pneumonia in Wuhan that was later identified as a novel strain of coronavirus, SARS-CoV-2, isolated from the respiratory epithelium of patients. SARS-CoV-2 is a single-

---

* **Corresponding author Tahira Khan:** Department of Pharmacology, SPER, Jamia Hamdard, New Delhi, India; E-mail: Indiatahirakhan45@gmail.com

stranded RNA virus of the genus Beta coronavirus. It is considered to be an extremely contagious and pathogenic coronavirus [1 - 4].

The disease caused by the new coronavirus, originally known as 2019-nCoV, was referred to as coronavirus disease 2019 or COVID-19 until it was officially renamed SARS-CoV-2 on February 11, 2020, by the WHO and the International Committee on Taxonomy of Viruses (ICTV) (2019-nCoV or COVID-2019) [1, 5, 6].

The severe acute respiratory syndrome coronavirus 2 (SARS-CoV-2) is the causative factor behind COVID-19 infection. Since its discovery, SARS-CoV-2 has been responsible for millions of deaths worldwide. The World Health Organization (WHO) declared it a pandemic due to the virus' unprecedented global impact. Until the outbreak in Guangdong, China, the SARS-CoV virus was primarily believed to infect animals only, but later it was transmitted to and among humans [7]. The SARS-CoV-2 virus first impacted the lower respiratory tract in humans in the Chinese province of Guangdong in 2002, and then again in Wuhan in 2019. It was found that the Huanan seafood wholesale business was associated with the hospitalization of patients in Wuhan. There was a possibility of zoonotic infection from the market because live animals including chicken, bats, snakes, frogs, rabbits, marmots, and hedgehogs were sold there. In addition, the National Health Commission of the People's Republic of China disclosed that human interaction with wild bats was the most likely route for the transmission of SARS-CoV-2 [1 - 4].

Transmission Cycle

When the SARS-CoV-2 virus infects patients, it causes pneumonia symptoms along with alveolar injury that eventually results in acute respiratory distress syndrome (ARDS). When an individual eats an infected animal as food, this results in the virus transmission from the animal to the human. Furthermore, when an infected person comes in close contact with a healthy individual, the virus is transmitted among them as well [5].

Furthermore, the process by which the coronavirus transmits from a vertebrate species (animals) to a human host is known as "zoonotic spillover." The CoV genome underwent continual recombination and evolution, which caused cross-species transmission and contributed to the virus' recurrent emergence as a pandemic [4].

To develop viable therapies against SARS-CoV-2 and preventive approaches to contain the progression of the disease, it is important to determine the source of origin and the transmission of the virus [5]. The transmission of the SARS-CoV-2 virus is primarily linked to Wuhan's seafood market, which has spread substantially to cause an outbreak of the pandemic. Several coronaviruses are believed to be transmitted by bats, which also are considered to be the major source of SARS-CoV and SARS-CoV-2 in humans. Although the underlying mechanisms for virus zoonotic spillover is unrecognized yet, it is thought that from this region, the spillover actually occurred from bats to civets and eventually to the neighboring residents or was attributed to involvement in the trade of diseased animals [4].

SARS-CoV-2 is primarily transmitted by three factors: the host, the environment, and the virus [10]. The novel coronavirus is believed to spread between humans by respiratory droplets that are released through an infected person's sneeze or cough [4].

The transmission cycle for SARS-CoV-2 is illustrated in Fig. (**1**).

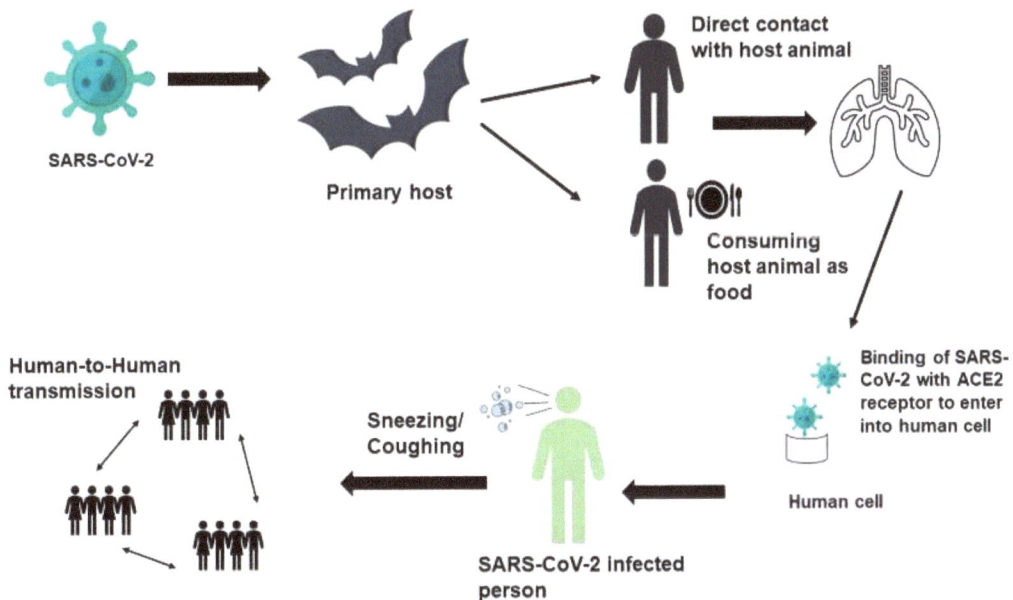

Fig. (1). Transmission cycle of SARS-CoV-2.

Although the transmission cycle is still unknown, scientists have identified particular pattern to limit the transmission of disease. Considering these patterns, some strategies were made by WHO to obstruct the transmission of coronavirus, which are mentioned at the end of the chapter.

MECHANISM OF SARS-COV-2 ENTRY INTO THE HUMAN CELL

The SARS-CoV-2 virus causes infection by binding to the specific host receptors that facilitate its cell membrane fusion. The virus spike contains a receptor-binding domain (RBD) to bind with the ACE2 receptor of the potential host cell, which aids in the transmission of SARS-CoV-2 between humans. Also, the spikes of SARS-CoV-2 and SARS-CoV have similar RBD sequences, which further suggests that they share the same entry route into the host cells through the ACE2 receptor [8, 9].

This binding of the viral spike or S protein to the host's ACE2 receptor is considered a very crucial step for the virus entry into the cell. Therefore, the distribution of the host's ACE2 receptor determines the viral tropism. The early stages of the illness have the highest viral loads in the upper area of the respiratory tract, specifically the oropharynx and nasal passages. Thus, this shows that the virus replication begins in the upper respiratory system before the infection progresses to the lower part of the respiratory system [10].

Modes of Transmission

In order to develop measures to cease the transmission of the virus and contain the infection, it is imperative to identify the source of origin and the methods by which the SARS-CoV-2 virus spreads [5].

Animal-to-Human Transmission

The outbreak of the SARS-CoV-2 in the Wuhan region of China is linked with the wet animal market. The majority of those who initially contracted the disease were found to have been exposed to the virus mostly through the wet animal market [4]. During the onset, researchers believed that raccoon dogs and palm civets were the key carriers for infection. But later on, based on the results of viral RNA detection from the samples collected from civets at the food market, it was suggested the palm civets might be secondary hosts [5].

Coronavirus consists of a huge family of viruses containing single-stranded RNA found in several species, such as birds, camels, cattle, cats, pigs, and bats; some of these species are carriers of the virus, as well. Out of all the animal species, the rhinolophid bats are particularly considered the most dangerous carriers of the virus. These bats do not show any clinical signs of infection. However, in other animal species, the virus is believed to have caused severe ailments, including infectious bronchitis sickness in chickens, which would lead to economic losses to the poultry sector if not controlled [6].

Additionally, anti-SARS-CoV antibodies in rhinolophid bats suggested that they were also a source of viral replication. According to a recent study, the Middle East Respiratory Syndrome (MERS) coronavirus, which first appeared in dromedary camels in Saudi Arabia in 2012, was also discovered in Pipistrellus and Perimyotis bats, further supporting the theory that bats were the infection's primary hosts and means of transmission [5].

Therefore, both SARS and MERS CoVs originate from bats and later pass through palm civets and camels (intermediate hosts). SARS-CoV-2 and coronavirus from bats have a genetic similarity of more than 95% based on recent research studies, which indicated that bats were likely to be the primary hosts for SARS-CoV-2. In conclusion, SARS-CoV-2 also originates from bats, just like SARS-CoV and MERS-CoV [2, 4].

Since humans and bats did not interact directly, there was a low likelihood that humans would become infected with the bat coronavirus. Researchers believed that a host between bats and humans served as an intermediary for the SARS-CoV-2 transmission. Bats are believed to be the main source of SARS-CoV-2 transmission in humans even if the specific route of virus zoonotic spillover has not yet been determined. This is because bats are known to have a range of coronaviruses. There is some evidence that SARS-CoVs in the nearby population of bats underwent recombination events. Additionally, upon analysis of genomic sequences of coronaviruses, it was found that SARS-CoV-2 was a recombinant virus made from combining bat coronavirus and a coronavirus with an unidentified origin. Due to changes in the S-glycoprotein and N-protein, the virus has evolved the capacity to infect humans, distinguishing it from other SARS-like CoVs seen in bats. This analysis suggested that the virus zoonotic spillover occurred from bats to civets and was then transferred to the local population or among people engaged in the trafficking of diseased animals [2, 4, 11].

There are various consecutive events that take place for the spillover to occur that ultimately facilitate the transmission of CoVs in humans and cause infection. For the prevalence of animal-to-human transmission, different contributory parameters include disease patterns in an animal population, the amount of virus exposure, and the percentage of the population that is virus-susceptible. All of these parameters can be grouped into three main phases that showcase how the transmission of the virus takes place. The first phase or the primary stage is when the virus interacts with humans. At this stage, the proportion of viruses that interact with humans at any given time is determined by virus prevalence and propagation from the host animal. The virus then survives, develops, and spreads outside of the animal host. In the second phase, the behavior of humans and the vector plays key roles in determining the likelihood of virus exposure, the route of virus entry, and the virus load. The genetic, physiologic, and immunologic state of the human host, as well as second-stage factors, determine whether an infection will occur and how severe it will be. When a spillover occurs, the virus usually manages to get past all of these obstacles to infect the next host. Each of these steps establishes a barrier for the virus transmission to the next level [4, 12, 13]. Fig. (**2**) illustrates the animal-to-human transmission of SARS-CoV-2.

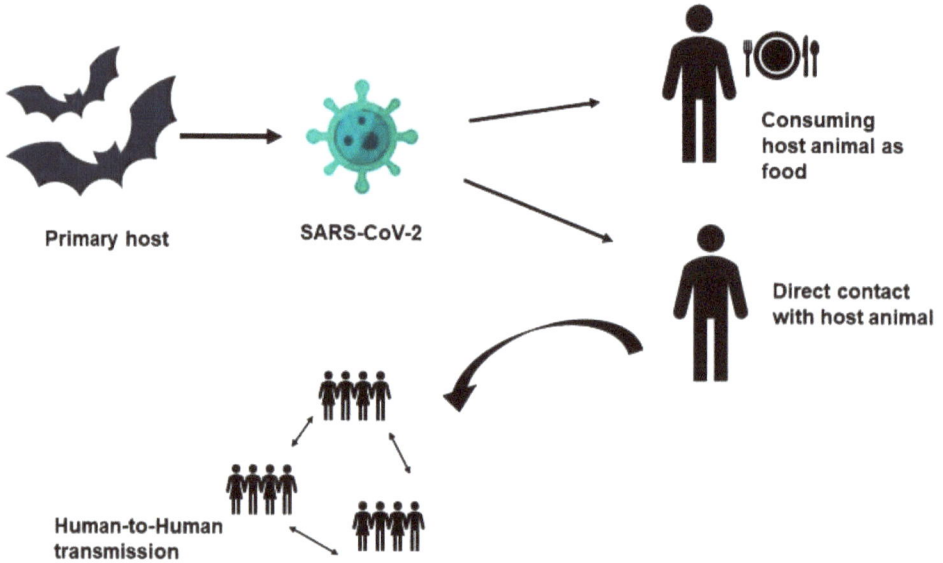

Fig. (2). Animal to human transmission of SARS-CoV-2.

The primary mechanism by which SARS-CoV-2 penetrates the cells is by the formation of a link between its S-protein and the angiotensin-converting enzyme 2 (ACE2) host cell receptor. SARS-CoV-2 has developed the potential to not only infect people but also to facilitate transmission between humans. It can recognize the ACE2 from various animal species In addition to that, SARS-CoV-2 has a greater binding capacity to human ACE2 than SARS-CoV, which substantiates the possibility of transmission and uncontrollable spread of the SARS-CoV2 virus in cross-species [2].

Human-to-Human Transmission

SARS-CoV-2 in humans is primarily spread via respiratory secretions, however, aerosol, exposure to polluted surfaces directly and fecal-oral transmission are also reportedly other possible modes of transmission [14].

The major routes for human-to-human transmission can be subdivided into the following:

1. Horizontal transmission
2. Fomite transmission
3. Nosocomial transmission
4. Oral fecal route of transmission

Horizontal Transmission

The SARS-CoV-2 virus can transmit from infected people via direct, indirect, or intimate contact with them. When a diseased person coughs, sneezes, or talks, the infected secretions like saliva, respiratory secretions, or respiratory droplets come out. These respiratory droplets contain the SARS-CoV-2 virus that can reach the healthy individual in close proximity (approximately, within one meter) via nose, mouth, or eyes and can therefore result in infection. Additionally, the virus may spread to a healthy individual through indirect contact, in which the vulnerable host comes into contact with a contaminated object or surface [10]. Fig. (**3**) illustrates the human-to-human transmission of the SARS-CoV-2 process.

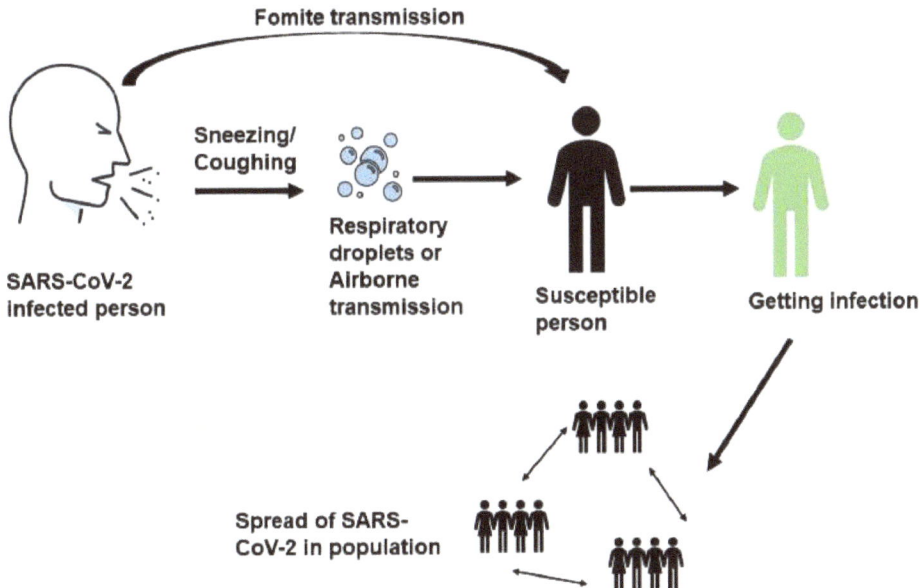

Fig. (3). Human-to-Human transmission process of SARS-CoV-2.

Another route for human-to-human transmission is airborne transmission. In this transmission route, the infectious agent spreads through the dissemination of droplet nuclei, also known as aerosols. These aerosols are known to remain infectious even when they are present in the air for a long distance and time. The spreading of SARS-CoV-2 via the airborne route can occur during medical procedures that lead to the generation of aerosols. WHO, along with other scientific communities, is actively evaluating if the dissemination of SARS-Co--2 occurs via aerosols even in the indoor environment with inadequate ventilation.

There are several theories regarding the possible mechanisms through which the dissemination of SARS-CoV-2 occurs via aerosols. According to these theories, microscopic aerosols of less than 5μm are generated by several respiratory droplets through evaporation, and aerosols can be released during normal breathing and conversing. When these aerosols contain enough viruses and a vulnerable person breathes them in, the virus can infect the person, making them ill. Yet, with SARS-CoV-2, it is unclear how much proportion of the infectious dose of the virus has to be present in exhaled respiratory droplets that evaporate to form aerosols to cause an infection in another person [15].

Certain experimental studies have been conducted that generated aerosols of the infectious sample with the help of high-powered jet nebulizers in a controlled laboratory environment. The studies reported that the SARS-CoV-2 pathogen was present in aerosolized air samples for up to 3 and 16 hours. However, since these results were obtained from experimentally induced aerosols, they cannot be considered synonymous with normal cough conditions in humans [16]. According to a recent clinical report, no evidence of droplets or aerosol transmission was observed, when the health workers came in contact with SARS-CoV-2 infected people while wearing protective gear, including medical masks and personal protective equipment (PPE). It revealed that the transmission via the airborne pathway might be decreased by avoiding contact and appropriately applying droplet precautions [17, 18].

Additionally, short-range transmission occurs through infected individuals in crowded indoor areas like restaurants, cafes, gyms, etc., especially poorly ventilated for an extended period of time. In-depth analyses of these clusters have indicated that human-to-human transmission within these clusters may also be mediated by droplet and fomite transmission. Moreover, these clusters are in a close contact environment that facilitates the transmission of the SARS-CoV-2 virus from a small group of people to a larger number. Such an occurrence is sometimes known as a super spreading event, especially if proper hand sanitization, wearing a mask, and physical distance, are not followed [19].

According to some researchers, the transmission of SARS-CoV-2 from human to human can occur if a healthy person comes into prolonged, unprotected contact with an infected person. In this scenario, ongoing pathogen pressure develops the infection and ultimately, disease [20].

So far, it is believed that a person affected with SARS-CoV-2 is a major source of infection. Respiratory particles, together with aerial particles and intimate contact between infected and uninfected people, are thought to be the main methods of CoV transmission [21].

Fomite Transmission

Fomite or direct contact transmission is another possible route for the propagation of SARS-CoV-2 in humans, however, there is no concrete proof. For instance, several people reported infection in a Chinese mall, and many people with coronavirus infection claimed that they had no direct contact with other patients. Later, it was observed that the infected individual utilized communal spaces, such as restrooms, where it is possible that respiratory or fomite transmission occurred. In contact transmission, it is important to maintain proper health hygiene to avoid the likelihood of SARS-CoV-2 spreading. Conclusively, poor hand hygiene increases the risk of contracting and spreading the infection, while cleaning solutions with chlorine or ethanol reduces the risk [10].

Oral-Fecal Route of Transmission

Recent studies have revealed that SARS-CoV-2 may be found in patient feces, indicating that the virus can also spread orally via feces via the fecal-oral route as well. This confirms that the virus can produce gastrointestinal symptoms and is present in the gastrointestinal tract. However, it is debatable whether eating food contaminated with a virus might result in infection and transmission [4].

The exact mechanism for SARS-CoV-2 transmission via the oral-fecal route is not established. However, a study on 96 patients in China reports a high percentage of viral load in the fecal samples of COVID-19- patients. There were some cases where the SARS-CoV-2 virus was isolated from feces, which survived in the feces for 1 to 2 days. Therefore, it is possible that the virus can further contaminate sewage, water bodies, and food supplies and cause contamination at bathroom sites through fecal-aerosol transmission [22, 23].

Nosocomial Transmission

Nosocomial infections are healthcare-associated infections acquired while receiving healthcare, especially in the healthcare delivery system. The route of transmission is known as the nosocomial transmission route. This transmission can occur in hospitals, clinics, and care facilities. The global burden of the coronavirus pandemic on hospitals and healthcare organizations enhanced the probability of nosocomial infection and outbreak in non-COVID patients or healthcare workers [24].

While providing care to COVID-19 patients, healthcare workers are exposed to the SARS-CoV-2 virus and are at increased probability of getting the infection. However, the accurate epidemiological data regarding the dissemination of SARS-CoV-2 to healthcare service providers are limited to the data from cross-sectional studies, small cohort studies, and reports from government agencies [24].

The infections caused by the novel coronavirus, SARS-CoV-2, include exogenous and endogenous infections. These infections are the reason for the potential threat to not only inpatients but also healthcare professionals and their accompanying staff. Exogenous infection, commonly referred to as cross-infection, is caused by pathogens that can infect humans through the hands of healthcare workers, contaminated objects or surfaces, or directly from the environment while providing care. Contrarily, in the event of endogenous infection, patients with impaired immune systems become infected by germs from the hospital or the patients' normal flora [25].

Since several hospitals accept patients who are both SARS-CoV-2 infected and healthy in the same areas, high pressure of colonization is generated in hospital settings. This practice exposes susceptible patients and healthcare workers to SARS-CoV-2 infection. Despite the fact that the recent medical recommendations and guidelines emphasize the necessity to keep COVID-19 patients away from susceptible non-COVID-19 patients, it may not always be possible to isolate them completely [24].

Environmental Transmission

The environmental factor is one of the many elements that affect the propagation of SARS-CoV-2. The SARS-CoV-2 ability to persist as an infectious agent, the extent to which it will spread, and the rate at which it does so are all influenced by the environment's air quality and surface contamination. When these environmental factors persist over a long time, they influence the spread of COVID-19. According to an outbreak on a cruise ship, the gene material of SARS-CoV-2 was discovered on the surface of the bathroom, bedroom, phone, and television, among other items, even after 17 days of the rooms being vacated. Although it is unknown if those materials were contagious, the SARS-CoV-2 outbreak on the cruise ship undoubtedly significantly contaminated the surroundings, especially those infected with the novel coronavirus [26].

The environmental factors responsible for the SARS-CoV-2 transmission are categorized below:

1. Air pollution
2. Water Pollution
3. Weather-related parameters

The environmental transmission of SARS-CoV-2 is illustrated in Fig. (4).

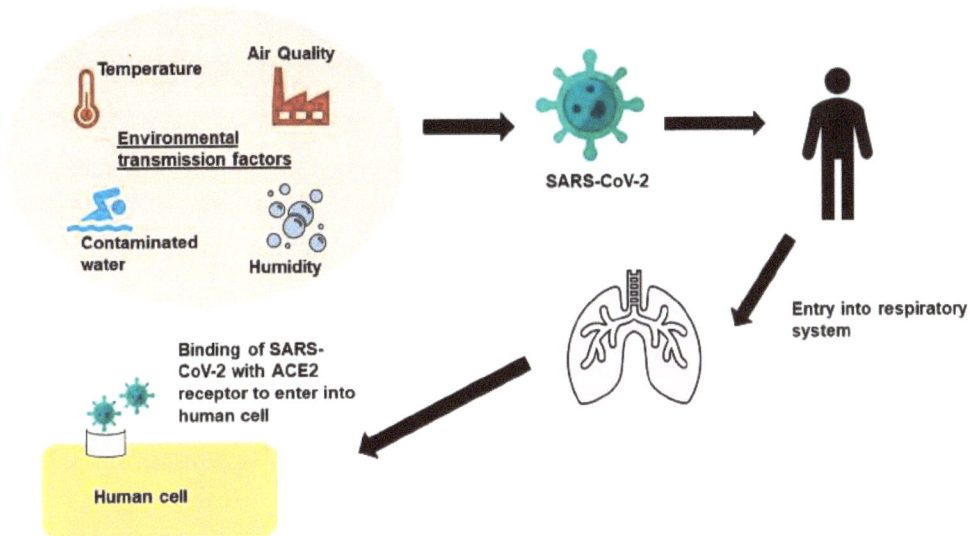

Fig. (4). Environmental transmission of SARS-CoV-2.

Air Pollution

Researchers also discovered that spread of SARS-CoV-2 in humans has intensified in high-pollution locations. It is also known as airborne viral infectivity. In addition to that SARS-CoV-2 can be distributed in the environment through water, bio aerosols, and food. These factors can also be considered potential agents for the transmission of the virus [27].

One of the main risk factors for respiratory infections, particularly those caused by SARS-CoV-2, is air pollution. When air pollutants, including potent oxidants, enter a person's system, it can have a toxic and dangerous effect on their respiratory and cardiovascular systems, which leads to a cascade of immunological disorders and diseases. These air pollutants are also known to impact and suppress the early immune responses of the body toward the infection. According to a study, patients with SARS-CoV-2 infection residing in an area with a high air pollution index had an 84% higher risk of mortality, compared to people living in areas with a lesser level of air pollution. There is a direct association between high-level air pollutants and the mortalities caused by respiratory viral infections. It is also evident that the Lombardy and Emilia Romagna regions of Italy, the most polluted areas of Europe, had the most COVID-19-related fatalities worldwide [27 - 29].

Water Pollution

Waterways could also be a route for SARS-CoV-2 transmission, although more research is needed to explore the same. There are circumscribed findings on the environmental resistance of SARS-CoV-2, but some research has shown the presence and survival of other coronaviruses in the water environment at various temperatures. Although it is well known that SARS-CoV-2 can be found in sewage and wastewater, it is debatable if this virus can constitute a concern to the population exposed to the water cycle because the pathogenicity of viral particles has not been reported yet in these matrices. Furthermore, additional research is necessary to ascertain the effect of environmental factors on the occurrence of SARS-CoV-2 infections, such as temperature, light exposure, organic matter, etc [27, 29].

Weather-related Parameters

The intensity of transmission, persistence in the environmental matrices, and the tendency to cause infection of the SARS-CoV-2, depend on various factors. Certain factors, such as the biological properties of SARS-CoV-2, its incubation state, and its effect on infected and vulnerable individuals, remain the same for all regions. While factors like longevity, transmission capacity, and ability to cause infection of SARS-CoV-2 differ from region to region. As a result, a number of variables, including the level of air pollution, weather, atmospheric conditions, population density, access to healthcare, cultural traits, and personal safety precautions, affect the rate of SARS-CoV-2 infection transmission [27].

During the transmission of SARS-CoV-2 infection, weather-related parameters like the variability of temperature due to change of season, solar radiation, relative humidity, etc., have enormous importance. Recent studies of SARS-CoV-2 cases showed that climatic factors such as specific humidity, and temperature were associated with positive COVID-19 cases in particular geographic areas. However, other research showed that a location's environment only had a little impact on the COVID-19 outbreak in some local areas. Additionally, it hypothesized that the global network of travelers delayed the COVID-19 outbreak in some areas with warmer climates, supporting the idea that the environment influences the spread of SARS-CoV-2. Until July 5, 2020, there were 218 countries and territories worldwide affected by SARS-CoV-2 transmission.

Among these countries and territories, various areas experienced active community transmissions. Additionally, all these areas or regions have diverse climate zones ranging from hot and humid to cold and dry. Therefore, it is important to examine the relationship between weather-related conditions and SARS-CoV-2 transmission and survival [27].

PREVENTIVE MEASURES TO COMBAT TRANSMISSION

To reduce the frequency of SARS-CoV-2 transmission on a global scale, the WHO, local governments, and disease control and prevention centers suggest infected individuals maintain self-quarantine or home isolation [30]. Other safety guidelines to combat coronavirus transmission executed by governing authorities are:

- Wearing a mask in public places to cover the nose and mouth, especially in hospitals and while in close proximity to infected individuals.
- Washing hands regularly.
- Sanitizing household.
- Consuming properly cooked meat and eggs.
- Extra precautions by the children and elderly in order to avoid COVID-19 infection.
- Restricting travel, especially to and from China.
- Imposing lockdown to control the spread of the virus.

CONCLUSION

This chapter extensively examined the multifaceted aspects of COVID-19, shedding light on its origins, pathways of transmission, and potential strategies to mitigate its dissemination. The emergence of the novel coronavirus, SARS-Co--2, as the trigger for a global pandemic, has underscored the critical need to comprehend its genetic makeup, source, and modes of propagation. The virus's ability to spread through respiratory droplets and aerosols has necessitated unprecedented public health interventions to curtail its expansion.

Furthermore, this chapter effectively underscored that the transmission of COVID-19 is not confined to a single route but encompasses various other modes that are equally crucial for containment. The dissemination of the disease through diverse sources, including animals, humans, and even fecal matter, was also prominently addressed. Additionally, the influence of environmental factors on the transmission of SARS-CoV-2 was thoroughly explored.

Raising greater awareness about the potential pathways of disease transmission and its propagation is essential not only for curtailing its spread but also for effective management

TAKE HOME MESSAGE

The most catastrophic pandemic in recent human history is probably COVID-19. SARS-Cov-2 viral transmission can happen between humans, animals, and the environment. Aerosols, droplets, direct contact with patients, and indirect contact through fomite or nosocomial transmission are the ways by which viral particles might spread. WHO suggested a list of guidelines to stop the spread of the COVID-19 infection and transmission. Conclusively, the unpredictable course of a pandemic requires careful monitoring, individualized health plans, the implementation of control measures, a distinct legal and bioethical framework, and particular medical prescriptions to direct our actions.

REFERENCES

[1]   Xu J, Zhao S, Teng T, *et al.* Systematic comparison of two animal-to-human transmitted human coronaviruses: SARS-CoV-2 and SARS-CoV. Viruses 2020; 12(2): 244.
[http://dx.doi.org/10.3390/v12020244] [PMID: 32098422]

[2]   Mahdy MAA, Younis W, Ewaida Z. An overview of SARS-CoV-2 and animal infection. Front Vet Sci 2020; 7: 596391.
[http://dx.doi.org/10.3389/fvets.2020.596391] [PMID: 33363234]

[3]   Jackson CB, Farzan M, Chen B, Choe H. Mechanisms of SARS-CoV-2 entry into cells. Nat Rev Mol Cell Biol 2022; 23(1): 3-20.
[http://dx.doi.org/10.1038/s41580-021-00418-x] [PMID: 34611326]

[4]   Yadav T, Saxena SK. Transmission cycle of SARS-CoV and SARS-CoV-2 InCoronavirus Disease 2019 (COVID-19). Singapore: Springer 2020; pp. 33-42.

[5]   Shereen MA, Khan S, Kazmi A, Bashir N, Siddique R. COVID-19 infection: Emergence, transmission, and characteristics of human coronaviruses. J Adv Res 2020; 24: 91-8.
[http://dx.doi.org/10.1016/j.jare.2020.03.005] [PMID: 32257431]

[6]   Rahman HS, Aziz MS, Hussein RH, *et al.* The transmission modes and sources of COVID-19: A systematic review. International Journal of Surgery Open 2020; 26: 125-36.
[http://dx.doi.org/10.1016/j.ijso.2020.08.017] [PMID: 34568614]

[7]   Yesudhas D, Srivastava A, Gromiha MM. COVID-19 outbreak: history, mechanism, transmission, structural studies and therapeutics. Infection 2021; 49(2): 199-213.
[http://dx.doi.org/10.1007/s15010-020-01516-2] [PMID: 32886331]

[8]   Wan Y, Shang J, Graham R, Baric RS, Li F. Receptor recognition by the novel coronavirus from Wuhan: an analysis based on decade-long structural studies of SARS coronavirus. J Virol 2020; 94(7): e00127-20.
[http://dx.doi.org/10.1128/JVI.00127-20] [PMID: 31996437]

[9]   Jaimes JA, Millet JK, Stout AE, André NM, Whittaker GR. A tale of two viruses: the distinct spike glycoproteins of feline coronaviruses. Viruses 2020; 12(1): 83.
[http://dx.doi.org/10.3390/v12010083] [PMID: 31936749]

[10]   Meyerowitz EA, Richterman A, Gandhi RT, Sax PE. Transmission of SARS-CoV-2: a review of viral, host, and environmental factors. Ann Intern Med 2021; 174(1): 69-79.

[http://dx.doi.org/10.7326/M20-5008] [PMID: 32941052]

[11] Singla R, Mishra A, Joshi R, *et al.* Human animal interface of SARS-CoV-2 (COVID-19) transmission: a critical appraisal of scientific evidence. Vet Res Commun 2020; 44(3-4): 119-30.
[http://dx.doi.org/10.1007/s11259-020-09781-0] [PMID: 32926266]

[12] Zhou P, Shi ZL. SARS-CoV-2 spillover events. Science 2021; 371(6525): 120-2.
[http://dx.doi.org/10.1126/science.abf6097] [PMID: 33414206]

[13] Plowright RK, Parrish CR, McCallum H, *et al.* Pathways to zoonotic spillover. Nat Rev Microbiol 2017; 15(8): 502-10.
[http://dx.doi.org/10.1038/nrmicro.2017.45] [PMID: 28555073]

[14] Harrison AG, Lin T, Wang P. Mechanisms of SARS-CoV-2 transmission and pathogenesis. Trends Immunol 2020; 41(12): 1100-15.
[http://dx.doi.org/10.1016/j.it.2020.10.004] [PMID: 33132005]

[15] Gralton J, Tovey ER, McLaws ML, Rawlinson WD. Respiratory virus RNA is detectable in airborne and droplet particles. J Med Virol 2013; 85(12): 2151-9.
[http://dx.doi.org/10.1002/jmv.23698] [PMID: 23959825]

[16] van Doremalen N, Bushmaker T, Morris DH, *et al.* Aerosol and surface stability of SARS-CoV-2 as compared with SARS-CoV-1. N Engl J Med 2020; 382(16): 1564-7.
[http://dx.doi.org/10.1056/NEJMc2004973] [PMID: 32182409]

[17] Wong SCY, Kwong RT-S, Wu TC, *et al.* Risk of nosocomial transmission of coronavirus disease 2019: an experience in a general ward setting in Hong Kong. J Hosp Infect 2020; 105(2): 119-27.
[http://dx.doi.org/10.1016/j.jhin.2020.03.036] [PMID: 32259546]

[18] Durante-Mangoni E, Andini R, Bertolino L, *et al.* Low rate of severe acute respiratory syndrome coronavirus 2 spread among health-care personnel using ordinary personal protection equipment in a medium-incidence setting. Clin Microbiol Infect 2020; 26(9): 1269-70.
[http://dx.doi.org/10.1016/j.cmi.2020.04.042] [PMID: 32360779]

[19] Adam DC, Wu P, Wong JY, *et al.* Clustering and superspreading potential of SARS-CoV-2 infections in Hong Kong. Nat Med 2020; 26(11): 1714-9.
[http://dx.doi.org/10.1038/s41591-020-1092-0] [PMID: 32943787]

[20] Ghinai I, McPherson TD, Hunter JC, *et al.* First known person-to-person transmission of severe acute respiratory syndrome coronavirus 2 (SARS-CoV-2) in the USA. Lancet 2020; 395(10230): 1137-44.
[http://dx.doi.org/10.1016/S0140-6736(20)30607-3] [PMID: 32178768]

[21] Jin YH, Cai L, Cheng ZS, *et al.* A rapid advice guideline for the diagnosis and treatment of 2019 novel coronavirus (2019-nCoV) infected pneumonia (standard version). Mil Med Res 2020; 7(1): 4.
[http://dx.doi.org/10.1186/s40779-020-0233-6] [PMID: 32029004]

[22] Hindson J. COVID-19: faecal–oral transmission? Nat Rev Gastroenterol Hepatol 2020; 17(5): 259.
[http://dx.doi.org/10.1038/s41575-020-0295-7] [PMID: 32214231]

[23] Guo M, Tao W, Flavell RA, Zhu S. Potential intestinal infection and faecal–oral transmission of SARS-CoV-2. Nat Rev Gastroenterol Hepatol 2021; 18(4): 269-83.
[http://dx.doi.org/10.1038/s41575-021-00416-6] [PMID: 33589829]

[24] Abbas M, Robalo Nunes T, Martischang R, *et al.* Nosocomial transmission and outbreaks of coronavirus disease 2019: the need to protect both patients and healthcare workers. Antimicrob Resist Infect Control 2021; 10(1): 7.
[http://dx.doi.org/10.1186/s13756-020-00875-7] [PMID: 33407833]

[25] Du Q, Zhang D, Hu W, *et al.* Nosocomial infection of COVID-19: A new challenge for healthcare professionals (Review). Int J Mol Med 2021; 47(4): 31.
[http://dx.doi.org/10.3892/ijmm.2021.4864] [PMID: 33537803]

[26] Azuma K, Yanagi U, Kagi N, Kim H, Ogata M, Hayashi M. Environmental factors involved in SARS-

CoV-2 transmission: effect and role of indoor environmental quality in the strategy for COVID-19 infection control. Environ Health Prev Med 2020; 25(1): 66.
[http://dx.doi.org/10.1186/s12199-020-00904-2] [PMID: 33143660]

[27]   Kumar S, Singh R, Kumari N, *et al.* Current understanding of the influence of environmental factors on SARS-CoV-2 transmission, persistence, and infectivity. Environ Sci Pollut Res Int 2021; 28(6): 6267-88.
[http://dx.doi.org/10.1007/s11356-020-12165-1] [PMID: 33387315]

[28]   Carraturo F, Del Giudice C, Morelli M, *et al.* Persistence of SARS-CoV-2 in the environment and COVID-19 transmission risk from environmental matrices and surfaces. Environ Pollut 2020; 265(Pt B): 115010.
[http://dx.doi.org/10.1016/j.envpol.2020.115010] [PMID: 32570023]

[29]   Al Huraimel K, Alhosani M, Kunhabdulla S, Stietiya MH. SARS-CoV-2 in the environment: Modes of transmission, early detection and potential role of pollutions. Sci Total Environ 2020; 744: 140946.
[http://dx.doi.org/10.1016/j.scitotenv.2020.140946] [PMID: 32687997]

[30]   Rasmussen SA, Gerber SI, Swerdlow DL. Middle East respiratory syndrome coronavirus: update for clinicians. Clin Infect Dis 2015; 60(11): 1686-9.
[http://dx.doi.org/10.1093/cid/civ118] [PMID: 25701855]

CHAPTER 5

Symptoms and Diagnostic Techniques of COVID-19

Mohammad Sufian Badar[1,2,3,4,*], **Aamir Nehal**[5], **Barka Basharat**[6] and **Nushrat Jahan**[6]

[1] *Department of Bioengineering, University of California, Riverside, CA, USA*

[2] *Universal Scientific Education and Research Network (USERN), Tehran, Iran*

[3] *Director (Academic), SPI Darbhanga, India*

[4] *Department of Computer Science and Engineering (Bioinformatics), School of Engineering Sciences and Technology (SEST), Jamia Hamdard, New Delhi, India*

[5] *Consultant Physiotherapist, Bank Road, Motihari, Bihar, India*

[6] *Department of Biotechnology, Jamia Hamdard, New Delhi, India*

Abstract: COVID-19, an outbreak that has disrupted people's normal lives and lifestyles worldwide, has evolved to rank among the top few major causes of death. The virus spreads through direct and contact transmission and is thought to have a zoonotic origin. Fever, cough, and myalgia are symptoms of the symptomatic phase, which progresses to severe respiratory failure. It also includes pulmonary symptoms, which involve the severe acute respiratory syndrome coronavirus 2.

Human antibody detection, viral antigen detection, and viral gene detection are used as the foundation for the diagnostic tools developed thus far; however, viral gene detection via RT-PCR has proven to be the most reliable method. It is one of the more delicate approaches, which is also well-known for being highly advised for both qualitative and quantitative products. There is another sensitive method too that can precisely amplify a target nucleic acid known as loop-mediated isothermal amplification or LAMP.

On the other hand, amplification of nucleic acid tests is the test that identifies COVID-19, which works by identifying the RNA (ribonucleic acid) sequences responsible for generating the viral genetic material. Diagnostic systems based on CRISPR for COVID-19 have advantages like early screening (30 minutes from crude extract to result), sensitivity and accuracy, mobility, and the absence of specific laboratory equipment. Some other diagnostic techniques are CBNAAT and TruNAT, along with some other serological assays that use the ELISA KIT. Lateral flow immunoassay, Enzyme-linked immunosorbent assay, and chemiluminescence immunoassay (CLIA) are some of the other reliable diagnostic techniques.

---

* **Corresponding author Mohammad Sufian Badar:** Department of Bioengineering, University of California, Riverside, CA, USA: E-mail: sufianbadar@gmail.com

Keywords: Computed tomography, COVID-19, CBNAAT, CRISPR, CLIA, diagnostic techniques for COVID-19, iFlash assay, Isothermal amplification, Manifestations of COVID-19, RT-PCR, SARS-CoV-2, TruNat, Spike protein, (crRNA).

INTRODUCTION

COVID-19 cases are divided into three categories: mild, severe, and critical.

Critical patients experienced respiratory failure, acute cardiac injury, septicemia, and numerous organ failures whereas, serious patients displayed dyspnoea, increased respiration rate, and blood oxygen levels, whereas patients with mild symptoms developed mild pneumonia.

The emergence of new and evolving SARS-CoV-2 variants has increased the requirement for better, more flexible diagnostic techniques for the detection of SARS-CoV-2 infections. On the other hand, it is currently more difficult to develop quick and effective diagnostic technologies because of novel variations and the range of symptoms presented by infected individuals. At least 65 million people are expected to be affected by Long COVID, and the incidence is continuously increasing. Medical science has made tremendous progress in defining the illness, treating various physiological and pathological alterations and comorbidities, and showing its similarities to other colds and flu, such as postural orthostatic tachyarrhythmia disease and so forth. It also includes pulmonary symptoms, which involve the severe acute respiratory syndrome coronavirus 2. (SARS -CoV-2). Its other symptoms involve endocrinology manifestations along with neurological symptoms and olfactory dysfunction. As mentioned in Fig. (**1**), there are various diagnosis techniques which are useful for detecting the presence of a virus in a body. The virus can potentially enter the central nervous system of the human body and lead to primary and secondary encephalopathy. One typical symptom seen in COVID-19 patients is myalgia. Systemic inflammation and a cytokine storm have also been suggested as the pathophysiological underpinnings of myalgia.

Those who suffer from serious COVID-19 disease have elevated levels of lactate dehydrogenase and serum creatinine. Endothelial dysfunction, venous and arterial micro- and macrovascular problems, and stroke caused by SARS-CoV-2 can result from endothelial cell infection. It causes vasculitis and localized inflammation in the cerebral artery walls. Recently, post-mortem findings in the pulmonary, renal, heart, and colon following SARS-CoV-2 infection have revealed an inflammatory response and the death of endothelial cells. Pro-inflammatory cytokines collecting in the arterial endothelium may raise the blood-to-brain shield's permeability. It has been studied that COVID-19 patients who arrive with severe meningeal encephalitis do not exhibit SARS-CoV-2 or any other viral pathogens in their CSF. Hence, the absence of SARS-CoV-2-RNA in the CSF may suggest that factors that go beyond a direct serious infection, such as an altered nervous system and peri-infectious irritation, may be involved.

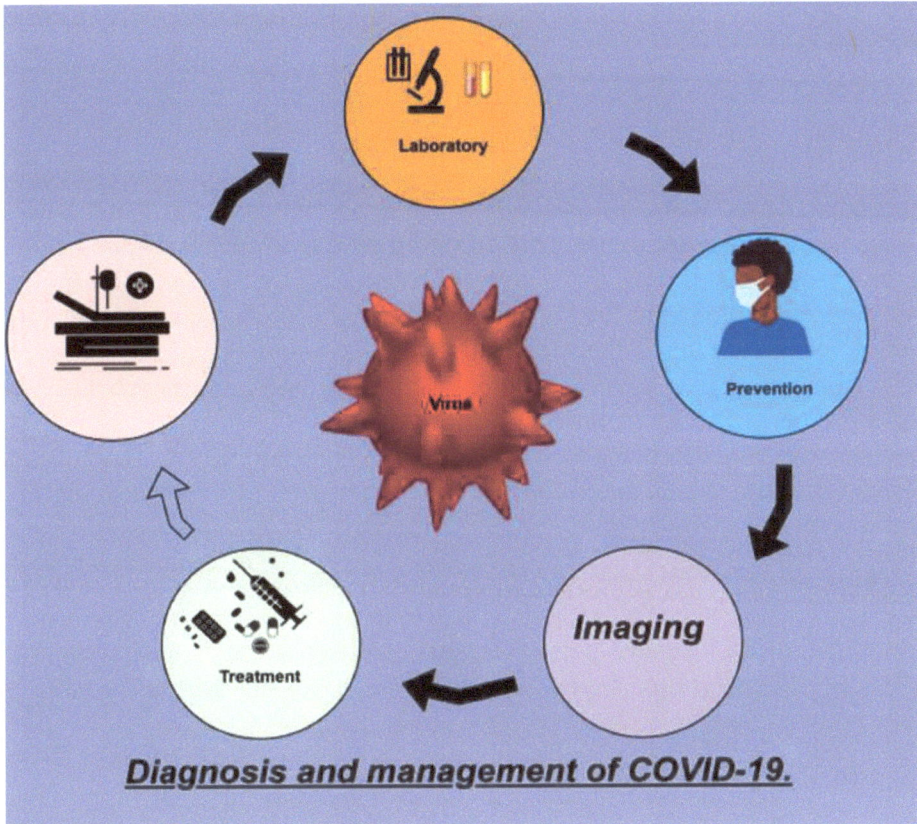

Fig. (1). Diagnosis and management of COVID-19.

In this review, we will focus mostly on the diagnostic methods of COVID-19 and manifestations. Several diagnostic methods have been demonstrated to be effective in identifying the illness; hence, we will focus on all methods that are efficient and regarded as the gold standard for the identification of COVID-19.

Asymptomatic Illness

A major issue has been COVID-19. Asymptomatic, mild, moderate, and critical symptoms have all been assigned to it. An asymptomatic illness exhibits no symptoms; according to a study, just one in five cases of illness exhibits signs.

COVID-19 symptoms are further divided into mild, moderate, and, in rare situations, severe and chronic illnesses. The moderate symptoms of COVID-19 are a temperature, a recent, persistent cough, and/or a decline in taste or smell.

Flu-like symptoms affect those who are only slightly ill. Examples of these include a dry cough and a mild temperature, but the fever may not reach above 37.8°C and there may occasionally be little to no coughing. You can have mood swings, and get melancholy [1].

Moderate Illness

If the lung edema worsens and lung problems like wheezing become more obvious, you can eventually advance to having a moderate case. One of the mild diseases is dyspepsia. The large airways, known as bronchi, the small ones, known as bronchioles, and the tiny air sacs, known as alveoli, at the end, where oxygen is extracted out of the air, make up the airways. They include a protein called surfactant, which gives the lungs flexibility and suppleness and helps to preserve the permeability of the air sacs. Moderate inflammation that COVID-19 individuals may experience may enter the bronchioles. They frequently experience increased exhaustion and a quicker heartbeat when moving around, particularly [2].

Severe Illness

Pneumonia indicates that a person is suffering from the severe symptoms of COVID 19 . Their oxygen levels may have fallen so the urge to breathe faster. Patients with severe COVID are very breathless [3].

Critical Illness

A phenomenon known as ARDS (acute respiratory distress syndrome) can appear in patients with severe infections. As a result of the virus, the little air sacs that line the lungs become so filled with inflammation that they often tend to close, and the amount of inflammation liquid in the alveoli prevents surfactant from working.

People who are at risk are generally those over-65s or people with medical conditions withaffected immune systems [4].

Other Symptoms

Endocrinology Manifestations.

Since COVID-19 first appeared, endocrinological relevance has been speculated about for many endocrine organs that are susceptible to COVID-19. The basic pathophysiological processes underlying endocrine malfunction in:

(1) Direct viral damage.

(2) Endothelial dysfunction is secondary to SARS-CoV-2-induced endothelitis.

(3) Immune-mediated organ damage brought on by cytokine release that is out of control.

(4) Deregulation of the Renin-Angiotensin-Aldosterone System (RAAS).

The two thyroid disorders that develop most frequently are subacute thyroiditis (SAT) and non-thyroidal sickness syndromes (NTIS). The involvement of the adrenal glands in COVID-19-related adrenal infarction and adrenal vein thrombosis may lead to adrenal insufficiency (AI). Acute diabetes, diabetic ketoacidosis (DKA), necrotizing pancreatitis, and impaired glucose tolerance have all been shown to affect the pancreas.

The gonads have been known to experience orchitis, epididymitis, epididymal-orchitis, necrotizing orchitis, gonadal vein thrombosis, changed semen parameters, and spermatogenesis. Prolactin, growth hormone (GH), and the hormones of the hypothalamus-pituitary axis (HP) can all be produced in a variety of ways. Additional COVID-19 HP-related adverse effects include hypophysitis, insufficient antidiuretic hormone secretion, central diabetes insipid us (CDI), and pituitary apoplexy [5].

Neurological Symptoms

Important and typical neurological symptoms, such as headache, myalgia, altered mental state, disorientation, delirium, and dizziness, are addressed in distinct sections. Seizures, meningoencephalitis, Guillain-Barré syndrome, Miller-Fisher syndrome, acute myelitis, and posterior reversible encephalopathy syndrome (PRES) are among the neurological signs and consequences that are addressed methodically.

The central nervous system (CNS), the peripheral nervous system (PNS), and the musculoskeletal system are the three separate systems that might be affected by neurological symptoms and manifestations [5]. The potential mechanisms of action causing COVID-19's neurological manifestations are described in several theories. SARS-CoV-2 appears to have two distinct pathways for entering the brain and causing damage: widespread hematogenous spread and neuronal retrograde dissemination.

Further study that examines the impact of neurological symptoms and manifestations on the disease's course is necessary to better comprehend and assess the association between neurological problems and the clinical outcome of COVID-19 patients. There are various symptoms that can be helpful in the diagnosis of the onset of COVID-19; some of them are present in Fig. (**2**). To prevent long-term repercussions, healthcare professionals must be able to identify potential neurological indications early and be aware of the neurological disorders and signs of COVID-19, which are becoming more prevalent [5].

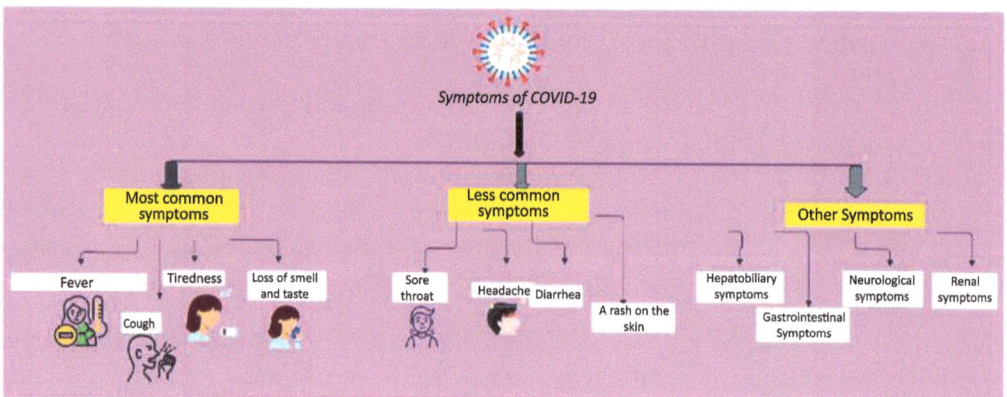

Fig. (2). Various symptoms of COVID-19.

Olfactory and Gustatory Dysfunction

A disorder of the olfactory and gustatory systems that affect the taste and smell (hyposmia/anosmia) and, smelling anomalies, which appear to emerge in the early stages of the illness and are therefore believed to be valuable diagnostic indications, are the most frequent sudden neurological manifestations of COVID-19 associated with PNS involvement.

SARS-CoV-2 cannot infect olfactory sensory neurons because these cells do not need to express ACE 2. This is based on early findings. Nonetheless, SARS-Co--2 invasion can occur because olfactory epithelium cells do express ACE 2. Injuries to the olfactory epithelium, not neuronal impairment, seem to be the root of anosmia [5].

Altered Mental Status/confusion/delirium

According to a case series from England, COVID-19 can have only one clinical sign without obvious pulmonary signs, which is severe disorientation or dementia.

The potential of SARS-CoV-2 to enter the CNS effectively through the incursion of the olfactory epithelium and secondary system-wide processes like inflammatory cytokines, hypoxia, and oxidative stress brought on by ARDS (acute respiratory distress syndrome) are among the primary neuro-invasive theories. They cause, alternately, both primary and secondary encephalopathy [5].

Myalgia

One typical symptom seen in COVID-19 patients is myalgia. Systemic inflammation and a cytokine storm have been suggested as the pathophysiological underpinnings of myalgia. It is currently unknown whether the muscle manifestation of COVID-19 is brought on by a generalized inflammatory process or a particular muscle invasion. Those who have serious COVID-19 disease have elevated levels of lactate dehydrogenase and serum creatinine.

According to some research, headaches are the most prevalent non-specific neurological complaint. The prevalence of headaches varies depending on how many instances were included in the study.

Cerebrovascular Diseases

Stroke

Endothelial dysfunction, venous and arterial micro- and macrovascular problems, and stroke can occur from endothelial cell infection. It causes a vasculitic process and localized inflammation in the cerebral artery walls. Recently, post-mortem findings in the pulmonary, renal, heart, and colon following SARS-CoV-2 infection have revealed an inflammatory response and the death of endothelial cells. Pro-inflammatory cytokines collecting in the arterial endothelium may raise the blood-to-brain shield's permeability.

It is thought that viral diseases trigger and start platelet aggregation and that there are intricate interactions between agglutination, blood clotting, and inflammation. Septicaemia, specifically caused by COVID-19, is characterized by prolonged prothrombin time, increased D-dimer values, and neutropenia despite hypofibrinogenemia [6].

Cerebral Venous (sinus) Thrombosis

This neurological action or event may happen to patients without even any prior risk factors for cerebral venous thrombosis, owing to the pro-thrombotic condition brought on by COVID-19. Early signs could consist of worsening pain, vision issues, swelling of the face, neurological symptoms such as impairments, reduced awareness, and seizures, which are all indications of elevated intracranial pressure (ICP). Haemorrhagic venous infarction with significant regions of necrosis can potentially make the identification of severe cerebral vein thrombus more challenging.

Encephalitis, Meninges-encephalitis, and Meningitis

This neurological sequel may occur in patients without any prior risk factors for cerebral venous thrombosis due to the pro-thrombotic condition induced by COVID-19 problems. The results of several case studies on COVID-19 patients point to meningitis and encephalitis.

Patients with COVID-19 can complain at first of a headache, fever, and a recent onset tremor. SARS-CoV-2 was discovered in the CSF of several COVID-19 patients, proving that the virus is to blame for this neurological symptom. It has additionally been noted that COVID-19 patients who arrive with severe meninges-encephalitis do not exhibit SARS-CoV-2 or any other viral pathogens in their CSF. Hence, the absence of SARS-CoV-2-RNA in the CSF may suggest that factors that go beyond a direct serious infection, such as an altered nervous system and peri-infectious irritation, may be involved in individuals with COVID-19 may have lymphocytic pleocytosis in their CSF.

Acute Myelitis

Throughout the continuing COVID-19 epidemic, there have been multiple reports of patients with transverse myelitis. Myelitis may first manifest as paresthesia and hypoesthesia in the feet that spread to the abdominal area. Total anesthesia below a particular spinal cord level can cause paralysis in the legs and feet that can quickly progress to paraplegia and finally sphincter dysfunction.

Gastrointestinal Manifestations

The cytoplasm of the stomach, duodenal, and rectal epithelium stained positively for the viral nucleocapsid protein upon histopathological analysis of the endoscopic samples. In the lamina propria of the stomach, duodenum, and rectum, there were many invading plasma

cells and lymphocytes with interstitial edema. A patient with mesenteric ischemia was hospitalized, and a small bowel hematological investigation revealed significant endothelial damage in the sub-mucosal arteries and apoptotic bodies.

In addition to coming before the normal respiratory symptoms, COVID-19 gastrointestinal symptoms may show up alone. It is interesting to note that the first COVID-19 case to be diagnosed in the US originally experienced gastrointestinal symptoms including severe diarrhea before experiencing respiratory issues [7].

Myocardial Symptoms

Patients recovering from the SARS-CoV-2 virus [1 - 3] and post-acute sequels of COVID-19 (PASC) [2] have reported persistent symptoms. At short- and long-term follow-up, acute COVID-19 infection is linked with multi-organ sequels, including pulmonary and cardiac, especially in those with serious disease. There is a higher-than-anticipated burden of myocarditis in our sample of recovered patients, handled in the community for initial COVID-19 infection and complaining of persisting symptoms, as evidenced by the existence of scar on LGE imaging by twelve months.

At the 12- to 16-week follow-up, complete lung function testing, and arterial blood gas analyses were completed. At 8 months following the COVID-19 infection, all patients underwent non-contrast computed tomography (CT) of the chest and histology for high-sensitivity troponin-I (hsTrI), C-reactive protein (CRP), and inflammatory cytokines [6].

Acute harm to the cardiac, pulmonary, and endothelial cells may be caused by the combination of SARS-CoV-2 with ACE2. A limited number of case reports have suggested that SARS-CoV2 may cause viral myocarditis by actively infecting the myocardium. Nevertheless, it has been found that in the majority of instances, the myocardial injury was brought on by a rise in the cardio-metabolic system caused by systemic infection and persistent hypoxia brought on by pulmonary disease, or ARDS [8].

Renal Manifestations

Since it contains all of the RAAS`s constituent parts, including renin, ACE, Ang II, and AT- 1 and AT2 receptors (AT1R and AT2R), the renal serves as both the source of RAAS and its destination organ [2]. As one of the organs with the highest concentrations of ACE2, the renal is also expressed primarily in the brush border of the proximal tubular cells and, to a lesser extent, in podocytes and vascular endothelial cells, whereas it is absent from glomerular endothelium and mesangial cells [9].

For example, unilateral ureteral obstruction and ischemia/reperfusion injury types of renal impairment with MasR loss reduced renal damage, but an infusion of Ang (1–7) to wild-type animals accentuated the pathological outcome by escalating the inflammatory reactions.

With an aim for novel treatment interventions in a wide range of kidney disorders, this axis should be emphasized because these findings are at odds with the majority of research results, which report positive effects of ACE2/Ang

(1–7)/MasR in assessing the balancing act between the intra renal impacts of angiotensin II and angiotensin (1-7) [10]. There is not a specific pharmaceutical remedy for COVID-19 at the moment. Thankfully, the bulk of infected patients generally exhibit minimal symptoms, and they are just given psychosocial support.

Hepatobiliary Manifestations

In 21-53% of COVID-19 patients, hepatobiliary symptoms of the disease have been documented [4 - 6]. The most often clinical signs were elevated levels of bilirubin, alanine aminotransferase (ALT), and aspartate aminotransferase (AST) [11]. COVID-19 commonly exhibits hepatic impairment, as shown by aberrant laboratory testing.

Furthermore, described histological abnormalities include lobular and portal inflammation. The majority of COVID-19-related liver dysfunction cases are minor and temporary, however, in a small subset of patients, a higher level of malfunction and liver enzyme metabolic derangement can be found. AST elevations are also more common than ALT, which is in contrast to the typical pattern of viral-induced liver injury [12].

There are many possible explanations for COVID-19-associated hepatic dysfunction. SARS-CoV-2 can directly infect hepatocytes and cholangiocytes, which also harbor the virus-specific ACE2 receptors [7]. A liver biopsy on the autopsy of COVID-19 patients shows microvesicular steatosis as well as lobular and portal inflammation [13].

In contrast to the pattern of liver damage often seen in viral hepatitis, AST rise is more frequently observed than ALT elevation. When zone 3 hepatocytes are involved in toxic and ischemic hepatotoxicity, preferential AST increases are more frequently observed. This conclusion is further supported by a greater prevalence of LFT anomalies in severe COVID-19 instances [14].

Diagnostic Techniques for COVID-19

Computed Tomography

Chest computed tomography (CT) is the foremost live imaging approach to analyze pneumonia-related maladies. It has been widely used previously for the detection of lung oddities in SARS and MERS [15]. The usage of CT scan images in straining for COVID-19 is important as diffuse ground glass-type opacities and nodules usually appear in the early stage of lung infections. Many results have been found to save more lives by using this technique, as it gives effective results.

It has also been found that the accuracy and effectiveness are far higher in CT scans than in other techniques. Ground-glass opacities (GGO), unification, and nodules exist as the main oddities that emerge after the manifestation outset in patients affected by COVID-19. So these oddities can easily be observed by using CT scans or deep learning techniques. CT scans are found to be more useful even in asymptomatic conditions because deep findings can scan lung abnormalities [16].

In recent studies, it has been found that CT scans may give false reports as the results might overlap with other symptoms like influenza, SARS, and MERS. So the health board newly led out chest CT scan as a criterion for analyzing suspected COVID-19 cases. Moreover, the combined usage of chest CT scans and RT-PCR strategies can confound the diagnosis [15].

Nucleic Acid Amplification Test

By identifying the RNA (ribonucleic acid) sequences responsible for generating the viral genetic material, nucleic acid tests identify COVID-19 [17].

It is also regarded as among the most effective methods for finding COVID-19. It is among the most accurate tests and can aid in the early detection of viral infection because viremia is typically seen in the beginning stages of the illness. The COVID-19 infectious gene is detected using the NAAT method by amplifying the specific genome and creating numerous copies of it. This detection technique is quite accurate and can examine even the short strand of the viral gene. NAAT is capable of utilizing a wide range of methodologies, such as RT-PCR, LAMP (loop-mediated isothermal amplification), and CRISPR (Clustered regularly interspaced short palindromic repeats) [16].

REVERSE TRANSCRIPTASE REAL-TIME POLYMERASE CHAIN REACTION (RT-QPCR)

One of the delicate approaches is PCR, which is also well-known for being highly advised for both qualitative and quantitative products. In essence, RT-PCR is a refinement of the PCR method that is proven to target the RNA responsible for the disease [18].

RT-PCR is regarded as among the best methods for analyzing COVID-19. The hallmarks of RT-qPCR experiments included the (RNA-dependent RNA polymerase (RdRp) RdRp, nucleocapsid (N), spike, envelope (E), and other genes. Given the likely dynamics of SARS-CoV-2 infection, it is not at all unexpected that RT-PCR testing in patients with SARS-CoV-2 infection, particularly in those who would later develop blatant COVID-19, may initially be negative. It is therefore not remarkable that at least 2 grey areas could be recognized, potentially afflicted by false SARS-CoV-2 negativity due to the low infection rates, especially in symptomless or moderately symptomatic patients, when combining this observational study's evidence with the analytical sensitivity of the currently used RT-PCR assays [19]. It would be tiresome and time-consuming to look through for further information given the ongoing introduction of probable cases all over the globe [19].

Although recognized by the CDC and WHO as the gold standard test for the confirmation of COVID-19 and having a moderate sensitivity and high specificity, this approach has produced a significant number of erroneous negative results that should be carefully addressed [19]. By concentrating on a region of the viral RNA genome that can recognize the virus at incredibly low quantities, this is easily preventable. An RT-PCR test uses extremely complex procedures, and the results are obtained in around 1-2 days. For RT-PCR experiments, modern amenities with BSL-2 form and properly educated staff are also necessary [20]. The test has a high degree of specificity and sensitivity, but it can still give patients who are symptomatic or have a positive CT scan incorrect negative results [20]. The effectiveness of the viral RNA has a major effect on the outcomes of RT-qPCR, and the test must occasionally be repeated multiple times for additional confirmation.

REVERSE TRANSCRIPTION LOOP-MEDIATED ISOTHERMAL AMPLIFICATION (RT-LAMP)

Loop-mediated isothermal amplification, or LAMP, is a sensitive method that can swiftly and precisely amplify a target nucleic acid. The LAMP response process amplifies DNA by the reverse transcriptase activity of the Bacillus stearothermophilus (BST) DNA polymerase in an isothermal environment rather than through a denaturation stage. Three sets of forward and reverse oligonucleotide primers are used, each one specific to one of six target gene series [15].

The efficient DNA amplification approach known as "loop-mediated isothermal amplification" (LAMP) has been used to identify viruses and other pathogens. The target DNA could be expanded in 30 minutes using the LAMP reaction, which usually occurs at a steady temperature. The specificity of the LAMP technique, which uses four or six primers to bind six sections of target DNA, is quite high. We created four sets of LAMP primers, designated as O117, N15, and N1, S17, which, target the RNA encoding Orf1ab, spike glycoprotein, and two sections of the SARS-CoV2 nucleocapsid protein, respectively.

For the quick (30–40 min) identification of SARS-CoV-2 in clinical specimens with a limit of detection of 10 copies per microliter, a combination of RT-LAMP and CRISPR-based Sensor technology was also created [15].

Yet, the RT-LAMP technique does not call for highly trained workers or expensive machinery. To make the most of the method, it is crucial to search for several SARS-CoV-2 targets. As the virus`s primers attachment region alterations will also impact the precision of RT-LAMP.

CRISPR-BASED DIAGNOSIS

Guide RNA is needed for CRISPR, which attaches to the complementary strand of the recipient and dissociates at the exact location. Biosensing nucleic acids from various pathogens, such as bacteria and viruses, is performed using CRISPR components. In the science realm, clustered regularly interspaced short palindromic repeats have become renowned as a tool for genome editing, but they are now slowly beginning to show promise for use in medical diagnostics.

The CRISPR-based detection technique for SARS-CoV-2 detection has been tried out by numerous researchers. For illustration, a work by Zhang et al. (2020b) combined a CRISPR-based detection approach (SHERLOCK) with isothermal recombinase polymerase amplification (RPA) to identify a single component per milliliter in less than an hour (Zhang et al. 2020a). The initial CRISPR product on the market with FDA approval was this Sherlock Biosciences assay. Mammoth Biosciences, a different CRISPR-based diagnostics business, used RT-LAMP with a CRISPR-cas12-based method to detect 10–100 copies of viral RNA per µl in 40 minutes. The severe acute respiratory membrane gene is the target of this procedure, and the outcomes can be examined using the lateral flow method or fluorescence [15].

A naturally occurring genome editing system that bacteria deploy as an immunological response is the basis for CRISPR-Cas9. Bacteria that are virus-infected seize tiny bits of the virus's DNA and splice it onto their DNA in a specific pattern to form sections known as CRISPR arrays. The bacteria can understand the viruses thanks to the CRISPR arrays (or closely related ones). In the event of a subsequent virus attack, the bacteria create RNA segments from CRISPR arrays that can recognize and bind to particular sections of the viral DNA. The virus is then rendered inoperable by the bacteria's employment of Cas9 or a related enzyme to split the DNA [21].

Since December 2019, the coronavirus illness 2019 (COVID-19) has affected more than 88 million individuals worldwide and killed close to 2 million people, caused by the severe acute respiratory Disorder coronavirus 2 (SARS-CoV-2).

Type V and Type VI CRISPR enzymes are DNA- and RNA-targeting, RNA-guided effectors that enable targeted gene silencing. The CRISPR proteins Cas12 and Cas13 are effective tools for identifying and thwarting single-stranded RNA (ssRNA) viruses. By focusing on RNAs that complement the CRISPR RNA, the fully programmable nature of these proteins paves the path for the identification and destruction of RNA viruses (crRNA). SsRNA genomes are present in almost two-thirds of viruses that cause illness. Such methods include CRISPR-Cas-based identification and digital PCR, many of which are pending medical certification from competent authorities [22].

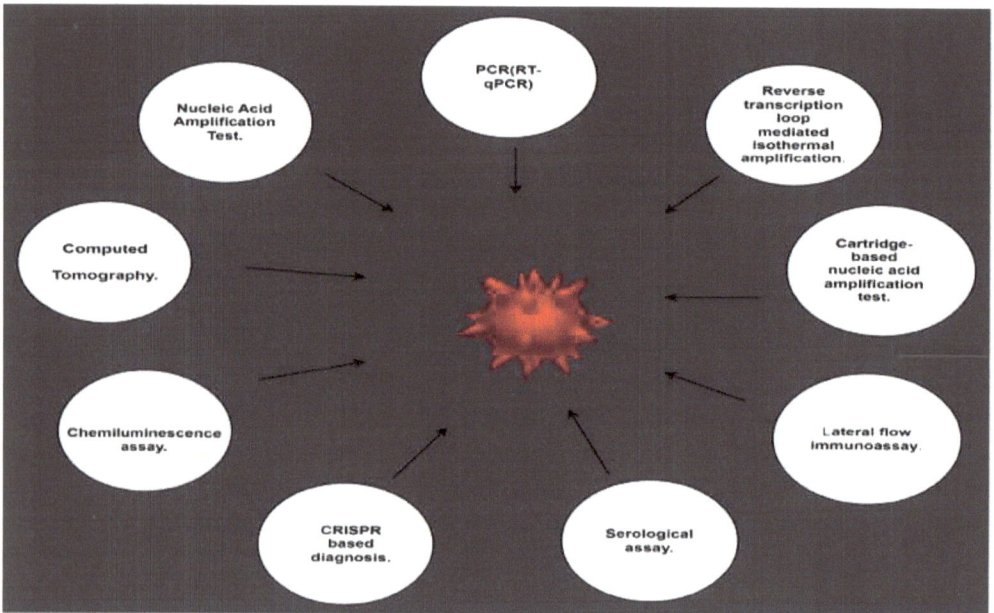

Fig. (3). Diagnostic techniques of COVID-19.

This study highlights the rapidly growing range of current and future diagnostic techniques/tests that may be utilized to determine SARS-CoV-2 infection in both clinical and academic contexts [23].

Diagnostic systems based on CRISPR for COVID-19 have advantages like early screening (30 minutes from crude extract to result), sensitivity and accuracy, mobility, and the absence of specific laboratory equipment. Here, we cover recent research on COVID-19 detection using CRISPR technology. The creation of CRISPR-based diagnostic technologies has changed molecular diagnostics. CRISPR stands for clustered regularly interspaced short palindromic repeats.

Scientists have been motivated to create CRISPR-based diagnostics because of the advantages of CRISPR, such as its quickness, precision, selectivity, power, effectiveness, and adaptability [24].

It is crucial to realize juncture diagnostics and CRISPR/Cas-based detection methods have the ability to become easier, more dependable, more inexpensive, and speedier in the near term. There are various methods to diagnose the COVID-19 like, PCR, nucleic acid amplification, and computed tomography as mentioned in Fig. (**3**). It can be used to identify any infection, virus, or fungus that could endanger people, farming, and the food industry in environments with few resources [25].

CARTRIDGE-BASED NUCLEIC ACID AMPLIFICATION TEST (CBNAAT)

The laboratories receive the nasopharyngeal/oropharyngeal swabs in a viral dispersing agent after they are collected at specimen collection centers. The samples go via CBNAAT. N2 and E gene detection is done by real-time polymerase chain reaction with Xpert Xpress SARS-Cov-2 (rt-PCR). The samples that were deemed positive have independent ct values for the detection of the N2 and E genes.

The number of primers needed for a PCR product's fluorescence to be detected crossing a threshold that exceeds the signal is known as the Ct value. Positive results are reported for samples with a ct value between 12 and 45. The viral load is assessed by Ct values, which are classified as high [22], medium (25.1–32), or low (32) when standard categories for samples exposed to CBNAAT are not accessible. Repeated CBNAAT/Rt-PCR was carried out on the specimens that amplified only one gene rather than both (indicating a guarantee of success) to verify the prognosis [4].

TRUNAT

A local testing phase TruNat, which was first developed for tuberculosis testing, has been studied and is presently used for COVID-19 testing in India. The sensor real-time PCR assay known as the TruNat beta COVID-19 test has a comparatively short test period of only one hour.

The Truelab workstation (Molbio Diagnostics, India) comprises parts for a reusable kit, a method for the extraction of RNA, RT-PCR equipment, and sample processing. It is a mobile, rechargeable, totally automated, real-time quantitative PCR machine that weighs approximately 3 kilos. This system has network data transmission capabilities and automatic reporting, and it may be used in remote areas. The benefit of TruNAT is that the virus is lysed during testing, reducing the possibility of contamination and transmission [4].

The TruNat test is a two-step, quasi-real-time PCR assay. An E-gene screening assay is the first step. It is proper to treat all negatives as real negatives. Step-2 RdRp gene confirmation assays ought to be employed to confirm any positive cases. By this assay, every data point that tests positive is regarded as a true positive. For samples that are positive following Step 2 of the TruNat assay, additional RT-PCR-based confirmation is not necessary, a thorough assay is conducted for testing and confirming.

To develop the TruNAT test for COVID-19 identification, state health authorities have been-collaborating with the National Tuberculosis Elimination Project (NTEP). Particularly, in places without access to sophisticated facilities, the TruNAT test is beneficial. In collaboration with the DST, ICAR, CSIR, DBT, DRDOL, and so on, the ICMR has expanded the number of COVID-19 testing facilities [4].

SEROLOGICAL ASSAYS

While the system is combating an illness like COVID-19, antibodies in the blood can be found.-The most effective form of antibody for identifying a current illness is IgM, one of the earliest-types to be generated. In the early stages of an illness, when the body's adaptive immune-the response is still developing, antibodies may not be detectable.-IgM antibodies against SARS-CoV-2 have been found to be present for 7 to 10 days following-the first appearance of symptoms. As a result, SARS-CoV-2 infections are not solely-diagnosed or ruled out via serology-based antibody screening. Yet, by assisting medical-practitioners in identifying patients who have an adaptive immune response to SARS-CoV-2,-antibody testing may contribute to the fight against COVID-19.-Also, the findings of these tests can be used to locate people who might donate-convalescent plasma, which might be used to treat COVID-19 patients who are very ill. Rapid-antibody testing is advised by the ICMR for use as a surveillance technique for diagnostic-purposes in critical areas and in similar locations where infections haven't yet surfaced. Theanti-SARS-CoV-2 human IgG ELISA test kit was effectively built and tested by ICMR-NIV for-the screening of COVID-19 antibodies.

In validation, the IgG ELISA kit's accuracy and specificity were determined to be 98.7% and 100%, respectively. In comparison to the real-time RT-PCR test, the ELISA test has the benefit of analyzing 90 samples simultaneously in a single session of a little over two hours. It also has less stringent biocompatibility and security criteria. It has been suggested that the IgG ELISA test could be employed to monitor the populations susceptible to SARS-CoV-2 coronavirus illness [18].

LATERAL FLOW IMMUNOASSAY

The material to be studied is poured on a test instrument, and the findings are shown within 5 to 15 minutes. This analysis operates on the theory of antigen-antibody responses [15].

Since they may swiftly identify new COVID-19 infections by examining particular SARS-like CoV-2 biomarkers, such as nucleic acids, antibodies, and antigens, LFA-based fast medical diagnostics have lately gained significant attention for halting the transmission and preventing a comeback of COVID-19 [26].

LFA coupled with RT-PCR amplification, LFA incorporated with isothermal amplification, LFA integrated with isothermal amplification and CRISPR, enhanced LFA by signalling amplification techniques, and other lateral flow Immunoassays are examples of lateral-flow assay methods for the identification of COVID-19.

Due to the low positive frequencies of molecular techniques, it is proven difficult to confirm the diagnosis of SARS-CoV-2 infections. Finding certain antibodies in the blood is a complementary test to the viral nucleic acid screening for SARS-CoV-2 infection. The immune system generates antibodies as a defense against the SARS-CoV-2 infection. Immune System response maturation often takes a while and is then followed by dynamic fluctuations in antibody levels.

IgA, IgM, and IgG are only a few of the unique immune globulins that are created in response to SARS-CoV-2 during this process, and they all appear and disappear at distinct times. So, in theory, COVID-19 can be diagnosed by targeting one or all immune globulins. This testing approach required the addition of 5–20 liters of serum to the sample well and 80–100 l of the product's buffer to an adjoining well, accompanied by an incubation time of 15 minutes. At room temperature, the outcome was determined by the presence of colored bands, which were labeled as authentic, illegitimate, or positive (control and test bands present)(no band, an absent control band, or a band in the wrong place).

The immediate visual evaluation of nucleic acid amplification data is possible with LFA. Recent advancements in sophisticated nucleic acid amplification-assisted LFA approaches for identifying viral RNA for SARS-CoV-2 have already been made possible by their major benefits of mobility, speed, economic viability, and user acceptance [26].

ENZYME-LINKED IMMUNOSORBENT ASSAY

To identify blood antibodies against SARS-CoV-2 in coronavirus illness victims in 2019 and assess the pattern of variations in antibodies, an enzyme-linked immunosorbent assay (ELISA) was developed by wrapping SARS-CoV-2 recombinant spike proteins [27]. Recombinant COVID-19 antigen that has been HRP-labeled will be used to detect the immunocomplex of "anti-hIgM" antibodies and COVID-19 IgM antibodies. The specificity and sensitivity of ELISA are good. Samples are put on a microtiter plate that has been pre-coated with antibodies against human IgM in this assay. Recombinant COVID-19 antigen that has been HRP-labeled will be used to identify the immune complex of the "anti-h IgM" antibody and COVID-19 IgM antibody.

IgM ELISA kit uses the "IgM detect" technique on microplate plate-based ELISA for the representative value of the COVID-19 IgM antibody in the serum samples, whereas the IgG ELISA kit uses an ELISA plate encased in SARS-CoV-2 recombinant nucleo-capsid protein to identify the presence of human IgG against SARS-CoV-2 in the test sample. It has been demonstrated that ELISA has a high level of specificity and sensitivity for identifying SARS-CoV-2 infections. There are just a few additional ELISA kits in addition to those described above that may be purchased by the industry to diagnose SARS-CoV-2 disease by evaluating IgM and IgG antibodies [15].

CHEMILUMINESCENCE IMMUNOASSAY (CLIA)

Chemiluminescence Immunoassay for Testing SARS-CoV-2 Specific Antibody

The Chinese Food and Drug Administration-approved iFlash immunoassay analyzer (Shenzhen Yhlo Biotech Co., Ltd., Shenzhen, China) and the iFlash-SARS-CoV-2 IgM sensing kit (Shenzhen Yhlo Biotech Co., Ltd., Shenzhen, China) were used to evaluate serum IgM immunoglobulin against the SARS CoV-2 N and spike proteins (cFDA).

It was a two-alternative immunoassay. To begin, SARS-CoV-2 IgM in the bloodstream binds to SARS-CoV-2 N and spikes proteins wrapped in paramagnetic micro particles to form a complex. After cleaning the unbound components in the magnetic field, an acridinium-labeled anti-human IgMA conjugated was placed for additional reactions to produce a new complex. Finally, following another wash, the pre-trigger and trigger solutions were added to the reaction mixture. It was an immunoassay with two alternatives. Initially, a complex is formed when the specific SARS-coCoV-2 IgM in the blood binds to the SARS-CoV-2 N and spikes proteins enclosed in paramagnetic tiny particles.

To create a novel complex, acridinium-labeled anti-human IgM conjugates were added after the elements had been released from their magnetic bonds. The pre-trigger and trigger solutions have now been incorporated into the reaction mixture after a second rinsing.

The Chinese Food and Drug Administration-approved iFlash-SARS-CoV-2 IgG detection kit (Shenzhen Yhlo Biotech Co., Ltd, Shenzhen, China) was used to measure serum IgG antibodies against the SARS-CoV-2 N and spike protein (FDA). IgG followed a similar theory and process as IgM. The manufacturer's recommended lower limit is 10 AU/ml [28].

Chemiluminescence Immunoassay for Testing Serum SARS-CoV-2 N Antigen

A two-antibody sandwich chemiluminescence immunoassay was used by the iFlash assay device to assess the amount of serum SARS-CoV-2 N protein antigen (Shenzhen Yhlo Biotech Co., Ltd., Shenzhen, China). After being cross-linked by N-ethyl-N'-(3-dimethylamino propyl) carbodiimide (Thermo Scientific) for the N protein antigen acquisition as described earlier, paramagnetic carboxylated microparticles (Thermo Scientific) were coated with one of 10 candidate-specific antibodies (Shenzhen YHLO Biotech Co., Ltd., Shenzhen, China).

To detect antigens, additional antibodies were conjugated with NSP-DMAE-NHS (Maxchemtech). The calibrators were recombinant SARS-CoV-2 nucleocapsid proteins (Shenzhen). YHLO Biotech) mixed in healthy serum samples. Following calibration, tests may be conducted. Paramagnetic carboxylated microparticles that were coated with the capture antibody in the tests gathered N-protein antigens. After removing the unbound material, the acridinium-labeled antibody interacted with the antibody-N protein antigen and captured antibody complexes. Under the influence of the magnetic field, the mixture remained in a tube. After that, pre-trigger and trigger solutions were added, and a 2-point calibration curve was used to determine the N protein antigen according to the obtained relative light units (RLUs) [28].

DISCUSSION

In young, otherwise healthy adults with COVID-19, persistent symptoms had no significant impact on markers of cardiac autonomic function (*i.e.*, HRV and cardiac BRS). Although there are several factors contributing to the heightened heart disease risk after COVID-19, we would argue that among young persons of college age, impaired cardiac function functioning is not a concern.

In this chapter, we have looked at various diagnostic methods for finding COVID-19 as well as how well they work for finding particular strains. Also, it should be highlighted that some diagnostic techniques detect illness by identifying gene alterations that could contribute to the development of COVID-19.

When it comes to asymptomatic illness, diagnostic procedures work wonders since they can identify genetic abnormalities and play a variety of roles in controlling the broad disease by providing information at the time of disease onset.

It became clear that precise and speedy diagnostic assays along with the development and testing of immunodiagnostic assays and other molecular strategies were required. Several recently created point-of-care molecular diagnostics are anticipated to be useful in pandemic management because they do not call for specialized operator expertise. Luckily, the US FDA has authorized the use of several serological tests for the identification of SARS-CoV-2 in an emergency circumstance.

CONCLUSION

COVID-19 signs and testing methods play a vital role in diagnosing and preventing the transmission of this extremely contagious viral disease. A broad range of indications related to COVID-19, from moderate to serious, highlight the disease's intricacy and ability to damage several systems of organs. Recognizing prevalent signs like coughing, fever, and other less prevalent signs such as loss of sensations of taste or smell, is critical for prompt discovery and treatment.

Since the beginning of the global epidemic, the testing methods for COVID-19 have changed dramatically. Initially reliant on experimental testing such as RT-PCR, technological developments have resulted in the introduction of quick antigen tests and serological assays which offer faster results and aid in mass screening initiatives. In extreme cases, imaging methods such as chest X-rays and CT scans have also been useful in determining the level of lung invasion.

WHAT YOU WILL LEARN

• A thorough understanding of COVID-19. A comprehensive knowledge of this disease's transmission and a concise explanation of its clinical symptoms.

• In-depth information on COVID-19 symptoms such as endocrinology, renal manifestations, gastrointestinal manifestations, hepatobiliary manifestations, and many more.

• In this review, we will focus mostly on the diagnostic methods of COVID-19 and its manifestations. Several diagnostic methods have been demonstrated to be effective in identifying the illness; hence, we will focus on all methods that are efficient and regarded as the gold standard for the identification of COVID-19.

• As asymptomatic patients are a constant source of worry when it comes to communicable diseases, we will also look more closely at the diagnostic methods for COVID-19, as there are numerous ways and assays to obtain accurate results, and these methods are frequently used in identifying the strains of Covid 19.

REFERENCES

[1]   Pollock AM, Lancaster J. Asymptomatic transmission of covid-19. BMJ 2020; 371: m4851.
        [http://dx.doi.org/10.1136/bmj.m4851]

[2]   https://www.frontiersin.org/journals/public-health/articles/10.3389/fpubh.2022.925492/full

[3]   https://patient.info/news-and-features/coronavirus-what-are-moderate-severe-and-critical-covid-19

[4]   Kumar KSR, Mufti SS, Sarathy V, Hazarika D, Naik R. An Update on Advances in COVID-19 Laboratory Diagnosis and Testing Guidelines in India. Front Public Health 2021; 9: 568603.
        [http://dx.doi.org/10.3389/fpubh.2021.568603] [PMID: 33748054]

[5]   Cha MH, Regueiro M, Sandhu DS. Gastrointestinal and hepatic manifestations of COVID-19: A comprehensive review. World J Gastroenterol 2020; 26(19): 2323-31.
        [http://dx.doi.org/10.3748/wjg.v26.i19.2323] [PMID: 32476796]

[6]   Krishnan A, Ellenberger KA, Phetsouphanh C, *et al*. Myocardial fibrosis occurs in non-hospitalised patients with chronic symptoms after COVID-19. Int J Cardiol Heart Vasc 2022; 39: 100964.
        [http://dx.doi.org/10.1016/j.ijcha.2022.100964] [PMID: 35097185]

[7]   https://www.wjgnet.com/2308-3840/full/v8/i5/348.htm

[8]   Basu-Ray I. N. k Almaddah, A. Adeboye, S. Vaqar, and M. P. Soos, 'Cardiac Manifestations of Coronavirus (COVID-19).StatPearls. Treasure Island, FL: StatPearls Publishing 2024.http://www.ncbi.nlm.nih.gov/books/NBK556152/ [Online]

[9]   Armaly Z, Kinaneh S, Skorecki K. Renal Manifestations of Covid-19: Physiology and Pathophysiology. J Clin Med 2021; 10(6): 1216.
        [http://dx.doi.org/10.3390/jcm10061216] [PMID: 33804075]

[10]   Esteban V, Heringer-Walther S, Sterner-Kock A, *et al*. Angiotensin-(1-7) and the g protein-coupled receptor MAS are key players in renal inflammation. PLoS One 2009; 4(4): e5406.
        [http://dx.doi.org/10.1371/journal.pone.0005406] [PMID: 19404405]

[11]   Hou Y, Hou D. Abstract B32: T cell receptor-like chimeric antigen-receptor to recognize neoepitopes derived from driver mutations. Cancer Immunol Res 2022; 10(12_Supplement) (_Suppl.): B32.

[http://dx.doi.org/10.1158/2326-6074.TUMIMM22-B32]

[12]   Garrofé AB, Picca M, Kaplan AE. Determinación de microdureza de resinas bulk-fill en diferentes profundidades. Acta Odontol Latinoam 2022; 35(1): 10-5.https://actaodontologicalat.com/wp-content/uploads/2022/05/aol_2022_35-1-03.pdf
        [http://dx.doi.org/10.54589/aol.35/1/10] [PMID: 35700536]

[13]   https://www.researchgate.net/publication/347091216_Gastrointestinal_and_hepatic_manifestations_of_COVID_-19_A_systematic_review_and_meta-analysis

[14]   Ferm S, Fisher C, Pakala T, *et al.* Analysis of Gastrointestinal and Hepatic Manifestations of SARS-CoV-2 Infection in 892 Patients in Queens, NY. Clin Gastroenterol Hepatol 2020; 18(10): 2378-2379.e1.
        [http://dx.doi.org/10.1016/j.cgh.2020.05.049] [PMID: 32497637]

[15]   Rai P, Kumar BK, Deekshit VK, Karunasagar I, Karunasagar I. Detection technologies and recent developments in the diagnosis of COVID-19 infection. Appl Microbiol Biotechnol 2021; 105(2): 441-55.
        [http://dx.doi.org/10.1007/s00253-020-11061-5] [PMID: 33394144]

[16]   Mustafa Hellou M, Górska A, Mazzaferri F, *et al.* Nucleic acid amplification tests on respiratory samples for the diagnosis of coronavirus infections: a systematic review and meta-analysis. Clin Microbiol Infect 2021; 27(3): 341-51.
        [http://dx.doi.org/10.1016/j.cmi.2020.11.002] [PMID: 33188933]

[17]   Perumal V, Narayanan V, Rajasekar SJS. Prediction of COVID-19 with Computed Tomography Images using Hybrid Learning Techniques. Dis Markers 2021; 2021(1): 1-15.
        [http://dx.doi.org/10.1155/2021/5522729] [PMID: 33968281]

[18]   Rahbari R, Moradi N, Abdi M. rRT-PCR for SARS-CoV-2: Analytical considerations. Clin Chim Acta 2021; 516: 1-7.
        [http://dx.doi.org/10.1016/j.cca.2021.01.011] [PMID: 33485902]

[19]   Lippi G, Simundic AM, Plebani M. Potential preanalytical and analytical vulnerabilities in the laboratory diagnosis of coronavirus disease 2019 (COVID-19). Clinical Chemistry and Laboratory Medicine (CCLM) 2020; 58(7): 1070-6.
        [http://dx.doi.org/10.1515/cclm-2020-0285] [PMID: 32172228]

[20]   Wu Y, Xu W, Zhu Z, Xia X. Laboratory verification of an RT☐PCR assay for SARS☐CoV☐2. J Clin Lab Anal 2020; 34(10): e23507.
        [http://dx.doi.org/10.1002/jcla.23507] [PMID: 32754967]

[21]   https://medlineplus.gov/genetics/understanding/genomicresearch/genomeediting/

[22]   Safari F, Afarid M, Rastegari B, Borhani-Haghighi A, Barekati-Mowahed M, Behzad-Behbahani A. CRISPR systems: Novel approaches for detection and combating COVID-19. Virus Res 2021; 294: 198282.
        [http://dx.doi.org/10.1016/j.virusres.2020.198282] [PMID: 33428981]

[23]   Sharma A, Balda S, Apreja M, Kataria K, Capalash N, Sharma P. COVID-19 Diagnosis: Current and Future Techniques. Int J Biol Macromol 2021; 193(Pt B): 1835-44.
        [http://dx.doi.org/10.1016/j.ijbiomac.2021.11.016] [PMID: 34774862]

[24]   Rahimi H, Salehiabar M, Barsbay M, *et al.* CRISPR Systems for COVID-19 Diagnosis. ACS Sens 2021; 6(4): 1430-45.
        [http://dx.doi.org/10.1021/acssensors.0c02312] [PMID: 33502175]

[25]   https://pubs.acs.org/doi/10.1021/acssensors.0c02312

[26]   Zhou Y, Wu Y, Ding L, Huang X, Xiong Y. Point-of-care COVID-19 diagnostics powered by lateral flow assay. Trends Analyt Chem 2021; 145: 116452.
        [http://dx.doi.org/10.1016/j.trac.2021.116452] [PMID: 34629572]

[27]   https://onlinelibrary.wiley.com/doi/10.1002/jmv.26741

[28]   Deng Q, Ye G, Pan Y, *et al.* High Performance of SARS-Cov-2N Protein Antigen Chemiluminescence
        Immunoassay as Frontline Testing for Acute Phase COVID-19 Diagnosis: A Retrospective Cohort
        Study. Front Med (Lausanne) 2021; 8: 676560.
        [http://dx.doi.org/10.3389/fmed.2021.676560] [PMID: 34336884]

CHAPTER 6

Treatment Options for COVID-19 Infected Patients

M. Anju[1], Vivas Salim[1], Azfar Kamal[2], Ekbal Ahmed[3] and Ravindra Kumar[1,*]

[1] Department of Bioscience and Engineering, National Institute of Technology Calicut, Kerala, India

[2] Postgraduate Diploma in Orthopedics, Senior Consultant, District Hospital, Sambhal, India

[3] Diwan of Royal Court, Muscat, Sultanate of Oman

Abstract: The world witnessed the outbreak of the most dreadful zoonotic infection, COVID-19, by the last month of 2019. The prompt dissemination of SARS-CoV-2 by intermediate hosts in the human community paved the way for the WHO declaration of a pandemic in 2020. In patients, the severity of this infection ranges from asymptomatic to critical state, leading to complications like acute respiratory distress syndrome (ARDS). The different diagnostics investigated the rapid spread and complexity of the disease. The omics and sequencing technologies helped to identify the virus's structure and potential targets for drug discovery against the virus. Different therapeutic agents like antivirals, antibiotics, *etc.*, are administered to reduce the infection. The various treatment options discussed in this chapter include different types of drugs and their combinational therapies, monoclonal antibodies, immune modulating treatments, promising vaccine developments, CRISPR-Cas13 therapy, experimental therapeutic interventions, non-pharmacological interventions, *etc.* This study also concentrates on the various challenges these clinical medications have faced. By rectifying each challenge, new beneficial treatments can be made possible with the fewest side effects.

Keywords: Antiviral, ARDS, Challenges, COVID-19, CRISPR-Cas13 therapy, Pharmacological interventions, Non-pharmacological interventions, SARS-Co--2.

INTRODUCTION

Even though there had been a history of the severe acute respiratory syndrome (SARS) and the Middle East Respiratory Syndrome (MERS) outbreaks in 2002 and 2012 respectively, the havoc caused by the Corona Virus Disease 2019 (COVID-19) in the human population is uncountable [1]. The three identified

* **Corresponding author Ravindra Kumar:** Department of Bioscience and Engineering, National Institute of Technology Calicut, Kerala, India; E-mail: ravindra@nitc.ac.in

Mohammad Sufian Badar (Ed.)

significant beta coronaviruses were SARS-CoV-1 which caused SARS, MERS-CoV which caused MERS, and SARS-CoV-2 which caused COVID-19. The source of these viruses was suspected to be from intermediate zoonotic hosts like civets, camels, bats, *etc*. Among these, due to the most dangerous and contagious actions of the SARS-CoV-2 virus, COVID-19 was declared a pandemic by WHO in 2020 [2]. However, the spreading of the community was caused by human-t--human interactions. Many strategies are being implemented to regulate the community's spread of COVID-19 [3] like contact tracing, quarantine, precise diagnostic testing, wearing face masks, *etc*.

Immunity is the ability of the host body to defend against infections caused by bacteria, viruses, toxins, *etc*. Simply, it is the disease resistance of the body. The body has two types of immunity, namely innate and acquired immunity. In the case of COVID-19 infection, both types play an important role. The first defense mechanism called innate immunity activates pathogen recognition receptors (PRR) and thereby facilitates natural killer cells (NK cells) and type 1 interferon (INF) production. Acquired immunity helps in the cytotoxic T cells (Tc) and B cell activation [4].

Coronaviruses are spherical, crown-shaped with many projections at their surface and a positive single-stranded RNA genome of 26-32 KB size. The virus contains 4 structural proteins, 9 accessory proteins, and 16 nonstructural proteins (NSP1 to NSP16). Structural proteins include spike glycoprotein (S), envelope protein (E), membrane protein (M), and nucleocapsid protein (N) [5]. About 16 nonstructural proteins formed from two open reading frames (ORF1a, ORF1b) and their respective Replicase polyproteins (pp1a, pp1ab). NSP forms a replicase-transcriptase complex with multiple enzymes like two cysteine proteases called the main protease (NSP5 or M^{PRO} or $3CL^{PRO}$) and papain-like protease (NSP3 or PL^{PRO}) [6]. Remaining are NSP7-NSP8 primase complex, NSP10 & NSP16 (methyl transferases), NSP12 (RdRp), NSP14 (exoribonuclease), NSP13 (helicase triphosphatase), and NSP15 (endonuclease) [7]. Highly variable accessory proteins (ORf3a & 3b, ORF6, ORF7a &7b, ORF8, ORF10, *etc*.) are formed by the interspersed ORF and they help in the formation of sub-genomic mRNAs (sg mRNAs) [8]. Among structural proteins, the S protein is involved in binding and cell membrane fusion with that of host cells as it contains 2 subunits namely, S1 and S2. The main functions of NSPs include viral replication, RTC formation, *etc*. Even if the exact molecular functions of accessory proteins are unknown, they are thought to be the major determinant of infection and will modulate the response of the host [8]. SARS-CoV-2 possesses ORF3b and ORF10 (complement of 3'ORF), which is the only difference noticed from SARS-CoV-1. The genomics helped to reveal the host range, cellular tropism, and mutations of coronavirus by sequence analysis of the S protein and its RBD (Receptor Binding Domain). The viral entry is through the host cell receptors like ACE2 (expressed in type 2 alveolar cells in the lung) and DPP4 (expressed in epithelial and endothelial cells of the lungs, liver, kidney, *etc.*) in SARS and MERS as they are highly conserved ectoenzymes in mammals, thus facilitating the interhuman transmission, respectively [9, 10].

Studies on the pathogenicity and viral features of COVID-19 have improved the pharmacological treatments and thus combat against this dreadful disease. Inhibiting the viral invasion, inhibiting the viral proliferation inside the host, and increasing the immunity of the host are the major methods that prevent and cure COVID-19. Such steps are being practiced in developing and discovering antiviral drugs by exploring the potent targets [11].

The proliferation and subsequent progression of coronavirus happen in the host body through different steps. The former step is the attachment between host-virus cell membranes due to viral invasion by receptor binding and receptor-mediated endocytosis [11]. For receptor binding, the viral body needs RBD, and endocytosis needs the S2 subunit or clathrin receptor. This will lead to viral nucleocapsid entry and its content release. The next step is the growth and establishment of the virus through processes like replication, transcription, and translation. The new viral particles are released, and they get transported *via* Golgi vesicles to the cell membrane surface, followed by exocytosis. This will cause community spread by aerosol transmission [3].

The interruption to any of these processes will inhibit the viral activity and thus prevent further transmission between individuals. So, the drugs that efficiently compete with RBD, drugs that inhibit endocytosis, the drugs that inhibit the replicase expression, replication, transcription, and translation, the drugs that interfere in viral assembly at ERGIC, the drugs that can activate the host's complement system, and IFNs are highly used in COVID-19 treatment. This study deals with various pharmacological and non-pharmacological interventions being used in the field of COVID-19 infection.

IMPORTANT TARGETS FOR PHARMACEUTICAL TREATMENT

About 26 viral proteins are expressed in COVID-19 affected humans and are found to interact with various human proteins in several biological processes [7]. These can be utilised for drug targeting as it is very important for the survival of viral metabolism inside host cells.

NSP1- involved in the replication of DNA

E protein, NSP8, NSP5, NSP13 – Involved in regulating the expression of genes

E, M, NSP2, NSP6, NSP7, NSP10, NSP13, NSP15, ORF3a and ORF8- Helps in vesicle transportation

S protein- priming for modification of lipids

N protein & NSP8 – Helps in RNA processing and its regulation

ORF10- Ubiquitination by ligases

ORF9b, NSP7, NSP8, NSP13, N protein - Signaling pathways and organization of Golgi, centrosome

ORF6, NSP9 & NSP15 – Involved in nuclear transportation

NSP1 & NSP13-maintenance of cytoskeleton, NSP4, NSP8 and ORF9c-mitochondrial formation, **NSP9**- formation of extracellular matrix

M protein- involved in the morphology of ER

NSP6 and ORF9c- involved in sigma factor interaction and stress response in ER

The discovery of new targets for SARS-CoV-2 was made possible by RNA sequencing and transcriptomics. The last open reading frame (ORF10) is suggested as a good target as its RNA expression is very low when compared with others and also due to the highest interaction with ubiquitination complex CUL2. This interaction will reduce the viral replication in the host body.

The ACE2 gene is normally found in the alveoli of humans helps to encode an enzyme called angiotensin-converting enzyme-2, which has an important role in the renal activity. ACE2 receptors are found to be the most efficient receptor for viral entry and binding. By RNA-Seq analysis, the ACE2 receptor was found also in the upper respiratory tract and enterocytes in the small intestine suggesting evidence of gastric issues related to COVID-19-infected patients.

The viral entry through ACE2 receptors is made possible by the S protein of the virus and serine protease2 (TMPRSS2). The subsequent priming of the S protein and its cleavage will produce two subunits called S1 and S2, which help in ACE2 interaction and cell membrane fusion respectively. Thus, S protein and TMPRSS2 are the potential targets for coronaviruses and can be used as protease inhibitors in the development of drug candidates [10].

The role of proteases is very important for viral entry and its replication. The different proteases present in the host cells help in the proteolytic processing of S protein leading to its activation and subsequent cleavage. Apart from TMPRSS2, there are other proteases like furin, TMPRSS11D, TMPRSS13, -11E, Cathepsin L/B (lysosomal protease), and 11F. All these proteases will have minor activity only when compared with TMPRSS2 [12].

After viral entry, it will be encapsulated in vesicles following the endosomal pathway. The endosomal pathway initiates viral replication by the acidification of endosomes and by glycoprotein cleavage through endosomal proteases. So, the candidates that target acidification and glycoprotein cleavage will be other potential drug molecules [13].

RdRp helps in catalyzing phosphodiester bonds for RNA replication. As the viral replication rate is directly proportional to disease severity, RdRp inhibitors can be used to reduce the replication process. However, it was found that the use of RdRp inhibitors does not suppress the replication rate, thus leading to resistance development. Hence, such anti-RdRp drugs are only used in the early stage of infection [14].

Viral proteases like Mpro and 3Clpro help in the maturation of viral proteins by converting the polyproteins into viral particles after the translation process. The main function of Mpro is the proteolytic release of nsp13, which controls NTPase and RNA helicase activity.

The viral proteins or kinases are targets of antiviral drugs, but they lack specificity and so kill healthy cells too. Hence, kinase inhibitors are least used for the mitigation of COVID-19 infection. However, newer PAK1 had an important role in the entry of the virus by micropinocytosis and viral replication [10]. Various drugs like Imatinib, Ruxolitinib, Silmitasertib, and Tofacitinib are kinase inhibitors that are now repurposed.

Tubulin polymerization is needed for the activity of endosomes so making it a target can reduce the early phase of infection to a great extent [15].

DPP4 is a potent and effective target as it is expressed in many human tissues like kidneys, lungs, heart, *etc.*, and is also involved in physiological and immunological processes. DPP4 will contribute to a cytokine storm leading to organ damage and fatal conditions. Hence, DPP4 inhibitors will reduce the inflammation in the respiratory tract even though they are not directly involved in receptor-binding activity [14].

Cathepsin is a protease that helps in S protein priming and protein degradation. In about 11 classes of cathepsin, CatB or L is reported to be a new therapeutic target as it is involved in the transmission of infection [14].

Apart from these, CD147 and CD26 are considered to be alternative receptors for viral entry and interactions with platelets [16].

TREATMENT STRATEGIES

Treatment strategies with minimal side effects are an urgent need due to the speedy spread and high mortality rates due to COVID-19. Researchers and clinicians are making continuous efforts to discover more effective treatments for coronaviruses. Here, different pharmacological and non-pharmacological interventions for the treatment of COVID-19 are being discussed. The mode of action for antiviral drugs will be different according to their targets. The potential targets of this virus include Papain-like proteases, RNA-dependent RNA isomerase, Helicase, S proteins, and ADP-ribose diphosphatase. Drugs that are used as RNA-dependent RNA inhibitors, protease inhibitors, spike inhibitors, endosomal pathway inhibitors, *etc.* help to terminate or prevent membrane attachment and entry, following proliferation, and assembly.

Pharmacological Interventions

Antiviral Drugs

The major RNA-dependent RNA polymerase inhibitors include Remdesivir, Favipiravir, and Ribavirin. The drug that inhibits the spike protein is the Camostat mesylate. Lopinavir or ritonavir are the major protease inhibitors. The major endosomal pathway inhibitors include Chloroquine, Teicoplanin, and Niclosamide [17].

Remdesivir blocks the proofreading of exoribonuclease and prevents new RNA synthesis by chain termination. Even if there exists the first success story of this drug in the United States, the usage of this drug has been stopped due to many reasons like the minimal level of exoribonuclease blocking as it has a very low affinity with human RdRp, a chance for developing resistance and undesirable side effects that happened [9]. Favipiravir shows activity against coronaviruses by RdRp inhibition. Initially, this drug was used to treat influenza viruses which is now used to treat Ebola and coronaviruses. This drug showed a significant decrease in viral load and proved to be effective in most cases [3]. Ribavirin is another RdRp inhibitor that was further incorporated into the HCV genome and induced mutations resulting in the death of viruses. But this drug had side effects like reduced haemoglobin level, hemolysis, increased bilirubin levels, *etc* [18].

Camostat mesylate is a potent prodrug associated with viral cell membrane and host cell membrane fusion. This drug will inhibit serine protease 2 (TMPRSS2) associated with the ACE2 receptor. As this inhibits TMPRSS2, the chance of developing viral resistance can be resisted. This drug is predicted to have a weak pharmacokinetic interaction with other available drugs as it is neither metabolizing nor inhibiting the CYP system. It will reduce different inflammatory markers IL6, TNFß, and TNFα, indicating a reduction in subsequent fibrosis and cure from inflammations. This drug can be provided in combination with other drugs like Remdesivir and corticosteroids to boost their action [12].

Nafamostat is another TMPRSS2 inhibitor that blocks the viral entry and also helps in diluting blood clots associated with ARDS. It is reported that this drug blocked the infection with higher efficiency than Camostat [19]. Such TMPRSS2 inhibitors will have a guanidinium group responsible for the association with this particular target [20].

Griffithsin is a potent drug that acts on oligosaccharides in S protein and affects the glycosylation sites (RBD) of the S1 subunit. In addition to GRFT, certain monoclonal antibodies (m336, m337, m338) and peptides (p4, p5) also target the RBD to prevent the invasion [11]. Recently, a pan coronavirus fusion inhibitor called EK1 was tested alone and in combination, and according to the result, EK1 showed more inhibitory properties when combined with GRFT. So, such combinations are being used in nasal sprays to have relief from corona infection [21].

Lopinavir or ritonavir has the potential to inhibit the effective targets called 3CL^{PRO} & M^{PRO} proteases. These can be used in combinations to increase the half-life. Ritonavir is a CYP3A inhibitor and HIV-1 protease inhibitor. The combination of Nirmatrelvir (the main protease inhibitor) and Ritonavir called Paxlovid is being administered to treat severe COVID infection [22].

Chloroquine and Hydroxychloroquine are the drugs that increase the endosomal pH, thereby inhibiting the replication of viruses. Hydroxychloroquine is its analog and is used in combination with antibiotic azithromycin for effective results. They interfere with the terminal glycosylation of the ACE2 receptor, alter post-translational modification by increasing pH, and thus disturb the assembly and protein synthesis. Gastrointestinal upset and retinal toxicity is the common side effect of this drug [23]. A combination of Remdesivir and chloroquine had better results in COVID-19 treatment [2].

Colchicine inhibits tubulin polymerization thus preventing endosomal proliferation and activity. Hence it is used for the early treatment of infection [15].

PAK1 inhibitors like 15K, Minnelide, and Frondoside A will prevent micropinocytosis of the virus and thus inhibit its entry. So they can be used as a potent therapeutic antiviral drugs [10].

Plitidepsin or Aplidin is a drug that inhibits the the ribosomal activity of the host by targeting the elongation factor eEF1A. Zotatifin is another drug that has the the same mode of mechanism but the the only difference is that it targets the elongation factor eEF4A [1].

Selinexor (SXR) is normally an anti-cancer drug that targets the mRNA nuclear export complex (XPO1 &SINE). XPO1 will trigger inflammation and oxidative stress. It will inhibit the protein transportation from the nucleus to the cytoplasm leading to the inhibition of proliferation. It also releases anti-inflammatory cytokines thus preventing the release of pro-inflammatory cytokines and the cytokine storm [24].

Rapamycin and FK506 are approved drugs that targets the mTOR enzyme and prevent protein synthesis and cytokine storms thus acting as immunosuppressants [25].

Metformin drug also targets the ACE2 receptor specifically to AMPK in hepatocytes and has an action in respiratory electron transport. This reduces TNFα and mortality rates [26].

Amiodarone and Verapamil are calcium channel inhibitors and have effects on endosome maturation. As calcium channels are required for viral entry, these drugs will inhibit viral entry [27].

These are some of the commonly trialed and repurposing antiviral drugs used in COVID-19 treatment. Apart from these drugs, there are many other pharmacological treatment strategies which add more effectiveness to modern treatment. Convalescent plasma therapy, monoclonal antibody therapy, vaccines, immunomodulators, CRISPR-Cas13 therapy, *etc.* are some of them.

Convalescent Plasma Therapy

Convalescent plasma treatment belongs to a passive immune therapy, which is used to make instant immunity through polyclonal antibody (Ab) administration in COVID-19 patients [28]. Convalescent plasma taken from COVID-19 survivors contains high quantities of neutralizing antibodies, which can improve immune response against coronavirus during the initial stage of their infection. According to the US-Food and Drug Administration guidelines, patients can receive convalescent plasma only from COVID-19 survivors with no clinical symptoms for a minimum of 28 days after COVID-19 recovery and must show two times negative results for either a nasopharyngeal swab test or molecular diagnostic test [29]. The proper dose of CCP is still a concern but many studies revealed that CCP with a high dose of neutralizing antibodies is effective against the SARS-CoV-2. In the majority of trials, CCP with a high level of antibody ranges between 200 to 600 mL *via* more than 2 units of plasma. The level and binding affinity of antibodies in CCP are heterogeneous and depend on the ABO blood group [30]. CCP transfusion in patients before undergoing mechanical ventilation is highly effective in lowering the mortality risk. Patients with mild COVID-19 symptoms respond well to CCP therapy, however, the early CCP transfusion prevents hospitalization and slows the development of severe respiratory disease in older patients [31]. Convalescent plasma therapy shows better results in oxygenation, neutralizing the SARS-CoV-2 particles, restricting entry to uninfected cells, and activating major immune mechanisms [32]. Furthermore, it has been shown that the CCP with high-level antibodies can facilitate Fc-dependent processes, such as phagocytosis, cellular cytotoxicity, and complement activation against SARS-CoV-2 [30].

Monoclonal Antibody Therapy

Antiviral monoclonal antibody (anti-mAbs) therapy is a passive immunization therapy to treat coronavirus. They are usually IgG1 subtype targeting RBD of the S-protein of SARS-CoV-2 virus [33]. By binding with the S protein, anti-RBD mAbs prevent the viral entry to the host cell by blocking its fusion with the ACE2 receptor on host cells. After targeting, mAbs are responsible for initiating either antibody-initiated cellular cytotoxicity or phagocytosis or inducing the affected cells to apoptosis [34]. The best candidates for this therapy are outpatients who are at severe risk of infection and do not require supplemental oxygen. Convalescent plasma (CP) from COVID survivors and humanized mouse antibody technology have been used to raise anti-viral mAbs against RBD of the Spike protein [35].

Bamlanivimab Plus Etesevimab: Etesevimab & Bamlanivimab are anti-viral IgG1 mAbs that contain a modified Fc region [35]. The U.S. FDA agreed with the use of Bamlanivimab alone in the therapy of various cases of COVID-19 in November 2020 and agreed to the combination therapy with Etesevimab in February 2021. The mechanism of action of both mAbs are the same, focusing the overlapping epitopes present in the RBD of the S protein [36] significantly in patients with moderate COVID-19 symptoms at day 11. The combination therapy is also effective for patients who express high risks such as diabetes mellitus, older age, cardiovascular diseases, pregnancy, lung, kidney, and neurological disorders associated with the development of severe disease [37].

REGN-COV2: REGN-COV2 includes a mixture of two G1 antibodies *i.e.,* Casirivimab and Imdevimab that are non-competing in nature, restrict the entry of SARS-CoV-2 virus to the host cell by binding specifically with two different non-overlapping epitopes in the RBD of S protein. REGEN-CoV-2 received authorization from US FDA to treat pediatric and adults' patients with mild to moderate disease in November 2020 [38]. The virus can escape from mAbs treatment by introducing mutations in the spike protein. All previous studies approved the ability of REGN-COV2 to retain its neutralizing capacity of all studied mutations in S protein [39]. In 2020, the dose of REGEN-CoV-2 given to high-risk outpatients was 2400 mg but nowadays the dose is limited to 1200 mg because the studies found that 1200 mg dose is enough to decrease the hospitalization and mortality rate. The same dose is again better for patients who express severe disease conditions. According to in vitro analysis, REGEN-CoV-2 can act against all of the SARS-CoV-2 variants except the Omicron variant [37]. Subcutaneous REGEN-CoV-2 treatment is effective for asymptomatic COVID-19 patients to lower the disease severity and duration of the sickness [40].

Sotrovimab: This is a derivative of S309 mAb in which the half-life period is extended by modifying the Fc region. S309 can bind both 'up' and 'down' conformations of the RBD in a single S trimer and neutralization is achieved by S trimer cross-linking. S309 is also responsible for initiating antibody-mediated cell cytotoxicity and cellular phagocytosis [41] Sotrovimab is efficient in minimizing the severity of COVID-19 and the chance of hospitalization (Sylwester). A single intravenous dose of 500 mg of Sotrovimab is effective for symptomatic patients with high disease progression [37].

Immunomodulator Therapy

After the SARS-CoV-2 viral entry, the host cell stimulates the immune system of the body by activating both innate and acquired immunity as a part of the defense mechanism [42]. CD4 + and CD8 + cells can synthesize cytokines, various interleukins, and TNF-α in cells in the presence of the virus. The overexpression of cytokines is called cytokine storm, which leads to damage in lung cells and lung tissues and also causes serious conditions or death. The immunomodulatory compounds can deactivate cytokines and prevent the action of other harmful compounds thereby reducing serious conditions in COVID-19 patients [43].

Tocilizumab: Interleukin 6 (IL-6) is a cytokine, that is over-expressed in affected patients and regulates the immune response of the host cell. The release of high concentrations of IL-6 is responsible for cytokine release syndrome [44]. In the classical approach to the immune response, the IL-6 binds with membrane-bound IL-6 receptor (mbIL-6), and this complex forms a ligand for Glycoprotein-130 (gp-130), which stimulates the immune response. Soluble receptor for IL-6 (srIL-6) is another target for IL-6, which is available on the surface of endothelial cells [43] Tocilizumab is an anti-IL-6R monoclonal antibody, which prevents the association between IL-6 and mIL-6R or sIL-6R receptors by blocking the binding site of IL-6 in the receptors (John). It is found that tocilizumab is only operative in a COVID-19 patient with a low level of lactate dehydrogenase or high CRP. According to the phase 3 trial, tocilizumab is not able to improve survival in the case of hospitalized COVID-19 patients with pneumonia. The action of tocilizumab is highly dependent on the conditions of COVID-19 patients [45]. Tocilizumab is very effective for COVID-19 severe patients to minimize the risk of mechanical intubation or death from 38% to 33% [46]. A dose of 400 mg tocilizumab is given to patients normally, and if it is found ineffective, one more administration will be permitted after 12 hours [47].

Baricitinib: Baricitinib or Olumiant, inhibits the function of Janus kinase (JAK) 1 and 2 enzymes and it is widely used to treat rheumatoid arthritis [43]. The partial inhibition of both enzymes regulates intracellular signaling which minimizes the phosphorylation and inactivates STAT proteins [48]. Baricitinib restricts the entry of viruses by blocking AP2-associated protein kinase (Eleanor). The combined therapy of Baricitinib or Remdesivir showed superior effectivity than Remdesivir alone in minimizing the time of recovery [45]. It decreased the need for mechanical ventilation and time for recovery in patients with high-flow oxygen [44].

Corticosteroids: Dexamethasone is an artificial glucocorticoid that belongs to the corticosteroid family and can minimize inflammation, decrease the overexpression of cytokines, and reduce immune system activity. It received approval for use in 1958 from the US-FDA. Dexamethasone is used for short periods in severe patients [43]. A dose of 12 mg of dexamethasone is very effective in reducing mortality rate up to 27% in COVID-19 patients with severe hypoxemia state [48].

CRISPR-Cas13 Therapy

CRISPR-Cas13 is another approach to make therapeutics against COVID-19. The principle of the mechanism is obtained from bacteria which protect the cell from bacteriophage infection by producing target-specific crRNAs [49]. In COVID-19 patients it is mediated by targeting CRISPR-Cas13 towards viral targets, for example, the ACE2 gene because the virus entry is facilitated by the recognition of the ACE2 receptor of the host cell membrane by the SARS-CoV-2 virus. In this case, the CRISPR-Cas13 technique leads to the synthesis of a condensed ACE2 receptor that is no longer recognized by the virus, and the entry is restricted as summarized in Fig. (**1a**). The other approach known as Prophylactic Antiviral CRISPR in huMAN cells (PAC-MAN) proposed by Abbott *et al.* based on the removal of the integrated virus genome from the host genome. Cas13 carries a guide RNA that can recognize and degrade the integrated provirus in the host genome without having any effect on the host. The small size (967 aa), strong catalytic power, and high specificity of Cas13 make it as a preferred choice to do the above process [50]. The source of the CRISPR-Cas13 system is *Ruminococcus flavefaciens* XPD3002. The CRISPR-Cas13 and guide RNAs are packaged into adeno-associated virus vectors and then introduced into infected cells. The guide RNAs associated with CRISPR-Cas13 target the peptide-encoding regions of the viral genome and a maximum of three such gRNAs are introduced to prevent any chance of resistance within the host cell. The removal of provirus is also mediated by transferring the CRISPR system in the form of DNA which encodes both Cas13 and crRNA in the host cell as shown in Fig. (**1b**). Delivery of CRISPR to infected cells without affecting nearby healthy cells is the main challenge in the process. This system helps to remove the RNA genome of the virus from infected host cells or can deactivate the transcription of many SARS-CoV-2 genes, for example, S-protein coding genes [51].

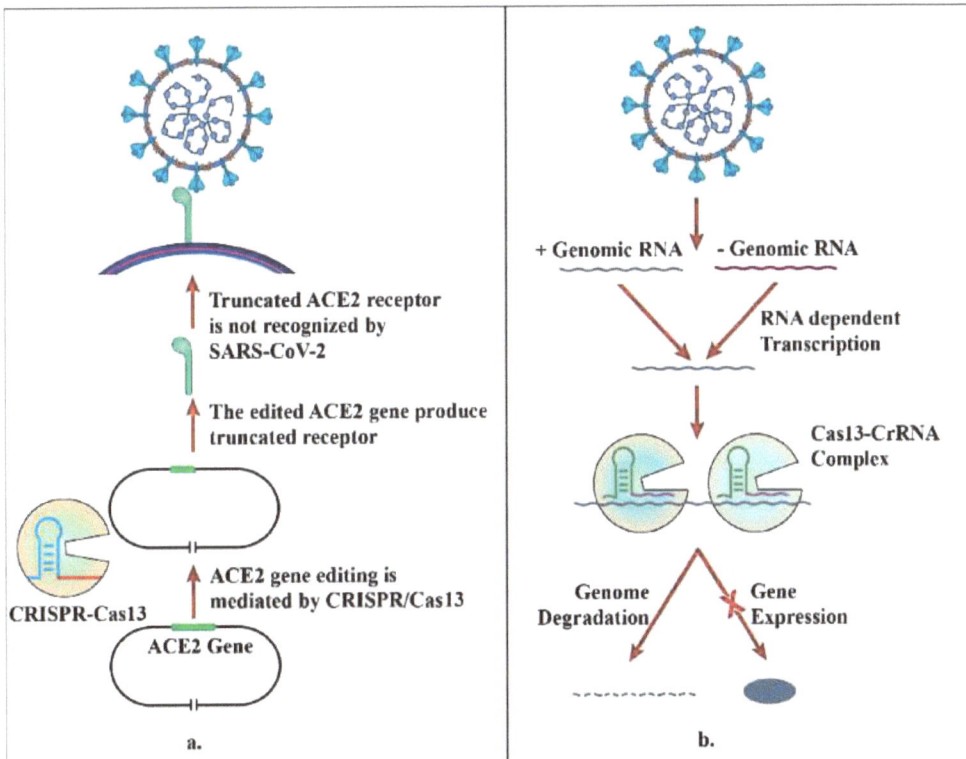

Fig. (1). Illustration showing the use of CRISPR-Cas13 therapy against SAR-CoV-2 virus. (**a**) indicates Genome editing using Cas13-crRNA to produce truncated ACE2 receptor and (**b**) indicates direct targeting of viral positive-sense RNAs by Cas13-crRNA complex and subsequent inhibition of viral functions.

The main targets of Cas13 are highly conserved sequences of the viral genome [52]. The comparative genomics analysis observed a higher-level conservativeness in the genes that express nucleocapsid proteins and RdRp in SARS-CoV-2 than in SARS-CoV-1 and MERS. So, it is somewhat easy to make a crRNA library with the help of a computational pipeline to target both nucleocapsid proteins and RdRp in various SARS-CoV-2 viruses without targeting the human genome. It is again proved computationally that a single cocktail with a maximum of three crRNAs is sufficient to associate with all the targets in SARS-CoV-2 [53]. The comparative analysis of all sequenced coronavirus genomes predicted a total of 6 crRNAs which can identify the genome of all coronaviruses through targeting conserved regions like RdRp, N genes, and ORF1ab; hence, these crRNAs are used in the PAC-MAN method [54].

CRISPR-Cas13 method will come at the top of COVID-19 treatment because it is very flexible in designing guide RNAs to all the variants of SARS-CoV-2 and has a high potential to cut target regions in single-stranded RNA. In CRISPR-Cas13 therapy, guide RNAs can be designed based on viral drug targets that are evolved and escape from the action of drugs. The average size of crRNAs is 20 bp but sufficient concentration of guide RNAs with longer than 20 bp is an option in the CRISPR-Cas13 system to produce better results [55]. The small size of Cas13 is again helpful to load more than two crRNAs in the adeno-associated virus system to ensure potent virus clearance and minimize the chance of evolving resistant strains. The PAC-MAN method will be a powerful antiviral approach to reduce the evolving strains of the virus and can be executed quickly during the pandemic [49].

Vaccines

Vaccines have a great role in public health especially during the outbreak of SARS-CoV-2 as they work with innate immunity and build protection against getting the infection. Effective vaccine development will therefore complement the antiviral drugs and is the most preventive option against SARS-CoV-2. The scientific and clinical community started working on various vaccines like inactivated, protein, live attenuated RNA-based, DNA-based, vector-based, subunit vaccines, *etc.* The vaccine development for SARS-CoV-2 has 4 different aspects.

✓ Suitable antigen epitope selection
✓ Overcoming of ADE (Antibody-Dependent Enhancement) issues
✓ Measuring of humoral and cell-mediated immunity
✓ Appropriate selection of technical route.

Even if all these aspects are cared for, before vaccine administration different problems like immune system failures, allergic inflammations in connection with Th2 immunopathology, variability of different titers of neutralizing antibodies, and immune complications associated with different clinical trials are also to be taken into consideration. Previous studies reported that in COVID-affected patients, there is great significance for cellular immunity as the SARS-specific IgG antibodies may vanish along with the disappearance of peripheral B memory cells but contrastingly will have long-lasting specific T cells memory response [56].

DNA Vaccines: Covigenix is a proteo-lipid vehicle using plasmid DNA with virus antigen and FAST proteins. The direct delivery of DNA will activate innate immunity, and show more stability. Large-scale production is possible as it does not involve any infectious agents. It showed high efficiency and immunogenicity in preclinical in vivo studies. The INO-4800 DNA vaccine delivers plasmids using the device CELLECTRA for making tiny pores in the membrane thus generating monoclonal antibodies.

mRNA Vaccines will have a genetic code of antigen S protein which is wrapped in a shell and is delivered by lipid nanoparticles. On injection, human cells utilize these viral antigens and produce corresponding antibodies. Pfizer-BioNTech (BNT162b1 and BNT162b2) and Moderna (mRNA 1273 vaccine) are the two promising vaccines approved by the US FDA. The essential components of mRNA vaccines include 5′ cap, 5′ UTR, ORF, 3′ UTR, and poly-A tail. By altering the sequences, mRNA vaccines can be modified. The cytokine production and elevated CD8+ and CD4+ cell responses, memory B cell production are the results of such vaccines [1]. BNT162b2 is with modRNA, full-length S protein, and RBD whereas mRNA 1273 vaccine is with stabilized S protein.

Viral vector vaccines will have DNA of the S protein antigen which is delivered by adenoviruses (vector). On injection, viral proteins are produced and immune responses are boosted up. It is safe and more immunogenic. Ad5-nCOV is the commonly used vaccine that had a strong immune response against COVID-19. CanSino Biologics & China's Institute of Biology at the country's Academy of Military Medical Sciences developed it. This vaccine is called a "specially needed drug" by the Chinese Military. AdCOVID is another adenoviral intranasal vaccine expressing S protein. Sputnik V is approved by the Russian Ministry proven to have strong immune responses [57].

Inactivated viral vaccines will have inactivated SARS-CoV-2 viruses (by using chemicals or radiation) as antigens. On injection, the corresponding antibody response happens and thus improves immunity. The main advantages are it is cheap, stable, and multivalent. CoronaVac vaccine showed neutralizing antibody induction against the virus. About 3 immunizations with 2 doses showed promising results with the least side effects. The Chinese Government provided emergency approval for limited usage.

Protein vaccines are predominantly humoral in nature. The main adjuvants added include inorganic compounds, bacterial compounds, *etc.* The plant-based corona vaccines are protein vaccines that utilize viral-like particles in *Nicotiana benthamiana.* As VLPs are without genetic material, they cannot replicate and at the same time can mimic like virus itself having the immune responses. COVID-19 S-Trimer is protein-based as well as a recombinant subunit vaccine based on S protein [57].

Apart from these vaccines, vaccines using Hyleukin-7 platform technology have been developed for hybridizing IgD and IgG4 for better immunity.

Non-Pharmacological Interventions

Apart from these pharmacological treatments, several other methods can reduce the horizontal transmission of SARS-CoV-2 viruses across the human community [10]. Some of the points are discussed below:

✓ Early case identification- identification of first contact will help to isolate that portion from the community so that he or she can be treated well without community spreading.
✓ Contact tracing- it should be done if the first person had contact with others or not. If yes, vigilant care should be taken for those individuals by observing symptoms if there or not.
✓ Travel restrictions- As it is an aerosol transmission pandemic, utmost care should be taken by avoiding traveling and isolating into own home is better till the COVID-19 cases decrease.
✓ Social distancing- Stringent measures should be taken by government officials to stop community gatherings like party meetings, festivals, different ceremonies, *etc.* so that the chance for disease contact can be reduced.
✓ Use of Hygienic masks- Different masks are made available for strict prevention of interhuman transmission. The proper disposal of used masks should be there and the continuous monitoring and fine system should be promoted so that everyone will wear the masks and have some sort of prevention of direct contact with viruses.
✓ Regular handwashing and sanitizer use- Hands should be washed frequently and ensure the use of hygienic sanitizer so that virus transmission gets reduced.
✓ Provision of e-learning from educational institutions and work at home from

companies- These will reduce the interaction with others along with regular workflow productivity. This will not hinder the academics and work for livelihood.

By taking care of all these points, the community spreading can be maintained and can reduce the mortality rate to a great extent. Only with therapeutics, the spread cannot be controlled. It needs proper non-pharmacological interventions also to reduce the speed of spreading as summarized in Fig. (**2**). By all these measures, the COVID-19 pandemic can be reduced and helped to bring life back to normal.

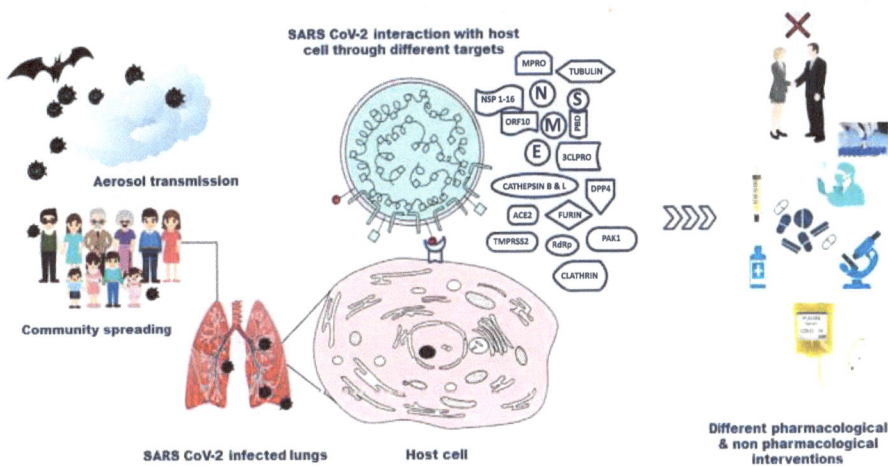

Fig. (2). Illustration showing how COVID-19 infection occurs in a community. By some vectors, the SARS-CoV-2 virus is entering the human community and is spreading through aerosol transmission. The respiratory system, mainly the lungs is infected much thus showing the binding of SARS-CoV-2 virus with host cells through different targets. If it continues, the entire community will be affected so different measures should be taken in pharmacological and non-pharmacological fields. This figure indicates different measures like preventing physical contact, wearing masks, carrying out different diagnoses and analyses, taking vaccines, antivirals, plasma therapy, and use of sanitizer.

CHALLENGES ASSOCIATED WITH VARIOUS TREATMENTS

The undesirable side effects and the resistance development are the two major issues connected with the use of antiviral drugs like Ribavirin, Favipiravir, *etc* [9]. The major limitation of employing PAC-MAN clinically is the development of active transfer methods of Cas13-crRNA to infected cells. Liposome or ribonucleoprotein-mediated delivery and engineered amphiphilic peptides are promising methods that could be used for this event. The other limitation is only cells expressing both Cas13 and crRNAs are protected from viral infection because it performs in a cell-autonomous manner. Therefore, to overcome SARS-

CoV-2, it seems to be expressed sufficiently in some percentage of cells and the range must be predicted experimentally [58]. It is noticed that the method is unsuccessful during the latent period of infection [59]. The occurrence of mutations at the target site of crRNA made by the virus in response to therapy is another limitation [60]. The source of Cas13 proteins is prokaryotes and therefore, the transport of these proteins in humans may result in toxicity, which leads to immune activation and the production of specific antibodies [61].

The first limitation of convalescent plasma therapy is about the dose of convalescent plasma to be imposed to neutralize viral infection and improve the patient's condition. Second, the same is less successful in patients during late in the course of the disease and need mechanical ventilation support [62]. The transfusion of convalescent plasma in high doses is ineffective for severe COVID-19 patients and less successful in reducing death rates, length of hospitalization, and period of mechanical ventilation [63]. Even if COVID-19 vaccines generated robust immunity for individuals, they had some limitations and challenges. In the case of DNA and RNA vaccines, the electroporation technique and temperature sensitivity were important issues, and no such vaccines were produced previously. Viral vector vaccines may worsen an individual's immune response due to pre-existing immunity. The inactivated vaccines like Sinovac had a limitation of weakened immunity and thereby had a possibility of disease risk [40].

Despite all these challenges and limitations, researchers, physicians, and pharmacists continue their stupendous efforts to develop many more ways to combat this virus by figuring out accurate targets.

TAKE HOME MESSAGE

A comprehensive exploration of various treatment strategies is needed to mitigate the COVID-19 infection impact. The majority of therapeutic targets discussed were proteins or receptors in the viral body that have potential effects in entry, proliferation, and assembly. According to those targets, the antiviral drugs are also broadly classified into three categories RNA dependent RNA inhibitors, protease inhibitors, spike inhibitors, and endosomal pathway inhibitors. Another strategy is to use recovered antibodies and engineered antibodies used in Convalescent Plasma Therapy (CCP) and Monoclonal Antibody Therapy (mAbs) respectively showed promising effects in reducing the risk, but the proper dosage and timing are very crucial for the effectiveness of treatment. Immunomodulator therapy will be more effective for severe patients as it directly targets cytokine storm and reduces lung tissue inflammation. The two strategies of CRISPR-Cas13, like ACE2 Receptor editing and Direct Viral RNA targeting, offer target specificity, and potential adaptability to new variants making it a promising toxin-free approach. In addition to this, the PAC-MAN method offers a long-term solution for preventing viral reservoirs. Vaccination is a powerful preventive approach and its selection should be careful by considering various side effects. Other non-pharmacological preventive measures like social distancing, mask-wearing, hand hygiene, remote work or e-learning, *etc.* are crucial for reducing the transmission rate. By integrating pharmacological interventions with effective public health strategies, we can better manage current and future infectious disease threats, ultimately enhancing global health resilience.

CONCLUSION

Repurposed drugs, Vaccines under clinical trials, Immunoglobulin therapy, Convalescent plasma treatment, Monoclonal antibody (anti-mAbs) therapy, and CRISPR-Cas13 technique are the different pharmacological interventions discussed in this study. Many more treatments like mesenchymal stem cell therapy, conventional herbal treatment, oxygen therapy, nanoparticle therapy, *etc.* are being developed to discover effective cures and control over SARS-CoV-2 virus. By rectifying various defects and limitations of different treatment approaches, new strategies are being developed day by day to deal with SARS-CoV-2 effectively. Along with pharmacological measures, some non-pharmacological interventions are also needed to vanish this dreadful virus as the phrase says "prevention is better than cure".

WHAT YOU WILL LEARN

• The specific viral proteins of SARS-CoV-2 and their roles in the virus's life cycle through different interactions.

• Fundamentals of key pharmacological strategies include repurposed drugs, monoclonal antibodies, convalescent plasma therapy, immunoglobulin therapy, as well as innovative methods like CRISPR-Cas13, and vaccine development.

• Specific biochemical pathways and cellular mechanisms of the virus's biology to treat COVID-19

• Non-pharmacological measures like early case identification, contact tracing, travel restrictions, social distancing, mask usage, and hand hygiene to reduce transmission.

• Challenges and limitations of various treatment strategies to combat SARS-CoV-2.

REFERENCES

[1]   Forchette L, Sebastian W, Liu T. A Comprehensive Review of COVID-19 Virology, Vaccines, Variants, and Therapeutics, Current Medical Science, Huazhong University of Science and Technology, 2021; 41(6): 1037–1051.
[http://dx.doi.org/10.1007/s11596-021-2395-1]

[2]   Guo Y R, *et al.* The origin, transmission and clinical therapies on coronavirus disease 2019 (COVID-19) outbreak- A n update on the status, Military Medical Research, BioMed Central Ltd., 2020; 7(1).
[http://dx.doi.org/10.1186/s40779-020-00240-0]

[3]   Parasher A. COVID-19: Current understanding of its Pathophysiology, Clinical presentation and Treatment," Postgraduate Medical Journal, BMJ Publishing Group, 2021; 97(1147): 312–320.
[http://dx.doi.org/10.1136/postgradmedj-2020-138577]

[4]   Zhong J, Tang J, Ye C, Dong L. The immunology of COVID-19: is immune modulation an option for treatment? Lancet Rheumatol 2020; 2(7): e428-36.
[http://dx.doi.org/10.1016/S2665-9913(20)30120-X] [PMID: 32835246]

[5]   Bergmann CC, Silverman RH. COVID-19: Coronavirus replication, pathogenesis, and therapeutic strategies. Cleve Clin J Med 2020; 87(6): 321-7.
[http://dx.doi.org/10.3949/ccjm.87a.20047] [PMID: 32366502]

[6]   Ghahremanpour MM, Tirado-Rives J, Deshmukh M, *et al.* Identification of 14 Known Drugs as Inhibitors of the Main Protease of SARS-CoV-2. ACS Med Chem Lett 2020; 11(12): 2526-33.
[http://dx.doi.org/10.1021/acsmedchemlett.0c00521] [PMID: 33324471]

[7]   Gordon DE, Jang GM, Bouhaddou M, *et al.* A SARS-CoV-2 protein interaction map reveals targets for drug repurposing. Nature 2020; 583(7816): 459-68.
[http://dx.doi.org/10.1038/s41586-020-2286-9] [PMID: 32353859]

[8]   V'kovski P, Kratzel A, Steiner S, Stalder H, Thiel V. Coronavirus biology and replication: implications for SARS-CoV-2 2021.
[http://dx.doi.org/10.1038/s41579-020-00468-6]

[9]   Felsenstein S, Herbert J A, McNamara P S, Hedrich C M. COVID-19: Immunology and treatment options 2020.
[http://dx.doi.org/10.1016/j.clim.2020.108448]

[10]   Uddin M, Mustafa F, Rizvi TA, *et al.*, SARS-CoV-2/COVID-19: Viral Genomics, Epidemiology, Vaccines, and Therapeutic Interventions. Viruses 2020; 12(5): 526.
[http://dx.doi.org/10.3390/v12050526]

[11]   Song L G, Xie Q X, Lao H L, Lv Z Y. Human coronaviruses and therapeutic drug discovery. Infect Dis Poverty 2021; 10: 28.
[http://dx.doi.org/10.1186/s40249-021-00812-9]

[12]   Breining P, Frølund AL, Højen JF, *et al.* Camostat mesylate against SARS-CoV-2 and COVID-19—Rationale, dosing and safety. Basic Clin Pharmacol Toxicol 2021; 128(2): 204-12.
[http://dx.doi.org/10.1111/bcpt.13533] [PMID: 33176395]

[13]   Shang C, Zhuang X, Zhang H, *et al.* Inhibitors of endosomal acidification suppress SARS-CoV-2 replication and relieve viral pneumonia in hACE2 transgenic mice. Virol J 2021; 18(1): 46.
[http://dx.doi.org/10.1186/s12985-021-01515-1] [PMID: 33639976]

[14]   Suvarnapathaki S, Chauhan D, Nguyen A, Ramalingam M, Camci-Unal G. Advances in Targeting ACE2 for Developing COVID-19 Therapeutics. Ann Biomed Eng 2022; 50(12): 1734-49.
[http://dx.doi.org/10.1007/s10439-022-03094-w] [PMID: 36261668]

[15]   Trougakos IP, Stamatelopoulos K, Terpos E, *et al.*, Insights to SARS-CoV-2 life cycle, pathophysiology, and rationalized treatments that target COVID-19 clinical complications. Biomed Sci 2021; 28(1): 9.
[http://dx.doi.org/10.1186/s12929-020-00703-5]

[16]   Campbell RA, Boilard E, Rondina MT. Is there a role for the ACE2 receptor in SARS-CoV-2 interactions with platelets? J Thromb Haemost 2021; 19(1): 46-50.
[http://dx.doi.org/10.1111/jth.15156] [PMID: 33119197]

[17]   Prabhakara C, Godbole R, Sil P, *et al.* Strategies to target SARS-CoV-2 entry and infection using dual mechanisms of inhibition by acidification inhibitors. PLoS Pathog 2021; 17(7): e1009706.
[http://dx.doi.org/10.1371/journal.ppat.1009706] [PMID: 34252168]

[18]   Ali M J, *et al.* Treatment Options for COVID-19: A Review, Frontiers in Medicine, vol. 7. Frontiers Media S.A., Jul. 31, 2020.
[http://dx.doi.org/10.3389/fmed.2020.00480]

[19]   Hoffmann M, Schroeder S, Kleine-Weber H, Müller MA, Drosten C, Pöhlmann S. Nafamostat Mesylate Blocks Activation of SARS-CoV-2: New Treatment Option for COVID-19. Antimicrob Agents Chemother 2020; 64(6): e00754-20.
[http://dx.doi.org/10.1128/AAC.00754-20] [PMID: 32312781]

[20]   Zhu H, Du W, Song M, Liu Q, Herrmann A, Huang Q. Spontaneous binding of potential COVID-19 drugs (Camostat and Nafamostat) to human serine protease TMPRSS2. Comput Struct Biotechnol J 2021; 19: 467-76.
[http://dx.doi.org/10.1016/j.csbj.2020.12.035] [PMID: 33505639]

[21]   Cai Y, Xu W, Gu C, *et al.* Griffithsin with A Broad-Spectrum Antiviral Activity by Binding Glycans in Viral Glycoprotein Exhibits Strong Synergistic Effect in Combination with A Pan-Coronavirus Fusion Inhibitor Targeting SARS-CoV-2 Spike S2 Subunit. Virol Sin 2020; 35(6): 857-60.
[http://dx.doi.org/10.1007/s12250-020-00305-3] [PMID: 33052520]

[22]   Lamb YN. Nirmatrelvir Plus Ritonavir: First Approval. Drugs 2022; 82(5): 585-91.
[http://dx.doi.org/10.1007/s40265-022-01692-5] [PMID: 35305258]

[23]   dos Santos W G. Natural history of COVID-19 and current knowledge on treatment therapeutic options, Biomedicine and Pharmacotherapy, vol. 129. Elsevier Masson SAS, Sep. 01, 2020.
[http://dx.doi.org/10.1016/j.biopha.2020.110493]

[24]   Mostafa-Hedeab G, Al-kuraishy HM, Al-Gareeb AI, Welson NN, El-Saber Batiha G, Conte-Junior CA. Selinexor and COVID-19: The Neglected Warden. Front Pharmacol 2022; 13: 884228.
[http://dx.doi.org/10.3389/fphar.2022.884228] [PMID: 35559257]

[25]   Patocka J, Kuca K, Oleksak P, *et al.* Rapamycin: Drug Repurposing in SARS-CoV-2 Infection. Pharmaceuticals (Basel) 2021; 14(3): 217.
[http://dx.doi.org/10.3390/ph14030217] [PMID: 33807743]

[26]   Li Y, Yang X, Yan P, Sun T, Zeng Z, Li S. Metformin in Patients With COVID-19: A Systematic Review and Meta-Analysis. Front Med (Lausanne) 2021; 8: 704666.
[http://dx.doi.org/10.3389/fmed.2021.704666] [PMID: 34490296]

[27]   Navarese EP, Musci RL, Frediani L, Gurbel PA, Kubica J. Ion channel inhibition against COVID-19: A novel target for clinical investigation. Cardiol J 2020; 27(4): 421-4.
[http://dx.doi.org/10.5603/CJ.a2020.0090] [PMID: 32643141]

[28]   Tiberghien P, de Lamballerie X, Morel P, Gallian P, Lacombe K, Yazdanpanah Y. Collecting and evaluating convalescent plasma for COVID-19 treatment: why and how? Vox Sang 2020; 115(6): 488-94.
[http://dx.doi.org/10.1111/vox.12926] [PMID: 32240545]

[29]   Majumder J, Minko T. Recent Developments on Therapeutic and Diagnostic Approaches for COVID-19, 2021.
[http://dx.doi.org/10.1208/s12248-020-00532-2]

[30]   Tobian AAR, Cohn CS, Shaz BH. COVID-19 convalescent plasma. Blood 2022; 140(3): 196-207.
[http://dx.doi.org/10.1182/blood.2021012248] [PMID: 34695186]

[31]   De Santis GC, Oliveira LC, Garibaldi PMM, *et al*, High-Dose Convalescent Plasma for Treatment of Severe COVID-19. Emerg Infect Dis 2022; 28(3): 548-5.

[32]   Brown BL, McCullough J. Treatment for emerging viruses: Convalescent plasma and COVID-19. Transfus Apheresis Sci 2020; 59(3): 102790.
[http://dx.doi.org/10.1016/j.transci.2020.102790] [PMID: 32345485]

[33]   Gavriatopoulou M, Ntanasis-Stathopoulos I, Korompoki E, *et al.*, Emerging treatment strategies for COVID-19 infection, Clinical and Experimental Medicine, Springer Science and Business Media Deutschland GmbH, 2021; 21(2): 167–179.
[http://dx.doi.org/10.1007/s10238-020-00671-y]

[34]   Menéndez R, González P, Latorre A, Méndez R. Immune treatment in COVID-19. Rev Esp Quimioter 2022; 35(Suppl 1) (Suppl. 1): 59-63.
[http://dx.doi.org/10.37201/req/s01.14.2022] [PMID: 35488829]

[35]   Taylor PC, Adams AC, Hufford MM, de la Torre I, Winthrop K, Gottlieb RL. Neutralizing monoclonal antibodies for treatment of COVID-19. Nat Rev Immunol 2021; 21(6): 382-93.
[http://dx.doi.org/10.1038/s41577-021-00542-x] [PMID: 33875867]

[36]   Forchette L, Sebastian W, Liu T. A Comprehensive Review of COVID-19 Virology, Vaccines, Variants, and Therapeutics, Current Medical Science, Huazhong University of Science and Technology, 2021; 41(6): 1037–1051.
[http://dx.doi.org/10.1007/s11596-021-2395-1]

[37]   Menéndez R, González P, Latorre A, Méndez R. Immune treatment in COVID-19. Rev Esp Quimioter 2022; 35(Suppl 1) (Suppl. 1): 59-63.
[http://dx.doi.org/10.37201/req/s01.14.2022] [PMID: 35488829]

[38]   Haddad F, Dokmak G, Karaman R. A Comprehensive Review on the Efficacy of Several Pharmacologic Agents for the Treatment of COVID-19. Life (Basel) 2022; 12(11): 1758.
[http://dx.doi.org/10.3390/life12111758] [PMID: 36362912]

[39]   Taylor PC, Adams AC, Hufford MM, de la Torre I, Winthrop K, Gottlieb RL. Neutralizing monoclonal antibodies for treatment of COVID-19. Nat Rev Immunol 2021; 21(6): 382-93.
[http://dx.doi.org/10.1038/s41577-021-00542-x] [PMID: 33875867]

[40]   Haddad F, Dokmak G, Karaman R. A Comprehensive Review on the Efficacy of Several Pharmacologic Agents for the Treatment of COVID-19. Life (Basel) 2022; 12(11): 1758.
[http://dx.doi.org/10.3390/life12111758] [PMID: 36362912]

[41]   Hwang YC, Lu RM, Su SC, *et al.* Monoclonal antibodies for COVID-19 therapy and SARS-CoV-2 detection. J Biomed Sci 2022; 29(1): 1-50.
[http://dx.doi.org/10.1186/s12929-021-00784-w] [PMID: 34983527]

[42]   Rizk JG, Kalantar-Zadeh K, Mehra MR, Lavie CJ, Rizk Y, Forthal DN. Pharmaco-Immunomodulatory Therapy in COVID-19. Drugs 2020; 80(13): 1267-92.
[http://dx.doi.org/10.1007/s40265-020-01367-z] [PMID: 32696108]

[43]   Rommasi F, Nasiri MJ, Mirsaeidi M. Immunomodulatory agents for COVID-19 treatment: possible mechanism of action and immunopathology features. Mol Cell Biochem 2022; 477(3): 711-26.
[http://dx.doi.org/10.1007/s11010-021-04325-9] [PMID: 35013850]

[44]   Quek E, Tahir H, Kumar P, Hastings R, Jha R. Treatment of COVID-19: a review of current and prospective pharmacotherapies. Br J Hosp Med (Lond) 2021; 82(3): 1-9.
[http://dx.doi.org/10.12968/hmed.2021.0112] [PMID: 33792391]

[45]   Hertanto DM, Wiratama BS, Sutanto H, Wungu CDK. Immunomodulation as a potent COVID-19 pharmacotherapy: Past, present and future. J Inflamm Res 2021; 14(July): 3419-28.
[http://dx.doi.org/10.2147/JIR.S322831] [PMID: 34321903]

[46]   Zhang Y, Chen Y, Meng Z. Immunomodulation for Severe COVID-19 Pneumonia: The State of the

Art. Front Immunol 2020; 11(November): 577442.
[http://dx.doi.org/10.3389/fimmu.2020.577442] [PMID: 33240265]

[47]   Rizk JG, Kalantar-Zadeh K, Mehra MR, Lavie CJ, Rizk Y, Forthal DN. Pharmaco-Immunomodulatory Therapy in COVID-19. Drugs 2020; 80(13): 1267-92.
[http://dx.doi.org/10.1007/s40265-020-01367-z] [PMID: 32696108]

[48]   Drożdżal S, Rosik J, Lechowicz K, *et al.* An update on drugs with therapeutic potential for SARS-CoV-2 (COVID-19) treatment. Drug Resist Updat 2021; 59(November): 100794.
[http://dx.doi.org/10.1016/j.drup.2021.100794] [PMID: 34991982]

[49]   Kumar P, Malik YS, Ganesh B, *et al.* CRISPR-Cas System: An Approach With Potentials for COVID-19 Diagnosis and Therapeutics. Front Cell Infect Microbiol 2020; 10(November): 576875.
[http://dx.doi.org/10.3389/fcimb.2020.576875] [PMID: 33251158]

[50]   Ama A, Ama A. Use of CRISPR to Enhance and Combat Human Viral Infections as HIV and SARS-Cov-2. J Emerg Dis Virol 2020; 5(2)
[http://dx.doi.org/10.16966/2473-1846.151]

[51]   He X, Zeng XX. Immunotherapy and CRISPR Cas Systems: Potential Cure of COVID-19? Drug Des Devel Ther 2022; 16(March): 951-72.
[http://dx.doi.org/10.2147/DDDT.S347297] [PMID: 35386853]

[52]   Abbott TR, Dhamdhere G, Liu Y, *et al.* Development of CRISPR as an Antiviral Strategy to Combat SARS-CoV-2 and Influenza. Cell 2020; 181(4): 865-876.e12.
[http://dx.doi.org/10.1016/j.cell.2020.04.020] [PMID: 32353252]

[53]   Gadwal A, Roy D, Khokhar M, Modi A, Sharma P, Purohit P. CRISPR/Cas-New Molecular Scissors in Diagnostics and Therapeutics of COVID-19. Indian J Clin Biochem 2021; 36(4): 459-67.
[http://dx.doi.org/10.1007/s12291-021-00977-y] [PMID: 33879980]

[54]   Najafabadi ZY, Fanuel S, Falak R, Kaboli S, Kardar GA. The Trend of CRISPR-Based Technologies in COVID-19 Disease: Beyond Genome Editing. Mol Biotechnol 2022; 2: M.
[http://dx.doi.org/10.1007/s12033-021-00431-7] [PMID: 35091986]

[55]   Lotfi M, Rezaei N. CRISPR/Cas13: A potential therapeutic option of COVID-19. Biomed Pharmacother 2020; 131: 110738.
[http://dx.doi.org/10.1016/j.biopha.2020.110738] [PMID: 33152914]

[56]   Zhu Y, Li J, Pang Z. Recent insights for the emerging COVID-19: Drug discovery, therapeutic options and vaccine development, Asian Journal of Pharmaceutical Sciences, Shenyang Pharmaceutical University, 2021; 16(1): 4–23.
[http://dx.doi.org/10.1016/j.ajps.2020.06.001]

[57]   Dube T, Ghosh A, Mishra J, Kompella U B, Panda J J. Repurposed Drugs, Molecular Vaccines, Immune-Modulators, and Nanotherapeutics to Treat and Prevent COVID-19 Associated with SARS-CoV-2, a Deadly Nanovector Advanced Therapeutics 2021; 4(2): Blackwell Publishing Ltd..
[http://dx.doi.org/10.1002/adtp.202000172]

[58]   Abbott TR, Dhamdhere G, Liu Y, *et al.* Development of CRISPR as an Antiviral Strategy to Combat SARS-CoV-2 and Influenza. Cell 2020; 181(4): 865-876.e12.
[http://dx.doi.org/10.1016/j.cell.2020.04.020] [PMID: 32353252]

[59]   Jorda A, *et al.* Convalescent Plasma Treatment in Patients with COVID-19: A Systematic Review and Meta-Analysis," Frontiers in Immunology, Frontiers Media S.A., 2022; 13.
[http://dx.doi.org/10.3389/fimmu.2022.817829]

[60]   Gadwal A, Roy D, Khokhar M, Modi A, Sharma P, Purohit P. CRISPR/Cas-New Molecular Scissors in Diagnostics and Therapeutics of COVID-19, Indian Journal of Clinical Biochemistry, Springer, 2021; 36(4): 459–467.
[http://dx.doi.org/10.1007/s12291-021-00977-y]

[61]   Kumar P, Yashpal SM, Ganesh B *et al.*, CRISPR-Cas System: An Approach With Potentials for

COVID-19 Diagnosis and Therapeutics. Front Cell Infect Microbiol 10: 576875.
[http://dx.doi.org/10.3389/fcimb.2020.576875]

[62]   Klassen SA, Senefeld JW, Senese KA, *et al.*, Convalescent Plasma Therapy for COVID-19: A Graphical Mosaic of the Worldwide Evidence. Front Med (Lausanne) 2021; 8: 684151.
[http://dx.doi.org/10.3389/fmed.2021.684151]

[63]   E. Salazar, Perez KK, Ashraf M, *et al.*, Treatment of Coronavirus Disease 2019 (COVID-19) Patients with Convalescent Plasma. Am J Pathol 2020; 190(8): 1680-90.

Challenges Posed by COVID-19

Mohammad Sufian Badar[1,2,3,4], **Waseem Ali**[5], **Onaiza Ansari**[6], **Asrar Ahmad Malik**[7], **Javaid Ahmad Sheikh**[6,*] and **Anam Mursaleen**[6]

[1] *Department of Bioengineering, University of California, Riverside, CA, USA*

[2] *Universal Scientific Education and Research Network (USERN), Tehran, Iran*

[3] *Director (Academic), SPI Darbhanga, India*

[4] *Department of Computer Science and Engineering (Bioinformatics), School of Engineering Sciences and Technology (SEST), Jamia Hamdard, New Delhi, India*

[5] *Department of Molecular Medicine, Jamia Hamdard, New Delhi, India*

[6] *Department of Biotechnology, Jamia Hamdard, New Delhi, India*

[7] *Department of Life Sciences, Sharda University, Greater Noida, UP, India*

Abstract: SARS-CoV-2, the viral inciting agent of one of the deadliest pulmonary infections known as novel Coronavirus Disease (COVID-19) has resulted in millions of deaths. With the first incidence being reported in the city of Wuhan, China, in December 2019 and dealing with a pathogen capable of quick as well as easy transmissibility, undefined symptoms, non-availability of therapeutics and acclimatization/adaptation to COVID-19 scenario can be acknowledged as the phase I challenges faced by the world. The novel and enduring COVID-19 pandemic that the world has been witnessing for the past few years has advanced to the huge and exhaustive phase II challenges that encompass the implementation of one of the longest complete global shutdowns, unusual practice of work-from-home practices, immense pressure on the healthcare sector, suspension of daily activities, majorly closing of schools and colleges, no social gatherings, the urgency to develop anti-COVID therapeutic/vaccine, lack of awareness/negligence, antimicrobial resistance and emergence of variants that fuelled the spread of the infection. Despite the combined efforts that might have flattened the curve of the infection, it remains a major trigger for rolling out post-COVID challenges, being a serious concern for every facet of the society that includes continuous deterioration of mental health, financial instability, and fear of death. This chapter focuses on addressing the challenges and threats that prevailed during and post-COVID period. Additionally, it also summarizes strategies to combat the setbacks posed by SARS-CoV-2 infection.

Keywords: COVID-19, Infection, Pathogen, Therapeutic, SARS-CoV-2, Vaccine, Variants.

---

* **Corresponding author Javaid Ahmad Sheikh:** Department of Biotechnology, Jamia Hamdard, New Delhi, India; E-mail: jasheikh@jamiahamdard.ac.in

INTRODUCTION

Individuals suffering from atypical viral pneumonia were initially observed at the centre of pandemic, Wuhan, China, towards the late 2019. Later, the International Committee on Taxonomy of Viruses (ICTV) and the World Health Organization (WHO) coined the disease and viral pathogen associated with it as Coronavirus disease-2019 (COVID-19) and Severe Acute Respiratory Syndrome Coronavirus 2 (SARS-CoV-2) [1]. According to the WHO update on COVID-19, the death toll stands at over 6.9 million with over 759 million confirmed cases **[Ref-Who Report https://covid19.who.int/].** The mode of transmission is primarily via respiratory droplets and contact routes, and the median latency period is around 4-5 days prior to symptom outset [2, 3]. The symptomatic COVID-19 patients often experience fever/chills, dry cough, shortness of breath(dyspnoea), upper airway congestion, loss of smell (anosmia) and loss of taste (ageusia) [1, 2]. Interaction of SARS-CoV-2 with the ACE2 receptor mediates its entry inside the pulmonary tract (the primary and potential target), wherein the virus replicates causing life-threatening acute respiratory distress syndrome (ARDS) [1, 4]. The underlying pathogenesis can be categorized into three stages: **a. Proliferative Stage**- the initial stage of the infection that is marked by SARS-CoV-2 infiltration into pulmonary parenchyma through the molecular gateway (ACE2 receptor). Activation of early innate defenses and the appearance of mild constitutional symptoms are hallmarks of this stage. **b. Pulmonary Stage-** the second stage of COVID-19 progression is defined by elevated signs of inflammation, tissue damage and impaired pulmonary function. **c. Hyper inflammatory Stage-** During this stage, the course of the disease advances to systemic inflammation, high levels of pro-inflammatory cytokines (IL-2, IL-6, IL-7, IL-10, C-reactive protein (CRP) thereby creating a '**Cytokine Storm**', a major cause of lung damage associated with life-threatening complexities including MOF, ARDS, septic shock, hemorrhage/coagulopathy, acute heart/liver/kidney injury, and secondary bacterial infections [1].

Due to the sudden outbreak worldwide, mass widespread and unknown outcomes of novel COVID-19, it was declared as a public health emergency on 30 January 2020 [5] followed by the very first shutdown in Wuhan on 23 Feb 2020 [4]. Owing to the health crisis globally and recurring COVID-19 waves, the world has faced multiple lockdowns/complete shutdowns for COVID-19 containment. Also, preventive guidelines were issued on a regular basis by competent authorities. Despite these efforts, COVID-19 continues to pose serious threats and challenges to public health. The deadly virus can be considered a global challenger as it has acutely affected different facets of society ranging from public health to the global economy. This chapter calls into question an in-depth understanding of these challenges, thereby necessitating appropriate measures to overcome these challenges as depicted in Fig. (**1**).

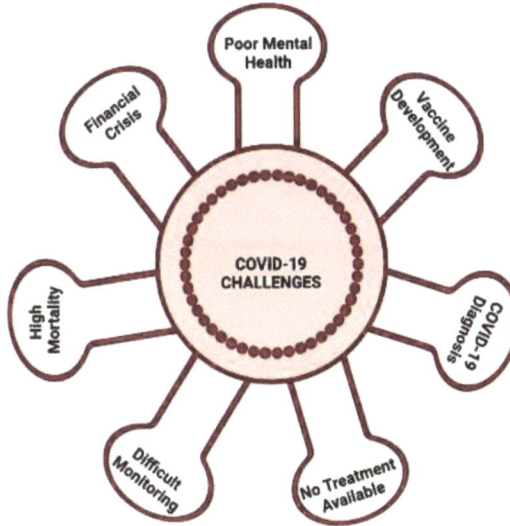

Fig. (1).   Depiction of different challenges posed by COVID-19 pandemic caused by novel SARS-CoV-2 virus.

The challenges posed by Coronavirus (COVID-19) pandemic are enlisted below-

Challenge: Mental Health of Healthcare Workers

COVID-19 can be attributed, credited, and regarded as a primary cause of disruption to health and health services worldwide. Frontline workers or health care workers (HCWs) including doctors, nurses have been 'diligent and committed heroes' in putting their undying efforts in the fight against ongoing COVID-19 pandemic [6]. Though being frontline fighters, HCWs have also been identified as a 'vulnerable/risk group' who suffered a decline in mental well-being/subjected to/prone to a decline in mental well-being [7]. HCWs can be described as the 'second victim' of COVID-19 pandemic as they have faced challenges not only limited to their professional space but at personal levels too, a reason for their mental health deterioration [6]. The tally of crisis for HCWs began with initial challenges, such as diagnosis, contact tracing, quarantine, and treatment of suspected or confirmed COVID-19 cases. With the upsurge in COVID-19 cases, HCWs faced mental challenges with meagre resources of personal protective equipment, patient overflow and continuous exposure to COVID-19 hot zones, prolonged work shifts, and extensive media coverage [8], clearly described in Fig. (**2**).

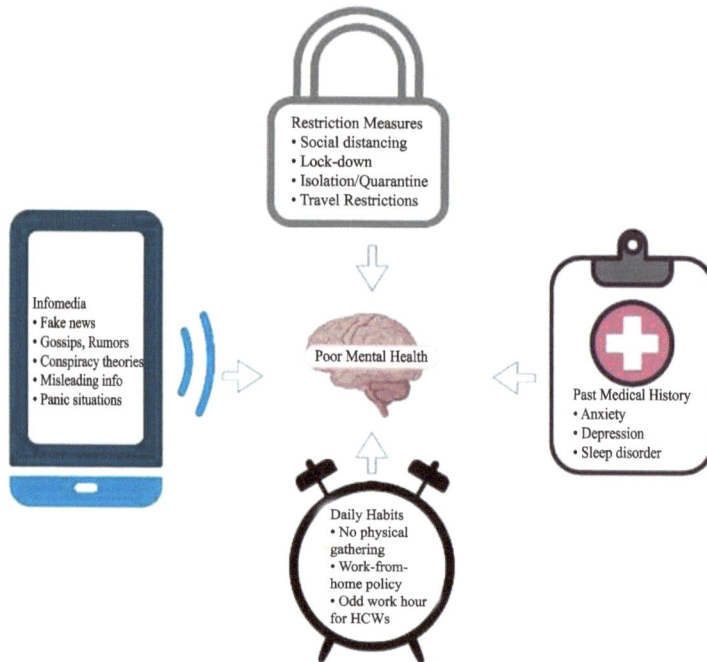

Fig. (2). Key stressors associated with poor mental health due to COVID-19.

Risk Factors Associated with Challenges Related to Mental Health Due to COVID-19 Outbreak
Infomania

Infomania is an obsessive urge to keep an update of information via digital platforms, including social media, instant messaging, online news, and e-mail. Therefore, infomania impairs concentration and leads to continuous stress [9]. A specific type of epidemic known as an infodemic—the accelerated diffusion of information of all kinds, including rumours, gossip, incorrect information, misinformation, and conspiracy theories is frequently linked to the rapid spread of COVID-19 [9].

A unique "infodemic" overloaded with mis/information in social media and internet increases a major risk to public and global mental health during this COVID-19 crisis as it promotes anxiety. For example, recent studies found that insufficient information or misinformation ('fake news') on COVID-19 was associated with poorer mental health and well-being. Social media has been a key stressor resulting in poor mental health outcomes amongst HCWs and younger generation [10].

Restriction Measures

Preventive restriction measures aimed at avoiding social/physical gatherings and staying indoor has proven to be an effective containment measure against the rapid dissemination of coronavirus infection/to flatten the curve of COVID-19 infection but it has also significantly ruled out negative impact on mental health particularly medical practitioners and nurses. Healthcare workers are more susceptible to anxiety and depression due to multiple reasons- non-availability of etiotropic therapy and efficient diagnostics tools and concerns about safeguarding their family members from the indirect transmission of the virus [8]. Furthermore, previous findings revealed engaging oneself in

COVID-19 environment with the insufficient supply of personal protective kit escalating fear levels concerning quick transmission and 47% HCWs faced sleep disturbances due to hectic schedules and over time [8]. The detrimental consequences/repercussion of restriction measures is not only limited to HCWs, but is also responsible for poor mental health of general population too. For instance, sudden shut-down and strict lockdowns have augmented mental stress and solitude amongst vulnerable risk groups. Therefore COVID-19 lockdowns leading to desolation/loneliness is a prognostic factor for anxiety and depression [11].

Changes in Daily Habits

COVID-19 pandemic has severely affected routine social behaviour of both non-healthcare and healthcare workers. During the initial phase of restriction impositions, work-from-home policies became popular but it soon turned out to worsen the mental well-being as it hampered physical gatherings leading to boredom, frustration, and social isolation. Comparatively, the pandemic compelled/demanded healthcare workers to be on toes round the clock resulting in anxiety and depression. In addition, with effect of lockdown curfews, disconnection with the loved ones especially nurses (female HCWs) has been a victim/sufferer of emotional distress and burnouts.

Current or Past Medical History-

Emergence of COVID-19 pandemic has elevated challenges for vulnerable group already dealing with serious mental illness. Due to exhausting work hours, HCWs are usual targets of anxiety, depression, and sleep disorders. Therefore, the pandemic has disproportionately aggravated mental trauma suffered by health care professionals. This has adversely compromised the quality of patient care [12]. Moreover, COVID-19 survivors exhibiting pre-mental illness has also been subjected to psychological problem such as post-traumatic syndrome disorder

(PTSD), acute and long-term cognitive disorders, substance abuse, behavioural addictions, self-harm, domestic violence, stigmatization, xenophobia, and emotional disorders both at personal and professional levels [12, 13].

Challenge: Vaccine

Vaccine development can be an effective therapeutic strategy in fighting against infectious diseases including novel coronavirus infection and paving the way to herd immunity without calamitous outcomes. Currently recommended treatment regimen to counter COVID-19 includes recovering therapy dependent on plasma of convalescent patient, recombinant antibodies, and repurposing pre-approved FDA-drugs. The SARS-CoV-2 pathogen can sow its infection due to the unavailability of the efficacious and safe vaccine resulting in high mortality rates. Though a new vaccine development is a resource-intensive process, the need of the hour is to identify the potential vaccine candidate for the betterment of the society [14]. Despite advances in research and 30 vaccines in clinical trials and approximately 200 potential vaccine candidates have been screened for vaccine development, a successful and fast-track COVID-19 vaccine remains to be a breakthrough for the researchers worldwide [15], because of the hurdles depicted in Fig. (3).

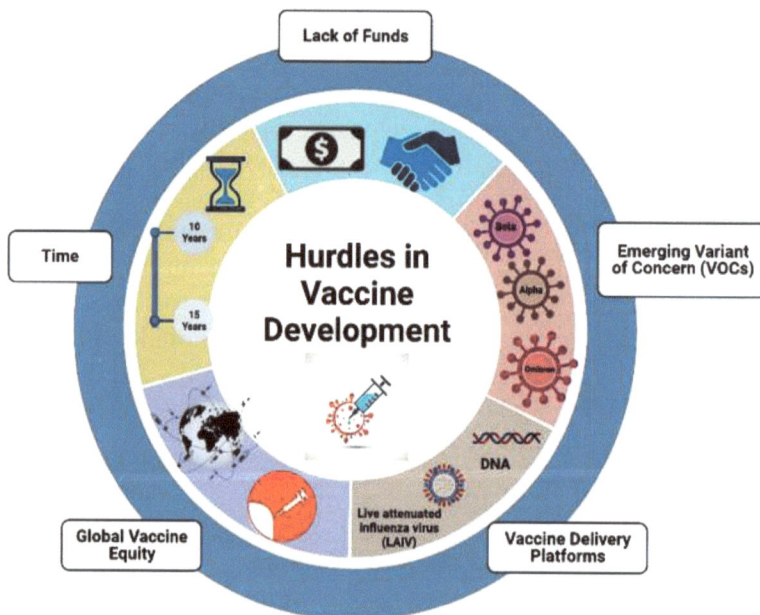

Fig. (3). Possible obstacles during development of a COVID-19 vaccine.

Major Hurdles in Vaccine Development against Global COVID-19 Pandemic

Lack of Proper Funds

A successful vaccine development is challenging due to mandatory clinical trials for its efficacy and safety surveillance. Thus, large scale/commercial investment is a pre-requisite for a vaccine development, production, equity, and distribution [15].

Time is a Barrier

Time is a barrier in the sense that the generation of a new vaccine is a gradual, and time-consuming process for any infectious disease. Conventionally, vaccine creation is a complex, long-lasting task which may take up to 10-15 years [15]. To date, the only fast-track vaccine that was developed in a span of 5-years was against mumps [15]. Undoubtedly, a highly immunogenic, safe and efficacious COVID-19 vaccine is a difficult job to be accomplished in a short time span of 12-24 months.

Emergence/Evolution of Variants of Concern (VOCs)

The different phenotypic lineages deriving out of parental SARS-CoV-2 wild type (WT) strain are a result of genomic alterations specifically amino acid substitution in spike protein (S-protein) [16]. These mutations have given an edge by aiding easy access inside the host upon interaction with the ACE2 receptor and raising an alarming threat. The appearance of four SARS-CoV-2 genomic variants designated by WHO as Alpha, Beta, Gamma and Delta are regarded as variants of concern (VOCs) [17]. The mutational complexities giving rise to VOCs are strongly associated with severe implications concerning increased transmission and virulence as well as a reduction in vaccine effectiveness (VE) and long-lasting immunity [18, 19]. Also as observed that post-vaccination, chances of re-infection are quite high due to circulating VOCs [17]. Evidence indicates that the emergence of VOCs is also contributing towards the growing resistance towards neutralization via convalescent and antibody therapies [20].

Some examples can be cited in correlation with strain-specific resistance and re-infection:

i. Gamma variants did not respond to monoclonal antibody (mAbs) treatment in comparison to beta strain [20].

ii. Also, gamma variant was responsible for recurring infection, dodging adaptive immunity, resulting in a rise in infected cases and burdening the healthcare system. system, as reported in Brazil towards the end of the first COVID-19 wave [19, 20].

iii. L452R mutation occurring in the RBD region of Delta variant contributed towards resistance developed against virus-neutralizing antibody, specifically Bamlanivimab [14].

Vaccine Equity

Unequal vaccine distribution is a potential barrier intensifying the challenges against global COVID-19 pandemic [21]. The unequal access to available vaccine by all income-group countries raises the concerns regarding vaccine production, public health equity, vaccine hesitancy, rate of vaccination making unvaccinated individuals as the primary targets of SARS-CoV-2 infection leading to a surge in the transmission and evolution of the pathogen [22, 23]. Invention of a successful vaccine will not guarantee an end of the current pandemic as the unequal vaccine distribution will promote continuity of social distancing and restriction norms followed by financial instability.

Different Vaccine Delivery Platforms

VE and safety largely depend on the technological platform employed for the vaccine delivery and development. Several platforms available for vaccine development have their advantages and disadvantages, making it a tough choice for the researchers and manufacturers, as summarized in **Table 1**.

Table 1. Major COVID-19 vaccine platforms with their advantages and disadvantages.

Vaccine Technology	Vaccine Name and Developed by	Advantages of the Technology Employed	Disadvantages
mRNA	BNT162b2 (Pfizer/BioNTech) and mRNA-1273 (Moderna/NIH)	• High efficacy • Versatile • Easy and quick production of vaccines against evolving variants. • Simple to design, elicit stronger immunologic response	• High freezing storage temperature affecting vaccine distribution. • Highly unstable, safety issues

(Table 1) cont.....

Vaccine Technology	Vaccine Name and Developed by	Advantages of the Technology Employed	Disadvantages
Nonreplicating viral vectors. (Adenoviral-based vaccines)	ChAdOx1 nCoV-19 (AstraZeneca/University of Oxfo	• Single dose regimen • Does not require deep freezing • Easy transportation and distribution • Safe to use	• Possibility of viral vector-neutralizing antibodies or pre-existing cell-mediated immunity • potential for displaying various immunological reactions
Protein Subunit (Recombinant protein)	Novavax NVX-CoV2373	• Simple storage • No logistic hurdles • Highly safe • Consistent/hassle-free manufacturing	• High cost • Lower immunogenicity • Multiple dose regimen requiring adjuvants
Inactivated virus	CoronaVac vaccine (Sinovac)	• Simple, quick and convenient to produce • Safe • High-levels of neutralizing antibodies	• Hypersensitivity

Challenge: COVID-19 Diagnosis

The ASSURED criteria (Affordable, Sensitive, Specific, User-friendly, Rapid, and Robust, Equipment-free and Deliverable to end-users), as outlined by WHO applicable to the duo *Mycobacterium tuberculosis* and SARS-Cov-2, is focused on discovering novel diagnostic tools [24, 25]. Speedy testing is a major point of concern to deal with highly contagious viral enemy SARS-CoV-2. Conventionally, clinical detection of SARS-CoV-2 relies on molecular tests (RT-PCR), serology test and radiological interventions such as computed tomography (CT) with their merits and demerits [26], as discussed in Fig. (**4**). Out of all detection methods, qPCR is regarded as **'gold standard molecular test'** due to its specific detection of viral genomic regions [27]. Moreover, in the absence of a preventive cure such as vaccine or a drug, the urgency of developing a rapid, accurate, sensitive, and specific diagnostic tools that can act as **'auxiliary tool'** can ensure proper surveillance and screening [27, 28]. Lack of reliable, high-performance, cost-effective diagnostic measure will also avoid long-term use of face masks, complete lockdown and social distancing and other threats for global public health [27].

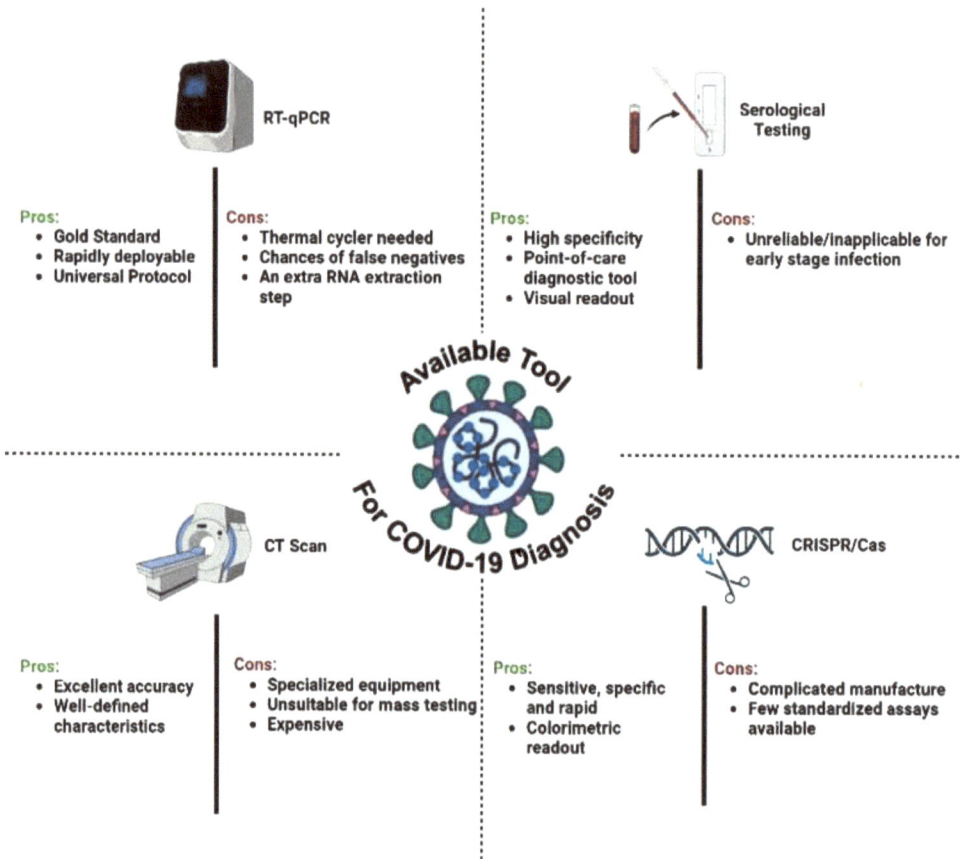

Fig. (4). Advantages and disadvantages of different diagnostic tools available for COVID-19.

Factors Interfering Diagnosis of COVID-19

Delay in diagnosis has been a major factor for a huge leap in COVID-19 cases. The possible reasons for the delay that can be considered comprises limited diagnostic tools, specialized laboratories- a prerequisite and various other factors that are represented in Fig. (**5**).

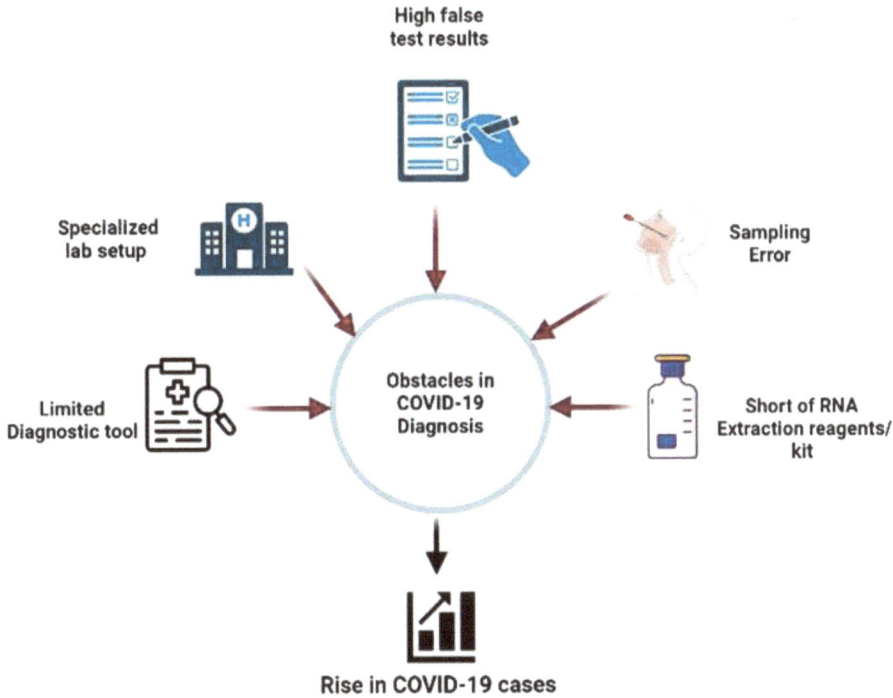

Fig. (5). Potential factors leading to delayed/mis-diagnosis of COVID-19, thereby resulting in upsurge of COVID-19 cases.

Unavailability of Effective Diagnostic Tool

Currently available testing tools including RT-PCR or serological assays are either low-performance or compromising the sensitivity or specificity, hindering the diagnosis of both symptomatic as well as asymptomatic individuals [29].

Specialized Laboratory Settings

SARS-CoV-2 being a highly contagious pathogen requires biosafety containment facility level-2 for procedures such as RNA extraction. Therefore, setting up of such containment facilities in a short span of time is an expensive business requiring technical as well as prior approval is needed from the competent authority [26].

False Results

Commercially available rapid antigen test kit and other serological assays are prone to either high false-positive negative result or failing to confirm the presence of the virus. It has worsened the screening of asymptomatic cases and leaving the infected cases untreated, thereby increasing the chances of transmission [30]. In accordance with the One Health Concept, the WHO advises anticipating future disease outbreaks before they reach pandemic levels and early diagnosis among carriers. However, it will be very challenging to screen people, especially in LMICs, because of the availability of tests with lesser sensitivity and higher costs (between $10 and $40 per test) [30].

Sampling Error

The type of sample, the right time of sampling with respect to the course of the disease is a constraint in correct and timely diagnosis of COVID-19 infection [26].

Shortage of kits/limited Supply of the Reagents

With a sharp rise in COVID-19 cases, there was a scarcity in medical supplies including RT-PCR, serological kits as well as reagents required for RNA extraction that ultimately delayed the diagnosis of COVID-19 patients affecting the course of the treatment [26].

Challenge: Identification of Potential of Drug Candidates Against COVID-19

Screening of drug candidate is itself challenging. The challenges for selecting drug candidates are the mechanism of action of drug candidates in different cell lines, poor clinical manifestations of human diseases in rodent or small-anima experimental models and undefined antiviral clinical trial endpoints associated with human testing [31], more precisely defined in Fig. (**6**).

Notably, following hallmarks are desired in a drug candidate to be considered as an 'antidote' against SARS-Cov-2 infection: 1. Easy/smooth administration via oral route, 2. Cost-effective and readily available to low-income countries, 3. Blocking advancement of COVID-19 to severe infection stages, and 4. Efficacy and potent against VOCs [32]. Therefore, to combat the disease, it is urgently required to develop a solution [33]. Therefore, scientists are working aggressively to develop new medicines to stop or lessen the increasing COVID-19 infections.

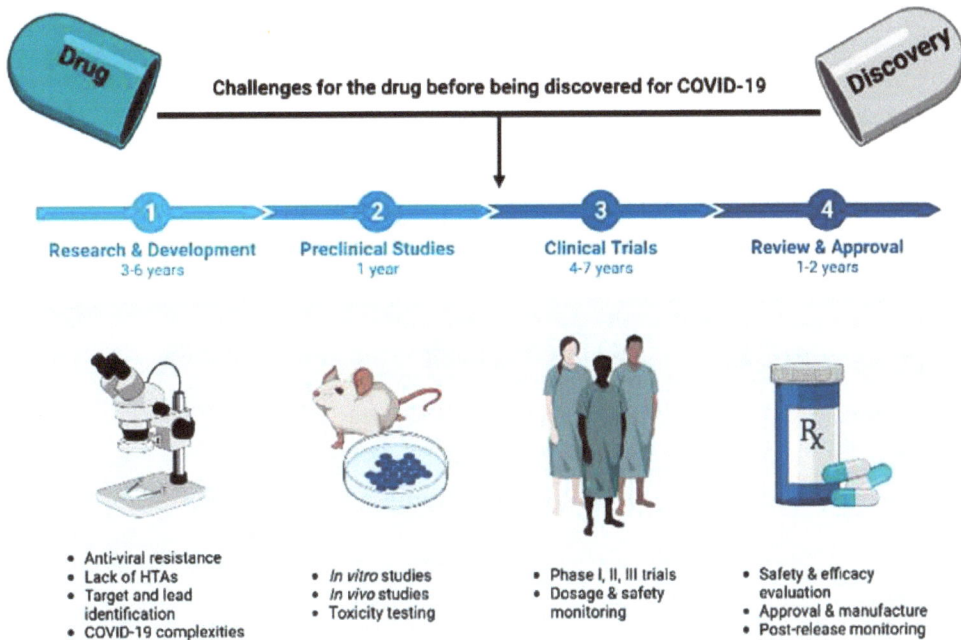

Fig. (6). Different stages of a drug-discovery process for SARS-CoV-2 infection.

Why Drug Discovery is a Challenge?

Mandatory Clinical Trials

The drug discovery is a long process and involves many steps: The first step, which takes an average of 6.5 years to complete, includes researching drugs in laboratories while using animals to test their safety followed by a 30-day safety review. Following animal studies, the next step is a human trial known as clinical research phase 1. This step, which lasts about 1.5 years focuses primarily on drug dose optimization, safety, pharmacokinetics, and pharmacology of the drugs on a small number of human volunteers followed by clinical research phase 2, which includes targeting a smaller group of patients with the targeted disease or condition, and the drug candidates showing safety for human use move to clinical research phase 3, which involves further testing on large number of patients throughout the country. Phase 2 and 3 takes around 5 years to be completed. Phase 4 of the process, which comes last, focuses on the frequency of rare adverse reactions and whether to keep marketing the drug [34 - 36]. Other factors that slow down the discovery of new drugs include uniformity and repeatability. Although duplication and reproducibility can be perceived as a waste of time and resources, they are, however, necessary to provide more records and proofs to validate the safety and effectiveness of the treatment before it is recommended to the general public [37].

Drug Designing Approaches

Structure-based drug design and artificial intelligence (AI) are modern computer-aided drug design (CADD) methods employed against novel SARS-CoV-2 coronavirus. Structure-based drug design (SBDD) is an in-silico strategy that potentially identifies different molecular fragments or lead compounds or small-molecule protein inhibitors as drug candidates by virtually screening large compound libraries [38]. SBDD has been helpful in FDA-approval of three drugs and in carrying out clinical trials for approximately 50 molecules against COVID-19 infection [38]. Whereas, AI-based strategy involves machine or deep-learning tools leading to the discovery of lead compounds upon screening large biochemical repositories via the implementation of various algorithms [38]. Moreover, SBDD is a target-protein interactive approach and AI is a target-drug interactive approach [38]. In the context of COVID-19 antiviral drug development, conventional SBDD approach results in challenges for drug development due to non-availability of 3-dimensional structure of target proteins [38, 39] and AI-based drug methods do not provide expected results because of the limited knowledge about the two-year old viral pathogen [38]. Hence, it has led to advancement in the challenges of drug development against the deadly SARS-CoV-2.

Lack of Host-targeting agents (HTAs) and Anti-viral Resistance

The current recommended COVID-19 regimen relies on FDA-approved repurposed direct acting antivirals (DDAs) such as Remdesivir (an intravenously injected drug), that helps in quick recovery but no survival benefits or no decline in mortality rate [31]. Recent studies have indicated that SARS-CoV-2 can develop resistance against Remdesivir [31, 40]. Consequently, WHO recommended conditional use of Remdesivir on in-hospital patients [31]. Another suitable therapeutic approach against COVID-19 is the development of potential broad-spectrum Host-targeting agents (HTAs) that modulate essential host cells utilised by the virus for its replication [31]. The reason behind fewer HTAs against COVID-19 is insufficient commercial investments, less public-private collaborations, and lack of knowledge about host-pathogen interaction [31]. These pitfalls drive the attention towards the development of potent DDAs as well as HTAs that can particularly fight against pan-coronavirus lineages that can be administered orally.

COVID-19 Complexities

With rapidly evolving SARS-CoV-2 genome and its associated complexities, there are obstacles in the path to drug development. As the disease progression is heterogeneous, targeting single SARS-CoV-2 is not a practical approach and targeting multiple proteins with emerging mutations and variants is a time-consuming/laborious drug development process [39, 41]. However, with limited information about the SARS-Cov-2 pathogenesis, drug designing for different stages or critically-ill patients with comorbidities is another hurdle for effective therapeutic against novel COVID-19 pandemic [31].

Cost and Risk

Large commercial investment greatly influences different aspects of drug development, for instance the amount required to conduct clinical trials. The average expenditure for developing a new drug can range nearly 1 billion to whopping 11.8 billion dollars or more. Subsequently, only around 10% of drugs undergoing human trials hardly reaches the market possibly due to insufficient efficacy, concerns for safety in human use, inadequate funds for ongoing trials or no commercial interest, non-adherence to good manufacturing practice (GMP) and FDA-guidelines as well as poor patient outcomes. Because of these setbacks during drug discovery process, the researchers are facing tough times to develop a COVID-19 drug with high potency, efficacy and safety [37].

Challenge: Antimicrobial Resistance

Antimicrobial resistance (AMR), another collaterally rising hidden pandemic is getting fuelled due to COVID-19 outbreak. AMR- the **'silent killing pandemic'** has sought to claim approximately 1.7 million deaths in 2019 [42] as well as predictable of leading to 10 million deaths by 2050 [43], potentially becoming a global public threat with disastrous outcomes. Following SARS-CoV-2 infection, the emergence of anti-microbial organisms (AROs) for example, extended-spectrum β-lactamase (ESBL)-producing *Klebsiella pneumoniae*, carbapenem-resistant New Delhi metallo-β-lactamase (NDM)-producing Enterobacterales, *Acinetobacter baumannii*, methicillin-resistant *Staphylococcus aureus* (MRSA), pan-echinocandin-resistant *Candida glabrata* and multi-triazole-resistant *Aspergillus fumigatus* has been markedly accelerated [44]. Additionally, multi-drug resistant TB (MDR-TB) has been the largest contributory factor towards the exacerbation of antimicrobial resistance (The Review on Antimicrobial Resistance, 2016). The greater number of incidence reported to occur via dissemination instead of acquired resistance during the course [45]. To better understand the above statement, social distancing and restriction measures opted during COVID-19 era have proven to be effective in reducing transmission rates at community level, yet escalated the household transmission [45]. Hence, the novel COVID-19 pandemic projects itself as a potential risk factor for evolving AMR burden worldwide.

FACTORS RESPONSIBLE FOR THE RISE IN AMR DUE TO COVID-19 PANDEMIC

High Rate of Antimicrobial Utilization

The widespread use of broad-spectrum antibiotics during SARS-CoV-2 infection promoting AMR can be attributable to the following: a. the clinical manifestations of COVID-19 (cough, fever, radiological infiltrates), that are also characteristic of other infections including malaria/TB. Therefore, this superimposition of symptoms, and lack of biomarkers specific to SARS-Cov-2 infection might be a reason for clinicians to mis-diagnose and prescribe broad-spectrum antibiotics despite speculation of a viral disease [44, 45] b. other possible major drivers implying high utilization of antibiotics may be influenced by the fear and apprehension surrounding the COVID-19 outbreak as well as the lack of efficient anti-SARS-CoV-2 medicines [44] c. prevalence of variable co-infections (bacterial, fungal, parasitic/secondary infections) along with COVID-19 makes it tough to distinguish amongst primary SARS-Cov-2 infection and co-infections [44].

Disruption of Healthcare

Clinical care and healthcare services were severely affected for the management of HIV, TB and malaria due to COVID-19 lockdowns or transforming hospitals to dedicated COVID-19 only facilities. The disruptions in the treatment course of such long-term diseases or on/off treatment course might be responsible for aggravating AMR or relapsing of the infection [45].

Antibiotic Availability

Sudden outbreak of COVID-19 has resulted in the closure of trade, import and export of pharmaceutics disturbing the supply and demand chains with no routine manufacturing of antibiotics, leading to knock-on changes in usage patterns [45]. For instance, the countries relying on the import of generic medicines such as UK faced delayed supplies owing to travel restrictions and the countries such as India, one of the largest manufacturers and exporters of medicines faced a hike in demand in home markets, thereby a decline in export [45]. Such uneven distribution or accessibility or acute shortage of antibiotics causes concern over AMR emergence due to suboptimal antimicrobial consumption [45].

Challenge: Economical Burden

• Besides afflicting community health, the ongoing pandemic also has substantial impacts on global economy. With the emergence of COVID-19 pandemic, developed and under-developed have enormously suffered the financial setback mainly due to the measures (complete and global shutdown) taken to mitigate the widespread infection. COVID-19 has disrupted demand and supply chain forcing the world to face 'COVID-19 recession' and the blockades of the recession has been elucidated in Fig. (**7**). Data strongly suggest that various economic sectors have suffered a hardest-hit due to the prevailing pandemic including aviation, hospitality and tourism, stock market, trade and petroleum industry [46].

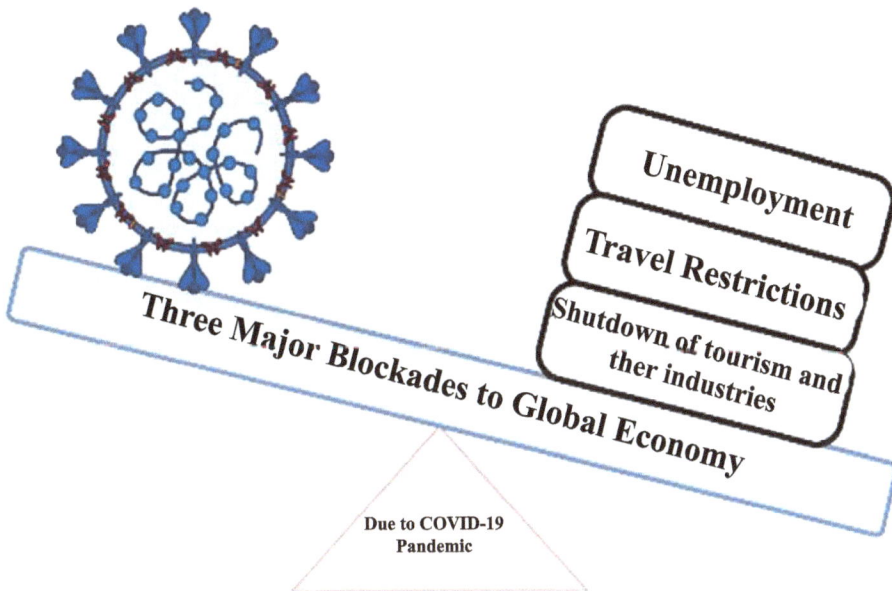

Fig. (7). Factors responsible for global economic burden due to novel COVID-19 pandemic.

Blockades Choking Global Economy Unemployment

With the outset of COVID-19, the global economy has shattered as it led to crashing of trade and business and millions of people faced unemployment [47]. In addition, telecommuting was advantageous to the skilled professionals but was a trouble maker for daily wagers. It also resulted in a hike in the unemployment rate as a single person became multi-tasking followed with lowered hiring and laying off employees [47], a major trigger for mental and psychological stress.

Travel Restrictions

The world economy was stagnant mainly due to mitigating measures of travel restrictions having impacted three major sectors- aviation, hospitality, and tourism. Being the highest revenue generating sectors, these industries were hardest-hit due to closing of borders, and experienced a fall in travel supply and demand and daily transactions, thereby crippling economic growth [48].

Impact on other Sectors

Sudden COVID-19 outbreak has considerably affected other sectors including healthcare, food, agriculture, petroleum, and oil industry; for instance, over-priced healthcare cost because of no routine OPD and hospital functioning, stockpiling of agricultural product, and reduced sales in petroleum and oil sector due to complete lockdown and immobilization [48]. Consequently, a parallel economic crisis is still prevalent along with COVID-19 pandemic.

Challenge: High morbidity and Mortality

As per WHO 2020 report, COVID-19 has become one of the highest death-causing pandemic of the century with over 1.6 million succumbed to death in a short span of time [49]. Acute symptoms of novel coronavirus infectious disease (COVID-19) can be correlated to increase in patients seeking intensive care unit (ICU) admissions as well as in-hospital deaths [50]. Therefore, it is a challenge for the healthcare sector, as illustrated in Fig. (**8**) with recurrent waves for better preparedness and arrangements needed for quality patient care.

Risk Factors Resulting in Higher Morbidity and Mortality Rates

Age

Severe COVID-19 disease is age-dependent. The factors making older population more vulnerable of developing chronic SARS-CoV-2 infection are- a decline in immunity with ageing, prevailing co-morbid conditions, and frequent hospital visits (a gateway for nosocomial infection) [51]. As per recent findings, geriatric population can be classified as 'high mortality group' [49, 52]. Although not only weakened immunity and comorbidity, also lack of cooperation is a major hurdle while treating older population.

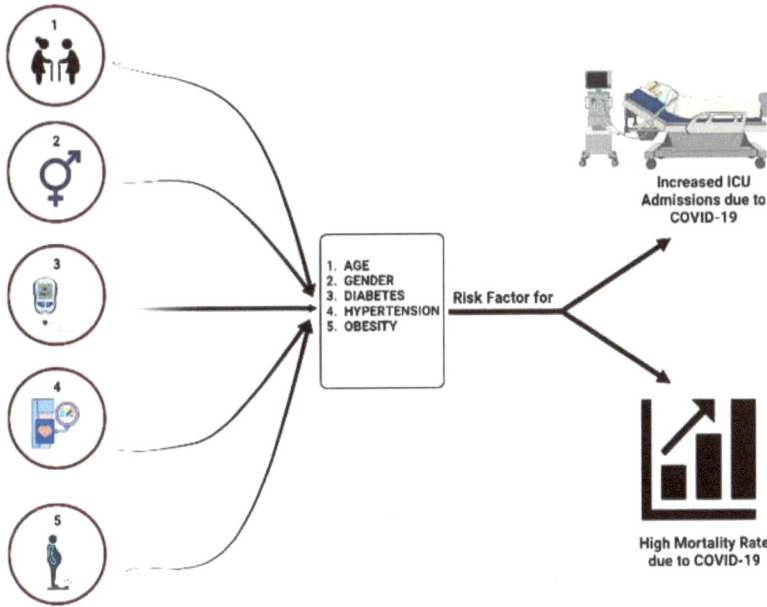

Fig. (8). COVID-19 risk factors associated with high ICU-admissions as well as mortality.

Gender

Male gender has also appeared to be a major risk factor for severe coronavirus infection, including higher hospitalization, and death rates in comparison to their female counterparts [52]. The driving force for the gender-biased COVID-19 deaths can be associated with the differential expression of ACE2 receptor on X and Y chromosomes [53]. As studied ACE2 gene is expressed on X chromosome, an added advantage for females as high coverage of the ACE2 receptor in the lungs could be a 'protective factor' against the severity of damage during COVID-19 infection [53]. Furthermore, females tend to elicit stronger innate as well as adaptive immune responses against invading pathogens and show higher vaccine efficacy in comparison to male counterparts making them a vulnerable victim of severe SARS-CoV-2 infection, resulting in higher male mortality ratio [53].

Co-morbidities: (Bacterial co-infection, viral co-infection, and non-communicable diseases)

Co-morbid disease and immunocompromised individuals are a vulnerable category to encounter severe COVID-19 infection and a major of reason for high mortality rate, a serious challenge posed due to novel COVID-19 global pandemic. The burden of affliction and rise in death toll can be seen as an additive effect of some common prevailing comorbidities- Hypertension (HTM), Diabetes Mellitus (DM), Obesity and Cardiovascular disease (CVD) amongst COVID-19 infected patients. As per statistics, severely ill COVID-19 patients with underlying comorbidities would 5 times more substantially need intensive care and ventilation and higher deaths have been reported in patients with no co-morbid conditions [53 - 55].

The Co-morbidities Associated with Severity and Greater Mortality during COVID-19 Pandemic

Obesity

Obesity is one of the co-morbid health issues concerning the severity of COVID-19 infection. Obesity is a contributing factor inducing metabolic complications resulting in diabetes mellitus type 2 and cardiovascular disease, which in turn highly impacts the lethality associated with COVID-19 [53, 56]. In addition, obesity is also a cause of chronic inflammation that in turn alters pulmonary physiology, upregulation of viral entry receptors, heterogeneous viral population, high viral titres, and extended viral shedding, worsening the SARS-CoV-2 pneumonia in obese individuals [57]. According to the world obesity federation 2021 report, the countries with obese population have experienced 10 times elevated mortality rates than countries having population exhibiting weight under normal range [53]. Therefore, obesity is a direct challenge in combating this viral infection due to increased demand of ventilation in obese people [53].

Hypertension

Hypertension and Cardiovascular diseases (CVD) are widely reported as the predominating comorbidities exponentially increasing the risk of developing a critical COVID-19 condition and mortality [58]. The plausible explanation can be the excessive use of hypertensive medication that includes inhibitors targeting renin-angiotensin system, such as ACE inhibitors (ACEI) and angiotensin-receptor blockers (ARB) that may significantly upregulate ACE2 receptors, a doorway for SARS-CoV-2 invasion [59]. Similarly, CVD comorbidity has also been a threatening condition associated with COVID-19 fatality possibly due to the use of the above-mentioned ACEI as well as ARB and secondly upregulation of ACE2 receptors in cardiovascular tissues [58]. Therefore, these pre-existing comorbidities can increase COVID-19 trajectory as such individuals are more susceptible and an easy target for SARS-CoV-2 infection.

Diabetes

Hyperglycaemia, repeatedly reported as the third most common comorbidity in severely ill COVID-19 patients [58]. Retrospective studies revealed that diabetes linked with obesity in older age group can be a **'risk predictor'** for COVID-19 progression and mortality [53, 60]. There has been growing evidence that glucose impairment is a cause for hyper-inflammation and increasing the risk for pulmonary infection, development of Adult Respiratory Distress Syndrome (ARDS) and multi-organ failure complications [58, 60, 61]. Another possible reason for increased COVID-19 susceptibility, severity and mortality in diabetogenic individuals is the use of anti-diabetogenic agents (DPP4 inhibitors) that are anti-inflammatory in nature resulting in decreased macrophage infiltration and dysregulated innate immune responses against COVID-19 pneumonia [58]. Hence, diabetic individuals require ICU admissions facing the mortal outcomes in comparison to non-diabetogenic counterparts, thereby compounding COVID-19 challenges for HCWs.

Bacterial/Viral co-infection

Pre-existing bacterial/viral respiratory ailments (for instance, Tuberculosis and HIV) worsen lung physiology and function [62, 63]. Therefore, impaired immune system and resistance co-infected such individuals who frequently develop ARDS and severe COVID-19 disease associated pneumonia. Meta-analysis, and systematic studies have revealed that pre-existing TB infection indicates two-fold jump in mortality in COVID-19 patients [63]. Likewise, disruptions in ART therapy for HIV patients contributed to high mortality beyond COVID-19 infection [64]. Hence, it can be speculated lung complications as a result of HIV-infection can also be a contributing factor for severe COVID-19 consequences. It can be concluded that TB and HIV co-pandemic can be a predisposing factor for exacerbating COVID-19 fatal outcomes, a grave concern for global public health.

COVID-19 Vaccination

Vaccine administration is a difficult task in immunocompromised individuals as well as in older age group, making them vulnerable to SARS-CoV-2 fatality [53]. According to recent studies, there is age-related decline in vaccine efficacy due to weakened innate and adaptive immunity that is a dual effect of inflamm-ageing and immunosenescence [53]. However, the profound challenge is to develop a safe and efficacious vaccine to combat SARS-CoV-2 infection, with a potential to produce adequate protection for every age group.

CONCLUSION

Since the outbreak of novel COVID-19 caused by deadly pathogen SARS-CoV-2 of unknown origin, with missing gaps about its pathogenesis, and continuously evolving different strains, this deadly viral disease has become a global threat by fuelling different challenges. This pandemic has forced the world to witness the longest ever lockdown of the century. The challenges evident the past 3 years of its emergence include crippled global economies, leaving millions of people unemployed. It has been a pressure builder on the healthcare systems as well as on healthcare staff, as they faced mental hardships due to prolonged working shifts and an imbalance in personal lives too. For general public and society, it has wreaked havoc in terms of anxiety, fear of losing their loved ones. Furthermore, with recurrent waves, it hampered the physical and social well-being. COVID-19 pandemic continues to be a challenger for pharma industry to come out with new, effective, and novel therapeutic options. In addition to its own damage, COVID-19 pandemic is speculated to burden humankind with another silently growing pandemic- AMR.

There are innumerable challenges the world is facing and struggling due to novel COVID-19 pandemic. This implies for better preparedness, awareness, and management strategies.

FUTURE PERSPECTIVES

Trust, respect, mutual understanding, and global unity can act as fundamental pillars to overcome the challenges posed by novel COVID-19 pandemic. The data related to COVID-19 disease should be shared on the common platform by all the nations accessible to all helping in tracking of active cases and better management. In order to conduct clinical studies, manufacture and distribute medical devices like anti-COVID-19 medications and vaccinations, testing supplies, respiratory machines, etc., international cooperation is mandatory.

The resolution that needs to be followed in the upcoming future for better management or to combat the challenges posed by novel COVID-19 pandemic includes:

Resilience, Rest and Recover

Resilience can be defined as the adaptability to changing situations and overcoming negative impacts of the adversities by making mental, emotional and psychological adjustments [65]. In COVID-19 times, resilience can be achieved at individual level by helping one another or showing empathy, at community level by applauding HCWs for their rigorous efforts and human resource supporting teammates emotionally by organizing virtual interactive sessions, at national level by co-operation between different states and at global levels by developed countries under-developed countries. In particular, HCWs should take proper rest to overcome psychological stress and night shifts or remote work duties should be scheduled in a 'work and break strategy' ensuring enough time with their families. Also, the positive workplace can act as an 'emotional first-aid' for HCWs. These conditions can include adequate supply of PPE that will help them handle their fear, and time-to-time updates about their progress that will boost their willingness towards their work resulting in improved patient care. For non-HCWs or general people in order to maintain mental-wellbeing, it is recommended to avoid using social media platforms or watching news for not more than 2 hours. For people in isolation or quarantine due to COVID, WHO has advised not to treat them with sympathy and stigmatization. Lastly, physical exercise and meditation should be included in daily routine as these may help in reducing stress levels and promote good mental as well as social health.

Vaccination Drives

Massive vaccination campaign organized globally has been a significant step to provide protection against COVID-19 infection especially for geriatric population. It is also recommended to organize awareness programme especially for school going children and elderly people to impart them knowledge about basic social distancing and protective measure, for example correct ways of using face mask, repeated use of hand sanitizers or hand wash and avoiding crowdy places. Moreover, such vaccination camps and awareness campaigns can also be beneficial in resolving issues related to vaccine uptake and hesitancy.

Multivalent Vaccine

The current challenges in vaccine formulation due to the emergence of VOCs can be overcome by updating present-day mRNA, protein and viral vaccines. These current vaccines can be modified by substituting the previous version of S-protein with that occurring in VOCs. Besides the modification of current FDA-approved vaccines, the alternative approach can be to design a 'multivalent/multi-epitope vaccine' that might be a combination containing both the old as well as new variant or recent mutations in the S-protein in a single vaccine.

Private-public Collaborations

Financial crisis has been a cause for some challenges posed by COVID-19 pandemic, for instance- drug/vaccine development and vaccine distribution as well as vaccine equity. Hence, the way to cope with prevailing financial setbacks is collaboration/alliance between private and public agencies or local and global organizations. One of the best examples is COVID-19 Vaccines Global Access (COVAX) program, an international collaboration between Gavi (the vaccine alliance), Coalition for Epidemic Preparedness Innovations (CEPI) and WHO to avoid vaccine inequity [66].

Monitoring Approaches

Digital platforms as well as smartphone applications are an efficient monitoring tool for contract tracing, maintaining records about vaccinated and non-vaccinated individuals. Mobile data and web-search queries have been a 'COVID-19 management tool' helping to keep a check on the transmission rate of the disease. Particularly, mobile apps such as 'aarogya setu' and many others designed for COVID-19 have proven to be crucial in monitoring symptomatic patients, their vaccination records and retrieval of physical co-location.

Drug Repurposing

With little knowledge of COVID-19 pathogenesis and a gradual time-intensive conventional drug development process, drug repurposing/repositioning of approved drug candidates is a fast-track as well as potent alternative to meet the urgency of therapeutics against fatal SARS-CoV-2 virus. Drug repurposing can be a practical approach and a quick solution to public health crisis because of several advantages that is FDA-approved drugs for other abnormalities can be screened and shortlisted using molecular docking techniques, these drugs have a 'green signal' in terms of safety;pharmacokinetics thereby enabling researchers to check for *in-vitro or in-vivo* antiviral efficacy avoiding pre-clinical stages and can directly enter in phase 2/3 clinical trials, which saves both time and money. Some of the initially FDA-authorized emergency drugs against SARS-CoV-2 infection are- Remdesivir, lopinavir/ritonavir, and chloroquine (or hydroxychloroquine) [32].

Point-of-care Diagnostic Devices/standardization of New Protocols for Better Diagnostic Approaches

Development of remote testing devices against SARS-CoV-2 infection can be a healthcare solution for asymptomatic, critically-ill patients as well as reducing burden on HCWs especially working in diagnostic facilities. To present an example, COVID-19 rapid antigen tests (RATs) kit developed for rapid and quick detection offered several advantages- no special/technical staff required for installation/implementation, user-friendly, cost-effective and swift results that are easy to interpret for layman. Moreover, the danger to HCWs can be reduced by standardizing one-step RNA extraction procedure, cell lysis-free techniques, accurate and reliable bioassays, and enhanced sample collection and processing techniques [21].

REFERENCES

[1]   Tsang HF, Chan LWC, Cho WCS, *et al.* An update on COVID-19 pandemic: the epidemiology, pathogenesis, prevention and treatment strategies. Expert Rev Anti Infect Ther 2021; 19(7): 877-88.
[http://dx.doi.org/10.1080/14787210.2021.1863146] [PMID: 33306423]

[2]   Lamers MM, Haagmans BL. SARS-CoV-2 pathogenesis. Nat Rev Microbiol 2022; 20(5): 270-84.
[http://dx.doi.org/10.1038/s41579-022-00713-0] [PMID: 35354968]

[3]   Rahman SA, Singh H, Singh J, *et al.* Mapping the genomic landscape & diversity of COVID-19 based on >3950 clinical isolates of SARS-CoV-2: Likely origin & transmission dynamics of isolates sequenced in India. Indian J Med Res 2020; 151(5): 474-8.
[http://dx.doi.org/10.4103/ijmr.IJMR_1253_20] [PMID: 32474554]

[4]   Zheng J. SARS-CoV-2: an Emerging Coronavirus that Causes a Global Threat. Int J Biol Sci 2020; 16(10): 1678-85.
[http://dx.doi.org/10.7150/ijbs.45053] [PMID: 32226285]

[5]   Note from the editors: World Health Organization declares novel coronavirus (2019-nCoV) 2019.

[6]   Vanhaecht K, Seys D, Bruyneel L, *et al.* COVID-19 is having a destructive impact on health-care workers' mental well-being. Int J Qual Health Care 2021; 33(1): mzaa158.
[http://dx.doi.org/10.1093/intqhc/mzaa158] [PMID: 33270881]

[7]   Aymerich C, Pedruzo B, Pérez JL, *et al.* COVID-19 pandemic effects on health worker's mental health: Systematic review and meta-analysis. Eur Psychiatry 2022; 65(1): e10.
[http://dx.doi.org/10.1192/j.eurpsy.2022.1] [PMID: 35060458]

[8]   Vindegaard N, Benros ME. COVID-19 pandemic and mental health consequences: Systematic review of the current evidence. Brain Behav Immun 2020; 89: 531-42.
[http://dx.doi.org/10.1016/j.bbi.2020.05.048] [PMID: 32485289]

[9]   Jakovljevic M, Bjedov S, Jaksic N, Jakovljevic I. COVID-19 Pandemia and Public and Global Mental Health from the Perspective of Global Health Securit. Psychiatr Danub 2020; 32(1): 6-14.
[http://dx.doi.org/10.24869/psyd.2020.6] [PMID: 32303023]

[10]   Suryavanshi N, Kadam A, Dhumal G, *et al.* Mental health and quality of life among healthcare professionals during the COVID-19 pandemic in India. Brain Behav 2020; 10(11): e01837.
[http://dx.doi.org/10.1002/brb3.1837] [PMID: 32918403]

[11]   Benke C, Autenrieth LK, Asselmann E, Pané-Farré CA. Lockdown, quarantine measures, and social distancing: Associations with depression, anxiety and distress at the beginning of the COVID-19 pandemic among adults from Germany. Psychiatry Res 2020; 293: 113462.
[http://dx.doi.org/10.1016/j.psychres.2020.113462] [PMID: 32987222]

[12]   De Kock JH, Latham HA, Leslie SJ, *et al.* A rapid review of the impact of COVID-19 on the mental health of healthcare workers: implications for supporting psychological well-being. BMC Public Health 2021; 21(1): 104.
[http://dx.doi.org/10.1186/s12889-020-10070-3] [PMID: 33422039]

[13]   Kassaeva P, Belova E, Shashina E, *et al.* Anxiety, Depression, and Other Emotional Disorders during the COVID-19 Pandemic: A Narrative Review of the Risk Factors and Risk Groups. Encyclopedia 2022; 2(2): 912-27.
[http://dx.doi.org/10.3390/encyclopedia2020060]

[14]   Chung JY, Thone MN, Kwon YJ. COVID-19 vaccines: The status and perspectives in delivery points of view. Adv Drug Deliv Rev 2021; 170: 1-25.
[http://dx.doi.org/10.1016/j.addr.2020.12.011] [PMID: 33359141]

[15]   Sharma O, Sultan AA, Ding H, Triggle CR. A Review of the Progress and Challenges of Developing a Vaccine for COVID-19. Front Immunol 2020; 11: 585354.
[http://dx.doi.org/10.3389/fimmu.2020.585354] [PMID: 33163000]

[16]   Sheikh JA, Singh J, Singh H, *et al.* Emerging genetic diversity among clinical isolates of SARS-Co-2: Lessons for today. Infect Genet Evol 2020; 84: 104330.
[http://dx.doi.org/10.1016/j.meegid.2020.104330] [PMID: 32335334]

[17]   Tatsi EB, Filippatos F, Michos A. SARS-CoV-2 variants and effectiveness of vaccines: a review of current evidence. Epidemiol Infect 2021; 149: e237.
[http://dx.doi.org/10.1017/S0950268821002430] [PMID: 34732275]

[18]   Hadj Hassine I. COVID-19 vaccines and variants of concern: A review. Rev Med Virol 2022; 32(4): e2313.
[http://dx.doi.org/10.1002/rmv.2313] [PMID: 34755408]

[19]   Zeng B, Gao L, Zhou Q, Yu K, Sun F. Effectiveness of COVID-19 vaccines against SARS-CoV-2 variants of concern: a systematic review and meta-analysis. BMC Med 2022; 20(1): 200.
[http://dx.doi.org/10.1186/s12916-022-02397-y] [PMID: 35606843]

[20]   Mistry P, Barmania F, Mellet J, *et al.* SARS-CoV-2 Variants, Vaccines, and Host Immunity. Front Immunol 2022; 12: 809244.
[http://dx.doi.org/10.3389/fimmu.2021.809244] [PMID: 35046961]

[21]   Tagoe ET, Sheikh N, Morton A, *et al.* COVID-19 Vaccination in Lower-Middle Income Countries: National Stakeholder Views on Challenges, Barriers, and Potential Solutions. Front Public Health 2021; 9: 709127.
[http://dx.doi.org/10.3389/fpubh.2021.709127] [PMID: 34422750]

[22]   Mohamed K, Rzymski P, Islam MS, *et al.* COVID-19 vaccinations: The unknowns, challenges, and hopes. J Med Virol 2022; 94(4): 1336-49.
[http://dx.doi.org/10.1002/jmv.27487] [PMID: 34845731]

[23]   Hyder AA, Hyder MA, Nasir K, Ndebele P. Inequitable COVID-19 vaccine distribution and its effects. Bull World Health Organ 2021; 99(6): 406-406A.
[http://dx.doi.org/10.2471/BLT.21.285616] [PMID: 34108746]

[24]   Visca D, Ong CWM, Tiberi S, *et al.* Tuberculosis and COVID-19 interaction: A review of biological, clinical and public health effects. Pulmonology 2021; 27(2): 151-65.
[http://dx.doi.org/10.1016/j.pulmoe.2020.12.012] [PMID: 33547029]

[25]   Sheikh JA, Malik AA, Quadir N, Ehtesham NZ, Hasnain SE. Learning from COVID-19 to tackle TB pandemic: From despair to hope. Lancet Regional Health - Southeast Asia 2022; 2: 100015.
[http://dx.doi.org/10.1016/j.lansea.2022.05.004] [PMID: 35769164]

[26]   Taleghani N, Taghipour F. Diagnosis of COVID-19 for controlling the pandemic: A review of the state-of-the-art. Biosens Bioelectron 2021; 174: 112830.
[http://dx.doi.org/10.1016/j.bios.2020.112830] [PMID: 33339696]

[27]   Yüce M, Filiztekin E, Özkaya KG. COVID-19 diagnosis —A review of current methods. Biosens Bioelectron 2021; 172: 112752.
[http://dx.doi.org/10.1016/j.bios.2020.112752] [PMID: 33126180]

[28]   Sreepadmanabh M, Sahu AK, Chande A. COVID-19: Advances in diagnostic tools, treatment strategies, and vaccine development. J Biosci 2020; 45(1): 148.
[http://dx.doi.org/10.1007/s12038-020-00114-6] [PMID: 33410425]

[29]   Alsharif W, Qurashi A. Effectiveness of COVID-19 diagnosis and management tools: A review. Radiography 2021; 27(2): 682-7.
[http://dx.doi.org/10.1016/j.radi.2020.09.010] [PMID: 33008761]

[30]   Donia A, Hassan S, Zhang X, Al-Madboly L, Bokhari H. COVID-19 Crisis Creates Opportunity

towards Global Monitoring & Surveillance. Pathogens 2021; 10(3): 256.
[http://dx.doi.org/10.3390/pathogens10030256] [PMID: 33668358]

[31]   Robinson PC, Liew DFL, Tanner HL, *et al.* COVID-19 therapeutics: Challenges and directions for the future. Proc Natl Acad Sci USA 2022; 119(15): e2119893119.
[http://dx.doi.org/10.1073/pnas.2119893119] [PMID: 35385354]

[32]   Kim S. COVID-19 Drug Development. J Microbiol Biotechnol 2022; 32(1): 1-5.
[http://dx.doi.org/10.4014/jmb.2110.10029] [PMID: 34866128]

[33]   Tayara H, Abdelbaky I, To Chong K. Recent omics-based computational methods for COVID-19 drug discovery and repurposing. Brief Bioinform 2021; 22(6): bbab339.
[http://dx.doi.org/10.1093/bib/bbab339] [PMID: 34423353]

[34]   Rao N, Poojari T, Poojary C, Sande R, Sawant S. Drug Repurposing: a Shortcut to New Biological Entities. Pharm Chem J 2022; 56(9): 1203-14.
[http://dx.doi.org/10.1007/s11094-022-02778-w] [PMID: 36531825]

[35]   Harrer S, Shah P, Antony B, Hu J. Artificial Intelligence for Clinical Trial Design. Trends Pharmacol Sci 2019; 40(8): 577-91.
[http://dx.doi.org/10.1016/j.tips.2019.05.005] [PMID: 31326235]

[36]   Schlander M, Hernandez-Villafuerte K, Cheng CY, Mestre-Ferrandiz J, Baumann M. How Much Does It Cost to Research and Develop a New Drug? A Systematic Review and Assessment. PharmacoEconomics 2021; 39(11): 1243-69.
[http://dx.doi.org/10.1007/s40273-021-01065-y] [PMID: 34368939]

[37]   Aghila Rani KG, Hamad MA, Zaher DM, Sieburth SM, Madani N, Al-Tel TH. Drug development post COVID-19 pandemic: toward a better system to meet current and future global health challenges. Expert Opin Drug Discov 2021; 16(4): 365-71.
[http://dx.doi.org/10.1080/17460441.2021.1854221] [PMID: 33356641]

[38]   Wang J, Zhang Y, Nie W, Luo Y, Deng L. Computational anti-COVID-19 drug design: progress and challenges. Brief Bioinform 2022; 23(1): bbab484.
[http://dx.doi.org/10.1093/bib/bbab484] [PMID: 34850817]

[39]   Yadav M, Dhagat S, Eswari JS. Emerging strategies on in silico drug development against COVID-19: challenges and opportunities. Eur J Pharm Sci 2020; 155: 105522.
[http://dx.doi.org/10.1016/j.ejps.2020.105522] [PMID: 32827661]

[40]   Stevens LJ, Pruijssers AJ, Lee HW, *et al.* Mutations in the SARS-CoV-2 RNA-dependent RNA polymerase confer resistance to remdesivir by distinct mechanisms. Sci Transl Med 2022; 14(656): eabo0718.
[http://dx.doi.org/10.1126/scitranslmed.abo0718] [PMID: 35482820]

[41]   Shariq M, Malik AA, Sheikh JA, Hasnain SE, Ehtesham NZ. Regulation of autophagy by SARS-Co--2: The multifunctional contributions of ORF3a. J Med Virol 2023; 95(7): e28959.
[http://dx.doi.org/10.1002/jmv.28959] [PMID: 37485696]

[42]   Langford BJ, So M, Simeonova M, *et al.* Antimicrobial resistance in patients with COVID-19: a systematic review and meta-analysis. Lancet Microbe 2023; 4(3): e179-91.
[http://dx.doi.org/10.1016/S2666-5247(22)00355-X] [PMID: 36736332]

[43]   Founou RC, Blocker AJ, Noubom M, *et al.* The COVID-19 pandemic: a threat to antimicrobial resistance containment. Future Sci OA 2021; 7(8): FSO736.
[http://dx.doi.org/10.2144/fsoa-2021-0012] [PMID: 34290883]

[44]   Lai CC, Chen SY, Ko WC, Hsueh PR. Increased antimicrobial resistance during the COVID-19 pandemic. Int J Antimicrob Agents 2021; 57(4): 106324.
[http://dx.doi.org/10.1016/j.ijantimicag.2021.106324] [PMID: 33746045]

[45]   Knight GM, Glover RE, McQuaid CF, *et al.* Antimicrobial resistance and COVID-19: Intersections and implications. eLife 2021; 10: e64139.

[http://dx.doi.org/10.7554/eLife.64139] [PMID: 33588991]

[46]   Su CW, Dai K, Ullah S, Andlib Z. COVID-19 pandemic and unemployment dynamics in European economies. Ekon Istraz 2022; 35(1): 1752-64.
[http://dx.doi.org/10.1080/1331677X.2021.1912627]

[47]   Blustein DL, Guarino PA. Work and Unemployment in the Time of COVID-19: The Existential Experience of Loss and Fear. J Humanist Psychol 2020; 60(5): 702-9.
[http://dx.doi.org/10.1177/0022167820934229]

[48]   Nicola M, Alsafi Z, Sohrabi C, *et al.* The socio-economic implications of the coronavirus pandemic (COVID-19): A review. Int J Surg 2020; 78: 185-93.
[http://dx.doi.org/10.1016/j.ijsu.2020.04.018] [PMID: 32305533]

[49]   Alam MR, Kabir MR, Reza S. Comorbidities might be a risk factor for the incidence of COVID-19: Evidence from a web-based survey. Prev Med Rep 2021; 21: 101319.
[http://dx.doi.org/10.1016/j.pmedr.2021.101319] [PMID: 33489728]

[50]   Elabbadi A, Turpin M, Gerotziafas GT, Teulier M, Voiriot G, Fartoukh M. Bacterial coinfection in critically ill COVID-19 patients with severe pneumonia. Infection 2021; 49(3): 559-62.
[http://dx.doi.org/10.1007/s15010-020-01553-x] [PMID: 33393065]

[51]   Riou C, du Bruyn E, Stek C, *et al.* Relationship of SARS-CoV-2–specific CD4 response to COVID-19 severity and impact of HIV-1 and tuberculosis coinfection. J Clin Invest 2021; 131(12): e149125.
[http://dx.doi.org/10.1172/JCI149125] [PMID: 33945513]

[52]   Carethers JM. Insights into disparities observed with COVID-19. J Intern Med 2021; 289(4): 463-73.
[http://dx.doi.org/10.1111/joim.13199] [PMID: 33164230]

[53]   Rea IM, Alexander HD. Triple jeopardy in ageing: COVID-19, co-morbidities and inflamm-ageing. Ageing Res Rev 2022; 73: 101494.
[http://dx.doi.org/10.1016/j.arr.2021.101494] [PMID: 34688926]

[54]   Singh AK, Gillies CL, Singh R, *et al.* Prevalence of co-morbidities and their association with mortality in patients with COVID -19: A systematic review and meta-analysis. Diabetes Obes Metab 2020; 22(10): 1915-24.
[http://dx.doi.org/10.1111/dom.14124] [PMID: 32573903]

[55]   Al Hussain O. Clinical characteristics and Co-morbidities among patients admitted with COVID-19. Ann Med Surg (Lond) 2022; 78: 103898.
[http://dx.doi.org/10.1016/j.amsu.2022.103898] [PMID: 35663125]

[56]   Petrakis D, Margină D, Tsarouhas K, *et al.* Obesity - a risk factor for increased COVID-19 prevalence, severity and lethality (Review). Mol Med Rep 2020; 22(1): 9-19.
[http://dx.doi.org/10.3892/mmr.2020.11127] [PMID: 32377709]

[57]   Zhou Y, Chi J, Lv W, Wang Y. Obesity and diabetes as high-risk factors for severe coronavirus disease 2019 (COVID -19). Diabetes Metab Res Rev 2021; 37(2): e3377.
[http://dx.doi.org/10.1002/dmrr.3377] [PMID: 32588943]

[58]   Callender LA, Curran M, Bates SM, Mairesse M, Weigandt J, Betts CJ. The Impact of Pre-existing Comorbidities and Therapeutic Interventions on COVID-19. Front Immunol 2020; 11: 1991.
[http://dx.doi.org/10.3389/fimmu.2020.01991] [PMID: 32903476]

[59]   Du Y, Zhou N, Zha W, Lv Y. Hypertension is a clinically important risk factor for critical illness and mortality in COVID-19: A meta-analysis. Nutr Metab Cardiovasc Dis 2021; 31(3): 745-55.
[http://dx.doi.org/10.1016/j.numecd.2020.12.009] [PMID: 33549450]

[60]   Varikasuvu SR, Dutt N, Thangappazham B, Varshney S. Diabetes and COVID-19: A pooled analysis related to disease severity and mortality. Prim Care Diabetes 2021; 15(1): 24-7.
[http://dx.doi.org/10.1016/j.pcd.2020.08.015] [PMID: 32891525]

[61]   Kumar A, Arora A, Sharma P, *et al.* Is diabetes mellitus associated with mortality and severity of

COVID-19? A meta-analysis. Diabetes Metab Syndr 2020; 14(4): 535-45.
[http://dx.doi.org/10.1016/j.dsx.2020.04.044] [PMID: 32408118]

[62] Gao Y, Liu M, Chen Y, Shi S, Geng J, Tian J. Association between tuberculosis and COVID-19 severity and mortality: A rapid systematic review and meta-analysis. J Med Virol 2021; 93(1): 194-6.
[http://dx.doi.org/10.1002/jmv.26311] [PMID: 32687228]

[63] Shariq M, Sheikh JA, Quadir N, Sharma N, Hasnain SE, Ehtesham NZ. COVID-19 and tuberculosis: the double whammy of respiratory pathogens. Eur Respir Rev 2022; 31(164): 210264.
[http://dx.doi.org/10.1183/16000617.0264-2021] [PMID: 35418488]

[64] Gatechompol S, Avihingsanon A, Putcharoen O, Ruxrungtham K, Kuritzkes DR. COVID-19 and HIV infection co-pandemics and their impact: a review of the literature. AIDS Res Ther 2021; 18(1): 28.
[http://dx.doi.org/10.1186/s12981-021-00335-1] [PMID: 33952300]

[65] Jakovljevic M. Empathy, Sense of Coherence and Resilience: Bridging Personal, Public and Global Mental Health and Conceptual Synthesis. Psychiatr Danub 2108; 30(4): 380-4.
[http://dx.doi.org/10.24869/psyd.2018.380] [PMID: 30439796]

[66] Sharun K, Dhama K. COVID-19 Vaccine Diplomacy and Equitable Access to Vaccines Amid Ongoing Pandemic. Arch Med Res 2021; 52(7): 761-3.
[http://dx.doi.org/10.1016/j.arcmed.2021.04.006] [PMID: 33941393]

CHAPTER 8

The Impact of COVID-19 on the Economy and Roadblocks to Recovery

Mohammad Sufian Badar[1,2,3,4], **Ankita Pati**[5,*], **Labeebah Rizwan Badar**[6] and **K. Shrutilekha**[7,8]

[1] *Department of Bioengineering, University of California, Riverside, CA, USA*

[2] *Universal Scientific Education and Research Network (USERN), Tehran, Iran*

[3] *Director (Academic), SPI Darbhanga, India*

[4] *Department of Computer Science and Engineering (Bioinformatics), School of Engineering Sciences and Technology (SEST), Jamia Hamdard, New Delhi, India*

[5] *Centre for Biotechnology, Siksha'O'Anusandhan University, Bhubaneswar, Odisha, India*

[6] *Badar Medical Centre, New Delhi, India*

[7] *Centre for One Health Education, Research, and Development (COHERD), Indian Institute of Public Health Gandhinagar (IIPHG), Gandhinagar, Gujarat, India*

[8] *IMS&SH, SOA University, Bhubaneswar, Odisha, India*

Abstract: An enormous global economic crisis was brought on by the COVID-19 epidemic, which first appeared in 2020. This paper analyzes the challenges standing in the way of an efficient recovery while also looking at the many economic effects. Severe economic contractions were first caused by widespread lockdowns and supply chain disruptions, mainly impacting the services, tourism, and hospitality industries. Fiscal and monetary measures were swiftly implemented by governments and central banks to lessen the effects, but a number of barriers to recovery have persisted.

In this research, several obstacles are outlined, such as unequal vaccination coverage, enduring health fears, and uneven economic recovery rates. The public's uneven adherence to safety measures and inconsistent worldwide response coordination have added to ongoing uncertainty. The pandemic has also highlighted pre-existing disparities and the need for extensive policy changes. In order to provide fair access to vaccines, the report promotes targeted aid for vulnerable sectors, investments in digital infrastructure, and international cooperation.

In conclusion, the COVID-19 outbreak highlighted weaknesses in the world's economies and prompted a reassessment of traditional economic paradigms. Despite continued recovery efforts, a number of challenges—from health issues to structural inequalities—remain in the way. Building a more robust and inclusive post-pandemic economy requires an integrated strategy that includes both short-term alleviation and long-term systemic improvements.

---

* **Corresponding author Ankita Pati:** Centre for Biotechnology, Siksha'O'Anusandhan University, Bhubaneswar, Odisha, India; E-mail: ankitapati689@gmail.com

Keywords: COVID-19, Economic impact of COVID-19, Macroeconomics, Microeconomics.

COVID-19 INFECTION

On 11th March 2020, the SARS-Cov2 Virus infection was declared a global pandemic by the World Health Organization. The SARS-CoV-2 virus brings on a highly contagious respiratory ailment called COVID-19. Since the disease's initial discovery in Wuhan, China in December 2019, it has spread worldwide and influenced almost every facet of life.

When an infected individual talks, coughs, or sneezes, respiratory droplets that are the primary means of COVID-19 transmission are released, it can spread through touch, mainly touching any parts of the face or contact with the nose, mouth or eyes epithelium after touching a surface exposed to the virus. Mild to severe COVID-19 symptoms might include fever, coughing, exhaustion, loss of taste or smell, and breathing difficulties. For elderly folks and those with existing medical issues, the illness can be more deadly. The mode of transmission of the virus is human-to-human transmission via droplets or direct contact; it has also been observed that this virus can show its effect even after 14 days.

STATISTICS OF COVID-19- MORBIDITY, MORTALITY

As the pandemic progresses, the figures for COVID-19 morbidity (the rate of illness incidence) and mortality (the rate of death due to the disease) constantly shift. According to WHO statistics from September 2021, over 4.5 million fatalities and over 220 million confirmed COVID-19 infections worldwide. These figures demonstrate the pandemic's intensity and substantially influenced world health.

The United States had the most confirmed cases and fatalities then, with over 40 million cases and 640,000 deaths. This placed a heavy load on the healthcare system, and the nation has been dealing with the pandemic's impacts for more than a year.

With over 33 million cases and 440,000 confirmed deaths in India, and over 21 million cases and 590,000 deaths in Brazil, respectively, both countries similarly experienced high rates of confirmed cases and fatalities. These nations had considerable increases in cases and deaths during the epidemic, straining their healthcare systems and highlighting the necessity of international collaboration in combating the pandemic.

The percentage of confirmed patients that pass away due to the illness is known as the case fatality rate (CFR). According to the global CFR average of 2%, there were two COVID-19-related deaths per 100 confirmed cases worldwide. The CFR varied significantly between nations, with some reporting more excellent rates than others. However, the CFR varied according to several variables, such as age, underlying medical disorders, and access to treatment.

The risk of developing serious disease and passing away from COVID-19 was greater in older persons and those with underlying medical disorders. Efforts have been made to prioritize vaccination and other preventive measures for these susceptible groups. It is crucial to remember that anybody can get COVID-19, therefore, preventative measures including social isolation, mask use, and immunization remain crucial.

In conclusion, the figures on COVID-19 morbidity and death show how seriously the pandemic has affected the world's health and the necessity for ongoing efforts to stop the disease's spread through vaccines, preventative measures, and international collaboration.

THE OVERALL IMPACT OF COVID-19

The overall impact of COVID-19 has been widespread and multifaceted, affecting nearly every aspect of life worldwide. Some of the key impacts of COVID-19 include:

1. Public health impact: With millions of verified cases and fatalities globally, the epidemic has devastated public health. In several nations, the epidemic has overburdened healthcare systems, causing a lack of medical supplies, hospital beds, and healthcare professionals. The epidemic has also interfered with standard medical care, which might have long-term health effects including delayed diagnosis and treatments.

2. Economic impact: COVID-19 has had a considerable negative economic impact, especially on small enterprises and low-income workers. Many firms' closures or reduced capacity has resulted in job losses and financial difficulties. The epidemic has also impacted global supply networks, resulting in some goods and services shortages.

3. Social effect: COVID-19 has altered social behaviour, resulting in lockdowns and social distance measures that influence people's everyday routines and activities. Social disparities, notably those related to access to healthcare, education, and work prospects, have also been brought to light by the epidemic.

4. Educational impact: The epidemic has disrupted education systems worldwide, posing difficulties for students, instructors, and parents due to school closures and remote learning. The epidemic has also brought attention to the disparities in access to technology and educational resources in the education world.

5. Technological impact: COVID-19 has sped up the use of digital technology, especially in the areas of healthcare, online education, and remote employment. The epidemic has also brought attention to the digital gap, with certain communities being unable to access the tools and services they require.

6. Political impact: Government goals and strategies have changed due to COVID-19, with a stronger emphasis now placed on economic recovery and public health initiatives. The epidemic has also brought attention to the necessity of international collaboration and readiness to address new public health concerns.

In summary, the impact of COVID-19 has been far-reaching and multifaceted, affecting nearly every aspect of life worldwide. The pandemic has highlighted existing social, economic, and health inequalities and underscored the need for greater preparedness and global cooperation to respond to public health crises.

Global lockdowns, travel bans, and social segregation policies have all been implemented during the pandemic to contain the transmission of the infection. These measures have a huge influence on the economy and health of the world. The high mortality in the initial days, lack of knowledge about the treatment, and the positivity that the pandemic could be contained, thanks to the development of vaccinations and their widespread distribution. Despite this, the pandemic persists, and it is crucial to adhere to public health recommendations to stop the spread of COVID-19. The effects of COVID-19 on the economy and global health have been significant. The epidemic has burdened healthcare systems and resources, causing millions of illnesses and deaths globally. Additionally, due to the pandemic, basic medical exams and non-urgent medical treatments have been delayed, which might have detrimental long-term effects on health.

Because of lockdowns and other social segregation measures, COVID-19 has significantly disrupted the economy, forcing many enterprises to close or operate at reduced capacity. Job losses and economic instability have resulted in tourism, hospitality, and retail industries. Additionally, the epidemic has revealed and widened alreadyexisting social and economic inequities, with underprivileged populations being disproportionately impacted. In addition, the epidemic has raised government expenditure on healthcare and stimulus programmes, pushing up public debt levels. Concerns regarding the long-term viability of government finances and the likelihood of upcoming economic upheaval have been expressed.

Overall, the COVID-19 pandemic has had far-reaching and long-lasting effects on global health and the economy, and its impact may not be fully understood for some time.

IMPACT OF COVID-19 ON MACROECONOMICS AND MACROECONOMICS

Gross Domestic Product

The pandemic brought our lives to a standstill. The lack of economic response globally led to chaos in the economies of countries around the world. Almost all studies carried out in the world indicated Gross Domestic product losses up to 10% [1]. GDP is a measure to value the final goods and services produced in a given period of time in a fixed geographic region.

OECD analyzed 20-25% losses in GDP globally due to the shutdowns during the 1st year of the pandemic. The countries' economies stabilized during the later part of 2021 and remained at par with the GDP of 2019. Fig. (**1**) shows a change in GDP in the G20 countries and the world during the pandemic.

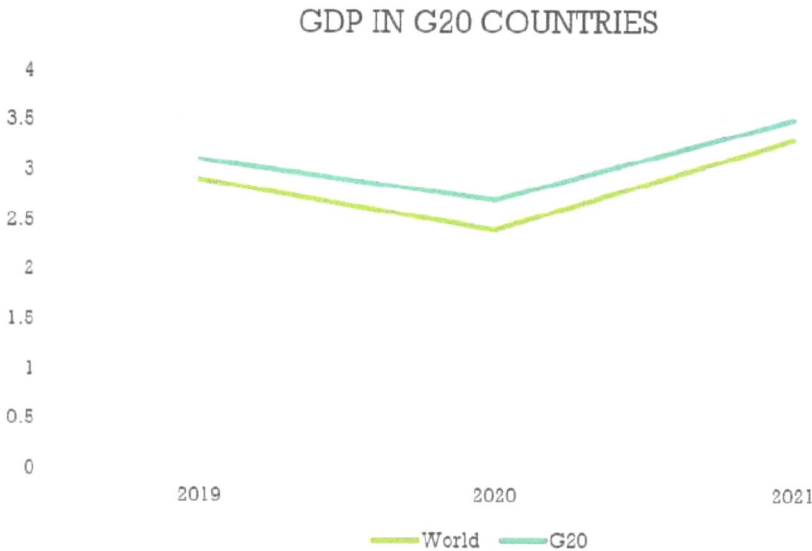

Fig. (1). The chart showing change in GDP in the G20 countries and the world during the pandemic.

Manufacturing

The lockdowns and shutdowns restricted the movement of labour and raw materials. The unavailability of raw materials and the differential demand due to the anxiety of the lockdown led to a change in the manufacturing trends. There was a decrease in the production of various products associated with industries like fashion, construction and other luxury items, whereas there has been a sudden boom in the healthcare industry. This includes the rising demand for sanitizers, masks and medicines used to treat COVID-19 patients systematically. The development and production of COVID-19 vaccine changed the expenditure dynamics as well as the prioritization of the governments of various countries towards the domains of expenditure.

Employment

Employment declined during the pandemic. The small eateries, roadside street vendors, and the workers involved in transport or construction did not work during the pandemic. Thus this led to a decline in the employment status of the departments and portfolios other than health. The worldwide decline in employment also led to a decrease in the income of the country as well as the enterprise.

Travel

The movement restrictions caused a decrease in international and domestic travel. UNWTO estimated that there was a 30% decline in the International tourism [2]. The profits of the aviation industry declined. This led to losses to the aviation industry along with the capping of prices of flight tickets. The dynamic pricing related to flight tickets was removed in India. Medial tourism was worse hit and it deprived many people of their right to seek care. The decrease in travel and tourism impacted the hotel industry as well as the food industry. The losses incurred by the hospitality industry led to the closure of many establishments. Few of the establishments functioned as isolation centres for international travels or COVID-19 positive patients. This helped them to survive the losses.

Economic activities

The economic investments of the government in the health sector increased multifold where as the investments decreased in other sectors dramatically during the pandemic. The health sector investments were focused on managing and treating the individuals with COVID-19 along with the vaccine production. The government outlays and investment in waving off loans increased drastically. The loans increased due to a decrease in income.

RESPONSE TO THE IMPACT OF COVID-19 ON MACROECONOMICS AND MICROECONOMIES BY AUTHORITIES

Several central agencies or banks expanded the liquidity of funds. They expanded their investments in the private sector. Governments of many countries responded aggressively to manage the effects of the pandemic. They entailed excessive spending on tax relief. The governments also faced added expenditure of providing relief to the unemployed people and helping them sustain the interest of people below the poverty line. Many governments addressed this issue through additional spending. VAT exemption on essential goods was an important measure adopted by many countries. Many countries like Argentina adopted additional benefits for the employees of small and medium enterprises. The Austrian government took 100% liability for emergency loans. The new models of employment were developed to ensure employment. Country-wise measures to deal with the Economic crisis during the COVID-19 Pandemic are documented in Table **1**. These are the measures undertaken by a few countries to manage the COVID crisis. The policies were to manage the situation as well as build the economy back.

Table 1. Country-wise measures to deal with Economic crisis during the COVID-19 Pandemic.

S.No.	Countries	Policy Measures Taken
1	Argentina	1. Credit insurance for loans from banks to MSMEs for the manufacture of food and essentials. 2. The following actions have been taken to encourage bank lending: - Banks require less stringent funds lending to individuals and SMEs. - Laws that restrict banks' ability to hold central bank paper to make room for SME lending. - A temporary relaxation of the requirements for bank provisioning and the classification of bank loans (i.e., an additional 60 days for non-performing loans). - A moratorium on closing bank accounts as a result of returned checks and the denial of credit to businesses that owe back payroll taxes.
2	Australia	1. Small and medium-sized firms (SMEs) which are eligible are provided with financial support of up to AUD 100,000 to help them continue their operations, including paying the rents, and power bills, giving salaries to employees and other obligations. Two cash flow increases will be used to accomplish this, the first of which will be made available beginning on April 28, 2020, through credits in the activity statement system (a tax withholding form). 2. To encourage banks to lend more to SMEs, the central bank has also set up a term funding facility with a minimum of AUD 90 billion for three-year financing at 25 basis points.

(Table 1) cont.....

S.No.	Countries	Policy Measures Taken
3	Austria	1. A 2 billion euro hardship fund was established. About 2 billion EUR hardship fund may provide assistance to sole proprietorships, small firms that have up to 9 employees, or those individuals who are newly self-employed, and freelancers. 2. Corona aid fund of up to 15 billion EUR is established to support businesses (both small and large ones) that have seen severe sales decreases as well as industries where policies like entry bans, travel restrictions, and meeting prohibitions have particularly impacted.
4	Bangladesh	The central bank has created an array of refinancing schemes totalling BDT 415 billion, a 360-day tenor special repo facility, and a loan guarantee plan for exporters, farmers, and Businesses to aid in implementing the government's stimulus strategies.
5	Bhutan	The government established the National Loan Guarantee Scheme to encourage investments in small and medium-sized businesses by reducing the need for collateral and offering a sizable loan guarantee.
6	China	1. About 1.8 million increase in re-lending and re-discounting has been created by the central bank to support the agriculture industry, micro, small, and medium-sized businesses, and producers of everyday necessities at cheap interest rates. 2 To encourage banks to allocate cash more effectively and strengthen the actual economy, the central bank reduced the interest rate on excess reserves from 72 to 35 basis points. 3. Policy banks boosted their 350 billion RMB lending resource in order to provide MSEs with favourable interest rates.
7	Colombia	1. Through Bancoldex (the Colombian Development Bank), The Colombian government has devised a credit guarantee programme worth USD 3 billion and soft loans of USD 150 million to finance SMEs' payroll and working capital. 2. New credit lines and load repayments for SMEs were carried out through additional financial support through the National Guarantee Fund.
8	Egypt	1. A new programme was introduced by MSME development authority to fund small initiatives impacted by the coronavirus, including financing for small and medium-sized businesses. MSMEDA and Banque du Caire inked two agreements of EGP 620 million to support and fund micro enterprises.
9	Finland	1. Working capital requirements brought on by the COVID-19 epidemic may be covered by Finnvera's Start Guarantee, SME Guarantee, and Finnvera Guarantee. - Companies that have been in operation for more than three years are eligible for the SME Guarantee. It may be applied to a maximum EUR 150,000 loan. The bank also applies this guarantee on your company's behalf. When Finnvera's Start Guarantee or SME Guarantee are inappropriate for the company's circumstances, it is possible to employ the Finnvera Guarantee instead. 2. The government increased its coverage of credit and guarantee losses at the agency from 50% to 80%. The Export Credit Agency of Finland is raising its lending and guarantee capacity to SMEs by 10 billion to 12 billion euros.
10	Hong Kong SAR	Increasing the maximum guaranteed loan amount per enterprise, offering interest subsidies for one year, expanding the eligibility requirements to include publicly traded enterprises annually and extending the term for relaxation for the SME Financing Guarantee Scheme.

(Table 1) cont.....

S.No.	Countries	Policy Measures Taken
11	India	1. Regulatory measures have been implemented by the central bank, including regulatory easing on asset categorization of loans to MSMEs and real estate developers, to promote credit flows to the retail sector and MSMEs. 2. The administration unveiled the following business-focused initiatives on May 13, 2020: - A financing scheme without collateral that is fully guaranteed. • Subordinate loans for struggling MSMEs with a partial guarantee. - A programme to partially indemnify public sector banks for borrowings from non-bank financial companies, home finance companies, and microfinance institutions. 33. The government also disclosed creating a Fund of Funds for the equity infusion of MSMEs; a special purpose vehicle (SPV) for the exclusive goal of purchasing short-term debt from housing finance companies and non-bank financial companies that meet certain criteria, with full government guarantee. 4. As of March 1, 2020, the central bank authorized banks to restructure existing loans to MSMEs classified as "standard" without requiring a change in asset classification. This authorization took effect on August 6, 2020. By March 31, 2021, the borrower account is expected to be reorganized. 5. The government lowered the eligibility restrictions and extended the Emergency Credit Line Guarantee Programme (ECLGS) for MSMEs through September 30, 2021.
12	Japan	1. The number of relaxations for credit facilities (interest-free loans without collateral) was increased by the government and made available through the Japan Finance Corporation and other institutions. The government also improves access to guaranteed loans from local financial institutions under the same terms. It assisted mainly for micro, small, and medium-sized firms affected by COVID-19. 2. The stimulus package also included cash transfers to SMEs experiencing sales losses and tax and social security payment postponements. 3. The central bank announced a new fund-provisioning policy to help primarily SMEs' lending.
13	Malaysia	MYR ten billion worth of stimulus package was revealed by the government; it contained incentives for smaller SMEs, enhanced pay subsidies, and a 25% discount on the expenses of hiring foreign labour. 2. Banks have also promised to provide debtors affected by COVID-19 with flexible repayment options, such as permitting interest-only payments in the interim and extending the payback period. 3. Relief and Recovery Facility (TRRF) of MYR 2 billion and, High Tech Facility (HTF) worth MYR 500 million and improvement of 110 MYR to the current Micro Enterprise Facility was announced by the Central bank.

(Table 1) cont.....

S.No.	Countries	Policy Measures Taken
14	Mauritius	1. From 23 March 2020 to 31 July 2020, a Special Relief Amount of MUR 5.0 billion will be given, according to a central bank announcement to help local businesses, notably SMEs, with their cash flow and working capital needs. This credit is available for 30 months, with a-6 month freeze on capital and interest payments throughout that time. Customers will be able to access the money at a 1.5 percent annual interest rate. 2. The State Investment Corporation would provide up to 60% of the security for government loans to SMEs. Furthermore, the Corporation will risk-weight the share of claims it secured at 0 percent when calculating the corresponding capital adequacy ratios. 3. Additionally, the central bank launched a $300 million Special Foreign Currency (USD) Line of Credit aimed at local business owners who generate foreign currency, especially SMEs. From 24 March 2020 until 30 June 2020, commercial banks will be able to use the line of credit. 4. Parastatal organizations have established a COVID-19 "Plan de Soutien" Cell to provide SMEs and other companies with a variety of supports. 5. SME Mauritius has introduced many brand-new programmes, including (a) the Internal Capability Development Scheme, (b) the Technology and Innovation Scheme, (c) the SME Marketing Support Scheme, (d) the Inclusiveness and Integration Scheme, and (e) the SME Utility Connection Assistance Scheme. 6. The Central bank has extended the Moratoriums given to SMEs, households, and individuals under its COVID-19 Support Program until the end of the calendar year.
15	Myanmar	A COVID-19 Fund of MMK 400 billion has been formed at the Myanmar Economic Bank to offer lenient loans to impacted companies at reduced interest rates, especially those in the key garment and tourism industries and SMEs.
16	Nepal	1. On March 29, the central bank boosted the amount of the Refinance Fund in order to offer banks subsidized capital if they are prepared to lend to priority sectors, such as small and midsize businesses hit by the epidemic and who are willing to accept loans at a concessional rate. 2. A loan programme for cottage, small, and medium-sized businesses and those in the tourist industry was launched on May 28, 2020.
17	New Zealand	1. The financial aid package includes a six-month principal and interest payment relief for mortgage owners and SME clients whose incomes have been disrupted by the COVID-19 economic disruption. 2. A business Finance Guarantee Scheme worth NZD 6.25 billion has been implemented for small and medium-sized businesses. 3. You should also take into account the Small Business Cash Flow Loan Scheme, under which the government provides loans to SMEs with 50 or fewer full-time employees. 4. Additionally, a number of financial efforts to aid SMEs and homeowners have been announced by the government, the central bank, and the New Zealand Bankers Association. Deferrals of principal and interest payments for six months are available to mortgage holders and SMEs affected by COVID-19 and the BFGS. Up to March 31, 2021, loans with deferred repayment had favourable regulatory treatment.

(Table 1) cont.....

S.No.	Countries	Policy Measures Taken
18	Saudi Arabia	The small and medium-sized business stimulus plan includes SAR 50 billion. - Loan deferral programme: Banks and financing firms will be given SAR 30 billion to postpone loan payments for SMEs for six months. - Lending Programme: Bank loans for small and medium-sized businesses (SMEs) would be provided with SAR 13.2 billion. - Loan guarantee programme: SAR 6 billion was used to exempt SMEs from KAFALA programme finance fees to reduce financing costs and make access to financing easier.
19	South Africa	1. There are funds available to assist struggling SMEs, mainly in the tourism and hospitality sectors, as well as small-scale farmers in the poultry, cattle, and vegetable sectors. A new loan guarantee programme is helping businesses with sales below a certain threshold access bank financing for operating expenses. 2. The debt relief finance strategy for small, medium, and micro enterprises (SMME) aimed to assist with working capital in the current environment. The intended budget of ZAR 200 million for the scheme was later increased to ZAR 500 million. 3. The revenue administration is expediting reimbursements and tax credits, allowing SMEs to postpone certain tax obligations, and has compiled a list of essential products eligible for a full customs duty refund and import VAT exemption. In addition, a four-month tax break on the skills development levy is being established.
20	Spain	1. The government is offering loan guarantees of up to 100 billion euros, including up to 80% coverage for independent contractors and small and medium-sized businesses (SMEs). 2. Loan guarantees through the Compaa Espaola de Reafianzamiento for SMEs and self-employed people (EUR 1 billion). 3. Extending to May 30, the due dates for SMEs and self-employed people to file their tax returns and self-assessment paperwork. 4. Permitting self-employed people and small business
21	Sri Lanka	1. There has been a significant reduction in the amount of back taxes owed by SMEs, as well as the granting of more accommodating payment terms and the suspension of legal action against non-payers. 2. Bank loans to the tourism, apparel, plantation, and information technology industries as well as SMEs are not repayable for six months, and the central bank is providing refinancing and concessional lending facilities of 1% of GDP, which are partially backed by a central bank guarantee. 3. The CBSL has recently introduced priority sector lending objectives for bank credit to MSMEs and provides refinancing and concessional lending facilities of 1% of GDP that are partially guaranteed.
23	Sweden	1. A government guarantee programme for bank loans to small- and medium-sized firms that have suffered financial harm as a result of the coronavirus pandemic has been formed by the National Debt Office. The guarantee user may also request postponed payments on other obligations. 2. Small and medium-sized firms that have suffered financial harm as a result of the coronavirus outbreak are receiving bridging loans from the government-controlled company Almi. 3. Corona crisis-affected businesses may be granted a tax respite in certain circumstances, albeit interest is charged on the amount of the reprieve.

(Table 1) cont.....

S.No.	Countries	Policy Measures Taken
24	Switzerland	Guaranteed bridging loans provided by the federal government, a COVID-19 refinancing facility established by the SNB, and some temporary regulatory amendments made by the Swiss Financial Market Supervisory Authority (FINMA) all contribute to liquidity support for SMEs. Companies in Switzerland affected by COVID-19 can access federal government-guaranteed bridging credits. During the initial wave of the epidemic, the Federal Council launched a variety of federal-level assistance packages, including CHF1 billion in financial aid to adversely afflicted enterprises and CHF580 million in loan guarantees for SMEs - A second package contained a CHF20 billion guarantee initiative to help SMEs with bridging loans.
25	United Kingdom	Small and medium-sized firms with up to GBP 45 million in annual turnover are eligible for government-backed loans of up to GBP 5 million under the Coronavirus Business Interruption Loan Scheme. For businesses, interest payments and any lender-imposed costs will be covered for the first twelve months. The government will guarantee loans up to 80% to enhance lenders' confidence in financing SMEs. 2. The government fully backs the Bounce Back Loan Scheme. Businesses can borrow between £2,000 and £50,000 over a six-year period. The government will cover all interest and fees for the first year, with no repayments necessary. The programme runs till November 4th, 2020. 3. On March 11, the central bank introduced a new Term Funding Scheme for SMEs (TFSME), which provides specific incentives for banks to increase lending to SMEs in order to strengthen the transmission of monetary policy. At interest rate at or close to the Bank Rate, the TFSME will provide funding throughout the next 12 months for at least 10% of the participants' stock of real economy loans. Banks will receive additional funding if they increase lending, particularly to small and medium-sized firms.
26	United States of America	The central bank launched the Main Street Lending Programme in order to acquire new or expanded loans to small and medium-sized businesses.

IMPACT OF COVID-19 AT AN INDIVIDUAL LEVEL

The pandemic chaos accelerated the crisis. Loss of jobs, shutdown of businesses, and decreased sales reduce the monthly income. The infection added to the woes. The burden of covid 19 as an infection was also hugefor many. The cost of COVID-19 is the direct cost of treatment, indirect cost of treatment and intangible cost associated with the condition. The direct medical cost includes the cost of diagnosis, treatment, hospitalization and rehabilitation where whereas the direct non-medical cost includes the cost of transport to a health care facility, and costs associated with the food. Indirect cost consists of the cost associated with the loss of livelihood of the individuals and the loss of income of the family member or primary caregiver. The intangible cost is associated with the social and psychological costs associated with the infection.

In case of COVID-19, the indirect and intangible costs were high due to the mandatory 14 days and seven days of isolation of the primary contacts of the individual with COVID-19. The stigma and the social stressors associated with the disease were also high.

The awareness regarding the transmission cycle, the concessions on the treatment of private hospitals, and the capping of costs were a few of the measures which relieved the burden associated with the cost of COVID-19. Many NGOs have come up front to help people with COVID-19. The families of the patients with COVID-19 were provided with financial benefits and other help to manage the situation.

WHAT YOU WILL LEARN

1. The basic of COVID-19 infection.

2. Impact of COVID-19 on the Macroeconomy and microeconomy.

3. Impact of COVID-19 on Individuals

4. Coping of Individuals towards the economic burden of COVID-19 pandemic

REFERENCES

[1]   Rungcharoenkitkul P. Macroeconomic effects of COVID-19: A mid-term review *. Pac Econ Rev 2021; 26(4): 439-58.
[http://dx.doi.org/10.1111/1468-0106.12372]

[2]   https://www.unwto.org/COVID-19-and-tourism-2020 in review

CHAPTER 9

AI-Based Diagnosis of Novel Coronavirus Using Radiograph Images

Mohammad Sufian Badar[1,2,3,4,*], **Aisha Idris**[5], **Areeba Khan**[5], **Md Mustafa**[5] and **Farheen Asaf**[6]

[1] *Department of Bioengineering, University of California, Riverside, CA, USA*

[2] *Universal Scientific Education and Research Network (USERN), Tehran, Iran*

[3] *Director (Academic), SPI Darbhanga, India*

[4] *Department of Computer Science and Engineering (Bioinformatics), School of Engineering Sciences and Technology (SEST), Jamia Hamdard, New Delhi, India*

[5] *Department of Biotechnology, Jamia Hamdard, New Delhi-India*

[6] *Max Super Speciality Hospital, New Delhi, India*

Abstract: The therapeutic value of artificial intelligence (ML) in the diagnosis of viral illnesses has been illustrated by the outbreak of COVID-19. This chapter digs into the modern uses of Artificial Intelligence and Machine Learning (ML) algorithms for COVID-19 diagnosis, with a focus on chest imaging procedures like as CT and X-rays. Additionally, we explored ML's strengths, such as its capacity to analyze enormous datasets and detect patterns in medical imagery. But there are still issues to deal with, like the scarcity of data, privacy issues, and machine learning's incapacity to evaluate the severity of health conditions. However, several machine learning methods, such as decision trees, random forests, and convolutional neural networks, are reviewed in this research concerning COVID-19 diagnosis. Subsequently, we highlight the efficacy of several models in COVID-19 screening, such as XGBoost and Truncated Inception Net. Moreover, the chapter discusses potential strategies for machine learning in COVID-19 diagnosis, emphasizing the crucial role of collaboration among data scientists and healthcare experts. It is imperative to confront data bias and incorporate more comprehensive patient data than just chest imaging. All things considered, machine learning presents a potential pathway toward quick and precise COVID-19 diagnosis; nonetheless, conquering existing obstacles is necessary for ML to be widely used in healthcare institutions.

---

[*] **Corresponding author Mohammad Sufian Badar:** Department of Bioengineering, University of California, Riverside, CA, USA; E-mail: sufianbadar@gmail.com

Keywords: Artificial Intelligence (AI), COVID-19, Chest X-ray, Computed Tomography (CT), Computer-aided Diagnosis (CAD), Deep Learning (DL), Diagnostic Imaging, Ground-Glass Opacity (GGO), Machine Learning (ML), Radiological Analysis, Variants of Concern (VOC).

INTRODUCTION

With the outbreak in December 2019, there have been almost 776 million officially verified cases of COVID-19 worldwide [1]. The World Health Organisation(WHO) proclaimed it a global pandemic in March 2020 following the first report in December 2019, and on April 21, 2020, two million cases and 120,000 fatalities were reported [2]. The Severe Acute Respiratory Syndrome Coronavirus-2 (SARS-CoV-2) was the new coronavirus that triggers COVID-19 [3]. However, SARS-CoV and Middle East Respiratory Disease Coronavirus (MERS-CoV) are two other coronaviruses that have previously been identified [4]. SARS-CoV-2 is thought to be less lethal but much more contagious than earlier coronaviruses [3]. The primary transmission pathways for SARS-CoV-2, the etiological agent of COVID-19, are predominantly through the inhalation of respiratory droplets and aerosols. These particles are expelled by an infected individual during respiratory activities such as coughing, sneezing, or speaking [5]. Consequently, implementing measures to curb the spread of SARS-CoV-2 was challenging due to the virus's high transmission capability. Furthermore, SARS-CoV-2 has been associated with several distinct variants including delta, omicron, and delta-cron (a combination of Delta and Omicron variants) [6]. Furthermore, the rapid mutational capacity of SARS-CoV-2 is exacerbating public health challenges and exerting a significant toll on the global economy and healthcare infrastructure [7]. However, respiratory difficulties, fever, body aches, coughing, and other symptoms are common with COVID-19, and they can lead to multi-organ failure or even death. Given that the initial symptoms of COVID-19 are similar to those of the ordinary influenza, prompt diagnosis at an early stage is essential [8]. Subsequently, early and efficient large-scale screening for SARS-CoV-2 infection, coupled with the rapid implementation of appropriate medical interventions, remains a cornerstone in mitigating the impact of the COVID-19 pandemic. The RT-PCR test, while serving as the current gold standard for diagnosing active COVID-19 infection, presents limitations. These include being labor-intensive, requiring specialized equipment and trained personnel, and potentially yielding false-positive (FP) or false-negative (FN) results [9 - 11]. However, the limitations of RT-PCR testing, particularly sensitivity and turnaround time, can be particularly concerning during periods of exponential viral spread. Additionally, supply chain disruptions and resource limitations may further exacerbate these issues, hindering timely identification and isolation of infected individuals. This, in turn, can contribute to ongoing community transmission due to both false-negative results allowing unknowingly infectious individuals to remain unisolated and delays in testing allowing the virus to propagate [12].

While RT-PCR remains the gold standard for diagnosing active SARS-CoV-2 infection, chest imaging modalities such as computed tomography (CT) and chest X-ray can play a complementary role. These imaging techniques may provide valuable insights into lung involvement and disease progression, aiding in patient management and treatment decisions [13]. While chest imaging, particularly computed tomography (CT), can be a valuable tool in managing patients suspected of COVID-19 infection, it is not a definitive diagnostic test for the virus itself. RT-PCR remains the gold standard for diagnosing active SARS-CoV-2 infection. However, chest CT findings, such as Ground-Glass Opacity (GGO), can be suggestive of COVID-19 pneumonia, particularly when presenting with a characteristic bilateral, peripheral, and multifocal distribution. It is important to note that GGO is a non-specific finding and can be seen in other respiratory illnesses. In some cases, particularly in the early stages of the disease, GGO may appear as a solitary lesion in the lung periphery [14]. Moreover, the high volume of chest CT scans generated during COVID-19 outbreaks presents a significant workload for radiologists. Manual analysis of these images is labor-intensive, prone to inter-reader variability, and susceptible to observer fatigue. This can lead to missed or misdiagnosed cases, particularly when COVID-19 pneumonia mimics other viral infections. Furthermore, subjective interpretation can lead to inefficient allocation of healthcare resources. Subsequently, advancements in artificial intelligence (AI)-powered Computer-Aided Diagnosis (CAD) systems offer promising solutions [15].

COVID 19- ETIOLOGY, CLINICAL IMAGING, AND PROGNOSIS

Coronaviruses are named for their characteristic crown-like appearance under an electron microscope. This crown-like morphology is due to the presence of spike proteins projecting from their outer lipid envelope. Among the six identified genera of coronaviruses, only the α-coronavirus and β-coronavirus genera encompass strains known to infect humans. Within these two genera, there are seven human coronaviruses identified [16]. The above-mentioned classification is shown in the following Table **1** [17]:

Table 1. Classification of Coronaviruses into Different Genus and Human-Infecting Strains

Genus	Human-infecting Coronavirus	Affect
α-coronavirus	HCoV-229E, HCoV-NL63	Common cold viruses
B-coronavirus	HCoV-OC43, HCoV-HKU1, SARS-CoV, SARS-CoV-2, MERS-CoV	SARS-CoV, SARS-CoV-2 and MERS causes respiratory diseases in humans
γ-coronavirus		
δ-coronavirus		

Human coronaviruses such as 229E, NL63, OC43, and HKU1 typically induce mild symptoms upon infection and are considered minimally pathogenic. However, a significant concern arises from the potential for coronavirus strains that primarily infect animals to undergo mutations enabling them to infect humans, resulting in severe illness. Notable examples include MERS-CoV, SARS-CoV and SARS-CoV-2, also known as COVID-19. Among these, MERS-CoV and SARS-CoV are associated with severe infections. In comparison, while SARS-CoV-2 is less fatal, it exhibits high contagiousness [18]. As discussed earlier in the chapter, SARS-CoV-2, the virus responsible for COVID-19 exhibiting high transmissibility, making the disease control challenging, there are several variants of concern (VOCs) emerged globally, including Delta, Omicron, and the recently identified recombinant strain Deltacron. The rapid mutation rate of the virus contributes to immune escape and ongoing transmission. Moreover, genomic sequencing reveals approximately 85% homology between SARS-Co--2 and bat SARS-like coronaviruses. While they share some amino acid and protein similarities, there are also key differences that influence their pathogenicity in humans. Both viruses are believed to originate in bats, and ACE-2 serves as their cellular receptor for entry into host cells. Additionally, the transmission of SARS-CoV-2 primarily occurs through the inhalation of respiratory droplets and aerosols expelled by infected individuals when coughing, sneezing, or even talking. The risk of infection is particularly high in enclosed environments with poor ventilation and during prolonged close contact with an infectious person. Exposure to the virus through contaminated surfaces is also a possibility, but considered a less significant route of transmission. The clinical presentation of COVID-19 can vary widely, ranging from asymptomatic infection to severe respiratory illness [8, 19]. Children, elders and immunocompromised individuals and individuals with terminal illness are at high risk. The disease is diagnosed through chest imaging techniques, including X-rays, CT scans, and Lung Ultrasound [13].

Chest Imaging

In the early stages of COVID-19, chest X-rays often have limited sensitivity and may appear relatively normal. This can lead to false-negative results. However, as the disease progresses, chest X-rays may show characteristic findings such as bilateral multifocal airspace opacities, which can be a helpful tool for initial evaluation, particularly in resource-limited settings. In contrast, chest CT scans offer superior sensitivity and resolution compared to X-rays, making them a more preferred modality for diagnosing COVID-19 pneumonia, particularly in equivocal cases. Common CT findings associated with COVID-19 pneumonia include and also shown in the Fig. (**1**)

Ground-glass opacity (GGO)

This appears as a hazy haziness in the lung tissue on CT scans.

Peripheral or posterior distribution

GGO opacities are often more prominent in the outer (peripheral) regions of the lungs or the lower lobes (posterior distribution).

Crazy-paving appearance

This describes a mosaic pattern of GGO and consolidation (complete airspace opacification) on CT scans.

Air bronchograms

These are visualized as branching air-filled structures within areas of consolidation.

Fibrous lesions

These may develop in later stages of the disease and indicate lung scarring.

Halo sign

This finding consists of a ground-glass opacity surrounding a central area of consolidation [14].

In the early stages of COVID-19 pneumonia, ground-glass opacity (GGO) on chest CT scans may appear unifocal, typically in the lung periphery. This suggests limited viral involvement, possibly restricted to a single bronchopulmonary segment. As the disease progresses, GGO often becomes multifocal, bilateral, and peripheral. These findings are indicative of more widespread viral invasion of the bronchiolar epithelium and alveolar cells. Viral replication disrupts the alveolar-capillary barrier, leading to leakage of fluid and protein into the alveolar spaces.

This accumulation of fluid manifests as GGO on CT scans. The ongoing inflammatory response can also contribute to thickening of the alveolar walls.

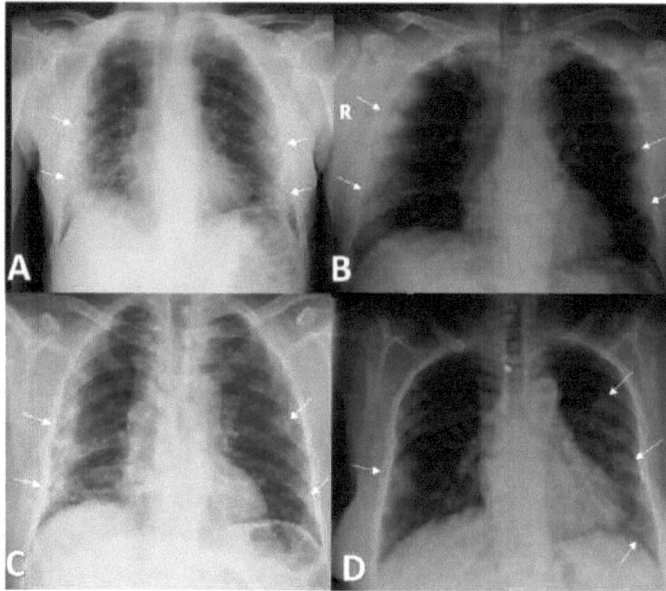

Fig. (1). ***Four patients tested positive for COVID-19*** [20]. ***(a)****72-year-old man reported having a fever and a cough. Bilateral peripheral mid and lower zonal air space consolidation opacities were visible on the first chest X-ray (arrows). Total severity Score (TSS) was 4 because each lung had a severity value of 2.****(b)****44-year-old man reported having fever, SOB, and a cough. In the initial chest X-ray, both lungs' periphery was opaque due to bilateral peripheral zonal air space consolidation (arrows). Each lung had a severity value of 2, resulting in a TSS of 4.****(c)****63-year-old man reported having a cough and a fever. The initial chest X-ray revealed minor patches of consolidation on the side and right peripheral mid and lower zonal air space consolidation opacities (arrows). The right lung's severity score was 2 and the left lung's severity score was 1, resulting in a TSS of 3.****(d)****63-year-old guy reported feeling feverish and coughing. The initial chest X-ray showed right peripheral mid and lower zonal air space consolidation opacities and little areas of consolidation on the side (arrows). The severity scores for the right lung were 2 and the left lung was 1, yielding a TSS of 3.*

White lungs in the images are seen as a result of inflammation by alveoli and mucosal ulcers. Upon disease progression; air bronchus signs which include – the low-density shadowing are visible leading to thickening and swelling of the bronchial walls without blocking the bronchioles. In the later stages of the infection, paving is seen which has an identical pattern to paving stones. This appears due to the superimposition of thickened lobular internal, interlobular line and GGO. Vascular thickening is visualized in all the stages of the disease. Scars are created when fibrous lesions replace the usual cellular components in lung hyperplasia. A circle of cloud called a Halo is formed in GGO as the density of the lesion diminishes from the centre to the edges. As the disease progresses, pleural effusion, lymphadenopathy, cavitation, CT halo sign and pneumothorax are visible in the CT images [21]. Lung ultrasound can be used during the first 24 hours of the illness. This method helps to study the disease progression in children, infants and adults. Pleural lines, B lines, deep vein blockage, thickening and consolidation of the lungs are the primary characteristics. Thick broken up and asymmetrical pleural lines are seen as well. B lines can stack together to create white lungs. These B lines are visible during the early stages of the infection. White lung and thickening occur further leading to consolidation upon disease progression. According to how severe the disease is, proportionate alterations in B lines and consolidation can be noticed. In extreme conditions; B lines and confluent B lines are the major features. In critically ill COVID 19 patients, pleural ebullition and deep vein blockage are important ultrasound imaging indicators.

COMPUTATIONAL DIAGNOSIS FOR COVID-19

Various identification methods for COVID-19 include: Rapid antigen test, antibody detection, RT-PCR (Reverse transcriptase polymerase chain reaction), next generation sequencing, X-Rays, and computed tomography (CT) [22]. The RT-PCR test is used as confirmatory test. However, the rate of positive result of RT-PCR from the throat and the nasopharyngeal swabs is only 30% to 70%. Although, few false negative results are also reported. Of the various pathological tests, CT scans of the chest and X-rays are said to have 98% and 69% sensitivity, respectively. Researchers are also working oncreating universal diagnostic systems that can be used for various COVID-19 variants diagnosis. One of the innovative methods that use prior experiences and accelerate the diagnosis of COVID-19 without explicit programming is the AI- Artificial Intelligence. The tracking, diagnosis and treatment process have become much easier and faster with the help of the two subsets of AI; which include; ML (Machine Learning) and DL (Deep Learning). Machine learning depends upon the machine intelligence from the previous reference datasets. There are 2 broad classifications of ML: Supervised and Unsupervised. In supervised learning, the data are labelled, the computer is trained under supervision using classification and regression techniques. In contrast to this, in the unsupervised learning, multiple techniques are used to train machines without any real direction or labelled data. With the analysis of CT scan and X-ray images; both machine learning and deep learning are used to diagnose patients. These also assist in tracking the epidemiological trend.

Techniques Used in Diagnosis of Covid 19

Several preventative measures such as the identification of viral antigen and their antibodies or viral nucleic acids have been implemented for the prompt detection of the SARS-CoV-2 genome. Early detection and prompt treatment can determine the quarantine duration to halt the spread and improve cure rates. Since the onset of the pandemic, researchers have routinely and efficiently used immunoassays, nucleic acid assays, and radiological imaging techniques for the clinical prediction of COVID-19 infection. All other methods to detect and diagnose COVID-19 are shown below in Table **2** and Fig. (**2**).

Table 2. A few COVID-19 detection techniques are detailed below.

COVID-19 Diagnostic Methods	Techniques	Elucidation
Nucleic Acid Amplification Tests	RT-PCR	The reverse transcription polymerase chain reaction (RT-PCR) is a laboratory technique for detecting viral genomes [23].
	CRISPR-related amplification	The molecular diagnostics method has been reformed by this diagnostic approach, which is based on interspaced short palindromic repeats [24].
	Loop-Mediated Isothermal Amplification	A quick diagnostic method for COVID-19 is the LAMP. It employs 4-6 primers that may identify various target DNA regions [25].
Serological Tests	ELISA	Antibodies and antigen-measuring techniques are used in the enzyme-linked immunosorbent assay to identify COVID-19 infection [26].
	CLIA	The Clinical Laboratory Improvement Amendments programme is used to test human specimens and deliver accurate, reliable, and exact patient test findings [27].
	LFIA	The lateral flow immunoassay is an antigen test that is used to detect active coronavirus infections [28].
Biosensors		The signals from the biomolecules are paired with a sensor transduction system in biosensors, which are systematic devices that are analysed by an analyser [29].
Radiology Imaging	CT	Patients who have recovered from COVID-19 can undergo chest computed tomography scans to screen lung fibrosis [30].
	CXR	Chest X-rays create images of the heart, lungs, airways, and bones in the chest and spine and are a reliable tool to assess the health of the lungs (https://www. mayocl inic.org/ tests-procedures/chest -x-rays/ about /pac- 20393494).
Micro fluid Approach		Microfluidic techniques include instruments for manipulating small amounts of fluids to influence biological, chemical, and physical processes [31].
ML-Based Approaches		The ML methodology uses a variety of statistical, probabilistic, optimization, and computational tools and algorithms to draw lessons from the past and find patterns in massive, complicated datasets [32].

Nucleic Acid Amplification Test

The detection and identification of the SARS CoV-2 viral genome from the infected patient can be done using NAAT. It is a diagnostic test used to detect viral genome. Primary step includes the amplification of the genomic material from the specimen of the infected patient. NAAT can detect even small amounts of the viral genome. Distinct amplification methods used in NAAT include 5 techniques:

I. **RT-PCR:** - Reverse transcriptase PCR is used to detect viral genome.

II. **CRISPR (Clustered Regularly Interspaced Short Palindromic Repeats) related amplification:** - this technique is based on the interspaced short palindromic repeats.

III. **Loop mediated isothermal amplification: - LAMP** is a rapid technique which uses 4-6 primers that recognize different regions of the target DNA [33].

• NAAT also include **Rolling circle Amplification (RCA) and Recombinase Polymerase Amplification (RPA).**

Serological tests

These tests have become more popular as an RT-PCR substitute for the diagnosis of acute infections. This method uses various techniques such as:

I. **CLIA (Clinical Laboratory Improvement Amendments):** - this test human specimens and provide reliable and accurate results.

II. **ELISA (Enzyme Linked Immunosorbent Assay)**: - this is used to estimate antibodies in a qualitative or semi quantitative manner. In this method, the antigen protein on the microplate wells binds to the target antibody.

III. **Lateral Flow Immunoassay (LFIA):** - it is an antigen test, which is used to identify any active coronavirus infection.

The most promising test is the LIFA; which has the lowest technical requirements, lowest risk for sample and specimen preparation, lowest cost and the highest specificity and sensitivity. LIFA offers result in just 15 minutes.

Biosensors

Biosensors are systematic devices that measure the signals from biomolecules also referred to as bio recognition elements. The fundamental idea behind biosensors is the ability to distinguish between two complementary hybridized nucleic acid strands, the interaction of monoclonal antigen specific antibodies to detect antigen proteins and the diagnosis of antibodies through interactions with recombinant antigen and target neutralizing antibodies. The most popular electrochemical biosensors are affordable, simple to use and well-suited for large production. For the diagnosis of COVID-19, neutralizing antibodies such as IgM or IgG, the SARS-CoV RNA genome and particular antigen protein should all be used in the construction of biosensors.

Radiology Imaging

Radiology imaging uses chest radiography (CXR) and chest computed tomography (CT) techniques to take images of body's internal structure, which helps in the early screening of the disease. However, the problem is that they fail to detect the type of virus. Chest CT Scans help in detection of lung fibrosis in COVID-19 recovered patients. CT imaging is used for the diagnosis of COVID-19 due to its rapid accessibility and high sensitivity. Chest X-rays produce images of the lung, heart, airways and bones of the lung and the spine. This is reliable in detecting chronic lung state. Compared to CT, CXR is cheaper and more accessible. However, it is prone to errors and less accuracy due to radiologist's manual examination and interpretation of the diseased image. These limitations can be easily curbed through the use of highly accurate AI based strategies.

Microfluidic approach

The biological, chemical, and physical processes can be controlled using tools for microfluidic techniques that deal with small amounts of fluids. Segmented flow microfluidics, which removes hydrodynamic dispersion and creates an isolated response vessel, is the most often used type of microfluidics for fluid manipulation. Microfluidic technology has recently advanced to the point where it can be used for illness diagnosis and therapy, which can produce statistically significant data for study.

Fluorescence-based antibody (microfluidic double-antigen bridging immunoassay technique (DA-D4), which detects the total antibody count as well as its subclasses and isotypes), antigen and nucleic acids (such as RT-qPCR and RT-LAMP based amplification,) detection, spectrometer and image analysis-based detection techniques are all used. According to reports, SARS-CoV-2 kits using microfluidic technology have greater sensitivity and specificity.

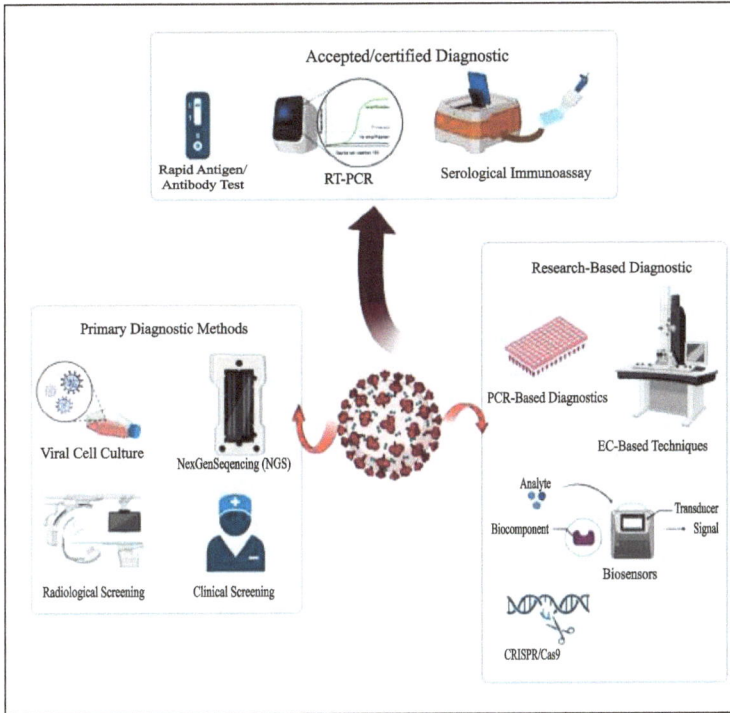

Fig. (2). Several methods of COVID-19 diagnosis are shown in the example [34].

ML BASED APPROACHES [35]

The goal of machine learning (ML) is to create tools that can learn from experience and get better without being explicitly programmed. For patients with COVID-19 infections, ML methods can successfully be utilised to increase the effectiveness of diagnosis and therapy delivery. The following section contains a detailed discussion of the circumstantial use of ML in COVID-19 detection.

Role of ML in COVID-19 Diagnosis

The world has learned from the COVID-19 pandemic about the shortcomings of contemporary healthcare systems that can be applied to the control of any disease epidemic. The key causes of rapid global spread of COVID-19, which is impeding global economic growth, are the slow development of conventional treatment protocols, slow illness tracking, and late discovery of the infected patient. Unnecessary antibiotic use has increased as a result of growing ignorance regarding treatment technique, which accelerates the development of antibiotic resistance.

Circumstantial Use of ML

Researchers use ML to help with the outbreak management after having trouble containing the COVID-19 outbreak. ML could be useful in the drug development process from the perspectives of patient disease diagnosis, tracking, and surveillance [35].

Patient Diagnosis through Radiology Images

Early detection of COVID-19 prevents serious sickness in the patients, thereby lowering fatality rates. RT-PCR has traditionally been used to confirm the illness. Yet, the unfavourable nature of RT-PCR results from its unavailability and lengthy process. In addition, the viral load plays a key role in generating a positive RT-PCR result. For gathering of samples, the design of experiments, and the analysis, qualified personnel are needed. Thus, patient detection utilising radiological images is the most typical application of ML in COVID-19. Images from CT scans and X-rays can help accurately identify COVID-19 with the aid of ML and DL [35]. An AI programme called COVID-NET analyzes data from patients' lung X-rays to aid in diagnosis with a 92.4% accuracy rate. Another application of convolutional neural networks (CNNs) that separate COVID-19 pneumonia from influenza or other lung disorders is COV-Net19. In binary categorization of COVID and non-COVID chest X-ray pictures, it achieved 99.71% accuracy. When Jin *et al.*, 2020 tested their artificial intelligence system on more than 10,000 CT volumes, they discovered that it performed two orders of magnitude more quickly than radiologists and looked to be more accurate. These several models demonstrate how AI might be useful in COVID-19 diagnosis. The disease's spread can be stopped with proper implementation, which can hasten patient diagnosis.

Tracking of COVID-19

For the treatment of any disease epidemic, early patient diagnosis, surveillance, and disease transmission predictions are essential. It is essential to track patient data, anticipate illness transmission, and control communal transmission of the highly contagious COVID-19. In the healthcare industry, AI has been crucial due to a lack of human resources. Several AI-based models that have been developed by scientists can assist governing bodies in taking the essential actions. Berlin, for instance, employs the epidemiological SIR model, which oversees the Government's allotted containment orders and draws further conclusions. A similar model that monitors illness transmission is GLEAM viz. an infection tracker model called Meta biota that can predict the onset of the disease. A few algorithms are frequently employed in ML to forecast and track disease data in addition to these applications. To predict the pandemic trajectory, Zhan, Zheng, *et al.* used a random forest bagging approach in conjunction with a comprehensive understanding in 2020. This model seemed to be very precise and predictably strong. Additional investigations that assisted in predicting the spread of the illness used a long short-term memory (LSTM) model in a Python simulation environment. Despite being highly accurate, these models were only tested on a short dataset; therefore, to corroborate the results, they must be evaluated on a larger dataset.

Tracking Patient Health Condition

Monitoring the patient's health is essential following the diagnosis of COVID-19 infection to increase treatment effectiveness and decrease mortality. Although a CT scan of the patient's lungs could be utilized to evaluate their health, these examinations are expensive. Hence, using ML approaches, researchers discovered a few blood test characteristics that might forecast the patient's health. Three variables—lactic dehydrogenase, lymphocytes, and high affectivity C-receptive protein—along with the XGBoost model were employed in a study to predict the mortality risk of patients with good accuracy and efficiency. Another study used the CNN model and variables such as patient body temperature, oxygen saturation point, heart rate, and audio signals to categorize patients' health. Salp optimization behavior was utilised to update the neural network parameters while classifying the patients. With an accuracy rate of 98.79%, this system is capable of accurately predicting the patient's state of health.

Use of ML in Vaccine and Drug Development

Drug and vaccine development typically takes a long time and is expensive. Accelerating the medication discovery process is crucial at the start of every epidemic, though. Recently, during the COVID-19 outbreak, researchers used AI to assist in the creation of both vaccines and medications. Information about the nucleic acid sequence or protein component is needed for vaccine development. By examining genomic sequences, ML can assist in forecasting 3D protein architectures. An example of ML technology that makes use of genetic or amino acid sequence data to forecast the function of proteins is the alpha fold model.

To forecast the protein's 3D atomic maps, it makes use of an important ResNet architecture. Six predicted proteins for COVID-19 (SARS-CoV-2 membrane protein, protein 3a, Nsp2, Nsp4, Nsp6, and papain-like proteinase) will aid in the prediction of the treatment.

Drug identification, pre-clinical research, clinical research, and FDA approval are the four stages of developing a novel medicine. The molecular level of AI is utilized in drug-target interaction. Drugs for COVID-19 were found using a deep learning (DL) model called Molecule Transformer Drug Target Interaction (MT-DTI). This model predicts target proteins using amino acid sequences and SMILES strings, and it identifies the drug atazanavir as a powerful inhibitor of COVID-19. KronRLS and SimBoost are two other similarity-based models that are applied to drug discovery. A network-based DL model called DeepDR was utilized for in-silico medication repurposing, and the AUC obtained was 90.08% greater than that of other models.

ML Algorithms Used to Combat COVID-19

The ML technique uses a variety of statistical, probabilistic, optimization, and computational tools and algorithms to extract patterns from huge and complicated datasets and learn from previous experiences. These algorithms have been successfully used for a variety of tasks, including automatic text cataloging, disease modeling, network infringement detection, junk email filtration, and many more. Supervised learning, unsupervised learning, reinforcement learning, and deep learning are the four basic categories into which machine learning approaches can be separated. By learning from previous datasets that supervise in the form of the labels in the training phase, supervised learning involves algorithms that predict opposing classes for the unseen data (algorithms classified under classifications) or foresee future occurrences (regression). By comparing its output to the inputs, the supervised learning paradigm, also known as exemplar-based learning, learns to respond precisely. Unsupervised learning is to gather data into similar clusters without any prior knowledge (clustering techniques can be either hierarchical or partition-based). It extracts from the data the hidden patterns that can be utilized to create rules. This statistical method is designed to discover and learn about the issue of the unidentified structure in the unlabelled data.

Reinforcement learning, on the other hand, is regarded as a category of intermediate learning that focuses solely on determining the accuracy of the output by investigating alternative options. This method of instruction is referred to as "learning with a critic" because it has no implications. A subset of machine learning called "deep learning" employs a range of algorithms to effectively combat the new coronavirus. It deals with medical imaging, tracking diseases, analyzing protein structures, finding new drugs, and comprehending the severity and contagiousness of the virus. COVID-net, a convolutional neural network-based system, Deep Pneumonia, which used ResNet to extract complex features from the CT samples, CoroNet, an Xception-based model for diagnosing coronavirus from the X-ray images, and many other deep learning-based systems are among the systems used to diagnose COVID-19. Convolutional neural networks (CNNs), commonly referred to as CovNets, are a popular deep learning technique that classifies data in the order of complexity [36]. Deep learning (79%) and supervised learning (16%) are the two main machine learning (ML) approaches utilized to address COVID-19. Deep learning can efficiently form neural networks with several hidden layers and can make judgements to provide a high-quality outcome. Unsupervised learning techniques in this situation, meanwhile, have not yet been recognized. The AI classification is shown in Fig. (3).

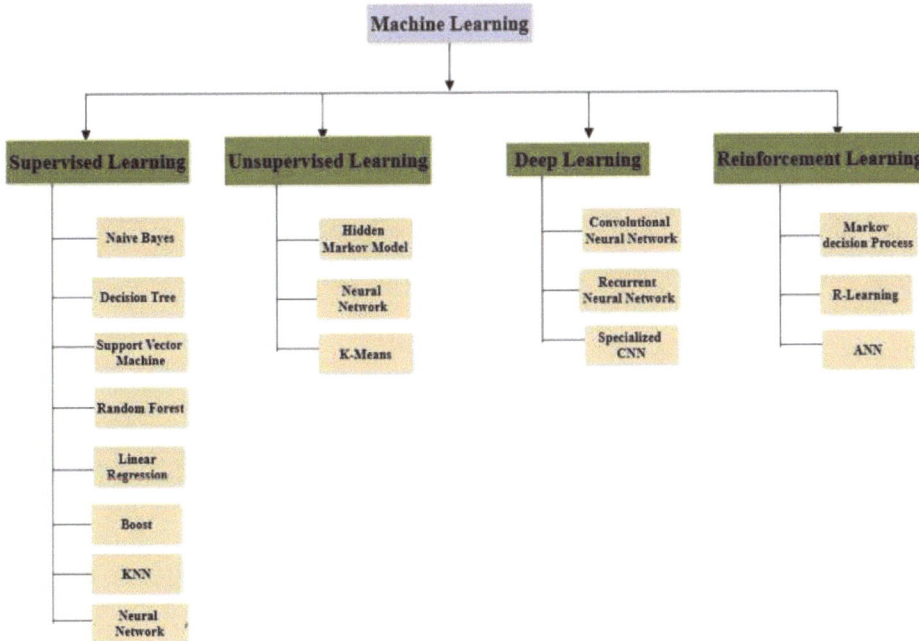

Fig. (3). Machine Learning Algorithm Classification [37].

Decision tree

A tree-structured model reflecting the learned functions is produced by the decision tree, which is a supervised learning algorithm. Two entities are the leaves and nodes of a decision tree. While the data is divided into decision nodes based on feature values, the leaves of the tree signify the outcome or choice. The root node, also known as the decision node, is where the data classification process begins. Until it reaches the leaf node, the tree traverses the edge based on the node's value. The leaf node represents the trio's decision.

Random Forest

For classification and regression, the ensemble-based Random Forest (RF) technique is employed. The datasets are used to generate numerous decision trees that are then integrated to produce the final decision tree [38]. The RF two-staged algorithm creates a random forest in the first stage, which is then utilized to make predictions in the second stage.

Naive Bayes

The Bayes theorem of probability is applied via the Naive Bayes ML algorithm [39]. Since the probability of an event B is known, Bayes' theorem calculates the following probability of an event A, where P(A/B) is as follows:

$$P\left(\frac{A}{B}\right) = \frac{P\left(\frac{B}{A}\right)P(A)}{P(B)}$$

Here, events A and B are involved. P(A) and P(B) represent the probabilities of events A and B separately. P(A/B) represents the likelihood that A will occur if B is accurate. P(B/A) represents the likelihood that B will occur if A is true. When the inputs have a high degree of dimension, the Naive Bayes classifier is frequently utilized.

Support vector machine

One of the top supervised learning methods for situations with vast amounts of data sorting is the support vector machine. It serves as a classification tool. The margin calculation that is made between the classes is the foundation of SVM. The margin's separation from the classes reduces classification error and boosts efficiency.

k-Nearest-Neighbor (KNN)

Another supervised learning technique used in data mining and machine learning is kNN. The assumptions about the distribution of the data are false since this learning strategy is unfocused and unparameterized. Models can be created using the indolence loading of the kNN without any training data. The testing process is slowed down and becomes more expensive as a result of the training data being used later in the testing phase.

Gradient-boosted Decision Tree (GBDT)

The ensemble method-based set of trees that the GBDT algorithm focuses on building sequentially is a set of trees. The algorithm creates decisions individually such that each iteration's trees perform better than the one before it in terms of performance. The effective GBDT method is used extensively in both the business and academic worlds [40].

Logistic regression

Based on the relationship between the numerical variable and the label, the logistic regression algorithm predicts the class of the variable. The likelihood of the independently featured data points can be utilized to construct models. These models are then employed to forecast the likelihood that a given data point will belong to a particular class. The construction of the regression model depends heavily on the sigmoid function. It is presumed that the data points adhere to a linear function. The mathematical formulation of the LR is $\log\left(\frac{p(X)}{1-p(X)}\right) = \beta_0 + \beta_1$

Where p is the probability of X belonging to class C, and $\beta_0 + \beta_1$ are the model parameters.

Artificial Neural Network

In several fields, the use of artificial neural networks (ANN) for classification, clustering, pattern recognition, and prediction is common. An intricate, multilayered deep learning algorithm called ANN aims to imitate the functioning of the human brain. It figures out the input scores for every class connected to the input object. The output of one layer in the ANN is coupled to the input of the one below it. The ANN is a multi-layered system. The weights and activation function given to each layer are used to calculate the final score. Different models of artificial neural network are listed in Table 3.

Different Models and Networks of ML Used in COVID-19 Diagnosis

LR Model

Researchers use powerful ML algorithms, such as linear regression (LR), to predict and diagnose various diseases. LR is a predictive technique that focuses on predicting the effect of certain factors on COVID-19 outbursts. Different researchers have used the linear regression model to predict COVID-19-infected patients. A comparative study shows that the LR model outperforms various other models with a high accuracy rate [41].

XGBoost Model

A widely used gradient-boosted decision tree technique is XGBoost, commonly referred to as extreme gradient boosting. The well-known XGBoost tool is renowned for managing missing data naturally, quickly, and in parallel. The optimized distributed gradient boosting library's high competence, flexibility, and portability make it suitable for usage in a variety of domains, including data mining and recommendation systems. As follows is the definition of the gradient advancing decision tree's goal function:

$$\pounds(\emptyset) = \sum_{i=1}^{n} loss\left(yi_{\hat{y}i}\right) + \sum_{k=1}^{k} \Omega(f_k)$$

The complexity of the tree is represented by and k is the total number of trees in the model. Loss in this equation stands for the loss in training. By reducing the objective function, this model's efficiency can be increased through optimization. The Sequential Organ Failure Assessment (SOFA) score variation of the critically ill can be predicted using the XGBoost model, which can be utilized to highlight the nonlinearity in the time series of COVID-19 cases [42], and determine how the properties of C-reactive protein, lymphocyte ratio, lactic acid, and serum calcium affect the extrapolative prediction of COVID-19 [43 - 45].

Boosted RF Model

Several decision trees that perform classification and regression and help determine the output are included in the Random Forest Classifier. The accuracy of the model is mostly determined by the effectiveness of the tree classifiers and their relationship [46]. The AdaBoost algorithm, on which the boosted RF model is built, leverages the geographic, travel, health, and demographic information of the COVID-19-infected individuals to forecast the severity of the infection and the likelihood of survival or death. The F1 score, which is the most important metric used to assess the model's effectiveness in categorizing COVID-19 patients, is 0.86, while the accuracy of the boosted RF model is 94% [47].

Deep Forest Model

The ensemble-based deep forest model, or DF, uses three classifiers (additional trees, XGBoost, and LightGBM) to increase variety and performance. The model's experimental examination shows that it has 99.5% accuracy, 95.28 sensitivity, and 99.96% specificity, which are all high-performance measures. In areas without access to diagnosis technology, this model can be a quick screening tool for COVID-19 infection [47, 48].

Truncated Inception Net

For COVID-19 screening, Das *et al.* suggested a computationally effective CNN-based model called the Truncated Inception Net. This model is derived from the intricate ImageNet database's Inception Net V3 architecture. To lessen its complexity and overfitting concerns, a truncated version of the Inception Net V3 model was created. The best categorization results were deferred at the point chosen as the truncation point. To find COVID-19, this shortened model functions as a binary classifier of CXR pictures. Truncated Inception Net is a breakthrough for COVID-19 screening [49].

Table 3. Different ML Algorithm Models (Deep Learning is a widely used model in COVID-19 diagnosis.

Machine Learning Algorithms	Models Based on Different Learning Algorithms
Deep Learning	COVID-Net [50], Truncated Inception net [49], Inception V3 [51], DenseNet169 [52], InceptionResNetv2 [52], NASNetLarge [52], VGG16 [53], DenseNet161 [53], COVID-CAPS, SqueezeNet, DRE-Net [54], COVNet [55], DarkCovidNet [56], POCOVID [57], LSTM [58]
Supervised Learning	SVM model [59], Linear regression model [60], XGBoost [61], LASSO [41], SEIR model [62], AdaBoost [63], RF model [63]
Unsupervised Learning	K-means clustering model

CASE STUDIES

CASE I

In the management of COVID-19, ML is frequently employed in several situations. Yet the two most common uses of ML are in diagnostics and the creation of vaccines. To diagnose CT scan lung images of COVID-19 patients, a few researchers from Tianjin Medical University Cancer Institute and Hospital created a CNN-based model utilising the RAD Logics algorithm. The photos demonstrated an accuracy of 89.5% when compared to individuals who had been admitted with severe pneumonia before the pandemic. The software accurately diagnosed patients using lung CT scan pictures, outperforming professional radiologists with a diagnosis rate of 55% [64].

CASE II

Software for peptide-based vaccine creation was created by MIT researchers. The developed programme, called "OptiVax," produces new vaccinations in huge quantities using immunoinformatic techniques and data from already-existing vaccines [65].

CASE III

A team of Indian researchers created the AI model "Waskaro" to combat the panic and falsehoods brought on by COVID-19 infection. Waskaro may be used to monitor and follow those who spread false information about the virus. It is a tool for self-evaluation that aids in automatically recording results and raising user self-awareness [66].

CASE IV

Another example of a multiple epitope vaccination case study was when DeepVacPred[i], a deep learning framework, was employed by researchers to create a vaccine. It produces a 26-subunit vaccine from the SARS-CoV2 spike protein that comprises B-cell, cytotoxic T lymphocyte, and helper T lymphocyte epitopes. The top 11 subunit vaccinations out of 26 were sorted. A 694Aa multi-epitope vaccine that has been refined and has 16 B-cell epitopes, 89HTL epitopes, and 82 CTL epitopes was created. The process of developing the vaccine was accelerated by the in silico deep learning network, and it was determined that the generated vaccine was effective against potential RNA mutations [67].

CHALLENGES AND FUTURE DIRECTIONS

AIML, as previously indicated, has tremendously aided in the detection and treatment of COVID-19 as well as the creation of an ML vaccine against SARS-CoV-2, but there are certain difficulties that these computer-aided methods confront that must be resolved.

• The existing data is the ML's key source of dependence. Little datasets and information ambiguity, however, are the two key factors that affect how ML models perform. The lack of coordination between disease biology and the computational framework has surfaced as a key concern for ML-based models, nevertheless, as ML is a new edge method and there are substantially fewer trained persons.

• There is a serious worry surrounding the privacy of patient data, which needs to be handled properly, as ML models are largely supervised learning models where the data need to be labelled.

• The majority of COVID-19 infection patients diagnosed to date rely on chest and lung pictures generated by CT or CXR techniques. However, research has shown that SARS-CoV-2 also has an impact on other organs, including the heart, gastrointestinal tract, and others. However, no ML procedures have been documented that incorporate the examination of several bodily organs [68].

• For patients to receive effective care, it is essential to comprehend the degree of the disease's severity as caused by the SARS-CoV-2 virus. However, ML is unable to determine the infection's severe level, necessitating extra care [68].

• ML use was challenging in disease outbreaks like COVID-19 due to the increased unpredictability of disease variables like patient symptoms.

Yet, the difficulties posed by ML can be readily addressed with a lot of hard work and attention from researchers. Excellent efficiency has been demonstrated by ML and DL models, which has to be evaluated on large datasets. In the future, ML will be a useful tool for forecasting pandemics and monitoring the effects of vaccines created against viruses that can lengthen human lifespans, together with the deployment of modern networks with great accuracy and flexibility.

TAKE AWAY HOME MESSAGE

Machine learning (ML) and artificial intelligence (AI) have played crucial roles in addressing COVID-19, contributing significantly to diagnostics, treatment strategies, and vaccine development. However, several critical challenges must be addressed to optimize their efficacy. Firstly, the performance of ML models is highly dependent on the quality and quantity of available data. Limited datasets and data ambiguity significantly impact model accuracy and robustness. Additionally, there is a notable gap between the biological understanding of SARS-CoV-2 and the computational models designed to study it, further complicated by a shortage of experts in this interdisciplinary field. Patient data privacy is a significant concern, as most ML models require extensive labeled datasets, raising ethical and legal issues regarding data protection. Moreover, current ML applications predominantly utilize imaging data from chest X-rays (CXR) and computed tomography (CT) scans to diagnose COVID-19, despite the virus affecting multiple organs, including the cardiovascular and gastrointestinal systems. This narrow focus restricts the holistic assessment of the disease's impact. ML models also face challenges in accurately assessing disease severity, which is essential for tailoring patient management and treatment plans. The variability and unpredictability of clinical presentations and disease progression in COVID-19 patients add another layer of complexity to ML applications in pandemic scenarios.

Future directions in ML research should focus on overcoming these challenges through rigorous data curation, integration of multimodal datasets, and development of more sophisticated models. Evaluating ML and deep learning (DL) models on larger and more diverse datasets will enhance their predictive power and reliability, making them invaluable tools for pandemic forecasting and vaccine efficacy monitoring. The COVID-19 pandemic has highlighted the potential for enhanced collaboration between data scientists, clinicians, and healthcare professionals. Such interdisciplinary efforts are essential for developing robust ML algorithms capable of accurate diagnosis, prognosis, and risk stratification. Addressing selection bias through methodological advancements is critical for ensuring the generalizability and applicability of ML models.

Moreover, integrating diverse data types—including clinical records, symptomatology, and demographic information—from multiple sources will significantly improve the predictive accuracy of ML models in managing COVID-19 and future pandemics. This integrative approach represents a promising avenue for further research and practical application in the field of AI-driven healthcare.

CONCLUSION

The emergence of variants of the SARS-CoV-2 isolates has resulted in high contagion, and this has resulted in mutations that have greatly impacted diagnosis and treatment choices. The ongoing COVID-19 pandemic presents an exceptional opportunity to accelerate collaboration between data scientists, clinicians, radiologists, and other healthcare professionals to understand the potential of machine learning in health care, i.e. the development of algorithms, which could aid in the diagnosis and prediction of the severity and mortality risks associated with SARS-CoV-2 infection. However, researchers created a few predictive models using several cutting-edge ML algorithms that helped analyse large-scale datasets and produce accurate inferences quickly. In this chapter, we have only shown how various ML techniques can be applied to the context of COVID-19 and its management. One of the most significant applications is the consistency of capturing findings diagnostic and prognostic features of the ML models that are present in medical literature, indicating the relevance of using ML algorithms to thoroughly analyse patient data, distinguish patterns, and support decision-making. Moreover, selection bias occurs when imbalanced datasets are used in the majority of current studies, which encourages the creation of some practical methods to address this problem. Despite recent developments in various machine learning techniques, no supervised learning algorithms have been used in practical applications since it is difficult to choose the appropriate models for COVID screening. For this reason, it is crucial to combine several data types, such as clinical details, symptom information, and other demographic data from many sources, so that the prediction of COVID-19 would be worth further investigating.

WHAT YOU WILL LEARN

• **Applications of AI and ML in COVID-19 Diagnosis:** Insight into how Artificial Intelligence (AI) and Machine Learning (ML) algorithms are employed to diagnose COVID-19, with a focus on chest imaging techniques such as CT scans and X-rays.

• **Capabilities of Machine Learning:** Understanding ML's strengths, including its ability to analyze large datasets and identify patterns in medical images.

• **Challenges and Limitations:**

- Limited availability of high-quality data for training models.

- Privacy concerns related to patient data.

- ML's current limitations in assessing the severity of health conditions.

• **Review of ML Methods for COVID-19 Diagnosis:**

- Examination of various ML techniques like decision trees, random forests, and convolutional neural networks (CNNs).

- Assessment of the performance of models such as XGBoost and Truncated Inception Net in COVID-19 screening.

• **Strategies for Effective ML Implementation:**

- Emphasizing the importance of collaboration between data scientists and healthcare professionals.

- Addressing data bias.

- Integrating comprehensive patient data, beyond chest imaging, for more accurate diagnosis.

• Future Directions and Potential of ML in Healthcare:

- Exploring the potential of ML for rapid and accurate COVID-19 diagnosis.

- Discussing the steps needed to overcome current challenges for broader adoption in healthcare settings.

REFERENCES

[1]   'Coronavirus' Accessed: Mar 04, 2023 [Online] Available: https://wwwwhoint/health-topics/coronavirus

[2]   Sharma A, Tiwari S, Deb MK, Marty JL. Severe acute respiratory syndrome coronavirus-2 (SARS-CoV-2): a global pandemic and treatment strategies. Int J Antimicrob Agents 2020; 56(2): 106054.
        [http://dx.doi.org/10.1016/j.ijantimicag.2020.106054] [PMID: 32534188]

[3]   Cui J, Li F, Shi ZL. Origin and evolution of pathogenic coronaviruses. Nat Rev Microbiol 2019; 17(3): 181-92.
        [http://dx.doi.org/10.1038/s41579-018-0118-9] [PMID: 30531947]

[4]   'Disease Transmission: Direct Contact vs Indirect Contact' Accessed: Mar 04, 2023 [Online] Available: https://wwwhealthlinecom/health/disease-transmission

[5]   Aleem A, Akbar Samad AB, Slenker AK. Emerging Variants of SARS-CoV-2 And Novel Therapeutics Against Coronavirus (COVID-19).StatPearls. Treasure Island, FL: StatPearls Publishing 2022. http://www.ncbi.nlm.nih.gov/books/NBK570580/ [Online]

[6]   Sonnleitner ST, Sonnleitner S, Hinterbichler E, *et al.* The mutational dynamics of the SARS-CoV-2 virus in serial passages in vitro. Virol Sin 2022; 37(2): 198-207.
        [http://dx.doi.org/10.1016/j.virs.2022.01.029] [PMID: 35277373]

[7]   'Different Symptoms for COVID-19, Flu, Allergies, and Cold' Accessed: Mar 04, 2023 [Online] Available: https://wwwhealthlinecom/health-news/flu-allergies-coronavirus-different-symptoms

[8]   Maharjan N, Thapa N, Pun Magar B, Maharjan M, Tu J. COVID-19 Diagnosed by Real-Time Reverse Transcriptase-Polymerase Chain Reaction in Nasopharyngeal Specimens of Suspected Cases in a Tertiary Care Center: A Descriptive Cross-sectional Study. JNMA J Nepal Med Assoc 2021; 59(237): 464-7.
        [http://dx.doi.org/10.31729/jnma.5383] [PMID: 34508439]

[9]   Arevalo-Rodriguez I, Buitrago-Garcia D, Simancas-Racines D, *et al.* False-negative results of initial RT-PCR assays for COVID-19: A systematic review. PLoS One 2020; 15(12): e0242958.
        [http://dx.doi.org/10.1371/journal.pone.0242958] [PMID: 33301459]

[10]   Habibzadeh P, Mofatteh M, Silawi M, Ghavami S, Faghihi MA. Molecular diagnostic assays for COVID-19: an overview. Crit Rev Clin Lab Sci 2021; 58(6): 385-98.
        [http://dx.doi.org/10.1080/10408363.2021.1884640] [PMID: 33595397]

[11]   'Infection prevention and control GLOBAL' Accessed: Mar 04, 2023 [Online] Available: https://wwwwhoint/health-topics/infection-prevention-and-control

[12]   Benmalek E, Elmhamdi J, Jilbab A. Comparing CT scan and chest X-ray imaging for COVID-19 diagnosis. Biomedical Engineering Advances 2021; 1: 100003.
        [http://dx.doi.org/10.1016/j.bea.2021.100003] [PMID: 34786568]

[13]   Cozzi D, Cavigli E, Moroni C, *et al.* Ground-glass opacity (GGO): a review of the differential diagnosis in the era of COVID-19. Jpn J Radiol 2021; 39(8): 721-32.
        [http://dx.doi.org/10.1007/s11604-021-01120-w] [PMID: 33900542]

[14]   Sabetkish N, Rahmani A. The overall impact of COVID-19 on healthcare during the pandemic: A multidisciplinary point of view. Health Sci Rep 2021; 4(4): e386.
        [http://dx.doi.org/10.1002/hsr2.386] [PMID: 34622020]

[15]   'Coronavirus | Definition, Features, and Examples | Britannica' Accessed: Mar 05, 2023 [Online] Available: https://wwwbritannicacom/science/coronavirus-virus-group

[16]   'Human coronavirus types' Accessed: Jun 01, 2024 [Online] Available: https://stackscdcgov/view/cdc/84531

[17]   Donnelly CA, Malik MR, Elkholy A, Cauchemez S, Van Kerkhove MD. Worldwide Reduction in MERS Cases and Deaths since 2016. Emerg Infect Dis 2019; 25(9): 1758-60.
        [http://dx.doi.org/10.3201/eid2509.190143] [PMID: 31264567]

[18]   Huang C, Wang Y, Li X, *et al.* Clinical features of patients infected with 2019 novel coronavirus in Wuhan, China. Lancet 2020; 395(10223): 497-506.

[http://dx.doi.org/10.1016/S0140-6736(20)30183-5]

[19]   Yasin R, Gouda W. Chest X-ray findings monitoring COVID-19 disease course and severity. Egypt J Radiol Nucl Med 2020; 51(1): 193.
[http://dx.doi.org/10.1186/s43055-020-00296-x]

[20]   'The Radiology Assistant : COVID-19 Imaging findings' Accessed: Mar 05, 2023 [Online] Available: https://radiologyassistantnl/chest/COVID-19/covid19-imaging-findings

[21]   Zhao W, Jiang W, Qiu X. Deep learning for COVID-19 detection based on CT images. Sci Rep 2021; 11(1): 14353.
[http://dx.doi.org/10.1038/s41598-021-93832-2] [PMID: 34253822]

[22]   Emery S L, Erdman DD, Bowen MD, *et al.* Real-Time Reverse Transcription–Polymerase Chain Reaction Assay for SARS-associated Coronavirus. Emerging Infectious Diseases journal 2004; 10(2).
[http://dx.doi.org/10.3201/eid1002.030759]

[23]   Rahimi H, Salehiabar M, Barsbay M, *et al.* CRISPR Systems for COVID-19 Diagnosis. ACS Sens 2021; 6(4): 1430-45.
[http://dx.doi.org/10.1021/acssensors.0c02312] [PMID: 33502175]

[24]   Werbajh S, Larocca L, Carrillo C, *et al.* Colorimetric RT-LAMP Detection of Multiple SARS-CoV-2 Variants and Lineages of Concern Direct from Nasopharyngeal Swab Samples without RNA Isolation. Viruses 2023; 15(9): 1910.
[http://dx.doi.org/10.3390/v15091910] [PMID: 37766315]

[25]   Alharbi SA, Almutairi AZ, Jan AA, Alkhalify AM. Enzyme-Linked Immunosorbent Assay for the Detection of Severe Acute Respiratory Syndrome Coronavirus 2 (SARS-CoV-2) IgM/IgA and IgG Antibodies Among Healthcare Workers. Cureus 2020; 12(9): e10285.
[http://dx.doi.org/10.7759/cureus.10285] [PMID: 33047077]

[26]   'Clinical Laboratory Improvement Amendments (CLIA) | CMS' Accessed: Oct 12, 2023 [Online] Available: https://wwwcmsgov/medicarc/quality/clinical-laboratory-improvement-amendments

[27]   Alhabbab RY. Lateral Flow Immunoassays for Detecting Viral Infectious Antigens and Antibodies. Micromachines (Basel) 2022; 13(11): 1901.
[http://dx.doi.org/10.3390/mi13111901] [PMID: 36363922]

[28]   'Sensors | Free Full-Text | Electrochemical Biosensors - Sensor Principles and Architectures' Accessed: Oct 12, 2023 [Online] Available: https://wwwmdpicom/1424-8220/8/3/1400

[29]   Garg M, Prabhakar N, Bhalla A, *et al.* Computed tomography chest in COVID-19: When & why? Indian J Med Res 2021; 153(1): 86-92.
[http://dx.doi.org/10.4103/ijmr.IJMR_3669_20] [PMID: 33402610]

[30]   Scott S, Ali Z. Fabrication Methods for Microfluidic Devices: An Overview. Micromachines (Basel) 2021; 12(3): 319.
[http://dx.doi.org/10.3390/mi12030319] [PMID: 33803689]

[31]   Uddin S, Khan A, Hossain ME, Moni MA. Comparing different supervised machine learning algorithms for disease prediction. BMC Med Inform Decis Mak 2019; 19(1): 281.
[http://dx.doi.org/10.1186/s12911-019-1004-8] [PMID: 31864346]

[32]   'Loop-Mediated Isothermal Amplification | NEB' Accessed: Mar 05, 2023 [Online] Available: https://internationalnebcom/applications/dna-amplification-pcr-and-qpcr/isothe-mal-amplification/loop-mediated-isothermal-amplification-lamp

[33]   Falzone L, Gattuso G, Tsatsakis A, Spandidos D, Libra M. Current and innovative methods for the diagnosis of COVID□19 infection (Review). Int J Mol Med 2021; 47(6): 100.
[http://dx.doi.org/10.3892/ijmm.2021.4933] [PMID: 33846767]

[34]   Zoabi Y, Deri-Rozov S, Shomron N. Machine learning-based prediction of COVID-19 diagnosis based on symptoms. NPJ Digit Med 2021; 4(1): 3.

[http://dx.doi.org/10.1038/s41746-020-00372-6] [PMID: 33398013]

[35]   'What are Convolutional Neural Networks? | IBM' Accessed: Mar 05, 2023 [Online] Available: https://wwwibmcom/topics/convolutional-neural-networks

[36]   Aldahiri A, Alrashed B, Hussain W. Trends in Using IoT with Machine Learning in Health Prediction System. Forecasting 2021; 3(1): 181-206.
[http://dx.doi.org/10.3390/forecast3010012]

[37]   'Machine Learning Random Forest Algorithm - Javatpoint' Accessed: Mar 05, 2023 [Online] Available: https://wwwjavatpointcom/machine-learning-random-forest-algorithm

[38]   'Naive Bayes Algorithm | Discover the Naive Bayes Algorithm', EDUCBA Accessed: Mar 05, 2023 [Online] Available: https://wwweducbacom/naive-bayes-algorithm/

[39]   'Gradient Boosted Decision Trees | Machine Learning', Google Developers Accessed: Mar 05, 2023 [Online] Available: https://developersgooglecom/machine-learning/decision-forests/intro-to-gbdt

[40]   Meraihi Y, Gabis AB, Mirjalili S, Ramdane-Cherif A, Alsaadi FE. Machine Learning-Based Research for COVID-19 Detection, Diagnosis, and Prediction: A Survey. SN Computer Science 2022; 3(4): 286.
[http://dx.doi.org/10.1007/s42979-022-01184-z] [PMID: 35578678]

[41]   Moreno R, Rhodes A, Piquilloud L, *et al.* The Sequential Organ Failure Assessment (SOFA) Score: has the time come for an update? Crit Care 2023; 27(1): 15.
[http://dx.doi.org/10.1186/s13054-022-04290-9] [PMID: 36639780]

[42]   Yang M, Chen X, Xu Y. A Retrospective Study of the C-Reactive Protein to Lymphocyte Ratio and Disease Severity in 108 Patients with Early COVID-19 Pneumonia from January to March 2020 in Wuhan, China. Med Sci Monit 2020; 26.
[http://dx.doi.org/10.12659/MSM.926393]

[43]   Liu X, Xue S, Xu J, *et al.* Clinical characteristics and related risk factors of disease severity in 101 COVID-19 patients hospitalized in Wuhan, China. Acta Pharmacol Sin 2022; 43(1): 64-75.
[http://dx.doi.org/10.1038/s41401-021-00627-2] [PMID: 33742107]

[44]   Ustebay S, Sarmis A, Kaya GK, Sujan M. A comparison of machine learning algorithms in predicting COVID-19 prognostics. Intern Emerg Med 2023; 18(1): 229-39.
[http://dx.doi.org/10.1007/s11739-022-03101-x]

[45]   Krzywinski M, Altman N. Classification and regression trees. Nat Methods 2017; 14(8): 757-8.
[http://dx.doi.org/10.1038/nmeth.4370]

[46]   Iwendi C, Bashir AK, Peshkar A, *et al.* COVID-19 Patient Health Prediction Using Boosted Random Forest Algorithm. Front Public Health 2020; 8: 357.
[http://dx.doi.org/10.3389/fpubh.2020.00357] [PMID: 32719767]

[47]   AlJame M, Imtiaz A, Ahmad I, Mohammed A. Deep forest model for diagnosing COVID-19 from routine blood tests. Sci Rep 2021; 11(1): 16682.
[http://dx.doi.org/10.1038/s41598-021-95957-w] [PMID: 34404838]

[48]   Das D, Santosh KC, Pal U. Truncated inception net: COVID-19 outbreak screening using chest X-rays. Physical and Engineering Sciences in Medicine 2020; 43(3): 915-25.
[http://dx.doi.org/10.1007/s13246-020-00888-x]

[49]   Wang L, Lin ZQ, Wong A. COVID-Net: a tailored deep convolutional neural network design for detection of COVID-19 cases from chest X-ray images. Sci Rep 2020; 10(1): 19549.
[http://dx.doi.org/10.1038/s41598-020-76550-z] [PMID: 33177550]

[50]   'Classification of COVID-19 from Chest X-ray images using Deep Convolutional Neural Network | IEEE Conference Publication | IEEE Xplore' Accessed: Oct 12, 2023 [Online] Available: https://ieeexploreieeeorg/document/9344870

[51]   Punn NS, Agarwal S. Automated diagnosis of COVID-19 with limited posteroanterior chest X-ray

images using fine-tuned deep neural networks. Appl Intell 2021; 51(5): 2689-702.
[http://dx.doi.org/10.1007/s10489-020-01900-3] [PMID: 34764554]

[52]   'Chest X-ray Classification Using Deep Learning for Automated COVID-19 Screening | SpringerLink'
Accessed: Oct 12, 2023 [Online] Available: https://linkspringercom/article/101007/s42979-02-
-00695-5

[53]   Song Y, Zheng S, Li L, *et al.*, Deep Learning Enables Accurate Diagnosis of Novel Coronavirus
(COVID-19) With CT Images. IEEE/ACM Trans Comput Biol Bioinform 2021; 18(6): 2775-2780.
[http://dx.doi.org/10.1101/2020.02.23.20026930]

[54]   Li L, Qin L, Xu Z, *et al.* Using Artificial Intelligence to Detect COVID-19 and Community-acquired
Pneumonia Based on Pulmonary CT: Evaluation of the Diagnostic Accuracy. Radiology 2020; 296(2):
E65-71.
[http://dx.doi.org/10.1148/radiol.2020200905] [PMID: 32191588]

[55]   Ozturk T, Talo M, Yildirim EA, Baloglu UB, Yildirim O, Rajendra Acharya U. Automated detection
of COVID-19 cases using deep neural networks with X-ray images. Comput Biol Med 2020; 121:
103792.
[http://dx.doi.org/10.1016/j.compbiomed.2020.103792] [PMID: 32568675]

[56]   Born J, Brändle G, Cossio M, *et al.* 'POCOVID-Net: Automatic Detection of COVID-19 From a New
Lung Ultrasound Imaging Dataset (POCUS)'. arXiv 2004; 12084.

[57]   Chimmula VKR, Zhang L. Time series forecasting of COVID-19 transmission in Canada using LSTM
networks. Chaos Solitons Fractals 2020; 135: 109864.
[http://dx.doi.org/10.1016/j.chaos.2020.109864] [PMID: 32390691]

[58]   Yao H, *et al.* Severity Detection for the Coronavirus Disease 2019 (COVID-19) Patients Using a
Machine   Learning   Model   Based   on   the   Blood   and   Urine   Tests
https://wwwfrontiersinorg/articles/103389/fcell202000683 2020.
[http://dx.doi.org/10.3389/fcell.2020.00683]

[59]   Yue H, Yu Q, Liu C, *et al.* Machine learning-based CT radiomics method for predicting hospital stay
in patients with pneumonia associated with SARS-CoV-2 infection: a multicenter study. Ann Transl
Med 2020; 8(14): 859.
[http://dx.doi.org/10.21037/atm-20-3026] [PMID: 32793703]

[60]   'An interpretable mortality prediction model for COVID-19 patients | Nature Machine Intelligence'
Accessed: Oct 12, 2023 [Online] Available: https://wwwnaturecom/articles/s42256-020-0180-7

[61]   Pandey G, Chaudhary P, Gupta R, Pal S. 'SEIR and Regression Model based COVID-19 outbreak
predictions in India'. 2020.
[http://dx.doi.org/10.2196/preprints.19406]

[62]   'Detection of COVID-19 Infection from Routine Blood Exams with Machine Learning: A Feasibility
Study | SpringerLink'   Accessed: Oct   12,   2023   [Online]   Available:
https://linkspringercom/article/101007/s10916-020-01597-4

[63]   Wang S, Kang B, Ma J, *et al.* A deep learning algorithm using CT images to screen for Corona virus
disease (COVID-19). Eur Radiol 2021; 31(8): 6096-104.
[http://dx.doi.org/10.1007/s00330-021-07715-1] [PMID: 33629156]

[64]   Liu G, Carter B, Bricken T, *et al.* Computationally Optimized SARS-CoV-2 MHC Class I and II
Vaccine Formulations Predicted to Target Human Haplotype Distributions. Cell Syst 2020; 11(2):
131-144.e6.
[http://dx.doi.org/10.1016/j.cels.2020.06.009] [PMID: 32721383]

[65]   Pandey R, Gautam V, Pal R, *et al.* A machine learning application for raising WASH awareness in the
times of COVID-19 pandemic. Sci Rep 2022; 12(1): 810.
[http://dx.doi.org/10.1038/s41598-021-03869-6] [PMID: 35039533]

[66]   Yang Z, Bogdan P, Nazarian S. An in silico deep learning approach to multi-epitope vaccine design: a

SARS-CoV-2 case study. Sci Rep 2021; 11(1): 3238.
[http://dx.doi.org/10.1038/s41598-021-81749-9] [PMID: 33547334]

[67]   Bernheim A, Mei X, Huang M, *et al.* Chest CT Findings in Coronavirus Disease-19 (COVID-19): Relationship to Duration of Infection. Radiology 2020; 295(3): 200463.
[http://dx.doi.org/10.1148/radiol.2020200463] [PMID: 32077789]

[68]   Jaiswal A, Gianchandani N, Singh D, Kumar V, Kaur M. Classification of the COVID-19 infected patients using DenseNet201 based deep transfer learning. J Biomol Struct Dyn 2021; 39(15): 5682-9.
[http://dx.doi.org/10.1080/07391102.2020.1788642]

Use of Machine Learning in Diagnosing COVID-19 Infection

Mohammad Sufian Badar[1,2,3,4], **Bipasa Kar**[5], **Budheswar Dehury**[5,*], **Sarbani Mishra**[5] and **Shamim Ahmed Shamim**[6]

[1] *Department of Bioengineering, University of California, Riverside, CA, USA*

[2] *Universal Scientific Education and Research Network (USERN), Tehran, Iran*

[3] *Director (Academic), SPI Darbhanga, India*

[4] *Department of Computer Science and Engineering (Bioinformatics), School of Engineering Sciences and Technology (SEST), Jamia Hamdard, New Delhi, India*

[5] *Bioinformatics Division, ICMR-Regional Medical Research Centre, Odisha, India*

[6] *Department of Nuclear Medicine, AIIMS, New Delhi*

Abstract: The world has witnessed the most devastating pandemic due to the rapid spread of COVID-19, an infectious disease caused by severe acute respiratory syndrome coronavirus (SARS-CoV2 virus). The public health emergency of international concern arose due to the sudden outbreak of COVID-19 where both medical and socio-economic structures remain entirely altered not only in developed countries but also in developing countries. In this crucial scenario, advanced technologies like machine learning (ML) and deep learning (DL) assisted the researchers and helped governments and other health officials (including frontline workers) to manage the outbreak. ML is a sub-branch of computer science, where, machines can analyze large datasets and derive inference from that variable data structures. With the help of suitable algorithms, computers can imitate human behavior by analyzing results and the machines can perform in less time with great accuracy. During the pandemic, due to the scarcity of human resources, ML aided in the diagnosis of patients, forecasted communal transmission, and also helped in the development of effective antivirals and vaccines. In this chapter, we have highlighted the importance of various state-of-the-art ML tools, algorithms and computational models useful in the diagnosis and management of COVID-19. The circumstantial applications of ML are also discussed with real-time case studies. Lastly, the challenges faced by ML in COVID-19 supervision and future directions are also discussed. This chapter will help the researchers and students to understand how this powerful tool is employed to fight COVID-19 and can assist in future health emergencies due to emerging pathogens.

* **Corresponding author Budheswar Dehury:** Bioinformatics Division, ICMR-Regional Medical Research Centre, Odisha, India; E-mail: budheswar.dehury@gmail.com

Mohammad Sufian Badar (Ed.)

Keywords: Computers, Computational models, COVID-19, Deep learning, ML, Socio-economic, SARS-CoV-2, Vaccine development.

INTRODUCTION

The global pandemic, named coronavirus disease (COVID-19), has ruled the world for the past two years and was first reported in Wuhan, China, in December 2019. Since then, 627 million confirmed COVID-19 cases have been reported globally [1, 2]. After the first report in December 2019, in March 2020, it was declared a global pandemic by WHO, and on 21st April 2020, two million cases were reported associated with 120,000 deaths [3]. COVID-19 was caused by a novel coronavirus named severe acute respiratory syndrome coronavirus 2 (SARS-CoV2) [4].

Other coronaviruses were reported earlier: severe acute respiratory syndrome coronavirus (SARS-CoV) and Middle East respiratory syndrome coronavirus (MERS-CoV). Compared to the previous coronaviruses, SARS-CoV2 is considered less fatal but most contagious [5]. The plausible mode of transmission of COVID-19 can be either through direct contact or through the small aerosols released by the infected person while talking, sneezing, or coughing. The high transmission capacity of SARS-CoV-2 made it challenging to take control measures on the spread of the disease. Several different variants of SARS-CoV-2 (delta, omicron, and delta-cron (mixed infections arise due to delta and omicron variants) were also reported from other parts of the world. The fast mutating ability of SARS-CoV-2 is worsening the health status of individuals and also affects considerably health infrastructure and the global economy [6, 7]. The common symptoms of COVID-19 include coughing, fever, body ache, difficulty breathing, etc. where, patients with comorbidities are mostly affected, which could end up in multi-organ failure or death [8]. Due to the similarity of primary symptoms of COVID-19 matches with common influenza, it is mandatory to identify COVID-19 at the preliminary stage.

Several identification systems have been reported for COVID-19, which include rapid antigen tests, antibody detection, reverse transcriptase (RT) PCR, next-generation sequencing, computed tomography (CT) of the chest, and X-rays. Among the techniques mentioned above, RT-PCR tests are usually used as confirmatory tests. However, studies showed that RT-PCR from nasopharyngeal and throat swabs give positive results in only 30-70% of cases. There are few reports of false negatives being reported as well. Among the other pathological tests, CT scans of the chest and X-rays are proclaimed to have 98% and 69% sensitivity, respectively. But identifying infection through CT-scan and X-rays requires expert radiologists [9, 10]. There are several kit-based identification methods also available in the market which are routinely used for the detection of COVID-19. But the positivity yield associated with those kits focuses on the demand for developing more advanced, accurate techniques to help patients in the early phases of diagnosis and prevent rapid dissemination.

In searching for more modern and accurate diagnostic techniques, researchers from different parts of globe try their best to develop universal diagnostic systems that apply to other variants of COVID-19 diagnosis. AI (AI) is one of the promising techniques that utilize previous instances, and without explicit programming, it speeds up the diagnosis process of COVID-19. With the help of two subsets of AI *i.e.* ML (ML) and deep learning (DL), the tracking, diagnosis, and treatment process have become much easier and faster [11]. ML is a system that depends upon machine intelligence based on the previous reference datasets, and deep learning (DL) is an advanced system that simplifies the learning of the machines [12]. ML approaches can be sub-divided into two broad categories viz. supervised and unsupervised learning. In supervised learning, the data are labeled, and it trains the machine in a guided manner, and two algorithms are used namely classified and regression. In unsupervised learning, without actual guidance and labeled data, different algorithms are employed for the training of machines. The algorithms employed could be subdivided into clustering and association [13]. Both machine and deep learning are used for patient diagnosis through the analysis of images of CT scans, and X-rays and they also help to track the epidemiological trend. In this chapter, we have highlighted the importance of ML techniques in the diagnosis of COVID-19 and illuminated new insights into the real-world applications of ML with some real-time case studies.

ROLE OF MODERN TECHNIQUES IN THE DIAGNOSIS OF COVID-19

The COVID-19 pandemic has wreaked havoc all over the world in the past two years. Different preventive measures have been taken for the early detection of the SARS-CoV-2 viral genome to control the outbreak, such as the detection of the viral antigen and their antibodies or viral nucleic acids. Furthermore, detecting the infection in its early stage [14 - 16] and its timely treatment can decide the quarantine period to stop the infection chain, increase the cure rates, and reduce the treatment costs of other serious ailments. However, the shortage of medical centres, dependable caretakers, and deficiency of diagnosis equipment creates difficulty in tracking down the infection and monitoring the pandemic. Recent advances in the technologies and healthcare sectors, along with the widespread use of smartphones, give rise to the development of various effective diagnosis equipment to fight against the current pandemic. Since the beginning of the pandemic, researchers have successfully implemented nucleic acid assays, immunoassays, and radiological imaging techniques for early diagnosis of COVID-19 infection (Table **1**) [10, 17, 18].

Table 1. List of different techniques used for the detection of COVID-19.

Methods used for COVID-19 Diagnosis	Techniques	Description
Nucleic acid amplification Tests	RT-PCR	The reverse transcription polymerase chain reaction is a lab-based technique used to detect the viral genome.
	CRISPR-related amplification	This diagnostic system is based on interspaced short palindromic repeats that have restructured the molecular diagnosis technique [19].
	Loop-Mediated Isothermal Amplification	The LAMP is a rapid diagnostic technique for COVID-19. It uses 4-6 primers that recognize the different regions of the target DNA.
Serological tests	ELISA	The enzyme-linked immunosorbent assay uses antibodies and antigen-measuring techniques to detect COVID-19 infection.
	CLIA	The Clinical Laboratory Improvement Amendments is a program performed to test human specimens and provide accurate, reliable, and exact patient test results [20].
	LFIA	Lateral flow immunoassay is an antigen test used to diagnose any active coronavirus infection.
Biosensors		Biosensors are systematic devices where the signals from the bio-molecules are combined with a sensor transduction system is measured by an analyzer.
Radiology Imaging	CT	Chest computed tomography scans can detect lung fibrosis in COVID-19-recovered patients [21].
	CXR	Chest X-rays produce images of the heart, lungs, airways, and bones of the chest and spine and can reliably detect chronic lung state (https://www. mayoc linic.org/ tests-proc edures/chest-x-r ays/about/pac- 20393494).
Microfluidic approach		The microfluidic approaches include tools to deal with small volumes of fluids to control the biological, chemical, and physical processes.
ML based approaches		The ML technique employs various statistical, probabilistic, optimization methods and computational algorithms to learn from past experiences and identify patterns from large and complex datasets.

Nucleic acid Amplification Tests

The accuracy of the detection of SARS-CoV-2 infected patients is a crucial step towards managing the emerging pandemic. The development of the nucleic acid amplification test, also known as NAAT, was elevated due to the quick commencement of positive COVID-19 cases in the United States [22]. NAAT is a viral diagnostic test designed to detect the viral RNA genome that causes COVID-19. The first stage of the NAAT procedure involves amplification of the virus's genetic material in the patient's specimen (if any), which enables NAATs to detect the presence of even a small amount of SARS-CoV-2 (https://www.cdc.gov/coronavirus/2019-ncov/lab/naats.html). Among the different amplification methods used in NAAT reverse transcription polymerase chain reaction (RT-PCR), loop-mediated isothermal amplification (LAMP), clustered regularly interspaced short palindromic repeats (CRISPR), rolling circle amplification (RCA), recombinase polymerase amplification (RPA) and many others are the primarily used methods in clinical research [23].

The real-time RT-PCR assay of the viral nucleic acid has become the gold standard for the molecular diagnosis of COVID-19. However, this assay faces a lot of challenges while dealing with global supply, testing thousands of samples regularly, leading to the need for a quantitative evaluation of SARS-CoV-2 viral load and the high false negative rate, which requires professional equipment and operations [24]. To overcome the limitations of quantitative RT-PCR, digital droplet PCR (ddPCR) is used at a second diagnosis level as a golden standard to quantize the viral load accurately [25].

Serological Tests

Serological tests are prevailing tools for monitoring infectious diseases such as the COVID-19 and detecting host immunity. These tests have emerged as an alternative to the RT-PCR for the detection of acute infections. This technology aims at a qualitative or semi-quantitative estimation of antibodies using different techniques such as i) ELISA, where the antigen protein present on the surface of the microplate wells binds to the target antibody [25], ii) CLIA combined with chemiluminescence techniques showing immunochemical reactions [26] or iii) the lateral flow immunoassays (LIFA) [27]. The decrease in technical requirements, lower sampling and specimen preparation risk, low cost, and higher specific and sensitive detection make LIFA the most promising test. LIFA can deliver results within 15 min of testing [28].

Biosensors

Biosensors are systematic devices where the signals from the bio-molecules (also known as bio-recognition elements) combined with a sensor transduction system, *i.e.*, a physicochemical transducer, are measured by an analyzer [29]. The principle of biosensors lies in recognizing the two complementary hybridized nucleic acid strands [30, 31], the interaction of monoclonal antigen-specific antibodies to detect antigen proteins, and diagnosis of antibodies by interacting with recombinant antigen and target-neutralizing antibodies. Numerous signal conversion systems are involved in the development of biosensors. The predominantly used electrochemical biosensors are cost-effective, easy to use, and suitable for mass production [18]. The development of biosensors preferably uses the RNA genome of the SARS-CoV-2, specific antigen protein, and neutralizing antibodies such as IgM or IgG for COVID-19 diagnosis [32].

Radiology Imaging

Radiology imaging refers to the techniques such as chest radiography (CXR) and chest computed tomography (CT) used for taking images and visualizing the body's internal structure that serves in the early screening of any infectious disease such as COVID-19.This diagnosis technique improves the chances of maintaining social distance and managing the pandemic [33]. However, these imaging techniques fail to diagnose the type of virus [34, 35]. Reports suggest the effectiveness of CT imaging in diagnosing COVID-19 due to its high sensitivity and rapid access [36 - 38]. However, CT cannot be used as a first-line imaging modality because of the necessity of patient relocation from fever clinics due to a lack of equipment. CXR is a more widely available and cost-effective technique as compared to CT. Still, it is less sensitive and error-prone due to radiologists' manual examination and interpretation of the infected images [39]. Altogether, the limitations of imaging techniques can be overcome by using highly accurate AI-based strategies.

Microfluidic Approach

The microfluidic approaches include tools to deal with small volumes of fluids to control the biological, chemical, and physical processes [40]. Continuous flow microfluidics and segmented flow microfluidics are mainly put into practice for fluid manipulation, where the latter eliminates hydrodynamic dispersion and generates the isolated reaction vessel [41]. The recent developments in microfluidic technology enable their use in disease diagnosis and treatments, which can provide statistically meaningful data for analysis [42]. The use of microfluidics for SARS-CoV-2 includes fluorescence-based antibody (microfluidic double-antigen bridging immunoassay technique (DA-D4, which detects the total antibody count together with its subclasses and isotypes) and competitive immune-sensors based techniques) [29] antigen and nucleic acids (such as RT-qPCR [43 - 48] and RT-LAMP [35 - 37] based amplification) detection, spectrometer, image analysis-based detection techniques (microfluidic-based on-chip ELISA [49 - 55], paper-based pulling force spinning top microfluidic devices [56]), electrochemical based antigen detection and many others. The reports have suggested that SARS-CoV-2 kits involving microfluidic techniques show higher sensitivity and specificity [57]. The different widely used methods and approaches for COVID-19 diagnosis have been illustrated in Fig. **1**.

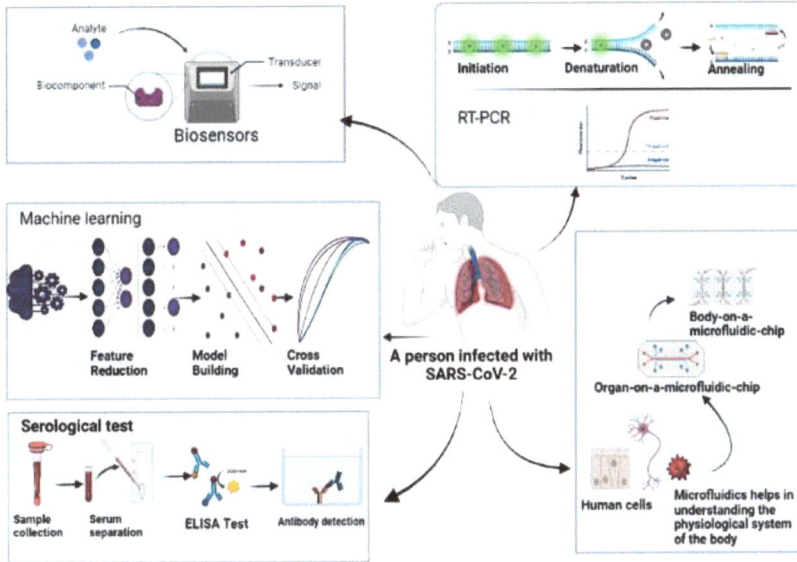

Fig. (1). Illustration of different techniques used for diagnosis of COVID-19.

ML based Approaches

ML (ML) focuses on producing techniques that can learn from the instances and improve without being programmed unambiguously [58]. ML techniques can be successfully used to improve the efficiency of diagnosis and administration of treatments for patients suffering from COVID-19 infections. The circumstantial use of ML in detecting COVID-19 has been discussed vividly in the following section.

ML AND ITS ROLE IN COVID-19 DIAGNOSIS

The COVID-19 pandemic has taught the world about the inefficiency of modern medical systems that can be used in the management of any disease outbreak. Late detection of the infected patient, inefficient disease tracking, and delay in developing standard treatment procedures are the critical factors for the rapid dissemination of COVID-19 globally, hampering the worldwide financial growth. Due to unawareness of the treatment procedure, inappropriate antibiotic consumption has increased, which enhances the emergence of antibiotic resistance as well [59].

Circumstantial use of ML

After facing difficulty in controlling the COVID-19 outbreak, researchers take the assistance of ML to ease the outbreak management. Through patient disease diagnosis, tracking, and surveillance, ML could also help in the drug development perspective [3]. The applications of ML in COVID-19 management are discussed below:

Patient Diagnosis Through Radiology Images

Early diagnosis of COVID-19 helps patients suffering from severe illness and eventually decreasing the mortality rates. Conventionally, RT-PCR is used to confirm the disease. But unavailability and time-consuming attributes of RT-PCR make it an unfavourable process. Besides that, the viral load is significant in getting the positive result in RT-PCR. It requires trained individuals for sample collection, experiment setting, and analysis. Thus, the most common use of ML in COVID-19 is the detection of the patient using radiology images. With the assistance of ML and DL, CT scans and X-ray images can help diagnose COVID-19 with accuracy.

COVID-NET is an AI application that uses the information from lung X-rays of patients and helps in diagnosis with an accuracy of 92.4% [60]. COV-Net19 is another convolutional neural network (CNN) application that distinguishes COVID-19 pneumonia from influenza or other lung diseases. It achieved 99.71% accuracy in binary classification between COVID and non-COVID chest X-ray images [61]. Jin *et al.*, 2020 developed an AI system where they tested more than 10,000 CT volumes and found that it operated at a two-order magnitude faster than radiologists and appeared more accurate [62]. These various models prove that AI can be helpful in the diagnosis of COVID-19. Proper implementation can fasten patient detection, preventing the disease's spread.

Tracking of COVID-19

Early diagnosis of patients, monitoring, and forecasting disease transmission are crucial for any disease outbreak management. The control of communal transmission of highly infectious COVID-19, tracking patients' data and predicting the disease transmission are necessary at its peak time. Due to a shortage of human resources, AI has played an important role in the healthcare sector. Scientists have developed different AI-based models that can help the governing organizations to take necessary measures. For example, Berlin uses the epidemiological SIR model, which supervises the Government allocated containment orders and derives further inference. Similarly, GLEAMviz is another model that tracks the transmission of infection. Metabiota is an infection tracker model that can forecast disease outbreaks [3].

Besides these applications, a few algorithms are frequently used in ML to predict and track disease data. Zhan, and Zheng, *et al.* 2020, utilized a random forest bagging approach associated with a broad understanding to forecast the pandemic trajectory. This model appeared to be highly accurate with great predictivity. Other studies have used long short-term memory (LSTM) model in a python simulation environment, which helped in predicting the dissemination of the infection. Although these models are highly accurate, they were only tested in a small dataset, which needs to be tested in a large dataset to confirm its outcome [7].

Tracking Patient Health Condition

After detecting COVID-19 infection in patients, monitoring patient's health condition is mandatory to improve the treatment efficacy and lessen the mortality rate. Though CT-scan of the lungs could be used to assess the patient's health condition, these tests are not easily affordable. So researchers identified a few blood test parameters with the help of ML techniques, which could predict the patient's health condition [63]. In a study, researchers have used three parameters (lactic dehydrogenase, lymphocyte, and high affectability C-receptive protein) and the XGBoost model to predict the patients' mortality risk with high accuracy and cost-effectiveness [64]. Another study employed parameters like patient's body temperature, oxygen saturation point, heart rate, and audio signals and employed the CNN model to classify patients' health. While classifying patients, Salp optimization behaviour was used to update the neural network parameters. This system is able to successfully predict the patient's health condition with 98.79% accuracy [65].

Use of ML in Vaccine and Drug Development

Generally, vaccine and drug development take a long time and are costly. But fastening the drug discovery process is very important at the onset of any pandemic. Recently during the COVID-19 outbreak, researchers employed the help of AI in both vaccine and drug development. Vaccine development requires information regarding the protein subunit or nucleic acid sequence. ML can help predict 3D protein structures by analyzing genetic sequences. Alphafold model is an example of an ML technique that utilizes the information of amino acid or genetic sequence and predicts the protein's function [66]. It uses significant ResNet architecture to predict 3D atomic maps of the protein. For COVID-19, six proteins (SARS-CoV-2 membrane protein, protein 3a, Nsp2, Nsp4, Nsp6, and papain-like proteinase) were predicted, which will help to predict the cures [3].

There are four steps for new drug development: drug identification, pre-clinical research, clinical research, and FDA approval. AI is used at the molecular level in drug-target interaction. A deep learning (DL) model named Molecule Transformer Drug Target Interaction (MT-DTI) was used to identify drugs for COVID-19 [67]. This model utilizes amino acid sequences and SMILES strings to predict target protein and identifies the compound atazanavir as a potent inhibitor of COVID-19 [63]. Two similarity-based models are also used for drug discovery: KronRLS and SimBoost [63]. For *in silico* drug repurposing, a network-based DL model named DeepDR was used, and the obtained AUC was 90.08% higher than other models [68].

ML Algorithms used to Combat COVID-19

The ML technique employs various statistical, probabilistic, optimization methods and computational algorithms to learn from past experiences and identify patterns from large and complex datasets [69]. These algorithms have been vividly applied for automated text cataloguing [70], network infringement detection [71], junk e-mail filtration [72], detection of credit card deception [73], disease modeling [74], and many more. ML techniques can be broadly divided into i) supervised learning, ii) unsupervised learning, iii) reinforcement learning, and iv) deep learning. The multiple ML algorithms have been discussed below (Fig. **2**).

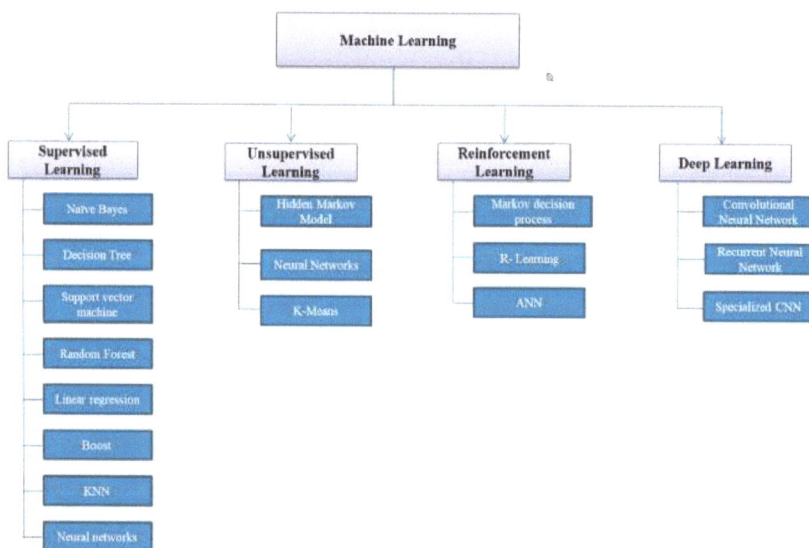

Fig. (2). The different classes of machine learning algorithms.

Supervised learning involves algorithms that predict opposite classes for the unseen data (algorithms categorized under classifications) or anticipate future occurrences (regression) by learning from prior datasets that supervise in the form the labels in the training phase [75]. The supervised learning paradigm is also known as exemplar-based learning, where it learns to retort precisely by comparing its output to those given as input [76].

Unsupervised learning intends to collect data into similar clusters (clustering techniques can be either hierarchical or partition clustering) without any further knowledge. It retrieves the unrevealed patterns from the data that can be used to develop rules. This is a statistical-based approach used for learning and finding the problem of the unidentified structure in the unlabelled data [76].

However, *reinforcement learning* is regarded as an intermediate learning category that focuses only on identifying the correctness of the output by exploring various possibilities. This learning approach does not provide any implication and is regarded as learning with a critic [76].

Deep learning is a subclass of ML that uses a variety of algorithms to fight efficiently against the novel coronavirus. It deals with medical imaging, disease tracking, protein structure analysis, drug discovery, and understanding the virus's severity and infectivity. The various deep learning-based systems used for COVID-19 diagnosis include COVID-net (a convolutional neural network-based system) [77], Deep Pneumonia (used ResNet to extract complex features from the CT samples) [78], CoroNet (an Xception-based model for diagnosing coronavirus from the X-ray images) [79] and many others. The widely used deep learning approach, *i.e.*, the convolutional neural network (CNN), also known as CovNets, categorizes information from the simplest to the most complex.

ML techniques used to deal with COVID-19 primarily include deep learning (79%) [80, 81], which can effectively create neural networks with multiple hidden layers and have the capability of making decisions to produce a high-quality result, followed by supervised learning (16%) and others. However, unsupervised learning algorithms in this context have not been highlighted so far [82].

Decision tree

The decision tree is a supervised learning algorithm that generates a tree-structured model representing the learned functions. A decision tree has two entities; leaves and nodes. The leaves denote the final decision of the tree or the outcome, whereas the data is split in the decision nodes based on feature values. The data classification starts at the root node, also called the decision node. The tree passes through the edge based on the node's value until it reaches the leaf node. The leaf node denotes the final decision of the tree [76].

Random forest

The ensemble-based Random Forest (RF) algorithm is used for classification and regression. It uses the datasets to create multiple decision trees combined to form a final decision tree. The RF two-staged algorithm first generates a random forest later used in the second stage to make predictions.

Naive Bayes

The Naive Bayes ML algorithm applies Bayes' theorem of probability. Bayes' theorem computes the subsequent probability of an event A when the probability of B is given, *i.e.*, P(A/B) is as follows:

$$P\left(\frac{A}{B}\right) = \frac{P\left(\frac{B}{A}\right)P(A)}{P(B)} \qquad (1)$$

Here, A and B are the events, P(A) and P(B) are the probabilities of events A and B independently, P(A/B) is the probability of A when B is accurate, and P(B/A) is the probability of B, given A is true. The Naive Bayes classifier is often used when the dimensionality of the inputs is high [83, 84].

Support Vector Machine

The Support Vector Machine is identified as one of the best-supervised learning algorithms that are capable of solving large data sorting-based problems. It is used for classification. The principle of SVM lies in the margin calculation, which is drawn between the classes. The distance between the margin and the classes minimizes the classification error and increases its efficiency [85].

k-Nearest-Neighbor (KNN)

kNN is another supervised learning algorithm used for data mining and ML. This learning approach is lethargic and non-parameterized, *i.e.*, the data distribution assumptions are invalid. The indolence loading of the kNN does not require any training data points for generating models. The training data later used in the testing phase slows down the testing procedure and makes it costlier than the training phase [83].

Gradient-boosted Decision Tree (GBDT)

The GBDT algorithm focuses on successively building a set of trees based on the ensemble method [86]. The algorithm builds decisions separately so that the performance of the trees generated in each iteration is improved from the previous iteration [5, 87]. The powerful GBDT technique is widely applied in commercial and academic fields.

Logistic Regression

The logistic regression algorithm predicts the class of the numerical variable based on its relationship with the label. It can be used to generate models based on the probability of the independently featured data points. These models are then used to predict the probability of the data point belonging to a specific class. The *sigmoid function* plays a critical role in building the regression model. The data points are assumed to follow a linear function. The LR can be mathematically described as follows:

Equation (2):

$$\log\left(\frac{p(X)}{1-p(X)}\right) = \beta_0 + \beta_1 X \qquad (2)$$

Where p is the probability of X belonging to class C, and $\beta_0 + \beta_1$ are the model parameters [5].

Artificial Neural Network

Artificial neural network (ANN) has been widely used for classification, clustering, pattern recognition, and prediction in various sectors. ANN is a complex multilayered deep learning algorithm that tries to mimic the working mechanism of the human brain. It calculates the input scores of each class associated with the input object [88, 89]. The ANN is a multiple-layered system where the output of one layer is connected to the input of the consecutive layer. The final score calculation is based on the weights and activation function assigned to each layer [82].

Different Models and Networks of ML used in COVID-19 Diagnosis
LR Model

Researchers use powerful ML algorithms, such as linear regression (LR), to predict and diagnose various diseases. LR is a predictive technique that focuses on predicting the effect of certain factors on COVID-19 outbursts. Different researchers have used the linear regression model to predict COVID-19-infected patients. A comparative study shows that the LR model outperforms various other models with a high accuracy rate [82].

XGBoost Model

XGBoost, also known as extreme gradient boosting, is a popularly used gradient-boosted decision tree algorithm. XGBoost tool is well known for handling missing data congenitally, with speediness and parallelization [90]. The characterization of optimized distributed gradient boosting library into high competence, flexibility, and portability [75] allows its use in many fields, such as data mining or recommendation systems. The objective function of the gradient advancing decision tree is defined in **Equation (3).**

$$£(\emptyset) = \sum_{i=1}^{n} loss\left(yi_{\hat{y}i}\right) + \sum_{k=1}^{k} \Omega(f_k) \qquad (3)$$

In this Equation, loss denotes the loss in training, and the complexity of the tree is symbolized as Ωfk and k is the total number of trees present in the model. This model can be optimized to increase efficiency by minimizing the objective function [91].

The XGBoost model can be used to reveal the nonlinearity in the time series of COVID-19 cases [92 - 95], to predict the variation in Sequential Organ Failure Assessment (SOFA) score of the critically ill COVID-19 patients [91], to identify the impact of C-reactive protein, the ratio of lymphocytes, lactic acid and serum calcium features on COVID-19 extrapolative prediction [96 - 100].

Boosted RF Model

The Random Forest classifier contains multiple decision trees that perform classification and regression and aid in determining the output [101]. The strength of the tree classifiers and their association are key factors determining the model's accuracy. The boosted RF model was proposed based on the AdaBoost algorithm that uses the geographical, travel, health, and demographic data of the patients infected with COVID-19 to predict the severity of the infection and the possibility of recovery or death. The accuracy of the boosted RF model is 94%, and the F1 score (the most significant measure used to evaluate the model's performance in classifying COVID-19 patients) is 0.86 [102].

Deep Forest Model

The deep forest model is based on the ensemble-based method, *i.e.*, deep forest (DF) which uses three classifiers (extra trees, XGBoost, and LightGBM) for increasing diversity and performance. The experimental analysis of the model demonstrates its high-performance metrics with 99.5% accuracy, 95.28% sensitivity, and 99.96% specificity. This model can be a fast screening tool against COVID-19 infection in places lacking diagnosis technologies [102].

Illustration of different models built based on ML algorithms (Deep learning algorithms are the most widely used models for COVID-19 diagnosis)

Machine Learning Algorithms	Models based on different learning algorithms
Deep Learning	COVID-Net [103], Truncated Inception net [104], Inception V3 [105], DenseNet169 [106], InceptionResNetv2 [106], NASNetLarge [106], VGG16 [107], DenseNet161 [107], COVID-CAPS, SqueezeNet, DRE-Net [78], COVNet [108], DarkCovidNet [109], POCOVID [110], LSTM [111]
Supervised Learning	SVM model [112], Linear regression model [113], XGBoost [114], LASSO [82], SEIR model [115], AdaBoost [116], RF model [116]
Unsupervised Learning	K-means clustering model

Truncated Inception Net

Das *et al.* proposed a computationally efficient CNN-based model, *i.e.*, the Truncated Inception Net, for COVID-19 screening. This model is derived from the complex Inception Net V3 architecture built for the ImageNet database [100]. Consequently, a truncation of the Inception Net V3 model was generated to reduce its complexity and overfitting issues. The point deferring the best classification results was chosen as the truncation point. This truncated model works as a binary classifier of CXR images to detect COVID-19. It is observed that the Truncated Inception Net acts as a breakthrough for COVID-19 screening [117].

CASE STUDIES

CASE I

There are several instances where ML is widely used in the management of COVID-19. But diagnosis and vaccine development are two main circumstances where ML is widely used. A few researchers from Tianjin Medical University Cancer Institute and Hospital prepared a CNN-based model using the RADLogics algorithm to diagnose CT scan lung images of COVID-19 patients. The images were compared with the patients who had severe pneumonia admitted before the pandemic and acquired 89.5% accuracy. Compared to trained radiologists with 55%, the model performed well in diagnosing patients with lung CT scan images [118].

CASE II

A group of MIT researchers developed software for peptide-based vaccine development. The designed software was named "OptiVax," which uses data from existing vaccines and immunoinformatic methods to create new vaccines in large numbers [119].

CASE III

To prevent rumors and fear associated with COVID-19 infection, a group of researchers from India developed an AI model named "Waskaro," which can track the person spreading misinformation about COVID-19 through recording. It is a self-assessment tool that helps to record symptoms automatically and increase self-awareness among people [120].

CASE IV

Another case study of multiple epitope vaccine development is that researchers used a deep learning approach and developed a vaccine using a framework named DeepVacPred. From the SARS-CoV2 spike protein, it generates 26 subunits vaccine, which contains B-cell, cytotoxic T lymphocyte, and helper T lymphocyte epitopes. From 26 subunit vaccines, the best 11 were sorted. After refinement, a 694Aa multi-epitope vaccine was generated, which contains 16 B-cell epitopes, 89HTL epitopes, and 82 CTL epitopes. The in silico deep learning network fastened the vaccine development process, and it was studied that the developed vaccine was effective against possible RNA mutations [121].

CHALLENGES AND FUTURE DIRECTIONS

The use of ML techniques has greatly contributed in COVID-19 screening, diagnosis as well as ML vaccine development against SARS-CoV-2 but there are specific challenges faced by these computer-aided techniques that need to be addressed.

i) ML mainly depends on the existing data. However, small datasets and ambiguity in information are the two main reasons for skewing the results of ML models. However, as ML is a new edge technique, hence trained individuals are significantly fewer in numbers, and a lack of coordination between disease biology and computational framework has emerged as significant a problem for ML-based models.

ii) As ML models are primarily supervised learning models where the data need to be labelled, there is a deep concern regarding patient data privacy, which needs to be handled carefully.

iii) Till date, the COVID-19 diagnosis of infected patients mostly depends on chest and lung images predicted via CT or CXR techniques. But studies have found that SARS-CoV-2 affects other different organs as well (such as the gastrointestinal tract, heart, *etc.*) . But there are no ML techniques reported so far that involves the inspection of different body organs except lungs and chest [122].

iv) Understanding the severity level of the disease caused by the SARS-CoV-2 is a crucial aspect for a proper treatment of patients. But ML lacks the ability to detect the severity level of the infection, which requires special attention [123].

v) In disease outbreaks like COVID-19, the variability of disease attributes like patient symptoms was higher, which made the application of ML difficult.

Nonetheless, with intense dedication and efforts by the researchers, the challenges associated with ML can be easily overcome. ML and DL models have shown excellent efficiency, which needs to be tested in large datasets. In the future, along with the application of modern networks with high flexibility and accuracy, ML will be an effective tool that will help forecast future pandemics and monitor the effects of vaccine developed against the virus, which can ultimately help increase human lifespan.

CONCLUSION

The high contagion nature and its associated mutations due to the emergence of variants of concern have affected diagnosis and treatment options against infection significantly. The ongoing COVID-19 pandemic offers a unique opportunity to fast-track collaboration between data scientists, clinicians, radiologists, and others associated with healthcare to comprehend the potential of machine learning in health care *i.e.* development of algorithms that could assist with diagnosis, and prediction of severity and mortality risks associated with SARS-CoV-2 infection. With the help of different state-of-art ML algorithms, researchers developed a few predictive models, which aided in the analysis of large-scale datasets and quickly developed an inference with accuracy. In this chapter, we have exclusively illustrated the applications of different ML methods in the milieu of COVID-19 and its management. One of the major applications includes the consistency of capturing diagnostic and prognostic features of the ML models, which exist in medical literature, signify the relevance of using ML algorithms to broadly analyze data of patients, discriminate patterns, and support the decision-making process. Furthermore, the use of imbalanced datasets in most of the existing studies suffers from selection bias, which advocates the development of some useful techniques to handle this issue. Despite recent advancements made in different machine learning approaches, none-of-the supervised learning algorithms have been deployed in real-world applications due to the challenges associated in determining the best models for COVID screening. Therefore, it is of immense importance to integrate multiple data types *i.e.* clinical information, symptoms and other demographic data from different sources for the prediction of COVID-19, which would be worth inspecting further.

REFERENCES

[1]   COVID-19 Weekly Epidemiological Update. World Heal Organ 2022; (August): 1-33.

[2]   Shereen MA, Khan S, Kazmi A, Bashir N, Siddique R. COVID-19 infection: Emergence, transmission, and characteristics of human coronaviruses. J Adv Res 2020; 24: 91-8.
[http://dx.doi.org/10.1016/j.jare.2020.03.005] [PMID: 32257431]

[3]   Kumar A, Gupta PK, Srivastava A. A review of modern technologies for tackling COVID-19 pandemic. Diabetes Metab Syndr 2020; 14(4): 569-73.
[http://dx.doi.org/10.1016/j.dsx.2020.05.008] [PMID: 32413821]

[4]   Cucinotta D, Vanelli M. WHO declares COVID-19 a pandemic. Acta Biomed 2020; 91(1): 157-60.
[http://dx.doi.org/10.23750/abm.v91i1.9397] [PMID: 32191675]

[5]   Alballa N, Al-turaiki I. ML approaches in COVID-19 diagnosis, mortality, and severity risk prediction: A review Norah. Informatics Med. Unlocked 2021; Vol. 24.

[6]   Gomes R, Kamrowski C, Langlois J, *et al.* A Comprehensive Review of Machine Learning Used to Combat COVID-19. Diagnostics (Basel) 2022; 12(8): 1853.
[http://dx.doi.org/10.3390/diagnostics12081853] [PMID: 36010204]

[7]   Heidari A, Navimipour NJ. ML applications for COVID-19 outbreak management 2022; 34.(18).

[8]   Rezasoltani S, Yadegar A, Hatami B, Asadzadeh Aghdaei H, Zali MR. Antimicrobial Resistance as a Hidden Menace Lurking Behind the COVID-19 Outbreak: The Global Impacts of Too Much Hygiene on AMR. Front Microbiol 2020; 11(December): 590683.
[http://dx.doi.org/10.3389/fmicb.2020.590683] [PMID: 33384670]

[9]   Mohammad-rahimi H, Nadimi M, Ghalyanchi-langeroudi A. Application of ML in Diagnosis of COVID-19 Through X-Ray and CT Images : A Scoping Review 2021; 8.
[http://dx.doi.org/10.3389/fcvm.2021.638011]

[10]   Udugama B, Kadhiresan P, Kozlowski HN, *et al.* Diagnosing COVID-19: the disease and tools for detection. ACS Nano 2020; 14(4): 3822-35.
[http://dx.doi.org/10.1021/acsnano.0c02624] [PMID: 32223179]

[11]   Peiffer-Smadja N, Maatoug R, Lescure FX, D'Ortenzio E, Pineau J, King JR. Machine Learning for COVID-19 needs global collaboration and data-sharing. Nat Mach Intell 2020; 2(6): 293-4.
[http://dx.doi.org/10.1038/s42256-020-0181-6]

[12]   Mondal M R H, Bharati S, Podder P. Diagnosis of COVID-19 Using ML and Deep Learning : A review Curr Med Imaging 2021; 17(12): 1-7.

[13]   Gangloff C, Rafi S, Bouzillé G, Soulat L, Cuggia M. Machine learning is the key to diagnose COVID-19: a proof-of-concept study. Sci Rep 2021; 11(1): 7166.
[http://dx.doi.org/10.1038/s41598-021-86735-9] [PMID: 33785852]

[14]   Sun K, Wang W, Gao L, *et al.* Transmission heterogeneities, kinetics, and controllability of SARS-CoV-2 Science. 2021; 371: p. (6526)eabe2424.
[http://dx.doi.org/10.1126/science.abe2424]

[15]   Alwan NA, Burgess RA, Ashworth S, *et al.* Scientific consensus on the COVID-19 pandemic: we need to act now. Lancet 2020; 396(10260): e71-2.
[http://dx.doi.org/10.1016/S0140-6736(20)32153-X] [PMID: 33069277]

[16] Lai S, Ruktanonchai NW, Zhou L, *et al.* Effect of non-pharmaceutical interventions to contain COVID-19 in China. Nature 2020; 585(7825): 410-3.
[http://dx.doi.org/10.1038/s41586-020-2293-x] [PMID: 32365354]

[17] Wiersinga WJ, Rhodes A, Cheng AC, Peacock SJ, Prescott HC. Pathophysiology, transmission, diagnosis, and treatment of coronavirus disease 2019 (COVID-19): a review. JAMA 2020; 324(8): 782-93.
[http://dx.doi.org/10.1001/jama.2020.12839] [PMID: 32648899]

[18] Cui F, Zhou HS. Diagnostic methods and potential portable biosensors for coronavirus disease 2019. Biosens Bioelectron 2020; 165: 112349.
[http://dx.doi.org/10.1016/j.bios.2020.112349] [PMID: 32510340]

[19] Rahimi H, Salehiabar M, Barsbay M, *et al.* CRISPR Systems for COVID-19 Diagnosis. ACS Sens 2021; 6(4): 1430-45.
[http://dx.doi.org/10.1021/acssensors.0c02312] [PMID: 33502175]

[20] CLIA Program & Medicare Lab Services 2021; (December): 1-8.

[21] Garg M, Prabhakar N, Bhalla A, *et al.* Computed tomography chest in COVID-19: When & why? Indian J Med Res 2021; 153(1): 86-92.
[http://dx.doi.org/10.4103/ijmr.IJMR_3669_20] [PMID: 33402610]

[22] Lephart PR, Bachman MA, LeBar W, *et al.* Comparative study of four SARS-CoV-2 Nucleic Acid Amplification Test (NAAT) platforms demonstrates that ID NOW performance is impaired substantially by patient and specimen type. Diagn Microbiol Infect Dis 2021; 99(1): 115200.
[http://dx.doi.org/10.1016/j.diagmicrobio.2020.115200] [PMID: 32980807]

[23] Kang T, Lu J, Yu T, Long Y, Liu G. Advances in nucleic acid amplification techniques (NAATs): COVID-19 point-of-care diagnostics as an example. Biosens Bioelectron 2022; 206: 114109.
[http://dx.doi.org/10.1016/j.bios.2022.114109] [PMID: 35245867]

[24] Zhao J, Yuan Q, Wang H, *et al.* Antibody responses to SARS-CoV-2 in patients with novel coronavirus disease 2019. Clin Infect Dis 2020; 71(16): 2027-34.
[http://dx.doi.org/10.1093/cid/ciaa344] [PMID: 32221519]

[25] Van Elslande J, Houben E, Depypere M, *et al.* Diagnostic performance of seven rapid IgG/IgM antibody tests and the Euroimmun IgA/IgG ELISA in COVID-19 patients. Clin Microbiol Infect 2020; 26(8): 1082-7.
[http://dx.doi.org/10.1016/j.cmi.2020.05.023] [PMID: 32473953]

[26] Xiao Q, Xu C. Research progress on chemiluminescence immunoassay combined with novel technologies. Trends Analyt Chem 2020; 124: 115780.
[http://dx.doi.org/10.1016/j.trac.2019.115780]

[27] Li F, You M, Li S, *et al.* Paper-based point-of-care immunoassays: Recent advances and emerging trends. Biotechnol Adv 2020; 39: 107442.
[http://dx.doi.org/10.1016/j.biotechadv.2019.107442] [PMID: 31470046]

[28] Peeling RW, Olliaro PL, Boeras DI, Fongwen N. Scaling up COVID-19 rapid antigen tests: promises and challenges. Lancet Infect Dis 2021; 21(9): e290-5.
[http://dx.doi.org/10.1016/S1473-3099(21)00048-7] [PMID: 33636148]

[29] Pohanka M. Progress in Biosensors for the Point-of-Care Diagnosis of COVID-19. Sensors (Basel) 2022; 22(19): 7423.
[http://dx.doi.org/10.3390/s22197423]

[30] Trotter M, Borst N, Thewes R, von Stetten F. Review: Electrochemical DNA sensing – Principles, commercial systems, and applications. Biosens Bioelectron 2020; 154: 112069.
[http://dx.doi.org/10.1016/j.bios.2020.112069] [PMID: 32056964]

[31] Pellitero MA, Shaver A, Arroyo-Currás N. Critical review—Approaches for the electrochemical

interrogation of DNA-based sensors: A critical review. J Electrochem Soc 2020; 167(3): 037529.
[http://dx.doi.org/10.1149/2.0292003JES]

[32]   Review SCS-A. Emerging Biosensors to Detect Severe Acute Respiratory. 2021; Vol. 2.

[33]   Tan BS, Dunnick NR, Gangi A, *et al.* RSNA international trends: a global perspective on the COVID-19 pandemic and radiology in late 2020. Radiology 2021; 299(1): E193-203.
[http://dx.doi.org/10.1148/radiol.2020204267] [PMID: 33289616]

[34]   Ai T, Yang Z, Hou H, *et al.* Correlation of chest CT and RT-PCR testing in coronavirus disease 2019 (COVID-19) in China: a report of 1014 cases. Radiology 2020; 296(2): E32-40.
[http://dx.doi.org/10.1148/radiol.2020200642] [PMID: 32101510]

[35]   Li K, Wu J, Wu F, *et al.* The clinical and chest CT features associated with severe and critical COVID-19 pneumonia. Invest Radiol 2020; 55(6): 327-31.
[http://dx.doi.org/10.1097/RLI.0000000000000672] [PMID: 32118615]

[36]   Mohammadi A, Wang Y, Enshaei N, *et al.* Diagnosis/Prognosis of COVID-19 Chest Images via Machine Learning and Hypersignal Processing: Challenges, opportunities, and applications. IEEE Signal Process Mag 2021; 38(5): 37-66.
[http://dx.doi.org/10.1109/MSP.2021.3090674]

[37]   Fang Y, Zhang H, Xie J, *et al.* Sensitivity of Chest CT for COVID-19: Comparison to RT-PCR. Radiology 2020; 296(2): E115-7.
[http://dx.doi.org/10.1148/radiol.2020200432] [PMID: 32073353]

[38]   Rafiee MJ, Babaki Fard F, Samimi K, Rasti H, Pressacco J. Spontaneous pneumothorax and pneumomediastinum as a rare complication of COVID-19 pneumonia: Report of 6 cases. Radiol Case Rep 2021; 16(3): 687-92.
[http://dx.doi.org/10.1016/j.radcr.2021.01.011] [PMID: 33437348]

[39]   Brady AP. Error and discrepancy in radiology: inevitable or avoidable? Insights Imaging 2017; 8(1): 171-82.
[http://dx.doi.org/10.1007/s13244-016-0534-1] [PMID: 27928712]

[40]   Yi C, Li CW, Ji S, Yang M. Microfluidics technology for manipulation and analysis of biological cells. Anal Chim Acta 2006; 560(1-2): 1-23.
[http://dx.doi.org/10.1016/j.aca.2005.12.037]

[41]   Streets AM, Huang Y. Chip in a lab: Microfluidics for next generation life science research. Biomicrofluidics 2013; 7(1): 011302.
[http://dx.doi.org/10.1063/1.4789751] [PMID: 23460772]

[42]   Siegel RA. Stimuli sensitive polymers and self regulated drug delivery systems: A very partial review. J Control Release 2014; 190: 337-51.
[http://dx.doi.org/10.1016/j.jconrel.2014.06.035] [PMID: 24984012]

[43]   Heggestad JT, Kinnamon DS, Olson LB, *et al.* Multiplexed, quantitative serological profiling of COVID-19 from blood by a point-of-care test. Sci Adv 2021; 7(26): eabg4901.
[http://dx.doi.org/10.1126/sciadv.abg4901] [PMID: 34172447]

[44]   Ji M, Xia Y, Loo J, *et al.* Automated multiplex nucleic acid tests for rapid detection of SARS-CoV-2, influenza A and B infection with direct reverse-transcription quantitative PCR (dirRT-qPCR) assay in a centrifugal microfluidic platform. RSC Advances 2020; 10(56): 34088-98.
[http://dx.doi.org/10.1039/D0RA04507A] [PMID: 35519051]

[45]   Dragoni F, Garofalo M, Trotti R, Liu Y, Cereda C, Gagliardi S. Comparison between Conventional qPCR and Microfluidic Chip-Based PCR System for COVID-19 Nucleic Acid Detection. Journal of Psychiatry and Psychiatric Disorders 2021; 5(6): 218-31.
[http://dx.doi.org/10.26502/jppd.2572-519X0147]

[46]   Xie X, Gjorgjieva T, Attieh Z, *et al.* Microfluidic nano-scale qPCR enables ultra-sensitive and quantitative detection of SARS-CoV-2. Processes (Basel) 2020; 8(11): 1425.

[http://dx.doi.org/10.3390/pr8111425]

[47] Fassy J, Lacoux C, Leroy S, *et al.* Versatile and flexible microfluidic qPCR test for high-throughput SARS-CoV-2 and cellular response detection in nasopharyngeal swab samples. PLoS One 2021; 16(4): e0243333.
[http://dx.doi.org/10.1371/journal.pone.0243333] [PMID: 33852580]

[48] Yang J, Kidd M, Nordquist AR, *et al.* A sensitive, portable microfluidic device for SARS-CoV-2 detection from self-collected saliva. Infect Dis Rep 2021; 13(4): 1061-77.
[http://dx.doi.org/10.3390/idr13040097] [PMID: 34940407]

[49] Soares RRG, Akhtar AS, Pinto IF, *et al.* Sample-to-answer COVID-19 nucleic acid testing using a low-cost centrifugal microfluidic platform with bead-based signal enhancement and smartphone read-out. Lab Chip 2021; 21(15): 2932-44.
[http://dx.doi.org/10.1039/D1LC00266J] [PMID: 34114589]

[50] Ramachandran A, Huyke DA, Sharma E, *et al.* Electric field-driven microfluidics for rapid CRISPR-based diagnostics and its application to detection of SARS-CoV-2. Proc Natl Acad Sci USA 2020; 117(47): 29518-25.
[http://dx.doi.org/10.1073/pnas.2010254117] [PMID: 33148808]

[51] Xiong H, Ye X, Li Y, Qi J, Fang X, Kong J. Efficient microfluidic-based air sampling/monitoring platform for detection of aerosol SARS-CoV-2 on-site. Anal Chem 2021; 93(9): 4270-6.
[http://dx.doi.org/10.1021/acs.analchem.0c05154] [PMID: 33635067]

[52] Funari R, Chu KY, Shen AQ. Detection of antibodies against SARS-CoV-2 spike protein by gold nanospikes in an opto-microfluidic chip. Biosens Bioelectron 2020; 169: 112578.
[http://dx.doi.org/10.1016/j.bios.2020.112578] [PMID: 32911317]

[53] González-González E, Garcia-Ramirez R, Díaz-Armas GG, *et al.* Automated ELISA on-chip for the detection of anti-SARS-CoV-2 antibodies. Sensors (Basel) 2021; 21(20): 6785.
[http://dx.doi.org/10.3390/s21206785] [PMID: 34695998]

[54] Liu Y, Tan Y, Fu Q, *et al.* Reciprocating-flowing on-a-chip enables ultra-fast immunobinding for multiplexed rapid ELISA detection of SARS-CoV-2 antibody. Biosens Bioelectron 2021; 176: 112920.
[http://dx.doi.org/10.1016/j.bios.2020.112920] [PMID: 33418184]

[55] Tan X, Krel M, Dolgov E, *et al.* Rapid and quantitative detection of SARS-CoV-2 specific IgG for convalescent serum evaluation. Biosens Bioelectron 2020; 169: 112572.
[http://dx.doi.org/10.1016/j.bios.2020.112572] [PMID: 32916610]

[56] Gong F, Wei H, Qi J, *et al.* Pulling-force spinning top for serum separation combined with paper-based microfluidic devices in COVID-19 ELISA diagnosis. ACS Sens 2021; 6(7): 2709-19.
[http://dx.doi.org/10.1021/acssensors.1c00773] [PMID: 34263598]

[57] Jamiruddin MR, Meghla BA, Islam DZ, *et al.* Microfluidics Technology in SARS-CoV-2 Diagnosis and Beyond: A Systematic Review. Life (Basel) 2022; 12(5): 649.
[http://dx.doi.org/10.3390/life12050649] [PMID: 35629317]

[58] Dargan S, Kumar M, Ayyagari MR, Kumar G. A survey of deep learning and its applications: a new paradigm to ML. Arch Comput Methods Eng 2020; 27(4): 1071-92.
[http://dx.doi.org/10.1007/s11831-019-09344-w]

[59] Lucien MAB, Canarie MF, Kilgore PE, *et al.* Antibiotics and antimicrobial resistance in the COVID-19 era: Perspective from resource-limited settings. Int J Infect Dis 2021; 104(52): 250-4.
[http://dx.doi.org/10.1016/j.ijid.2020.12.087] [PMID: 33434666]

[60] Wang L, Lin ZQ, Wong A. COVID-Net: a tailored deep convolutional neural network design for detection of COVID-19 cases from chest X-ray images. Sci Rep 2020; 10(1): 19549.
[http://dx.doi.org/10.1038/s41598-020-76550-z] [PMID: 33177550]

[61] Kedia P, Anjum , Katarya R. CoVNet-19: A Deep Learning model for the detection and analysis of

COVID-19 patients. Appl Soft Comput 2021; 104: 107184.
[http://dx.doi.org/10.1016/j.asoc.2021.107184] [PMID: 33613140]

[62]   Jin C, Chen W, Cao Y *et al.* Development and evaluation of an AI system for COVID-19 diagnosis. Nat Commun 2020; 11(1): 5088.
[http://dx.doi.org/10.1038/s41467-020-18685-1] [PMID: 33037212]

[63]   Chadaga K, Prabhu S, Vivekananda BK, Niranjana S, Umakanth S. Battling COVID-19 using ML : A review. Cogent Eng 2021; 8(1).
[http://dx.doi.org/10.1080/23311916.2021.1958666]

[64]   Chen T, Guestrin C. XGBoost: A scalable tree boosting system Proc ACM SIGKDD Int Conf Knowl Discov Data Min. 785-94.
[http://dx.doi.org/10.1145/2939672.2939785]

[65]   Jaber MM, Alameri T, Ali MH, *et al.* Remotely Monitoring COVID-19 Patient Health Condition Using Metaheuristics Convolute Networks from IoT-Based Wearable Device Health Data. Sensors 2022; 22: 1205.
[http://dx.doi.org/10.3390/s22031205]

[66]   Jumper J, Evans R, Pritzel A, *et al.* Highly accurate protein structure prediction with AlphaFold. Nature 2021; 596(7873): 583-9.
[http://dx.doi.org/10.1038/s41586-021-03819-2] [PMID: 34265844]

[67]   Shin B, Park S, Kang K, Ho JC. Self-Attention Based Molecule Representation for Predicting Drug-Target Interaction. Proc Mach Learn Res 2019; 106: 1-18.

[68]   Zeng X, Zhu S, Liu X, Zhou Y, Nussinov R, Cheng F. deepDR: a network-based deep learning approach to *in silico* drug repositioning. Bioinformatics 2019; 35(24): 5191-8.
[http://dx.doi.org/10.1093/bioinformatics/btz418] [PMID: 31116390]

[69]   Mitchell TM. Machine Learning. New York: McGraw-hill 1997; 1(9).

[70]   Sebastiani F. Machine learning in automated text categorization. ACM Comput Surv 2002; 34(1): 1-47.
[http://dx.doi.org/10.1145/505282.505283]

[71]   Sinclair C, Pierce L, Matzner S. An application of ML to network intrusion detection Proceedings 15th annual computer security applications conference (ACSAC'99). 371-7.
[http://dx.doi.org/10.1109/CSAC.1999.816048]

[72]   Sahami M, Dumais S, Heckerman D, Horvitz E. A Bayesian approach to filtering junk e-mail Papers from the 1998 workshop. vol. 62: 98-105.

[73]   Aleskerov E, Freisleben B, Rao B. Cardwatch: A neural network based database mining system for credit card fraud detection Proceedings of the IEEE/IAFE 1997 computational intelligence for financial engineering (CIFEr). 220-6.
[http://dx.doi.org/10.1109/CIFER.1997.618940]

[74]   Yao D, Yang J, Zhan X. A Novel Method for Disease Prediction: Hybrid of Random Forest and Multivariate Adaptive Regression Splines. J Comput (Taipei) 2013; 8(1): 170-7.
[http://dx.doi.org/10.4304/jcp.8.1.170-177]

[75]   Rustam F, Reshi AA, Mehmood A, *et al.* COVID-19 future forecasting using supervised ML models. IEEE Access 2020; 8: 101489-99.
[http://dx.doi.org/10.1109/ACCESS.2020.2997311]

[76]   Alzubi J, Nayyar A, Kumar A. Machine Learning from Theory to Algorithms: An Overview. Phys Conf Ser 2018; 1142: 012012.
[http://dx.doi.org/10.1088/1742-6596/1142/1/012012]

[77]   Gunraj H, Wang L, Wong A. COVIDNet-CT: A Tailored Deep Convolutional Neural Network Design for Detection of COVID-19 Cases From Chest CT Images. Front Med (Lausanne) 2020; 7: 608525.

[http://dx.doi.org/10.3389/fmed.2020.608525] [PMID: 33425953]

[78] Ying S, Zheng S, Li L, *et al.* Deep Learning Enables Accurate Diagnosis of Novel Coronavirus (COVID-19) With CT Images. IEEE/ACM Trans Comput Biol Bioinform 2021; 18(6): 2775-80

[79] Khan AI, Shah JL, Bhat MM. CoroNet: A deep neural network for detection and diagnosis of COVID-19 from chest x-ray images. Comput Methods Programs Biomed 2020; 196: 105581.
[http://dx.doi.org/10.1016/j.cmpb.2020.105581] [PMID: 32534344]

[80] Goodfellow I, Bengio Y, Courville A. Deep learning. MIT press 2016.

[81] Asraf A, Islam MZ, Haque MR, Islam MM. Deep Learning Applications to Combat Novel Coronavirus (COVID-19) Pandemic. SN Computer Science 2020; 1(6): 363.
[http://dx.doi.org/10.1007/s42979-020-00383-w] [PMID: 33163975]

[82] Meraihi Y, Gabis AB, Mirjalili S, Ramdane-Cherif A, Alsaadi FE. ML-Based Research for COVID-19 Detection, Diagnosis, and Prediction: A Survey 2022; 3.(4)

[83] Kavitha A. A Review on ML Algorithms and Their Applications. Int. Res. J. Eng. Technol 2020; pp. 4654-8.www.irjet.net [Online]

[84] Kothari D. A Review of Grey Scale Normalization in ML and AI for Bioinformatics using Convolution Neural Networks. Int J Res Appl Sci Eng Technol 2021; 9: 1306-10.
[http://dx.doi.org/10.22214/ijraset.2021.33316]

[85] Dey A. ML Algorithms: A Review. Int J Comput Sci Inf Technol 2016; 7(3): 1174-9. [Online]. [. Available: www.ijcsit.com.].

[86] Friedman JH. Greedy function approximation: A gradient boosting machine. Ann Stat 2001; 29(5): 1189-232.
[http://dx.doi.org/10.1214/aos/1013203451]

[87] Si S, Zhang H, Keerthi SS, Mahajan D, Dhillon IS, Hsieh CJ. Gradient boosted decision trees for high dimensional sparse output 34th Int Conf Mach Learn ICML 2017. vol. 7: 4899-908.

[88] Graupe D. Principles of artificial neural networks: basic designs to deep learning. World Scientific 2019.
[http://dx.doi.org/10.1142/11306]

[89] Travassos X L, Avila S L, Ida N. Artificial neural networks and ML techniques applied to ground penetrating radar: A review Appl Comput Informatics 2020.

[90] Nielsen D. "Tree boosting with xgboost-why does xgboost win" every" ML competition?. NTNU 2016.

[91] Nakamura M, Kajiwara Y, Otsuka A, Kimura H. Lvq-smote–learning vector quantization based synthetic minority over–sampling technique for biomedical data. BioData Min 2013; 6(1): 16.
[http://dx.doi.org/10.1186/1756-0381-6-16] [PMID: 23294634]

[92] Luo J, Zhang Z, Fu Y, Rao F. Time series prediction of COVID-19 transmission in America using LSTM and XGBoost algorithms. Results Phys 2021; 27: 104462.
[http://dx.doi.org/10.1016/j.rinp.2021.104462] [PMID: 34178594]

[93] Curran-Everett D. Explorations in statistics: the log transformation. Adv Physiol Educ 2018; 42(2): 343-7.
[http://dx.doi.org/10.1152/advan.00018.2018] [PMID: 29761718]

[94] Nishio M, Nishizawa M, Sugiyama O, *et al.* Computer-aided diagnosis of lung nodule using gradient tree boosting and Bayesian optimization. PLoS One 2018; 13(4): e0195875.
[http://dx.doi.org/10.1371/journal.pone.0195875] [PMID: 29672639]

[95] Mehta M, Julaiti J, Griffin P, Kumara S. Early stage ML–based prediction of US county vulnerability to the COVID-19 pandemic: ML approach. JMIR Public Health Surveill 2020; 6(3): e19446.
[http://dx.doi.org/10.2196/19446] [PMID: 32784193]

[96]   Liu X, Xue S, Xu J, *et al.* Clinical characteristics and related risk factors of disease severity in 101 COVID-19 patients hospitalized in Wuhan, China. Acta Pharmacol Sin 2022; 43(1): 64-75.
[http://dx.doi.org/10.1038/s41401-021-00627-2] [PMID: 33742107]

[97]   Rodriguez VA, Bhave S, Chen R, *et al.* Development and validation of prediction models for mechanical ventilation, renal replacement therapy, and readmission in COVID-19 patients. J Am Med Inform Assoc 2021; 28(7): 1480-8.
[http://dx.doi.org/10.1093/jamia/ocab029] [PMID: 33706377]

[98]   Wynants L, Calster BV, Collins GS, *et al.* Prediction models for diagnosis and prognosis of COVID-19: systematic review and critical appraisal BMJ 2020; 369: m1328.

[99]   Fernandes FT, de Oliveira TA, Teixeira CE, Batista A F de M , G. Dalla Costa, A. D. P. Chiavegatto Filho. "A multipurpose ML approach to predict COVID-19 negative prognosis in São Paulo, Brazil,". Sci Rep 2021; 11(1): 1-7.
[http://dx.doi.org/10.1038/s41598-021-82885-y] [PMID: 33414495]

[100]   Ustebay S, Sarmis A, Kubra G, Sujan M. A comparison of ML algorithms in predicting COVID - 19 prognostics. Intern Emerg Med 2022; (0123456789):
[http://dx.doi.org/10.1007/s11739-022-03101-x] [PMID: 36116079]

[101]   Xiong Y, Ma Y, Ruan L, Li D, Lu C, Huang L. Comparing different machine learning techniques for predicting COVID-19 severity. Infect Dis Poverty 2022; 11(1): 19.
[http://dx.doi.org/10.1186/s40249-022-00946-4] [PMID: 35177120]

[102]   Iwendi C, Bashir AK, Peshkar A, *et al.* COVID-19 Patient Health Prediction Using Boosted Random Forest Algorithm. Front Public Health 2020; 8: 357.
[http://dx.doi.org/10.3389/fpubh.2020.00357] [PMID: 32719767]

[103]   Wang L, Lin ZQ, Wong A. COVID-Net: a tailored deep convolutional neural network design for detection of COVID-19 cases from chest X-ray images. Sci Rep 2020; 10(1): 19549.
[http://dx.doi.org/10.1038/s41598-020-76550-z] [PMID: 33177550]

[104]   Das D, Santosh KC, Pal U. Truncated inception net: COVID-19 outbreak screening using chest X-rays. Physical and Engineering Sciences in Medicine 2020; 43(3): 915-25.
[http://dx.doi.org/10.1007/s13246-020-00888-x] [PMID: 32588200]

[105]   Asif S, Wenhui Y, Jin H, Jinhai S. Classification of COVID-19 from Chest X-ray images using Deep Convolutional Neural Network
[http://dx.doi.org/10.1109/ICCC51575.2020.9344870]

[106]   Punn NS, Agarwal S. Automated diagnosis of COVID-19 with limited posteroanterior chest X-ray images using fine-tuned deep neural networks. Appl Intell 2021; 51(5): 2689-702.
[http://dx.doi.org/10.1007/s10489-020-01900-3] [PMID: 34764554]

[107]   Shelke A, Inamdar M, Shah V, *et al.* Chest X-ray Classification Using Deep Learning for Automated COVID-19 Screening. SN Computer Science 2021; 2(4): 300.
[http://dx.doi.org/10.1007/s42979-021-00695-5] [PMID: 34075355]

[108]   Li L, *et al.* Using AI to Detect COVID-19 and Community-acquired Pneumonia Based on Pulmonary CT: Evaluation of the Diagnostic Accuracy. Radiology 2020; 296(2): E65-71.
[http://dx.doi.org/10.1148/radiol.2020200905] [PMID: 32191588]

[109]   Ozturk T, Talo M, Yildirim EA, Baloglu UB, Yildirim O, Rajendra Acharya U. Automated detection of COVID-19 cases using deep neural networks with X-ray images. Comput Biol Med 2020; 121: 103792.
[http://dx.doi.org/10.1016/j.compbiomed.2020.103792] [PMID: 32568675]

[110]   Born J, Brändle G, Cossio C, *et al.* POCOVID-Net: Automatic Detection of COVID-19 From a New Lung Ultrasound Imaging Dataset (POCUS) arXiv 2004; 12084.http://arxiv.org/abs/2004.12084

[111]   Chimmula VKR, Zhang L. Time series forecasting of COVID-19 transmission in Canada using LSTM

networks. Chaos Solitons Fractals 2020; 135: 109864.
[http://dx.doi.org/10.1016/j.chaos.2020.109864] [PMID: 32390691]

[112]   Yao H, Zhang N, Zhang R, *et al.* Severity Detection for the Coronavirus Disease 2019 (COVID-19) Patients Using a Machine Learning Model Based on the Blood and Urine Tests. Front Cell Dev Biol 2020; 8(July): 683.
[http://dx.doi.org/10.3389/fcell.2020.00683] [PMID: 32850809]

[113]   Yue H, Yu Q, Liu C, *et al.* Machine learning-based CT radiomics method for predicting hospital stay in patients with pneumonia associated with SARS-CoV-2 infection: a multicenter study. Ann Transl Med 2020; 8(14): 859.
[http://dx.doi.org/10.21037/atm-20-3026] [PMID: 32793703]

[114]   Yan L, Zhang H-T, Goncalves J, *et al.* An interpretable mortality prediction model for COVID-19 patients. Nat Mach Intell 2020; 2(5): 283-8.
[http://dx.doi.org/10.1038/s42256-020-0180-7]

[115]   Pandey G, Chaudhary P, Gupta R, Pal S. SEIR and Regression Model based COVID-19 outbreak predictions in India 1-10.2020; http://arxiv.org/abs/2004.00958 Online
[http://dx.doi.org/10.2196/preprints.19406]

[116]   Brinati D, Campagner A, Ferrari D, Locatelli M, Banfi G, Cabitza F. Detection of COVID-19 Infection from Routine Blood Exams with Machine Learning: A Feasibility Study. J Med Syst 2020; 44(8): 135.
[http://dx.doi.org/10.1007/s10916-020-01597-4] [PMID: 32607737]

[117]   Das D, Santosh KC, Pal U. Truncated inception net: COVID-19 outbreak screening using chest X-rays. Physical and Engineering Sciences in Medicine 2020; 43(3): 915-25.
[http://dx.doi.org/10.1007/s13246-020-00888-x] [PMID: 32588200]

[118]   Wang S, Kang B, Ma J, *et al.* A deep learning algorithm using CT images to screen for Corona virus disease (COVID-19). Eur Radiol 2021; 31(8): 6096-104.
[http://dx.doi.org/10.1007/s00330-021-07715-1] [PMID: 33629156]

[119]   Liu G, Carter B, Bricken T, *et al.* Computationally Optimized SARS-CoV-2 MHC Class I and II Vaccine Formulations Predicted to Target Human Haplotype Distributions. Cell Syst 2020; 11(2): 131-144.e6.
[http://dx.doi.org/10.1016/j.cels.2020.06.009] [PMID: 32721383]

[120]   Pandey R, Gautam V, Pal R, *et al.* A machine learning application for raising WASH awareness in the times of COVID-19 pandemic. Sci Rep 2022; 12(1): 810.
[http://dx.doi.org/10.1038/s41598-021-03869-6] [PMID: 35039533]

[121]   Yang Z, Bogdan P, Nazarian S. An in silico deep learning approach to multi-epitope vaccine design: a SARS-CoV-2 case study. Sci Rep 2021; 11(1): 3238.
[http://dx.doi.org/10.1038/s41598-021-81749-9] [PMID: 33547334]

[122]   Bernheim A, Mei X, Huang M, *et al.* Chest CT Findings in Coronavirus Disease-19 (COVID-19): Relationship to Duration of Infection. Radiology 2020; 295(3): 200463.
[http://dx.doi.org/10.1148/radiol.2020200463] [PMID: 32077789]

[123]   Jaiswal A, Gianchandani N, Singh D, Kumar V, Kaur M. Classification of the COVID-19 infected patients using DenseNet201 based deep transfer learning. J Biomol Struct Dyn 2021; 39(15): 5682-9.
[http://dx.doi.org/10.1080/07391102.2020.1788642] [PMID: 32619398]

CHAPTER 11

Future Technologies for Coronaviruses (COVID-19)

Mohammad Sufian Badar[1,2,3,4,*], **Alia**[5], **Kamakshi Srivastava**[5], **Zara Khan**[5], **Himanshu Dagar**[5], **Faiz Akram Siddiqui**[6], **Punit Kaur**[6] and **Nadeem Zafar Jilani**[7]

[1] *Department of Bioengineering, University of California, Riverside, CA, USA*

[2] *Universal Scientific Education and Research Network (USERN), Tehran, Iran*

[3] *Director (Academic), SPI Darbhanga, India*

[4] *Department of Computer Science and Engineering (Bioinformatics), School of Engineering Sciences and Technology (SEST), Jamia Hamdard, New Delhi, India*

[5] *Department of Computer Science, Jamia Millia Islamia, New Delhi, India*

[6] *AIIMS, New Delhi, India*

[7] *Department of Pediatric Emergency, Sidra Medicine, Ar-Rayyan, Qatar*

Abstract: The ongoing battle against coronaviruses demands innovative approaches and cutting-edge technologies to enhance our ability to detect, prevent, and respond to outbreaks effectively. This chapter explores the forefront of advancements in robotics, drones, Genetic Engineering technologies, and nano-technology, presenting a comprehensive overview of their potential roles in shaping the future of pandemic management. By embracing these innovative solutions, we have paved the way to not only enhance our response capabilities during the current pandemic but also to establish a robust framework for tackling future viral threats.

Keywords: Active and passive targeting, AMBU Ventilator, Autonomous-Robotics, COVID-19, CRN, CRISPR-Cas, Gene therapy, Mobile edge computing (MEC), Nanotechnology, Nanocarriers, Nano-based vaccines, Nanoparticles, RNAi, Telerobotic system, UAVs/Drones, Vaccine delivery methods.

EXPLORATION OF ROBOTICS IN PANDEMIC MITIGATION STRATEGIES

Integration of Robotics in Combating Coronaviruses

The workload of frontline personnel had been significantly reduced by the intelligent robot systems' capacity to assist in diagnosis, risk assessment,

---

* **Corresponding author Mohammad Sufian Badar:** Department of Bioengineering, University of California, Riverside, CA, USA; E-mail: sufianbadar@gmail.com

monitoring, telehealth care, disinfection, and various other tasks during this pandemic. The public and media have shown a great deal of interest in the use of robots in public areas, hospitals, and quarantine facilities. Although robots have been used in industrial settings such as automotive plants since the 1960s, they are now able to help us in places where humans are at high risk of being infected, like hospitals.

With robots and artificial intelligence (AI), humans are reducing the impact of coronaviruses, after two years of combating the virus. Professionals are replaced by robots as they have special benefits in enhancing the productivity and preventing the spread of viruses. Robots that measure temperature, such as the DROID team developed by UBTech Robotics in China, have monitored China, and have monitored people's health in public areas [1].

Robots used in telemedicine have the potential to reduce the direct contact between sick patients and their carriers. With a single sampling success rate of over 95%, the COVID-19 throat swab intelligent sampling robot has improved the standardisation of biological sample research topics and guaranteed specimen quality.

"This pandemic has created an interesting new landscape for advancements in consumer-facing robotics," says Bernd Schmitt, the Robert D. Calkins Professor of International Business and Faculty Director of the Centre on Global Brand Leadership at Columbia Business School. "Not only has the pandemic created many new immediate uses for robots, but I predict it will also change consumers' perceptions of service robots from one of relative skepticisms to acceptance, and more quickly than we previously expected."

Robotics Techniques and Tools

The most recent advancements in robotics research are the distribution of healthcare resources, diagnosis of symptoms or viruses, and detection techniques and tools.

COUGH RECOGNITION NETWORK (CRN)

A cough recognition network is built using an Mel-spectrogram and the CNN model. When compared to alternative techniques, CRN performs exceptionally well in cough recognition. Generalisation test findings indicate that CRN can adjust to cough monitoring in a variety of diverse everyday scenarios. The correct recognition rate of the datasets used is 98%. It can be seen that the model can still achieve good recognition performance even if a variety of different sounds are mixed. It is anticipated to lessen the exposure of healthcare workers and offer a viable option for managing illness during the COVID-19 pandemic [1].

AUTOMATED AMBU VENTILATOR

Automated AMBU Ventilator with Negative Pressure Headbox as shown in Fig. (**1**) and Transporting Capsule in Fig. (**2**) for COVID-19 patients transfer is a low-cost construction, flexible usage unit, and airborne prevention that could be manufactured without a high level of technology. It is possible to adjust the oxygen flow rate, rhythm, and volume using this automated AMBU ventilator. An HEPA filter was used to purify the dangerously expired air. The air treatment systems are integrated inside a small-sized patient transport capsule. The machine's future development concentrates on ensuring seamless integration with imaging technology, validating standardisation, conducting tests on human subjects, and eventually undergoing commercialization [2].

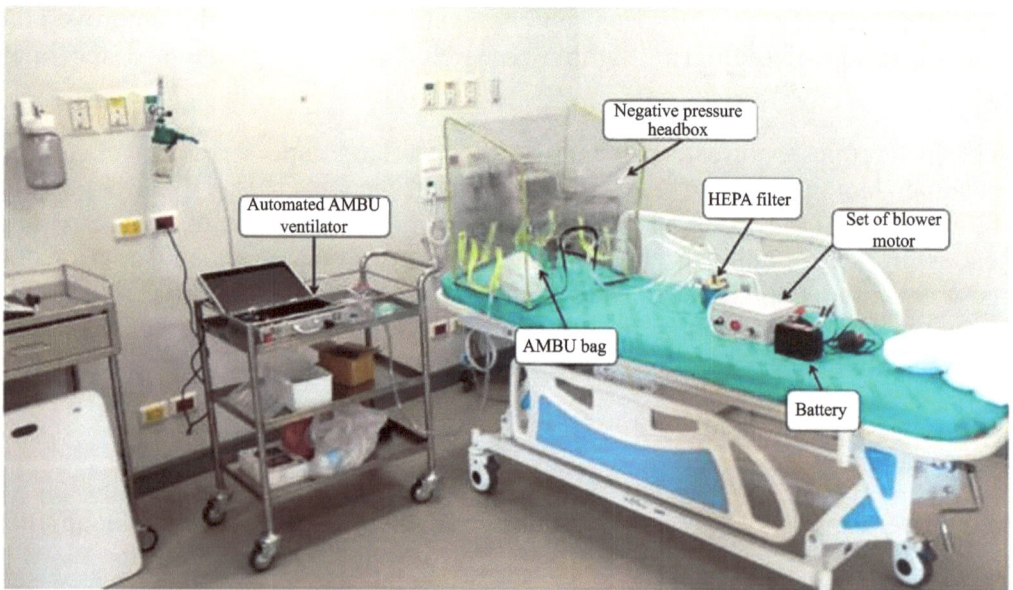

Fig. (1). Automated AMBU ventilator with the negative pressure headbox prototype.

AUTONOMOUS ROBOTIC POINT-OF-CARE ULTRASOUND IMAGING FOR MONITORING OF COVID–19–INDUCED PULMONARY DISEASES

An automated robotic system as shown in Fig. (**3**) makes it possible to stage and diagnose COVID-19 patients by POCUS (Point-of-care Ultrasound) scanning their lungs. An algorithm is created to determine the best orientation and position of an ultrasound probe on a patient during a CT scan to photograph target spots in the lungs. Given a model, a deep learning system can predict 3D landmark placements of a ribcage without the need for CT data. The outcomes show the system's initial viability and its potential to provide a way to lessen the spread of COVID-19 in places where people are vulnerable [3].

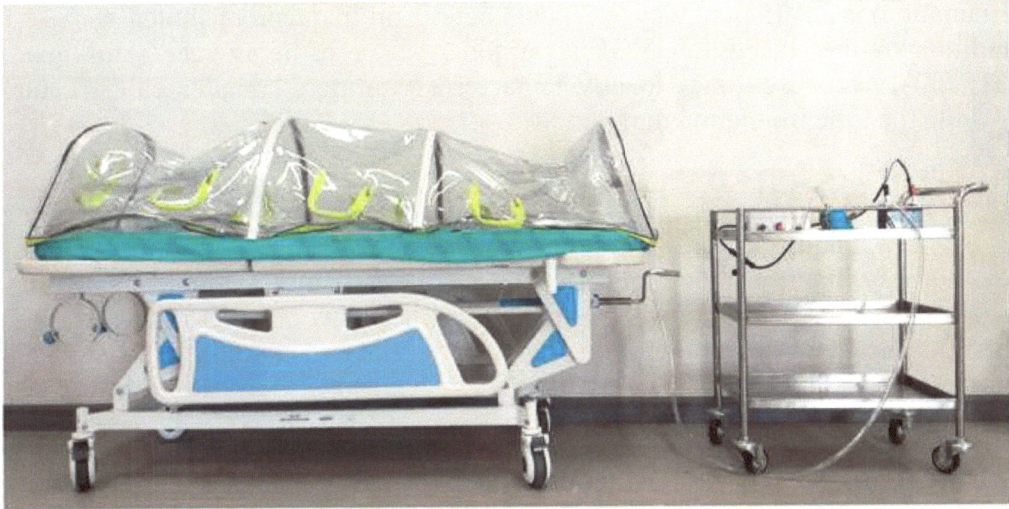

Fig. (2). Negative pressure transporting capsule with the set of the blower motor model.

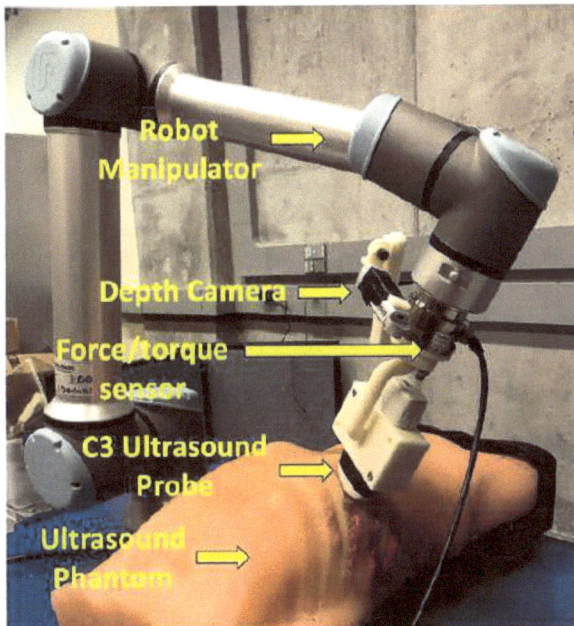

Fig. (3). Autonomous robotic system.

ROBOT-ASSISTED   ULTRAVIOLET   (UV)   DISINFECTION   IN RADIOLOGY

The technique can be used in close quarters with human workers or deployed independently. The findings demonstrate that UVGI (Ultraviolet Germicidal Irradiation) is an efficient way to render bacteria on frequently handled surfaces in radiology suites inactive. UVGI has a good chance of being successful against COVID-19 because it may inactivate bacteria with more complex cell structures despite the little irradiation duration [4].

ROBOTIC-ASSISTED SURGERY FOR AUTOPSY

A novel technique encourages mortuary workers to use robotic technology during the autopsy, mainly for cutting a cadaver's skull. It is a choice for protecting against any occupational damage among healthcare workers. It restricts aerosol particle discharge to amounts comparable to standard autopsy practices. This process lessens the amount of tiny, infectious dust, particularly amid the COVID-19 outbreak [5].

ULTRASOUND SCANNING ROBOT

In quick response to enabling physical distancing during the COVID-19 Pandemic, a robot-assisted device was developed. It automatically scans the tissue allowing for patient and sonographer separation. This device uses a nimble robot arm (Panda robot arm) as shown in Fig. (**4**) to hold the ultrasound probe as it autonomously scans the tissue, evaluating the quality of the ultrasound pictures in real-time. The quality assessment method indicates that this system is quick enough to be used in a robotic control loop and that it effectively maintains ultrasound picture quality [5].

MEDICAL TELEROBOTIC SYSTEMS

The need for intelligent robotic systems in healthcare is increasing. Specifically, the use of medical telerobotic systems can benefit patients receiving telemedicine who are not infected with COVID-19. Strategies based on control theory have been developed to solve problems with intrinsic robot control related to the motion of organs. The inherent benefits of medical robots, such as their steady hand, accuracy, motion scaling, and biomotion compensation enable them to further reduce the non-COVID-19 burden on healthcare systems during the global crisis and offer general support to patients and medical professionals [6].

DRONES REDEFINING PANDEMIC SURVEILLANCE AND RESPONSE

In the fight against COVID-19 epidemic, drones or UAVs (Unmanned Aerial Vehicles) proved to be a versatile and effective tool. Their ability to navigate restricted areas, carry payloads, and broadcast messages made them invaluable for tasks such as delivering medical supplies, disinfecting public spaces, monitoring social distancing, and raising awareness about the virus. Drones are also being used in hospital settings to transport patients, bring food and supplies to medical staff, and offer psychological support to isolated patients. Drones have received significant attention in various domains of civil and military operations because of their high mobility, enhanced stability, affordability, and high endurance in multiple tasks. Because of the integration of different developing technologies including 5G/B5G, artificial intelligence, the Internet of Things (IoT), and mobile edge computing, the use cases of UAVs are expanding significantly. The directions for future research on the use of drone technology to treat COVID-1--like illnesses will be discussed in this section.

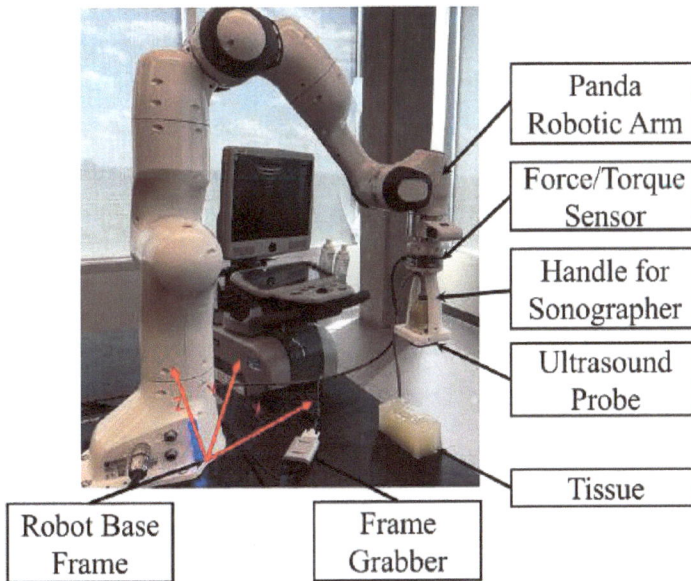

Fig. (4). US scanning assistant including Panda robot arm

Unmanned Aerial Vehicles (UAVs)

UAVs are remotely operated aircrafts which use sensors, microprocessors, and other hardware to assess their environmental condition and send these factors as signals to the operator for human intervention or action. To communicate with satellites or ground control stations (GCSs), such as computers or smartphones,

UAVs need communication connections. The UAVs must be remotely controlled by a human operator to conduct remote operations.

Due to the overwhelming interest in drones, several UAVs of varying sizes and forms as shown in Fig. (**5**) have been developed to perform a variety of tasks. Single-rotor, multi-rotor, fixed-wing, and hybrid UAVs have all been employed in industrial applications as well as the pandemic. Different characteristics of these UAVs are also summarized in Table **1** [7].

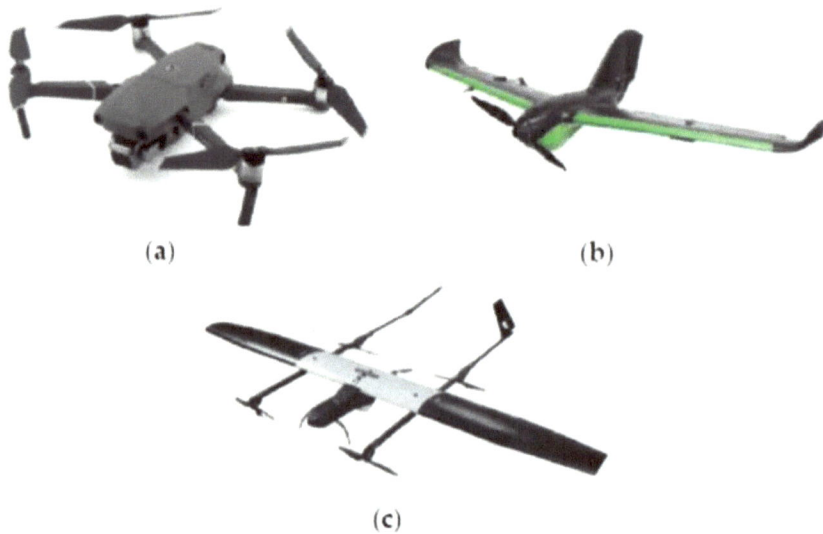

(a)　　　　　　　　　　　　　　(b)

(c)

Fig. (5). Different types of UAV: (**a**) rotary wing, (**b**) fixed wing, (**c**) fixed-wing hybrid

Tabel. 1. Characteristics of different UAVs [8].

Characteristics	Fixed Wing	Rotary Wing	Hybrid
Energy efficiency	High	Low	High
Flight system	Complicated	Simple	Complicated
Landing	Conventional	Vertical	Vertical
Autonomy	No	Yes	Yes
Hovering	No	Yes	Yes
Power supply	Battery, fuel	Battery	Battery, fuel
Endurance	60–3000 m	6–180 m	180–480 m
Payload	1000 kg	50 kg	10 kg
Weight	0.1–400,000 kg	0.01–100 kg	1.5–65 kg

Technological Advancements in Drones to Combat COVID-19

The COVID-19 pandemic has accelerated the advancement and assimilation of novel drone-related technologies to counteract viral transmission and enhance medical results. At present, several technologies are being used to combat COVID-19, including blockchain, smartphone applications, wearable sensing, artificial intelligence, machine learning, and edge computing.

BLOCKCHAIN

The prevention and control of epidemics can be greatly improved by using blockchain technology. This combination can guarantee the accuracy of the information gathered. Additionally, a blockchain can protect data against fraud and attack. It has several benefits, including security, immutability, and transparency [9].

WEARABLE SENSING

The development of wearable technology involves the integration of wearable sensors with the human anatomy. These technologies come in watches, bracelets, helmets, and spectacles. A patient under observation is monitored with wearable sensors. These wearables allow drones to gather patient data, which is subsequently saved in drone memory. These saved data are sent to big data via many servers. These servers process, model, profile, and analyse the data using edge, cloud, and fog computing. Refined data are provided to hospitals via appropriate laws and regulations issued by the medical board and government after a thorough study. When needed, the data are safely sent to media personnel [10, 11].

ARTIFICIAL INTELLIGENCE AND MACHINE LEARNING

With the rapid growth of artificial intelligence, researchers have started to integrate AI algorithms into drones and robotics for use in medical imaging and other healthcare applications. The potential of this technology can be validated in Scopus. Drones with AI capabilities have been used to locate hotspots. Without human assistance, UAVs with embedded sensors can collect the data needed to carry out essential tasks. This exciting technology can do multiple tasks to provide significant help to medical workers, and it has demonstrated impressive outcomes in the identification and treatment of infected patients. Drones with AI capabilities may be used for a variety of tasks, including physical inspection, transportation, and surveillance [12 - 14].

EDGE-COMPUTING-BASED DRONE TECHNOLOGY

Mobile edge computing (MEC) is proposed as an efficient way to deal with the issue of high computing resource requirements. Edge computing brings computing power closer to the source of data, while drones provide a unique aerial platform for data collection and processing. Together, they enable real-time data analysis, decision-making, and autonomous operations, significantly enhancing the capabilities of drones in various applications. Data processing is strengthened by edge computing, which does it without using internet bandwidth. It takes into account the 5G spectrum's flexible deployment of edge nodes and many drones. Drones can be networked together to exchange data or communicate with a central cloud server. The users at the particular location where detection is taking place are linked to this server. Several drones may be deployed on streets using this method to detect COVID-19 victims [15].

GENETIC ENGINEERING AT THE FOREFRONT: CRISPR-CAS, GENE THERAPY, RNAI

In three decades, biology has evolved into biotechnology and ultimately into bioinformatics. Many genetic engineering and genome editing techniques have been identified in vivo and modulated versions have been implemented in the study of diseases and treatments associated with them. Genetic engineering technologies are defined as techniques, that incorporate some foreign genetic material that is adding some coding sequence into the model organism whereas genome editing induces changes without any foreign element addition. They are quite overlapping fields and much less distinction is present, but the basic difference is stated here. When the modifying agent or complex operates on DNA, it results in a single or double-strand break, which disrupts cellular activity. The repair mechanism employed by the cell to restore cellular functions are of two types – 1.) NHEJ pathway (Non-Homologous End Joining Pathway) or 2.) Homologous-direct repair (HDR) pathway [16 - 18]. If the formal is performed, then the indels are induced into the genome. On the contrary, if the latter is executed then the insertion of correct or foreign genetic material is possible. The molecular mechanisms behind these mechanisms are beyond the scope of this chapter.

Gene therapy involves replacing the disease-causing gene with a healthy gene. RNAi silences the expression of genes by hybridizing siRNA with mRNA. CRISPR Cas9 systems induce DSBs in the genome. The repair mechanism employed by the cell can be programmed by supplying specific agents responsible for the regulation of environmental conditions resulting in cellular activity manipulation [20]. Hence CRISPR complexes are competent with both, i.e.,

NHEJ and HDR pathways [19]. Prime Base (PB) editing is based on the principle of CRISPR but induces single-strand break (SSB), only resulting in more stable editing techniques [21]. Although PB editing is still in the early stages, it could prove to be a game changer in the upcoming years. NICER is the most recently discovered genetic engineering technology. NICER is said to overcome the off-target activity of CRISPR technology and is under development [22]. During COVID-19, mRNA vaccines have shown a novel approach not just to fight against SARS-CoV2 but other diseases as well.

CRISPR/Cas9

CRISPR technology is an advanced genome editing technique inspired by the phenomenon of bacterial acquired immunity [23]. CRISPR (Clustered-Regularly Inter Spaced Palindromic Repeats) sequences in association with CRISPR-associated 9 (Cas9) protein are capable of performing guided targeted editing. CRISPR/Cas systems have been exploited in COVID-19 and other disorders such as cancer to understand the disease and its treatment to enhance the therapeutic effects to improve the survival rate of patients. CRISPR /Cas systems are not limited to genome editing. Their activity can also be used to screen disease-associated genes and diagnosis.

Diagnosis and Therapy

During COVID-19, different combinations of Cas12, Cas3, and Cas9 proteins were used to diagnose the infection in patients. Infection diagnosis techniques involving Cas12 protein are all-in-one dual CRISPR-Cas12a (AIOD-CRISPR) assay, CRISPR/Cas12a-NER (naked eye readout), iSCAN (in vitro specific CRISPR-based assay for nucleic acids detection) and STOP (SHERLOCK testing in one pot). Similarly, techniques related to Cas 3 and Cas9 are Cas3-operated nucleic acid detection (CONAN) and FnCas9 editor-linked uniform detection assay (FELUDA), respectively. AELUDA was initially developed to detect Zika virus presence, but the effective approach was immediately adopted by the developers to detect SARS-CoV2 as well [24, 25]. The techniques detect the viral genome with very low concentration, which gives them the edge over other techniques such as RT-PCR, which are prone to False Negatives in a low concentration of viral genome in the sample [24]. The activity of the CRISPR/Cas system involves two actions – 1) Identification of target sequence achieved by a single guide RNA (sgRNA), and 2) Double-stranded break induced by the Cas9 protein (endonuclease) at the target site [19]. The Protospacer Adjacent Motif (PAM) site present on the non-complementary strand is essential for DNA and Cas9 protein interaction *via* the PI domain of Cas9 protein. Once the PAM is found, hybridization between sgRNA and a complementary strand of DNA followed by the double-stranded break on the target site takes place [28, 29].

CRISPR-based therapeutic approaches are still developing under the principle of subjecting the viral genome to editing. This will lead to a cease of the functionality of translated protein if the editing takes place in the coding region. Some researchers have identified a few host genes that can also be targeted to reduce or avoid SARS-CoV-2 infection. They were found to be supporting elements in the virus life cycle by high throughput screening [24].

RNAi

RNAi stands for Ribonucleic- Acid Interference. As the name suggests, RNAi is a technique that interferes with the mRNA transcript of the gene that has to be regulated with the help of siRNA (Small Interfering RNA). The size of the siRNA varies in length from 21 to 25 nt long. Once siRNA reaches inside the cell, it hybridizes with the target mRNA [30]. Identification of mRNA is based on the number of mismatches. The higher the intolerance against non-complementary mismatches in the sequences, the more accurate the target identification is [31]. Many bioinformatics studies have claimed that the RNAi mediated by siRNA is capable of performing gene regulation by targeting various locations of viral genetic material, *i.e.*, ssDNA. Khandakar A.S.M. Saadat in one of his research studies identified 14 locations of the viral genome including ORF(s) that are said to be playing an important role in SARS-CoV-2 infection along with structural and functional proteins [32]. Another study led by João Pedro Viana Rodrigues and his team supported the idea with experimental data for in-vivo SARS-CoV-2 infection inhibition. This has streamlined the anti-viral medicine research towards finding more effective and cost-effective therapies [26, 27].

Gene Therapy

Gene therapy involves modifying vectors such as plasmids, bacterial vectors, deactivated adenoviruses, and adeno-associated viruses to carry corrected/functional genes inside the host cells or tissues. The expression of functional genes from the vector will overcome the deficiency and regulate cellular activity in a normal manner. This approach to gene therapy is known as Gene replacement therapy and is highly successful in treating disorders arising due to haploinsufficiency or recessive traits. To correct the issues related to dominant traits, CRISPR/Cas systems are a better choice providing the edge to correct the gene in the DNA of the cell. During COVID-19, SGT-53 gene therapy became popular as it supplies the vector into the cell to translate the P53 protein [33]. This protein is a hub protein and is an experimentally proven tumour suppressor as well as a viral infection modulator. SGT-53 is in phase II trials for cancer treatment[33]. During SARS-Cov-2 infection, the activity of P53 is inhibited by viral elements leading to the failure of cell-cycle arrest and apoptosis [34, 35]. Joe B Harford and his team support employing SGT-53 for COVID-19 treatment. It has a high chance of success based on the hypothesis that SGT-53 holds the capability to overcome the deficiency of P53 in cells during COVID-19 infection manifestation leading to health restoration [33]. Using SGT-53 for gene therapy is not harmful to patients with genetic disorders as well because the vector used for SGT-53 delivery is liposomes. The concern of genetic disorders patients across the globe arises due to the advancement of gene therapeutic approaches for COVID-19 through AAV. Because it is a virus-based vector, the recombination frequency is as high as 50%. For the patients who depend on these AAVs to be content with regular life, this can cause life-threatening conditions [36]. But gene therapy such as SGT-53 opens a way to ensure the health of all for a better tomorrow.

Repurposed Drugs

Drugs are another prospect of medical science, clinical studies, and pharmacology. Using drugs for some diseases that they were not designed to target initially is known as drug repurposing. It is not a new practice but its effects on COVID-19 are commendable. Favipiravir drug initially developed for Zika virus was repurposed for the COVID-19 treatment with success [37]. Many bioinformatic in-silico studies have provided solid evidence that ACE2, TMPRSS2, and BSG gene proteins are expressed together in lung cells [38]. The presence of TMPRSS2 is crucial for SARS-CoV-2 infection as it activates the spike protein by proteolytic activity leading to increased binding affinity for the ACE2 receptor. Hence, lung cells abundant with TMPRSS2 are prone to SARS-CoV-2 infection. Acetaminophen and curcumin are drugs that can target TMPRSS2 protein leading to the deactivation of protease leading to declined sensitivity of ACE2 towards spike protein [38, 39]. Further experimental confirmation through clinical trials is required but the principle is practical and rational.

RNAi, CRISPR/CAS systems, gene therapy, and drug repurposing have great potential to advance antiviral research. Their exploitation along with knowledge gathered by bioinformatic tools and algorithms opens several opportunities for young budding minds to explore the biological instances and their applications to improve the quality of life for all populations [40].

PRECISION PANDEMIC INTERVENTION THROUGH ADVANCED NANOTECHNOLOGY APPLICATIONS

During the pandemic, to detect viruses quickly, affordably, and accurately, researchers in the fields of nanoscience and nanotechnology are hard at work. To fight the deadly SARS-Cov-2 infection, nanotechnology has been extensively employed.

Nanotechnology deals with the manipulation, control, design, and synthesis of complex systems of atoms in the size range of 1 to 100 nanometers. Nanoparticles are small in size and have variable shapes, which can carry drugs, genetic editing agents, and environmental factors influencing the target cell or tissue. The development of nanocarriers is a crucial step to safeguard drug formulation against premature degradation leading to the risk of long-term toxicity. Nanocarrier activity is affected by many factors such as their structure, chemical composition, physical properties, and surface fabrication with coating materials. Despite their size, nanoparticles have a huge surface-to-volume ratio, which gives them a remarkable ability to combat COVID-19. Their flexibility to be programmed and interact with surroundings makes them useful techniques for in vivo delivery systems. Nanoparticles are roughly divided into organic nanoparticles and inorganic nanoparticles. Organic nanoparticles are compounds containing carbon, for example– liposomes, micelles, dendrimers, organic polymers, etc. Inorganic nanoparticles do not contain carbon-based materials; for example- gold nanoparticles, silver nanoparticles, quantum dots, metal oxide, etc. They are known for their unique applications. While organic nanoparticles are valuable for their biocompatibility and distribution in various applications, inorganic nanoparticles are valuable for their physical and chemical properties. Inorganic metal nanoparticles are more effective against COVID-19 [41].

Nanoparticles to Combat COV19/SARSCOV2

1. Lipid Nanoparticles: BioNTech SE and Pfizer developed four lipid nanoparticles (LNPs) encapsulating mRNA for the SARS-CoV-2 vaccine, known as BNT162a1, BNT162b1, BNT162b2, and BNT162c. These LNPs utilized two types of nucleoside-modified mRNA, one containing uridine and the other being self-amplifying. Phase 3 clinical trials for the BNT162b2 candidate have concluded, demonstrating the vaccine's safety and efficacy.

2. Gold Nanoparticles: The diagnostic kit utilizing gold nanoparticles simplifies the identification of SARS-CoV-2 antigens from a swab. The conjugate pad contains gold (Au) anti-SARS-CoV-2 antibodies. SARS-CoV-2 antigens present in the sample bind to these antibodies forming antigen-antibody complexes. As one gold nanoparticle attaches to multiple anti-SARS-2 antibodies, numerous antigens bind to one nanoparticle resulting in vivid colour test lines, which can be detected by colour change. This is considered an indication of the presence of SARS-CoV-2 antigen in the sample. The unbound Au anti-SARS-2 antibodies present in the control line emit different colours than antigen-antibody complexes, making these diagnostic kits straightforward for interpretation.

3. Silver nanoparticles: Silver nanoparticles (AgNPs) interact with the surface protein of extracellular viruses, inhibiting infection in the early stages. This inhibition can occur by damaging the surface proteins, affecting the ability to interact with the receptor ACE2. Previous research has demonstrated that AgNPs effectively suppress extracellular SARS-CoV-2 in virus pre-treatment assays (VPrA), protecting target cells from infection and pseudo-virus entry. AgNPs can also exert an intracellular antiviral effect by interacting with viral nucleic acid. The antiviral impact of silver nano-sponges is size-dependent, with particles around 10 nm in diameter being the most potent. Specifically, polyvinyl pyrrolidone-capped 10 nm silver nanoparticles (PVP-AgNP10) show highly promising anti-SARS-CoV-2 action. To address the COVID-19 pandemic, silver nanoparticles (AgNPs) can be utilized on various inanimate surfaces such as Ag-coated air filters in air conditioners and masks in suppressing SARS-CoV-2 suggesting a potential use for medical equipment. Studies have demonstrated that polycotton textiles combined with AgNPs can effectively prevent SARS-CoV-2 transmission. Nanomaterials can be developed using ACE2 receptors on their surface that can reduce infection rates by neutralizing viruses.

4. Nitrous Oxide (NO) Nanoparticles: Viruses typically range in size from 10 to 850 nm, and nitrous oxide (NO) has demonstrated efficacy in destroying various microorganisms, including bacteria, viruses, fungi, and tumour cells. The applications of nitrous oxide in conjunction with nanoparticles span across diverse fields. Combining NO with other medications has proven effective in treating individuals infected with MERS-CoV, showcasing promising results with minimal side effects. NO has been successfully employed in treating lung-related illnesses triggered by certain viruses. Investigations suggest that NO compounds may have the potential to halt SARS-CoV-2 replication. Specifically, S-nitroso--acetyl penicillamine, a nitrous oxide donor, effectively inhibited the SARS-Co--2 replication pathway [42].

Vaccine Delivery Methods via Nanocarriers

Overcoming resistance, systematic toxicity, and non-specificity of therapeutic agents are significant challenges in Drug Delivery Systems (DDSs). Different nanomaterials provide advantages and potential for smart DDSs because of their distinct nanoscale characteristics and certain bio-functions. The crucial feature of

DDSs based on nanoparticles, for instance, can attach to the disease target precisely and selectively accumulate while exhibiting regulated release behaviour. This section has examined the many ways that nanocarriers are used to target cells.

1. **Passive targeting:** Passive targeting involves the convection or passive diffusion of nanocarriers into the cells through leaky capillary fenestrations. This approach is common for large molecules to traverse large pores when net filtration is zero. Diffusion is the primary method for drug delivery. The Enhanced Permeability and Retention (EPR) effect can bring different alterations in the bio-distribution of DDS depending on the location or tissue, commonly known as passive targeting. This passive targeting mechanism significantly enhances the quantity of drug delivered to disease sites, including sites of inflammation and infection. The EPR effect leads to the selective accumulation of nanocarriers and drugs. The maximum impact of the EPR effect is achieved when nanocarriers can evade immune surveillance and circulate for an extended period.

2. **Active targeting:** Active or ligand-mediated targeting involves the incorporation of ligands targeting cell-specific receptors on nanoparticle surfaces to enhance their site-specific actions and accessibility. The ligand is chosen to bind to a receptor that has some special biological significance related to diseases that is the higher expression or specific expression on the cell surface. In locations where cells are easily accessible, high-affinity binding is preferable due to the complex flow conditions of the bloodstream. Actively targeted nanocarriers with their ability to provide intracellular medication offer a promising approach to addressing multidrug resistance [43, 44].

Future Prospect

Additional research is essential to gain an understanding of the process of immunization corresponding to nano-carriers. This ongoing investigation is critical for refining existing vaccines and has the potential to advance the field of immunization by improving vaccine design and delivery strategies. The transfer of technology is crucial for scaling up the manufacturing of nanoparticle (NP) vaccines, ensuring a widespread and abundant supply to the world. NP vaccines play a significant role in the treatment and prevention of COVID-19 by enabling controlled antigen release and interference with the viral entry. Clinical trials are essential to evaluate the efficacy, stability, and safety of NP vaccines. The rapid development and effectiveness of NP-based SARS-CoV-2 vaccines have contributed significantly to saving lives. However, the true potential and development of NP-based vaccines in future pandemics will be revealed over time [45, 46].

CONCLUSION

Nevertheless, like any promising medical interventions, some hurdles need attention. Subsequent research efforts can focus on refining the advancements taking place and provide a forward-looking perspective on the integration of technology in our arsenal against viruses in the future.

TAKE HOME MESSAGE

In the fight against the pandemic, robotics emerges as a crucial ally, significantly reducing the workload of frontline personnel. From intelligent robots aiding in diagnosis and disinfection to advanced tools like the Cough Recognition Network and Autonomous Robotic Point-of-Care Ultrasound, innovative technologies play a pivotal role in mitigating the impact of COVID-19, reshaping consumer perceptions and transforming healthcare strategies for the future. From delivering medical supplies to leveraging advanced technologies like blockchain, wearable sensing, artificial intelligence, and edge computing, the book highlights the versatile applications of UAVs in addressing public health crises. The convergence of biology, biotechnology, and bioinformatics is explored, revealing the intricate interplay between genetic engineering techniques like CRISPR/Cas9, RNAi, gene therapy, and drug repurposing. The book underscores their pivotal role in advancing antiviral research, showcasing their potential to revolutionize disease understanding, treatment, and the pursuit of a healthier future. In the race against the pandemic, nanoscience and nanotechnology are pivotal for quick, affordable, and precise virus detection. Nanoparticles, especially inorganic ones like gold and silver, showcase unique antiviral properties. Utilized in vaccine development and drug delivery systems, nanoparticles offer promising avenues in combating COVID-19, with ongoing research pointing towards their potential in future pandemics.

WHAT YOU WILL LEARN

The first section delves into the integration of robotics in healthcare, illustrating the most recent advancements in robotics research, which are the distribution of healthcare resources, diagnosis of symptoms or viruses, and detection techniques and tools.

Drones, the focus of the second section, emerge as invaluable tools for surveillance, logistics, and communication during pandemics. Their ability to cover vast areas efficiently makes them instrumental in monitoring public spaces, delivering medical supplies to remote locations, and even facilitating telemedicine services.

The third section investigates the revolutionary Genetic Engineering technologies, emphasizing their role in rapid and precise diagnostics, as well as potential applications in therapeutic interventions. This section sheds light on the development of CRISPR-based diagnostic tools, RNAi, and gene therapy-based approaches that promise quick and accurate treatment of viral infections, paving the way for targeted and efficient strategies.

Nano-technology takes centre stage in the final section, showcasing its potential in the development of antiviral coatings, drug delivery systems, and advanced diagnostics. Nano vaccines offer a unique platform for the targeted delivery of therapeutic agents. There are diverse applications of nano-technology in mitigating the impact of coronaviruses at both individual and community levels.

REFERENCES

[1]   Zhou Q, Shan J, Ding W, *et al.*, Cough Recognition Based on Mel-Spectrogram and Convolutional Neural Network. Front. Robot. AI, 07 May 2021. Sec. Smart Sensor Networks and Autonomy; 8: 2021.
[http://dx.doi.org/10.3389/frobt.2021.580080]

[2]   2. Automated AMBU Ventilator With Negative Pressure Headbox and Transporting Capsule for COVID-19 Patient Transfer. Front. Robot. AI, 29 January 2021. Sec. Biomedical Robotics 2021; 7.
[http://dx.doi.org/10.3389/frobt.2020.621580]

[3]   3. Autonomous Robotic Point-of-Care Ultrasound Imaging for Monitoring of COVID-19–Induced Pulmonary Diseases. Front. Robot. AI, 25 May 2021. Sec. Biomedical Robotics 2021; 8.
[http://dx.doi.org/10.3389/frobt.2021.645756]

[4]   Exploring the Applicability of Robot-Assisted UV Disinfection in Radiology Sec Biomedical Robotics 2021; 7.
[http://dx.doi.org/10.3389/frobt.2020.590306]

[5]   Robotic Ultrasound Scanning with Real-Time Image-Based Force Adjustment: Quick Response for Enabling Physical Distancing During the COVID-19 Pandemic | Front. Robot. AI, 22 March 2021. Sec. Biomedical Robotics. 2021; 8.
[http://dx.doi.org/10.3389/frobt.2021.645424]

[6]   COVID-19 Pandemic Spurs Medical Telerobotic Systems A Survey of Applications Requiring Physiological Organ Motion Compensation 2020; 7.
[http://dx.doi.org/10.3389/frobt.2020.594673]

[7]   Yaacoub JP, Noura H, Salman O, Chehab A. Security analysis of drones systems: Attacks, limitations, and recommendations. Internet of Things 2020; 11: 100218.
[http://dx.doi.org/10.1016/j.iot.2020.100218] [PMID: 38620271]

[8]   Role of Drone Technology Helping in Alleviating the COVID-19 Pandemic. 1593; 13(10).
[http://dx.doi.org/10.3390/mi13101593]

[9]   Alsamhi SH, Lee B, Guizani M, Kumar N, Qiao Y, Liu X. Blockchain for decentralized MULTI-DRONE to combat COVID-19 and future pandemics: Framework and proposed solutions. Trans Emerg Telecommun Technol 2021; 32(9): e4255.
[http://dx.doi.org/10.1002/ett.4255]

[10]   Nasajpour M, Pouriyeh S, Parizi RM, Dorodchi M, Valero M, Arabnia HR. Internet of Things for current COVID-19 and future pandemics: An exploratory study. J Healthc Inform Res 2020; 4(4): 325-64.

[http://dx.doi.org/10.1007/s41666-020-00080-6] [PMID: 33204938]

[11] Bai L, Yang D, Wang X, *et al.* Chinese experts' consensus on the Internet of Things-aided diagnosis and treatment of coronavirus disease 2019 (COVID-19). Clinical eHealth 2020; 3: 7-15.
[http://dx.doi.org/10.1016/j.ceh.2020.03.001]

[12] Artificial intelligence-powered decentralized framework for Internet of Things in Healthcare 4.0. Trans Emerg Telecommun Technol 2021; e4245.
[http://dx.doi.org/10.1002/ett.4245]

[13] Piccialli F, di Cola VS, Giampaolo F, Cuomo S. The role of artificial intelligence in fighting the COVID-19 pandemic. Inf Syst Front 2021; 23(6): 1467-97.
[http://dx.doi.org/10.1007/s10796-021-10131-x] [PMID: 33935585]

[14] Lv Z, Chen D, Feng H, Zhu H, Lv H. Digital twins in unmanned aerial vehicles for rapid medical resource delivery in epidemics. IEEE Trans Intell Transp Syst 2022; 23(12): 25106-14.
[http://dx.doi.org/10.1109/TITS.2021.3113787] [PMID: 36789134]

[15] Huda SMA, Moh S. Survey on computation offloading in UAV-Enabled mobile edge computing. J Netw Comput Appl 2022; 201: 103341.
[http://dx.doi.org/10.1016/j.jnca.2022.103341]

[16] Nuñez JK, Harrington LB, Kranzusch PJ, Engelman AN, Doudna JA. Foreign DNA capture during CRISPR–Cas adaptive immunity. Nature 2015; 527(7579): 535-8.
[http://dx.doi.org/10.1038/nature15760] [PMID: 26503043]

[17] Yeh CD, Richardson CD, Corn JE. Advances in genome editing through control of DNA repair pathways Nature Cell Biology. Preprint at 2019; Vol. 21.
[http://dx.doi.org/10.1038/s41556-019-0425-z]

[18] Li X, Heyer WD. Homologous recombination in DNA repair and DNA damage tolerance Cell Research. Preprint at 2008; Vol. 18.
[http://dx.doi.org/10.1038/cr.2008.1]

[19] Mishra G, Srivastava K, Rais J, *et al.* CRISPR-Cas9: A Potent Gene-editing Tool for the Treatment of Cancer. Curr Mol Med 2024; 23(2): 191-204.
[PMID: 36788695]

[20] Kelm JM, Samarbakhsh A, Pillai A, *et al.* Recent Advances in the Development of Non-PIKKs Targeting Small Molecule Inhibitors of DNA Double-Strand Break Repair. Front Onco 2022; 12.
[http://dx.doi.org/10.3389/fonc.2022.850883]

[21] Kantor A, McClements M E, Maclaren R E. Crispr-cas9 dna base-editing and prime-editing. International Journal of Molecular Sciences 2020; 21.
[http://dx.doi.org/10.3390/ijms21176240]

[22] Tomita A, Sasanuma H, Owa T, *et al.* Inducing multiple nicks promotes interhomolog homologous recombination to correct heterozygous mutations in somatic cells. Nat Commun 2023; 14(1): 5607.
[http://dx.doi.org/10.1038/s41467-023-41048-5] [PMID: 37714828]

[23] Mojica FJM, Díez-Villaseñor C, Soria E, Juez G. Biological significance of a family of regularly spaced repeats in the genomes of Archaea, Bacteria and mitochondria Molecular Microbiology. Preprint at 2000; Vol. 36.
[http://dx.doi.org/10.1046/j.1365-2958.2000.01838.x]

[24] Deol P, Madhwal A, Sharma G, Kaushik R, Malik YS. CRISPR use in diagnosis and therapy for COVID-19 in Methods in Microbiology . 2022; 50.

[25] Shademan B, *et al.* CRISPR Technology in Gene-Editing-Based Detection and Treatment of SARS-CoV-2 Frontiers in Molecular Biosciences. Preprint at 2022; Vol. 8.
[http://dx.doi.org/10.3389/fmolb.2021.772788]

[26] Ebrahimi S, Khanbabaei H, Abbasi S, *et al.* CRISPR-Cas System: A Promising Diagnostic Tool for

COVID-19. Avicenna J Med Biotechnol 2022; 14(1): 3-9.
[http://dx.doi.org/10.18502/ajmb.v14i1.8165] [PMID: 35509363]

[27]   Berber B, *et al.* Gene editing and RNAi approaches for COVID-19 diagnostics and therapeutics Gene Therapy. Preprint at 2021; Vol. 28.
[http://dx.doi.org/10.1038/s41434-020-00209-7]

[28]   Palermo G, Ricci CG, Fernando A, *et al.* Protospacer Adjacent Motif-Induced Allostery Activates CRISPR-Cas9. J Am Chem Soc 2017; 139(45): 16028-31.
[http://dx.doi.org/10.1021/jacs.7b05313] [PMID: 28764328]

[29]   Cencic R, Miura H, Malina A, *et al.* Protospacer adjacent motif (PAM)-distal sequences engage CRISPR Cas9 DNA target cleavage. PLoS One 2014; 9(10): e109213.
[http://dx.doi.org/10.1371/journal.pone.0109213] [PMID: 25275497]

[30]   Sajid MI, Moazzam M, Cho Y, *et al.* siRNA Therapeutics for the Therapy of COVID-19 and Other Coronaviruses. Mol Pharm 2021; 18(6): 2105-21.
[http://dx.doi.org/10.1021/acs.molpharmaceut.0c01239] [PMID: 33945284]

[31]   Wei N, Zhang L, Huang H, *et al.* siRNA has greatly elevated mismatch tolerance at 3′-UTR sites. PLoS One 2012; 7(11): e49309.
[http://dx.doi.org/10.1371/journal.pone.0049309] [PMID: 23145149]

[32]   Saadat KASM. RNAi-mediated siRNA sequences to combat the COVID-19 pandemic with the inhibition of SARS-CoV2. Gene Rep 2022; 26: 101512.
[http://dx.doi.org/10.1016/j.genrep.2022.101512] [PMID: 35071824]

[33]   TP53 Gene Therapy as a Potential Treatment for Patients with COVID-19. Harford, J. B., Kim, S. S., Pirollo, K. F. & Chang, E. H. Viruses 2022; 14.

[34]   Wang X, Liu Y, Li K, Hao Z. Roles of p53-Mediated Host–Virus Interaction in Coronavirus Infection. Int J Mol Sci 2023; 24(7): 6371.
[http://dx.doi.org/10.3390/ijms24076371]

[35]   Lodi G, Gentili V, Casciano F, *et al.* Cell cycle block by p53 activation reduces SARS-CoV-2 release in infected alveolar basal epithelial A549-hACE2 cells. Front Pharmacol 2022; 13: 1018761.
[http://dx.doi.org/10.3389/fphar.2022.1018761] [PMID: 36582523]

[36]   Aledo-Serrano A, *et al.* Aledo-Serrano, A. et al. Gene therapies and COVID-19 vaccines: a necessary discussion in relation with viral vector-based approaches. Orphanet Journal of Rare Diseases 2021; 16
[http://dx.doi.org/10.1186/s13023-021-01958-3]

[37]   Marlin R, Desjardins D, Contreras V, *et al.* Antiviral efficacy of favipiravir against Zika and SARS-CoV-2 viruses in non-human primates. Nat Commun 2022; 13(1): 5108.
[http://dx.doi.org/10.1038/s41467-022-32565-w] [PMID: 36042198]

[38]   Tarek M, Abdelzaher H, Kobeissy F, El-Fawal HAN, Salama MM, Abdelnaser A. Bioinformatics analysis of allele frequencies and expression patterns of ace2, tmprss2 and furin in different populations and susceptibility to sars-cov-2. Genes (Basel) 2021; 12(7): 1041.
[http://dx.doi.org/10.3390/genes12071041] [PMID: 34356057]

[39]   Contributions of human ACE2 and TMPRSS2 in determining host–pathogen interaction of COVID-19. Journal of Genetics 2021; 100.
[http://dx.doi.org/10.1007/s12041-021-01262-w]

[40]   Senapati S, Banerjee P, Bhagavatula S, Kushwaha P P, Kumar S. Contributions of human ACE2 and TMPRSS2 in determining host–pathogen interaction of COVID-19. Journal of Genetics 2021; 100.
[http://dx.doi.org/10.1007/s12041-021-01262-w]

[41]   Current and future nanoparticle vaccines for COVID-19. EBioMedicine.
[http://dx.doi.org/10.1016/j.ebiom.2021.103699]

[42]   An Encapsulation on Nano Drug Delivery Systems and their Probable Applications. NanoWorld J

9(S1): S444-9.

[43]   Wang EY, Sarmadi M, Ying B, Jaklenec A, Langer R. Recent advances in nano- and micro-scale carrier systems for controlled delivery of vaccines. Biomaterials 2023; 303: 122345.
[http://dx.doi.org/10.1016/j.biomaterials.2023.122345]

[44]   Nanoparticle against SARs-CoV-19: Applications for prevention, diagnosis, and treatment of COVID-19 and future perspectives. 2021; 4259-69.

[45]   Nanotechnology and COVID-19: Prevention, diagnosis, vaccine, and treatment strategies. Front.Mater., 11 January 2023.Sec. Biomaterials and Bio-Inspired Materials 2023; 9.
[http://dx.doi.org/10.3389/fmats.2022.1059184]

[46]   Shi Y, Wang G, Cai X, *et al.* An overview of COVID-19. J Zhejiang Univ Sci B 2020; 21(5): 343-60.
[http://dx.doi.org/10.1631/jzus.B2000083] [PMID: 32425000]

SUBJECT INDEX

A

Acid(s) 21, 102, 112, 113, 114, 118, 197, 199, 221, 223
  nucleic 21, 102, 113, 114, 118, 197, 199, 221, 223
  ribonucleic 102, 112
Activation 62, 64, 70, 71, 72, 74, 77, 129, 141, 149
  cytokine 70
  immune 141
  of Spike protein 62
Activity 17, 113, 128, 132, 191
  hemagglutinin-esterase 17
  renal 128
  respiratory 191
  reverse transcriptase 113
  ribosomal 132
Acute 46, 47, 69, 72, 75, 76, 86, 87, 105, 106, 108, 109, 110, 125, 149, 165
  kidney injury (AKI) 75, 76
  myelitis 106, 109
  respiratory distress syndrome (ARDS) 46, 47, 69, 72, 75, 76, 86, 87, 105, 108, 110, 125, 149
  symptoms of novel coronavirus 165
Adenoviral-based vaccines 156
ADP-ribose diphosphatase 130
Adult respiratory distress syndrome 168
Aerosol particle discharge 247
Air 96, 97, 245
  expired 245
  pollutants 96
  pollution 96, 97
  treatment systems 245
Amino acid(s) 12, 22, 23, 62, 63, 203, 227
  composition 23
  residue 62
  sequences 22, 62, 203, 227
  side chains 12
  tyrosine 63
Amplification test 222

Analyzer, immunoassay 119
Angiotensin 23, 38, 50, 76, 91, 111, 167
  -converting enzyme 23, 38, 50, 91
  -receptor blockers (ARB) 167
Anosmia 107, 149
Anti-viral resistance 161
Antibiotic 131, 224
  azithromycin 131
  consumption 224
Antibodies 40, 65, 72, 117, 118, 119, 120, 132, 133, 138, 155, 156, 199, 220, 221, 223
  acridinium-labeled 120
  fluorescence-based 199, 223
  polyclonal 132
  vaccination-derived 40
Antibody 65, 73, 154, 196, 219
  -dependant cell cytotoxicity (ADCC) 73
  -dependent phagocytosis (ADP) 65
  detection 196, 219
  therapies 154
Antigen 71, 197, 198, 199, 221, 222, 223
  -measuring techniques 197, 221
  -presenting cells (APCs) 71
  proteins 198, 199, 222, 223
Antiviral 133, 259
  coatings 259
  monoclonal antibody 133
Antiviral drugs 77, 127, 129, 130, 131, 132, 137, 140, 141
  therapeutic 131
Artificial intelligence 190, 201
  and machine learning 190
  system 201
Artificial neural networks (ANN) 206, 230
Avian infectious bronchitis virus (AIBV) 2, 19

B

Battery, power supply 249
Bayes theorem of probability 205

Beta-coronaviruses infect 29
Broncho-alveolar lavage fluid (BALF) 2, 13
Bronchoscopy 42

C

Cardiac 75
   biomarkers 75
   injury 75
Cardio-metabolic system 110
Cardiovascular 75, 96, 133, 167
   diseases 75, 133, 167
   systems 75, 96
Chemiluminescence immunoassay (CLIA)
   102, 103, 119, 120, 197, 198, 221, 222
Chest 193, 199, 212, 223
   imaging techniques 193, 212
   radiography 199, 223
Cholangiocytes 111
Chronic kidney dysfunction 75
Combat coronavirus transmission 98
Combating coronaviruses 243
Combination therapy 133
Computed tomography (CT) 110, 111, 156,
   161, 190, 191, 192, 196, 197, 199, 209,
   210, 219, 221, 223
   scans 197, 221
Computer-aided 161, 191, 192
   diagnosis (CAD) 191, 192
   drug design (CADD) 161
Conditions 20, 108, 109, 134, 254
   life-threatening 254
   pro-thrombotic 108, 109
   severe disease 134
   severe lower respiratory 20
Convalescent plasma (CP) 72, 117, 132, 133,
   141, 142
   treatment 132, 142
Convolutional neural networks (CNNs) 190,
   201, 203, 212, 225, 228
Corona 125, 131
   infection 131
   virus disease 125
Coronavirus 3, 11, 25, 26, 29, 31, 44, 45, 51,
   60, 67, 87, 94, 114, 187
   disease 87
   genome 60, 67
   infection 3, 11, 44, 45, 51, 94
   outbreak 187
   severe acute respiratory disorder 114

spike proteins 25, 26, 29, 31
CoV transmission 90, 94
COVID-19 40, 49, 50, 78, 86, 87, 109, 111,
   117, 126, 127, 129, 149, 152, 159, 161,
   166, 167, 168, 192, 194, 197, 201, 207,
   208, 221, 225, 232, 233, 251
   antibodies 117
   -associated hepatic dysfunction 111
   detection techniques 197
   environment 152
   gastrointestinal symptoms 109
   infection 86, 87, 126, 127, 129, 159, 161,
     166, 167, 168, 207, 208, 221, 232, 233
   infectious 225
   pneumonia 168, 192, 194, 201, 225
   progression 78, 149
   risk factors for 40, 49
   victims 251
   virus 50
CRISPR technology 115, 252
CXR techniques 209, 234
Cytokine(s) 69, 71, 72, 75, 77, 78, 79, 103,
   108, 110, 132, 134, 149
   anti-inflammatory 132
   inflammatory 71, 108, 110
   pro-inflammatory 71, 79, 103, 108, 132, 149
   release syndrome 134

D

Damage 47, 70, 71, 75, 77, 106, 110, 121,
   134, 166, 169
   pulmonary 75
   reduced renal 110
   virus-induced 71
Deep learning 112, 203, 209, 228, 232, 233,
   246
   algorithms 232
   -based systems 203, 228
   framework 209
   network 209, 233
   system 246
   techniques 112
Detection 102, 111, 112, 114, 116, 196, 198,
   199, 203, 220, 221, 222, 223, 225, 227,
   244, 258
   network infringement 203, 227
   techniques 112, 244, 258
   viral antigen 102
Diabetes mellitus (DM) 133, 167

Disease 38, 46, 47, 48, 49, 51, 71, 72, 79, 87,
 99, 110, 122, 153, 154, 159, 165, 166,
 178, 179, 194, 195, 201, 218, 222, 223,
 225, 252
  communicable 122
  infectious 47, 153, 154, 165, 218, 222, 223
  lung 47, 225
  noncommunicable 166
  pulmonary 110
  transmission 99, 225
Disorders 19, 96, 106, 107, 133, 152, 153,
 252, 253, 254
  emotional 153
  genetic 254
  immunological 96
  neurological 107, 133
  post-traumatic syndrome 152
  sleep 152
  thyroid 106
Disseminated intravenous coagulation (DIC)
 76
DNA 71, 113, 114, 115, 127, 136, 138, 141,
 251, 253
  and RNA vaccines 141
  plasmid 138
  polymerase 113
  viral 114

E

Economic growth 165
Endocytosis 127
Endoribonuclease 24
Endosomal pathway inhibitors 130, 141
Endothelial 103, 106, 108
  cell infection 103, 108
  dysfunction 103, 106, 108
Environment 39, 66, 75, 88, 93, 95, 96, 99,
 113, 116, 202, 226
  hypoxic 75
  indoor 93
  isothermal 113
  python simulation 202, 226
Enzyme linked immunosorbent assay 198
Epidemiologists 13
Epididymalorchitis 106

F

Fetal distress 44
Fibrosis, pulmonary 13
Food industry 116, 182
Function, cardiac autonomic 120
Fusion peptide (FP) 26, 27, 61, 65, 191

G

Gastrointestinal 4, 29, 43, 46, 51, 94, 109,
 131, 210
  distress 43
  symptoms 46, 51, 94, 109
  systems 4, 29, 210
Genes 112, 251
  disease-causing 251
  infectious 112
Growth hormone (GH) 106

H

Health, myocardial 75
Heart disease 47
Heat-shock proteins 71
Helicase triphosphatase 126
Hepatocyte growth factor (HGF) 72
Host cell 66, 68, 130
  machinery 66, 68
  membrane fusion 130
Host-targeting agents (HTAs) 161
Hypercytokinemia 75
Hyperglycaemia 168

I

Illness 37, 152, 201, 245
  life-threatening 37
  managing 245
  mental 152
  transmission 201
Immune 106, 125
  -mediated organ damage 106
  modulating treatments 125
Immune response 45, 48, 64, 69, 71, 72, 74,
 132, 134, 138, 139, 141, 168
  dysregulated innate 168
  humoral 72
Immune system 40, 70, 78, 118, 134, 135

activity 135
Immunity 72, 77, 126, 127, 138, 165
  humoral 72
Immunological reactions 156
Immunomodulator therapy 134, 141
Immunosenescence, age-related 45
Infect hepatocytes 111
Infected human macrophages 65
Infection 40, 44, 76, 111, 135, 148, 168, 193,
      256
  asymptomatic 193
  bacteriophage 135
  fetal 44
  inhibiting 256
  lung 111
  natural 40
  pulmonary 76, 148, 168
Infectious disease threats 142
Inflammasome(s) 73, 74, 79
  activation and immune response 74
  activation of 74
  downstream 74
Inflammation 47, 51, 72, 73, 74, 75, 105, 108,
      129, 131, 132, 135, 138, 141, 167
  allergic 138
  chronic 167
  lung tissue 141
Interferon-stimulated gene (ISGs) 71
Ischemic hepatotoxicity 111

L

Lactate dehydrogenase 74, 103, 108, 135
Lactic dehydrogenase 202, 226
LAMP 113
  reaction 113
  response process 113
  technique 113
Lateral flow immunoassay (LFIA) 102, 118,
      197, 198, 221, 222
Liver 44, 75, 76, 77, 79, 111, 127
  dysfunctional 44
  dysfunction 75
  enzymes 76, 111
Liver injury 75, 76, 111
  viral-induced 111
Lung 47, 77, 78, 105, 121, 195, 199, 201, 221
  disorders 201
  edema 105
  fibrosis 199, 221

hyperplasia 195
infiltrates 47
invasion 121
macrophages 77, 78
Lymphocytes 70, 71, 109, 202, 209, 226, 231,
      233
Lymphocytic pleocytosis 109
Lymphopenia 72

M

Machine intelligence 196, 220
Machine learning 190, 191, 196, 200, 203,
      205, 208, 210, 211, 212, 218, 227, 232,
      234, 250
  algorithms 227
  methods 190
  techniques 211
Machines, respiratory 169
Macrophage-colony-stimulating factor
      (MCSF) 72
Mannose-binding lectin (MBL) 71
Mediators, pro-inflammatory 66
Membrane fusion protein 29, 31
Meningitis 109
Meningoencephalitis 106
Methicillin-resistant Staphylococcus aureus
      (MRSA) 162
Micropinocytosis 129, 131
Middle East respiratory syndrome (MERS)
      11, 19, 21, 38, 39, 90, 111, 112, 125,
      126, 127
Mobile edge computing (MEC) 243, 248, 251
Molecule transformer drug target interaction
      (MTDTI) 203
Multiple organ dysfunction syndromes
      (MODS) 75, 79
Myocardial 75, 110
  infarction 75
  symptoms 110
Myocarditis, viral 110

N

Neural networks, artificial 206, 230
Next generation sequencing (NGS) 59
Non-thyroidal sickness syndromes 106
Nucleic acid 197, 202, 226
  assays 197
  sequence 202, 226

Nucleocapsid proteins 24, 60, 64, 126, 137

O

Obesity and cardiovascular disease 167
Olfactory dysfunction 103
Organ 46, 71, 75, 103
　dysfunction 75
　failure 46, 71, 103
Oxidative stress 108, 132

P

Peptidase 23
　protein 23
Peripheral nervous system (PNS) 106
Phagocytic cells 78
Phagocytosis 65, 71, 133, 134
　antibody-dependent 65
　cellular 134
Pneumonia 2, 11, 20, 21, 39, 46, 59, 86, 87,
　　105, 111, 135, 149, 168
　associated 168
　fatal 2, 11
　-related maladies 111
　symptoms 87
　viral 149
Pneumonitis 72
Polymerase chain reaction (PCR) 3, 59, 112,
　　116, 219
Porcine epidemic diarrhea CoV (PEDC) 2, 4
Posterior reversible encephalopathy syndrome
　　(PRES) 106
Postural orthostatic tachyarrhythmia disease
　　103
Production, cytokine 77, 138
Proteases, lysosomal 129
Proteasome 63
Protein 120, 129, 138, 253
　translated 253
　antigen 120, 138
　degradation 129
Public health 1, 149, 218
　emergency 149, 218
　systems 1

R

Random forest (RF) 190, 202, 204, 205, 207,
　　212, 226, 229, 231

Rapid antigen tests (RATs) 10, 171, 219
Recombinase polymerase amplification (RPA)
　　114, 198, 222
Renin-angiotensin-aldosterone system
　　(RAAS) 76, 106, 110
Respiratory 1, 11, 37, 42, 58, 86, 96, 193
　diseases 193
　infection 37, 96
　symptoms 42, 86
　syndrome 1, 11, 37
　tract infections (RTI) 58
　transmission 42
Reverse transcriptase (RT) 196, 219
　polymerase chain reaction 196
Rheumatoid arthritis 135
RNA-dependant RNA 66, 130
　polymerase 66
　isomerase 130

S

SAR-CoV-2 6, 23, 86, 87, 89, 90, 93, 94, 96,
　　97, 98, 136, 193, 256
　virus 136
　spike glycoprotein 23
　transmission 6, 87, 89, 90, 93, 94, 96, 97,
　　98, 193, 256
　transmission pathways 86
Sensor protein 73
Severe acute respiratory syndrome 5, 11, 12,
　　19, 22, 37, 38, 59, 71, 125
Signals, pro-inflammatory 76
Spermatogenesis 106
Sphincter dysfunction 109
Spike 4, 26, 28, 113, 126
　coronavirus protein 26
　glycoproteins 4, 113, 126
　glycoproteins protein 28
Spike protein 5, 14, 15, 28, 30, 60, 61, 62, 64,
　　65, 119, 120, 130, 133, 134, 254
　coronavirus protein 5
STAT proteins 135
Swine acute diarrhea syndrome (SADS) 1, 6

T

Techniques 111, 112, 141, 197, 198, 199, 203,
　　204, 208, 211, 212, 219, 221, 224, 226,
　　227, 252, 258
　antibodies and antigen-measuring 197, 221

electroporation 141
genetic engineering 258
immunoinformatic 208
microfluidic 197, 199, 224
Technology, microfluidic 199, 223
Thrombocytopenia 44
Tomography, computed 103, 110, 111, 116,
    191, 192, 196, 199, 210, 219, 223
Transcription 66, 67, 71
   factors 71
   mechanism 66
   regulatory sequence (TRS) 66, 67
Transcriptomics 128
Transmission 37, 41, 43, 44, 92, 94, 99
   nosocomial 92, 94, 99
   pathways 41
   sexual 37, 44
   transplacental 43

V

Vaccination camps 170
Vaccine 16, 156
   technology 156
   therapy 16
Viral 26, 27, 42, 62, 63, 64, 68, 69, 74, 77,
    108, 112, 127, 129, 138, 139, 140, 141,
    142, 163, 167, 192, 259
   diseases 108, 163
   infection 42, 64, 69, 74, 112, 140, 141, 167,
    192, 259
   -like particle (VLPs) 68, 139
   membrane fusion proteins 26, 27
   proteins 62, 63, 77, 127, 129, 138, 142
Viruses 17, 42, 130
  infectious peritonitis 17
  influenza 130
  live infectious 42

W

Withaffected immune systems 105

www.ingramcontent.com/pod-product-compliance
Lightning Source LLC
Chambersburg PA
CBHW050816220326
41598CB00006B/230